ON THE LAPS

OF GODS

ON THE LAPS
OF GODS

*The Red Summer of 1919
and the Struggle for Justice
That Remade a Nation*

ROBERT WHITAKER

CROWN PUBLISHERS | NEW YORK

Published in the United States by Crown Publishers, an imprint of the
Crown Publishing Group, a division of Random House, Inc., New York.

www.crownpublishing.com

Crown is a trademark and the Crown colophon is a registered trademark of
Random House, Inc.

Library of Congress Cataloging-in-Publication Data

Whitaker, Robert.
On the laps of gods : the Red Summer of 1919 and the struggle
for justice that remade a nation / Robert Whitaker.—1st ed.
Includes bibliographical references and index.
1. Elaine Race Riot, Elaine, Ark., 1919. 2. Riots—Arkansas—Phillips County—
History. 3. Jones, Scipio Africanus, 1863–1943. 4. African Americans—
Arkansas—Phillips County—History. 5. Phillips County (Ark.)
—Race relations—History—20th century. 6. Trials (Murder)—Arkansas—
Phillips County—History—20th century. 7. Phillips County (Ark.)—History. I. Title.
F417.P45W475 2008
976.7'88052—dc22   2007045820

ISBN 978-0-307-33982-9

Printed in the United States of America

DESIGN BY LEONARD W. HENDERSON

MAPS BY MAPPING SPECIALISTS, LTD.

10 9 8 7 6 5 4 3 2 1

First Edition

For Rabi, Zoey, and Dylan

Contents

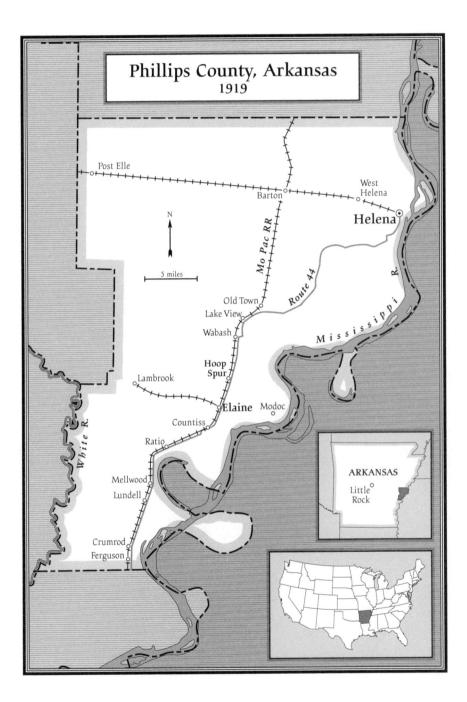

Phillips County, Arkansas
1919

Post Elle

West
Helena

Barton

Helena

N

Mo Pac RR

5 miles

Route 44

Old Town
Lake View

Wabash

Mississippi R.

Hoop
Spur

Lambrook

Elaine   Modoc

Countiss

Ratio

ARKANSAS

Little
Rock

Mellwood
Lundell

White R.

Crumrod
Ferguson

Now their was a riot down here among the wrases and it was a Good many of Negros down their killed and the white Peoples called for the troops from Little Rock and they went down their and killed Negros like they wont nothen But dogs and did not make no arest on the whites whatever while they arested and unarmed a lots of Negroes and left the white with their armes and the Negro with nothen But their Hands and face to stand all the punishment that the white wished to Give them.

—ANONYMOUS LETTER FROM A WORLD WAR I VETERAN TO
EMMETT J. SCOTT,
NOVEMBER 12, 1919

A Union in Hoop Spur

HOOP SPUR HAS LONG since disappeared from the maps of Phillips County, Arkansas, and even in 1919, when it could be found on such a map, it consisted of little more than a railroad switching station and a small store. But the cotton fields surrounding Hoop Spur were speckled with cabins, each one home to a family of sharecroppers, and on September 30 of that year, shortly after sunset, the black farmers began walking along dirt paths and roads toward a small wooden church located about one-quarter mile north of the switching station. For most, the church was a mile or two away, or even farther, and as they expected their meeting to run late into the night, they brought along sweaters and light coats for the walk back home. Many had their children with them, and a few, like Vina Mason, were carrying babies.

By 7:00 P.M., the first of the farmers had arrived, and they lit three lamps inside the Baptist church. The wooden benches began filling up rapidly. Sallie Giles and her two sons, Albert and Milligan, reached Hoop Spur around 8:00 P.M., and by then the "house was packed," she said. Paul Hall was there, and so too were "Preacher" Joe Knox and Frank Moore, along with their wives. At last, Jim Miller and his wife, Cleola, pulled up in a horse and a buggy. Miller was president of the Hoop Spur Lodge of the Progressive Farmers and Household Union, which for the past several months had been signing up sharecroppers throughout southern Phillips County.

The one person still missing was the lodge's secretary, Ed Ware.

He was, as he later admitted, thinking of quitting. The previous Thursday, September 25, sharecroppers in Elaine, a small town three miles to the south, had held a Progressive Farmers meeting, which he'd attended. The next day, white planters had singled him out and warned him not to go to any more such gatherings. He had reason to be afraid, but at last his wife, Lulu, insisted that they go, reminding him, as he later recalled, that "I had those [union] books and papers." Although they lived only one mile to the west of the church, they had to swing around to the south in order to get past the Govan Slough, a ditch lined by a thicket of trees, and it was nearly 9:00 P.M. by the time they arrived. Ware nodded at the nine or ten men milling around front, and then he shook hands with Lit Simmons at the door, both men twisting their fingers into the lodge's secret grip.

"We've just begun," Ware whispered.

That was the union's password, and everyone who had entered that night had uttered the same thing. Although the meeting was now in full swing, with, as one sharecropper put it, "two hundred head of men, women and children" inside, Simmons and the other men in the front yard remained where they were. William Wordlow, John Martin, John Ratliff, and Will Wright stood together in one group, about fifteen feet away from the door, while Alf Banks Jr., Albert Giles, and the three Beco brothers—Joe, Boisy, and Ransom— sat in Miller's buggy. At first glance, it all seemed so peaceful. The church lamps cast the yard in a soft glow and the men were speaking in low voices, or saying nothing at all. But not too many yards distant, the light petered out, and everyone had his eyes glued to the road that disappeared into that darkness. Route 44, which ran north 22 miles to Helena, the county seat, was a lonely county road, bordered on both sides by dense patches of rivercane. In the buggy, the Beco brothers fiddled with shotguns draped across their laps, while several others nervously fingered the triggers of their hunting rifles. Martin was armed with a Smith & Wesson pistol.

At the door, Simmons was growing ever more nervous. This was only the third time that the Hoop Spur lodge had met, and at the previous meeting, which had been Simmons's first, he'd asked why it was necessary to have men stand guard. "White people don't want the union and are going to get us," he'd been told. And on this night, Simmons knew, rumors were flying that whites "were coming there to break up the meeting, or to shoot it up."

The minutes passed slowly by. Everyone listened for the sound of an approaching car, but the only noises that Simmons and the others heard, other than the chirping of field crickets, rose from inside the church. Nine-thirty passed without incident, then ten and ten-thirty. The road remained dark and quiet, and yet, to Simmons, it seemed that this night would never end.

"The whites," he muttered, "are going to kill us."

MOST OF THE HOOP SPUR farmers in the church that night were middle-aged, in their thirties, forties, and fifties, and their religious faith was such that they began all of their meetings with a prayer. They all had migrated here during the past decade, as this was about as deep in the Mississippi Delta as you could get, the cotton fields having been a tangle of swampland and dense hardwood forests only ten to fifteen years earlier. Southern Phillips County was a floodplain for both the White and Mississippi rivers, and as a result it had been about the last stretch of delta land in Arkansas to be drained and cleared. It remained an inhospitable place to live, the woods thick with fever-carrying mosquitoes, and yet it offered the black families a new hope. The two rivers had deposited topsoil so rich in minerals that geologists considered it perhaps the most fertile land in the world.

The Hoop Spur farmers were mostly from Mississippi and Louisiana, although a few hailed from as far away as North Carolina. Their journeys here had been much the same. Most had arrived during the winter months, just after the end of a harvest, as this was moving season for sharecroppers throughout the South. The black farmers almost always ended the year in debt, and so, hoping that it might be different someplace else, many packed up their meager belongings every couple of years and moved to a distant county or to another state. Most of those who'd come to Hoop Spur had arrived—as a local scholar named Bessie Ferguson wrote in 1927—with "nothing of their own with the exception of their makeshift household furniture, a few ragged clothes, a gun, and one or more dogs, sometimes a few chickens or a hog."

They'd moved into cabins that were, even by the dismal housing standards of the time, a sorry lot. Plantation owners threw up cabins made from rough lumber for their sharecroppers, each one surrounded by the plot of land that was to be worked by a family, and typically they were so poorly constructed that, as the joke went, the sharecroppers "could study astronomy through the openings in the roof and geology through the holes in the floor." A sharecropper's cabin usually consisted of one large room, perhaps 18 by 20 feet in size, where the entire family would live and sleep, with a shed attached to the back. The main room would have a fireplace for heat and a couple of windows—with wooden shutters but no glass—for light. Because southern Phillips County was so vulnerable to floods, the landowners had erected cabins that were particularly flimsy, since they needed to be "so cheap that the loss from floods is small," Ferguson said.

During the winter months, the Hoop Spur sharecroppers did what they could to survive. Occasionally it would snow, and with nighttime temperatures regularly dipping to near freezing, they struggled mightily to stay warm. They patched up the drafty walls of their cabins with newspapers, and they collected firewood from the Govan Slough and other nearby stands of trees, although at times they grew so desperate, Ferguson wrote, that "garden or yard fences are used for fuel." Fortunately, there was plenty of fish and game to be had, which complemented whatever vegetables they had grown in their gardens the summer before and canned. The woods were filled with deer, wild turkeys, rabbits, squirrels, doves, quail, and geese, and those hunting with dogs could chase bears through the canebrakes. At last, March would come and the rains would turn the fields into bogs, and the sharecroppers would pray that the levees on the White and Mississippi rivers would hold and keep away the floods that could destroy their cabins.

Once the fields began to dry, usually by the end of March, the men began breaking up the soil, leaving their cabins before the first light of day to hook ploughs to their mules, their work hours stretching, as they liked to say, from "can see to can't see." This was particularly true for the Hoop Spur farmers, as most were working 15 to 30 acres, which were large plots for sharecroppers in the Mississippi Delta. After they finished turning up the soil, which took a couple of weeks, they would run a "middlebuster" over it to form furrows and mounds. By early May, they were ready to plant. They would dig a narrow trench in the mounds and, every 18 inches or so, drop in cottonseed.

As soon as the plants sprouted, they would work the fields with long-handled hoes, chopping the weeds that grew fast and thick in the humid air. Everyone in the family would help with this chore, even the younger children spending long hours in the hot sun. Daytime temperatures regularly soared into the nineties, and night brought little relief. Malaria was a constant problem in the delta, and at dusk, in order to drive off the mosquitoes and flies, the cabins had to be smoked or sprayed with insecticide, and with the doors and windows shuttered to keep out the pests, no one slept well in the stifling air.

The cotton plants, however, flourished. Early in the season, they produced a light-hued blossom that darkened, wilted, and dropped within a couple of days, which was all the time it took for pollination. A tiny green pod soon appeared at the base of the flower, and during July and August it swelled into a boll packed with seeds wrapped in willowy fibers, until at last, in late August, the bolls split open and the fields would be painted white.

Although the plants grew waist high, many of the bolls hung close to the ground, and so the sharecroppers moved through the rows stooped over or even on their knees. They fixed their fingers into claws to pluck the cotton from the bolls, and while one hand was plucking the other hand would be stuffing the cotton into a canvas sack they dragged behind them. The best sacks had tar covering the bottom to reduce the friction, but still, as the bags filled with a hundred pounds of raw cotton, the strap slung over the picker's back would cut into his or her shoulder. "Pulling the cotton out of the boll can work your fingers too," one sharecropper remembered. "The husks of the cotton boll are sharp and brittle." After years of picking, sharecroppers regularly ended up with arthritic hands, their fingers crippled at the joints.

The younger children, of course, had smaller sacks, and as the Hoop Spur families moved together through the fields, they would sing:

> I'm down here in this cotton field
> With a sack that's ten feet long
> Well my poor back is killin' me
> I'll be glad when this cotton's all gone.

A good picker could fill a hundred-pound bag in the morning, break for lunch, and then fill a second one by the end of the day. The cotton would be dumped onto a mule-drawn wagon, packed down, and taken to the nearest gin. There it would be vacuumed from the wagon through a suction pipe and run through a machine that, by means of narrowly spaced teeth, removed the seeds from the fiber. The cotton would then be funneled into a compressing room, where it was pressed into bales, wrapped in burlap, and tied together with steel bands.

The fertile fields around Hoop Spur yielded at least 1,500 pounds of raw cotton per acre, and that translated into one 500-pound bale of ginned cotton, ready for the market. A sharecropper who worked 10 acres could expect to produce ten bales of cotton, and the seeds could also be sold—the protein-rich hulls were fed to cattle, and the cottonseed oil was used in foods and cosmetics. However, the sharecroppers would have to make several passes through their fields to fully reap what the land had to offer, as not all of the cotton bolls ripened at the same time; thus it was late in November before the plantation owners and sharecroppers met to settle their accounts.

It was then that the sharecroppers' lot, at least from the black farmers' point of view, turned most unfair.

SHARECROPPERS THROUGHOUT THE MISSISSIPPI Delta proudly declared to census workers that they were "working on their own account" and were not plantation "employees." However, from the first moment of spring planting, their wishes conflicted with their landlords' desires. They wanted to plant large gardens, raise hogs and chickens, and grow both corn and cotton. However, the landowners, who often had overseers run their plantations, wanted their sharecroppers to keep their gardens small, and at times would insist that cotton be planted right up to the cabins' front porches. Not only did this maximize the cotton harvest, it minimized the amount of food the sharecroppers could grow, and that created an opportunity for the landowners to keep them in debt. The black farmers would be forced to buy most of their goods on credit at plantation commissaries, or at stores in nearby towns where the landlords had an account for their tenants, and in either case, the sharecroppers would be charged exorbitant amounts.

Many of the Hoop Spur families shopped at Dowdy and Longnecker's in Elaine, a town of four hundred people 3 miles to the south, and they paid 25 percent to 100 percent more than whites did for the same goods, the higher prices said to be a "carrying charge." A gallon of molasses that normally cost 85 cents was sold to the sharecroppers at $1.25 on credit. Work shoes that normally sold for $2.50 cost the sharecroppers $4. When it came time to settle, the plantation owner would deduct these expenses from his tenant's half share of the cotton crop, and more often than not, after he was done with the arithmetic, he would scribble a balance-due figure on a scrap of paper and hand it to the bewildered farmer.

"They didn't give no itemized statement," recalled one Arkansas sharecropper, Henry Blake. "No, you just had to take their word. They never give you no details. They just say you owe so much. No matter how good account you kept, you had to go by their accounts. . . . It's been this way for a long time."

The black families in Hoop Spur had a song for this moment as well:

> Nought's a nought
> An figger's a figger
> All fer de white man
> None fer de nigger.

Although they were regularly kept in debt, the Hoop Spur sharecroppers would usually return to their cabins with $50 to $100 in their pockets, as the landowners—most of whom lived in Helena—typically gave their tenants half of the money from the sale of the cotton seed. The landowners hoped this small amount of cash would suffice to keep the sharecroppers around until the following spring.

Five or so years earlier, the sharecroppers—even if they had been fairly treated—couldn't have expected to earn a great deal more than that. In 1914, cotton sold for 7 cents a pound, and at that price, it did not take much creative bookkeeping by a plantation owner to come up with a negative figure at settlement. But since then, the demand for cotton had steadily risen, largely because of World War I, and so had the price. By 1917, when the United States entered the conflict, cotton was fetching 24 cents a pound. At that price, a sharecropper who harvested fifteen ginned bales, which was a good crop for any one family, was due a half share of $900 before deductions, and his commissary bill, even given the inflated prices, should not have run much more than $200. That meant the sharecropper was due at least $700, which was a fair amount of money, given that a new Model T sold for only $350. But few sharecroppers in Phillips County—or anywhere else in the Mississippi Delta—received anywhere close to that amount in 1917. Indeed, since it was no longer so easy for plantation owners to turn that profit into a negative figure, many didn't bother settling their sharecroppers' accounts that fall, instead waiting until the spring to hand them their usual balance-due note, as that way it was too late for the sharecroppers to move to a new plantation. "The negro is then bound hand and foot and must accept the landlord's terms," the U.S. Department of Labor reported.

As a result, the government conceded, a state of "acute unrest" had begun to develop among sharecroppers in the Mississippi Delta. The conflict in Europe was creating a windfall opportunity for cotton farmers, and they were missing out on it. In 1918, the price of cotton rose higher still, to more than 30 cents a pound, and at the end of the year, black farmers in southern Phillips County and elsewhere in Arkansas became ever more insistent on claiming their rightful share. One sharecropper, having been told that he had no money coming to him, walked 122 miles to Little Rock to see if he could hire Ulysses S. Bratton, a former federal prosecutor, to sue his landlord. The sharecroppers, Bratton said, came "by the droves to my office, telling their stories as to how they were being robbed by the landlords, who took their crops at their own prices, charged whatever they saw fit for the supplies furnished, and as a final consummation of the whole thing, refused to make any kind of a settlement with them whatever." At the Theo Fathauer plantation in Ratio, which was 10 miles south of Hoop Spur, none of the sixty-eight tenants received a settlement in 1918, and when they finally did so in July 1919, the plantation manager, J. J. Petro, handed them a "statement, written upon blank tablet paper, showing 'balance due' in a lump sum," Bratton said.

Throughout southern Phillips County, sharecroppers in the summer of 1919 bitterly voiced the same complaint. Black farmers in Crumrod, Lundell, Mellwood, Ratio, Countiss, Elaine, Modoc, Lambrook, Wabash, and Hoop Spur all felt they had been cheated out of what had been due them from the 1918 harvest. Either they had not been given itemized accounts or their settlements had been deferred, and one way or another, the $1,000 and up they should have received from 30-cent-a-pound cotton had never materialized. This year, they vowed, would be different. The price of cotton was forecast to top 40 cents a pound, and to possibly even reach 50 cents a pound, and while many of the sharecroppers, having never had the chance to attend school, couldn't read or write, they could all calculate what 50-cent-a-pound cotton would mean for them. Their half share would bring more than $100 per acre, and all you had to do then was multiply that figure by the number of acres you were working. Frank Moore and his father, James, had 51 acres planted—their share was going to be worth more than $5,000. Paul Hall and his brother had 40 acres in the ground. Alfred Banks had 32, John Martin 22, Albert Giles 20, and William Wordlow 16. They were all working large plots. Even old Ed Coleman, who'd been born a slave in 1841, was working 18 acres. None had ever dreamed they would see cotton selling at prices this high, and as they labored in their fields in July and early August, spending ten to twelve hours a day in the hot delta sun chopping weeds, they believed, as they later said, that "their chance had come to make some money for themselves and get out from under the white landlord's thumb."

And it was at that moment, when the cotton bolls were just about ready to burst, that a slight, twenty-seven-year-old man, Robert Lee Hill, showed up in Hoop Spur. He had been recently discharged from the United States Army, and he came bearing literature that stated, in big bold letters, "We battle for the rights of our race."

WHILE DETAILS OF HILL'S early life are sparse, his military records show that he was born on June 8, 1892, in Dermott, Arkansas, a small town in the southeastern corner of the state. It appears that he grew up on plantations in that area, his parents most likely sharecroppers. By the end of 1917, he was married and working as a common laborer for the Valley Planting Company in Winchester, a cotton-growing town 60 miles southwest of Elaine. Able to read and write, he had taken to heart the teachings of Booker T. Washington, who had urged blacks to run their own businesses and to become more self-reliant. In early 1918, he and three others—one of whom, V. E. Powell, was a thirty-one-year-old physician who'd graduated from Meharry Medical College in Nashville, Tennessee—organized the Progressive Farmers and Household Union, drawing up a constitution and bylaws that surely would have met with Washington's approval. "The object of this organization," they said, "shall be to advance the interests of the Negro, morally and intellectually, and to make him a better citizen and a better farmer."

Secret fraternal organizations were extremely popular at the time, and Hill and the others adopted this model for their union. There would be a grand lodge in Winchester, they decided, with "chapter" lodges throughout the state. Members coming to chapter meetings would need to know a secret password and handshake, and there would be a doorkeeper to ensure that nonmembers were kept out. Every year the grand lodge would host a statewide meeting, which was to be marked by a great deal of pomp and circumstance along with the wearing of regalia, customs familiar to anyone who had ever attended a Shriners convention. All of the delegates from the local chapters would wear "the Grand Circuit badge, pinned in a conspicuous place on the Breast."

Hill and the other founders were also careful to ensure that their organization was properly registered with the state. They hired white attorneys from Monticello, Arkansas, to draw up the incorporation papers, which were dutifully filed with the county clerk and approved by a county judge. "We did all that the law required and was declared a legal body," Hill said proudly.

However, the war raging in Europe derailed the union's development in 1918. Hill was drafted into the army in June 1918, one of 17,500 Arkansas blacks to serve in the military during World War I, and it appears that he served overseas. "I lend my best services during the great war," he wrote. He returned to Arkansas in the spring of 1919, and since his mother was living in Ratio, in the southernmost part of Phillips County, he began his union-organizing efforts there.

The union, which by then had five officers, gave Hill the title of Grand Councillor, and paid him $2 for each chapter he organized. As a first step, Hill printed up a circular—one that broadcast a rousing call to change—to hand out to sharecroppers.

O you laborers of the earth hear the word. The time is at hand that all men, all nations and tongues must receive a just reward. This union wants to know why it is that the laborers cannot control their just earnings which they work for. . . . Why should we be cut off from fair play? Hear us, o God, hear us!

Hill's circular advised the sharecroppers to "get 15 men and 12 women" together, and then he would come "set them up" as a union chapter.

Dr. Powell accompanied Hill to the organizational meetings and would sit at a table, registering members. It cost the men $1.50 and women 50 cents to join, and Powell would ask them questions to determine their moral fitness. Did they believe in the Almighty God? Did they give respect to all humankind? Did they obey the law at all times? Did they go to church? The younger men had to attest that they had properly registered for the draft, and all had to know their preachers' names. Finally, they had to declare themselves American patriots by responding yes to this question: "Will you defend this Government and Her Constitution at all times?" Powell would then attest to their fitness and hand them a membership card.

Initially, neither Hill nor Powell stepped forward with a plan for helping the farmers settle their accounts. Instead, Hill focused on building the union. Those joining were asked if they would like to buy shares in the union, at $5 a share, with the money to be used to build the Grand Lodge's headquarters in Winchester and to buy land. Anyone buying $50 in shares, Hill said, would have his name inscribed in the building and be invited as a delegate to the union's inaugural state convention. He provided everyone who bought shares with a stock certificate, which stated that income from the building and land would be paid back to the union members on a per-share basis, and he deposited the money he collected into the union's account with the Bank of Winchester.

At the end of meetings, Hill asked everyone to stand, and it was then that he most powerfully stoked their emotions, leading them in a song he'd composed, set to the melody of "Maryland, My Maryland":

Ye farmers of this mighty land,
Organize, oh organize!
To firmly stand against each wrong
Organize, oh organize!
Your only hope is union strong
Organize, oh organize!
To break the bonds of slavery
That bind you now from sea to sea
And from oppression to be free,
Organize, oh organize!
Your calling was the first on earth
Organize, oh organize!
And ever since has proved its worth
Organize, oh organize!
Then come ye farmers, good and true
The die is cast—it's up to you
Organize, oh organize!

Hill must have known that he was treading on dangerous ground with such lyrics, and in late July, he took his rebellious talk a step further. After the sixty-eight black families on the Theo Fathauer plantation in Ratio received balance-due settlements from the 1918 harvest, Hill promised that he would find an attorney to help them get a proper settlement at the end of this year's season. While 1918 may have been a lost cause, 1919 did not have to be, and Hill began offering this attorney-finding service to all of the union lodges in Phillips County. "It was a fact that the people could not get statements of their accounts and the custom in that section was the landlord would take the cotton and seed and ship them away," Hill said. "I did what I thought was right in the matter. I advised people to get the help of some honest white lawyers."

Hill threw himself into this new task. He'd previously taken a correspondence course to become a private investigator, and he now fancied himself the "detective on the case." He contacted Ulysses Bratton, who had opened a branch office in Helena, and in mid-September, several of the Ratio farmers, acting upon his advice, traveled to Little Rock to confer with Bratton and to provide him with the balance-due stubs that documented their travails.

"They inquired of us as to whether or not they had any legal rights in the matter. We advised them that they did," Bratton said. He also told them how he would proceed. For a fee of $100 per farmer, with $50 up front, he would meet with Theo Fathauer or his agent and request an itemized account of their expenses in 1919. "If refused," he said, he "would immediately file suit in the Circuit Court of Phillips County."

News that the Ratio sharecroppers were planning to challenge their landlords in this way quickly spread to other union lodges, and on Thursday, September 25, Hill and Powell traveled to Elaine to talk to the members there about doing the same. It was declared an "open" meeting, with any farmer welcome to attend, and many of the Hoop Spur sharecroppers came. Hill, dressed as always in a frock coat, spoke in his usual animated way, and emotions rose as he called upon the men and women to rise up and "fight" for their legal rights. The sharecroppers tallied up twenty-one landlords who could be sued, and they discussed whether, on October 6, they would in unison ask their landowners for itemized accounts of their expenses. No one would give up his cotton until he received this information. Others spoke of holding back their cotton even longer. A World Cotton Conference was going to be held in New Orleans from October 13 to 16, and perhaps, with the federal government promoting cotton products to foreign buyers at that convention, the price of cotton would soar even higher.

"Let us see what Uncle Sam means!" Hill shouted. "Uncle Sam can help you when nobody else can!"

The Phillips County sharecroppers were thinking of doing the unthinkable. They were talking of holding back the cotton from their white landlords for days and even weeks. This was akin to going on strike, and perhaps a few even knew the history of how, in 1891, the Colored Farmers' Alliance, which claimed to have 1.2 million members throughout the South, had called for a national strike.

The labor stoppage mostly fizzled in the face of threats from white landowners, but about twenty-five cotton pickers in Lee County, Arkansas, just to the north of Phillips County, had gone ahead with it, and by the time the dust had settled, white posses had gunned down two of the men and lynched nine more, a killing spree that Southern newspapers applauded. "Negroes," the *Memphis Appeal-Avalanche* editorialized, "should be made to understand that they cannot commit these outrages with impunity, and that the penalty is very severe." Yet the sharecroppers in Elaine were now discussing committing just such an outrage, and the noise from the church, which was located on the far side of the colored section of town, adjacent to a cotton patch, carried all the way to the other end of town, where the whites—and several of the plantation owners—lived.

As the meeting drew to a close, Hill announced that the following Wednesday he would bring a representative from Bratton's law firm to Ratio. Bratton was ready to sign contracts with the sharecroppers. Hill and the lawyer would then come, either later that afternoon or early the next morning, to Elaine and Hoop Spur. Anyone wishing to hire Bratton could do so at that time. The sharecroppers' rebellion was reaching a point of no return, and Powell, as a final word of advice, told them that from now on they were "to keep their racks full." There was no mistaking what he meant: the guards, at all future union meetings, were to make sure their guns were fully loaded.

AFTER ED WARE ENTERED the Hoop Spur church that night of Tuesday, September 30, he sat at a table in front, just to the left of the pulpit, where Jim Miller was speaking, and facing the wooden benches. As the secretary for the lodge, he kept the membership lists and registration papers, and a number of farmers had come that night to join, queuing up in front of the table to hand over the $1.50 or 50-cent initiation fee. Ware, who had gone to school through the fourth grade, filled out the examination certificates for each of them, just as Dr. Powell usually did, asking them about their religious beliefs and their willingness to defend the Constitution, although he had difficulty gripping the pencil, as two of his fingers were crippled from his many years picking cotton. At times, he appeared distracted, for he was deeply troubled by his own thoughts. On the way to the church, he'd told Preacher Will McFarland, who'd walked over with him, that he was "going to resign."

In many ways, Ware was in a different boat than the others. Forty-eight years old, he'd come here from Louisiana, where he and his wife, Lulu, had suffered one heartache after another—all four of their children had died from fever and other illnesses. But he'd done well for himself in Hoop Spur, having scraped together enough money to buy a Ford, which he'd turned into a taxi, shuttling others back and forth to Elaine and Helena. The taxi service in turn had provided him with money to rent 120 acres outright, and while he worked some of the acreage himself, much of it was farmed by other black families, including Sallie Giles and her two sons, who were now *his* tenants. He owned two mules, a horse, a Jersey cow, eight hogs, 135 chickens, a wagon, and all of the farming tools he needed, and he'd turned his cabin into a nice home, furnished with several dressers and a nice mirror. When he smiled, he showed off five gold teeth, evidence that he, unlike most of the union members, could afford to go to a dentist.

Ware had joined the Hoop Spur lodge in early September, shortly after it had formed, and he knew that it was risky to be one of its officers. Twice in the past week he'd run into trouble because of the union. The previous Wednesday he'd been in the Elaine post office when a white landowner he knew, a man named McCullough, had curled his finger and said, "Ed, come here."

"Do you belong to the union?" McCullough asked.

"Yes sir. I am secretary of it at Hoop Spur."

"Tell me, what is that thing?"

"You know as much about it as I do. It is called the Progressive Farmers Household Union of America, as I understand it. It is to make better conditions among the farmers and that is why I belong to it."

"I hear you are the leader."

"No, I'm not."

"We hear that you boys are making the lodge to make strikes."

"That's not so."

"You get out of that thing, because it is going to cause trouble here."

"I mean to do the square thing."

"Well, you get in the square and get out of that thing."

Although the conversation unnerved him, Ware spent the next night ferrying farmers from Hoop Spur to the union meeting at the Elaine church, taking advantage of an opportunity, he later explained, "to make money." On Friday, he brought a wagon of cotton into town to have it ginned, only to be confronted once again, this time by merchants insisting that he sell them the cotton he'd just baled. "They offered me 24 cents and then 33 cents [a pound] for it," Ware said. "I refused to take it, and they said they were going to take the cotton at that price. I rejected their offer and said I'd take my cotton to Helena to sell. They then said they were going to mob me, but I was warned about it. So when they tried to fool me into their store so they could get me I refused to go in and kept out of their way."

Ware—having been threatened with a lynching—waited for the weekend to pass, and then he drove to Helena and gave his "business over to an attorney." He also noticed that Helena merchants were "paying 44.5 cents a pound for short cotton," confirmation that the Elaine merchants had been trying to cheat him.

The threat of Ware being "mobbed" wasn't the only sign that trouble was brewing. A number of union members were complaining that their landlords, in the past couple of weeks, had tried to chase them off. While much of the cotton still needed to be picked, a landowner could always get day laborers to handle this chore, and they could be hired for as little as a penny a pound. There would be no need then to quarrel with sharecroppers raising a fuss about being owed half of 50-cent-a-pound cotton. Both John Martin and Will Wordlow had been told to leave, as had Frank Moore and his father. The Moores were living on a 200-acre farm, run by a white man named Billy Archdale, where nine of the thirteen families had been forced to flee. Ware considered Moore, who was one of the leaders of the Hoop Spur lodge, "the bravest man" in the union, and yet even Moore was unsure of how long he could last now that Archdale "was threatening to run us away from our crops."

But Ware said nothing more about his worries during the meeting. Instead, he patiently stayed at the table, signing up new members, until at last, a few minutes before 11:00 P.M., the line of men and women waiting to join dwindled and came to an end. Ware closed the membership book and put away the examination forms. The money from the membership dues, he knew, would have to be sent to Winchester. Miller continued to talk, leading the discussion about what the lodge should do. Surely they had a right to hire Bratton, but did they dare? They all knew that there wasn't a plantation owner alive who wouldn't object to being called into court. And who were they to do such a thing? Most everyone in the church was dirt poor, and most were illiterate, and their own songs told everything you needed to know about their place in society—"None fer de niggers." Ware looked briefly at his friends sitting across from him— Frank Moore and Will McFarland and their wives and his wife, Lulu, were all together—and he was, as he later recalled, about to stand when he heard a knock on the rear window on the church's north side. It was Will Wright, and he had his face pressed up against the glass.

"A car has driven up and stopped," he said.

Outside, Lit Simmons and the others looked up the road, toward a small bridge about 40 yards away. A moment earlier, the car had pulled up before the bridge, turned off its engine, and cut its lights. And now it was just sitting there, in the darkness, waiting.

The Path to Hoop Spur

THE GUNFIRE THAT WAS about to erupt at Hoop Spur would prove, in the months and years ahead, to be a pivotal moment in the nation's history, and to understand why that is so, it is necessary to briefly backtrack to a specific date: December 4, 1865. That is the day that Congress met for the first time following the end of the Civil War. From there, it is easy to follow a path, one forged from politics, science, and U.S. Supreme Court decisions, to that fateful Tuesday night in 1919. When that car slid to a halt, all of America had reason to hold its breath for fear of what would happen next.

The Thirty-ninth Congress, in the winter of 1865, was faced with the daunting challenge of putting the country back together again, and at the heart of this reconstruction effort, the *New York Times* noted, was this pressing question: "What shall we do with the blacks?" Abraham Lincoln may have pronounced the 4 million slaves in Southern states free on January 1, 1863, but that left open the question of what rights they would have, and as Congress opened its session, there were three disparate visions on the table for resolving it: Southern whites had one point of view, blacks another, and Northern whites a third.

Although the South may have lost the war, whites there were already busily putting the chains back on the freedmen. The previous spring, President Andrew Johnson, acting without the advice and consent of Congress, which was not then in session, had issued a Proclamation of Amnesty whereby most former Confederates, so long as they swore an oath of loyalty to the Union, were pardoned and allowed to reclaim the land they'd owned prior to the war. Moreover, Johnson decreed that once a majority of a state's voters had taken this oath, they could form a state government and rejoin the Union. White Democrats in the South immediately took advantage of this proclamation to elect ex-Confederates as their leaders and enact "black codes" to regain their control over the freedmen. The state laws, among other things, allowed for blacks to be arrested as "vagrants" and forced to work, without pay, for whites that paid off their "fines." These laws, observed Massachusetts senator Henry Wilson, made the freedmen "the slaves of society."

Alarmed and frightened, blacks responded by holding Freedmen's Conventions during the summer and fall of 1865 to articulate their hopes for the future. The South Carolina convention eloquently summed up the dream of blacks everywhere:

> We simply ask that we shall be recognized as *men;* that there be no obstructions placed in our way; that the same laws which govern *white men* shall govern *black men;* that we have the right of trial by a jury of our peers, that schools be established for the education of *colored children* as well as *white,* and that the advantages of both colors shall, in this respect, be *equal;* that no impediments be put in the way of our acquiring homesteads for ourselves and our people, that in short, we be dealt with as others are—in equity and justice.

In short, the nation's 4.5 million blacks wanted full citizenship. However, while Abraham Lincoln, a year before his assassination on April 15, 1865, had declared that "the restoration of the Rebel States to the Union must rest upon the principle of civil and political equality of both races," this notion of equality was still viewed as radical by most white Northerners, including abolitionists. Most Northern states did not allow blacks to vote or provided them with only limited suffrage, and only one state—Massachusetts—allowed blacks to serve on juries. Nor, in many states, were blacks allowed to testify in court against whites. "If the color is not right," the Ohio Supreme Court had asserted in 1846, "the man can not testify. The truth shall not be received from a black man." The Thirteenth Amendment, which would soon be formally ratified, prohibited slavery and declared blacks to be free, but that did not mean that Northern whites were prepared to provide blacks with political equality.

As its first order of business in December 1865, the Thirty-ninth Congress refused to seat the delegates from the ex–Confederate states, thereby formally rejecting Johnson's restoration plan and serving notice that the black codes were not to be tolerated. While the vision that Southern whites had for the future had been summarily rejected, the "Negro question" still loomed. What federally guaranteed rights should the freed slaves have? And once that question was answered, how could those rights—given that the country had been born a federation of independent states—be secured?

Putting the country back together again, the 192 members of Congress realized, was going to require rethinking its fundamental makeup. To undertake this monumental task, Congress appointed a fifteen-member Joint Committee on Reconstruction, chaired by Maine senator William Fessenden and Pennsylvania congressman Thaddeus Stevens. In so many ways, the Thirty-ninth Congress faced a challenge equal to that confronted by the delegates to the Constitutional Convention in 1787, and it was best that it not rush ahead. "Let us rather make haste slowly," said House Speaker Schuyler Colfax, "and we can hope that the foundation of our Government, when thus reconstructed on the basis of indisputable loyalty, will be as eternal as the stars."

ALTHOUGH THE FOUNDING FATHERS waxed eloquent about protecting individual liberty and freedom, the Constitution they drew up in 1787 was, in essence, a pro-slavery document. Not only did it authorize slavery in the Southern states, but it made the federal government the guardian of the slave owner's property rights. Article IV, section 2, clause 3 of the Constitution declared that if a slave escaped into a Northern state, the state would have to hand over the person upon "claim to the party to whom such service or labor may be due." All states were duty-bound to cooperate with slave-catchers, which, prior to the war, had frustrated abolitionists to no end. The Constitution, thundered William Lloyd Garrison, was "a covenant with death, an agreement with hell."

The Committee on Reconstruction, as it began the process of breaking with this past, quickly realized that Lincoln, in arguing that the freedmen would need to be given *full* equality under the law, had been politically prescient. With slavery having been abolished, a black living in the South was no longer to be counted as three-fifths of a person, but rather as a full person for the purpose of calculating how many representatives a state sent to Congress. The number of congressmen from the Southern states, once they were readmitted to the Union, was due to increase dramatically, and if the four million blacks in the South were not allowed to vote, the five million whites in the South would have the representational power of nine million people, and all of the Southern congressmen were certain to be white Democrats. The North faced the prospect of winning the war but losing the peace, and the only possible solution, the Republicans in Congress came to realize, was to grant Negroes suffrage, and thus the rights of full citizenship.

"I admit that this species of legislation is absolutely revolutionary," thundered Maine senator Lot Morrill. "But are we not in the midst of a revolution?"

With that decision having been made, the committee turned its attention to securing those rights. The states—and not the federal government—had always been seen as the primary protector of civil liberties, and clearly whites in the ex–Confederate states could not be trusted with that responsibility. Although the Bill of Rights seemed to provide a national guarantee of civil liberties, the U.S. Supreme Court, in 1833, had ruled in *Barron v. Baltimore* that the ten amendments served as a curb only on the powers of the federal government. It did not similarly limit the states. They were free to abridge the fundamental rights of their citizens, and before the war Southern states had passed many laws that did just that, making it a crime, for example, to speak out against slavery. If blacks were to be made citizens and their rights secured against state abridgement, that legal precedent would have to be repudiated. "We must see to it that hereafter personal liberty and personal rights are placed in the keeping of the nation," said Ohio congressman James A. Garfield (who in 1880 would be elected president). "If our Constitution does not now afford all the powers necessary to that end, we must ask the people to add them."

Ohio congressman John A. Bingham, a lawyer who had been an early advocate of emancipation, took the lead in drafting a constitutional amendment that would achieve that end. If the federal government had enjoyed the power to enforce a slave owner's rights under the Constitution, surely it could now assert the power to protect personal liberty. The amendment, he reasoned, would need to "arm the Congress of the United States, by the consent of the people of the United States, with the power to enforce the Bill of Rights." He wrote:

> All persons born or naturalized in the United States and subject to the jurisdiction thereof, are citizens of the United States and of the State wherein they reside. No State shall make or enforce any law which shall abridge the privileges or immunities of citizens of the United States; nor shall any State deprive any person of life, liberty, or property, without due process of law; nor deny to any person within its jurisdiction the equal protection of the laws.

There could be no mistaking the dramatic effect that those eighty words, which constituted the first section of the proposed amendment, would have on the country. Blacks would become citizens. Black men would have the right to vote. States would be limited by the Bill of Rights. Whites and blacks would have equal rights under the law. Most profound, a federal government that previously had been the guardian of a slave owner's "property rights" would become the guardian of liberty and freedom.

"Why should this not pass?" asked Minnesota congressman Ignatius Donnelly as Congress debated the proposal. "Are the promises of the Constitution mere verbiage? Are its sacred pledges of life, liberty and property to fall to the ground through lack of power to enforce them? Or shall that great Constitution be what its founders meant it to be, a shield and a protection over the head of the lowliest and poorest citizen in the remotest region of the nation?"

Although it took two years and the passage of a Military Reconstruction Act that put the South under the control of federal troops, the Fourteenth Amendment was ratified by the requisite number of states and made a part of the Constitution on July 28, 1868. All of the ex–Confederate states, in order to be readmitted to the Union, were required to ratify it as well. Acceptance of this new principle of equality became the price of admission to the United States, and over the next ten years, the Republican-controlled Congress continued to erect an edifice of law to perfect this revolution. The 1867 Federal Habeas Corpus Act gave federal courts the right to review state criminal proceedings and determine whether people were being imprisoned "in violation of the Constitution, or of any treaty or law of the United States." The Fifteenth Amendment, which was ratified on March 30, 1870, prohibited states from denying citizens the right to vote on account of race, and thus further secured for black men the suffrage granted by the Fourteenth Amendment. Finally, in 1875, Congress passed a Civil Rights Act barring hotels, restaurants, theaters, and amusement parks from discriminating against blacks.

The revolution in law that blacks had hoped for had been achieved. As a result of the Fourteenth and Fifteenth Amendments, and the rest of the edifice of law that had been erected, the United States was now a far different country. "The black man is free, the black man is enfranchised, and this by the organic law of the land," exulted Frederick Douglass, the great black abolitionist. "Never was revolution more complete."

THE REVOLUTION WAS A PERIOD when this change in constitutional law enabled blacks to take their place in the body politic, and flourish in other ways as well. Armed with the vote, they elected sixteen of their peers to Congress between 1868 and 1877, and hundreds more to state legislatures. At the local level, blacks served as county coroners, tax assessors, and court clerks, found jobs as police officers and firefighters, and served on grand and petit juries. The freedmen also showed an uncommon passion for education, with children in rural areas often walking miles to attend newly opened schools. "They are *crazy* to learn, and will endure almost any penance rather than be deprived of this privilege," a North Carolina teacher said. This access to education proved to be a seed that produced, in the decades ahead, a black professional class that included doctors, teachers, and attorneys. Many blacks also became successful businessmen, owners of barbershops, cafes, saloons, and grocery stores. Together the educated professionals and the business owners came to form a black elite, which by the turn of the century had even taken on some of the airs of an upper-crust aristocracy.

And yet the opportunity for blacks to participate fully in American society always hung by a thread. The truth was that the North had imposed the Fourteenth Amendment on the South, the ratification process there involving the disenfranchisement of many ex-Confederates. Most whites in the South did not accept this principle of equality under the law, and certainly not the notion that blacks should vote, and they gathered under the umbrella of the Democratic party, vowing to resurrect a "white man's government in a white man's country." The Ku Klux Klan, which formed in the wake of the Civil War, acted in essence as the party's paramilitary arm. They killed white carpetbaggers and black political leaders; they terrorized blacks attempting to vote; they burned down black churches and schools; they chased away black teachers and ministers. "The time has arrived," the Klan in Arkansas boasted. "Blood must flow. The true must be saved."

In 1870, Congress held hearings on the white terrorist groups and compiled a thirteen-volume report on the atrocities they'd committed. Congress also passed three Federal Enforcement Acts that allowed for federal prosecution of terrorist groups, and over the next several years, U.S. prosecutors indicted hundreds of Klansmen and obtained a number of convictions, particularly when the juries included blacks. "We have broken up Ku Klux in North Carolina," Judge Hugh Bond reported in 1872. "Everybody now wants to confess and we are picking out the top puppies only for trial." But all-white juries also regularly declared the Klansmen innocent, and by the early 1870s, it was evident that the future of the South, and thus of the nation, was up for grabs. Would terrorism or the law triumph? The violent tactics of the Klan promised a future in which blacks would once again be a subjugated race, perhaps not enslaved but not citizens either, while an enforcement of Reconstruction law promised a society where blacks would enjoy at least a measure of justice, economic opportunity, and political representation. Two paths lay ahead of the South, and it was then, with the country's future in the balance, that the first Fourteenth Amendment case made its way to the U.S. Supreme Court.

REPUBLICANS HAD REASON TO be confident that their revolution in constitutional law was in good hands. Five of the justices had been appointed by Lincoln and three by Ulysses S. Grant, and the ninth justice, Nathan Clifford, while having been appointed by a Democrat, was from New Hampshire and thus not likely to be hostile to the Reconstruction amendments. This was a solid Republican Court, and the case before them was not, on the face of it, of great importance. In 1869, the Louisiana legislature had passed a law that required all butchers in New Orleans to set up shop in one location, but white butchers had filed suit, arguing that the law had taken away their property—that is, their butcher shops—without due process, violating their Fourteenth Amendment rights. At its core, this was a case about the powers of a state to regulate commerce. Numerous states had in fact passed such laws as public health measures, which the Supreme Court had previously ruled were constitutional. However, the Court had been waiting for a Fourteenth Amendment case to come its way, and Justice Samuel F. Miller, while writing up a 5–4 decision against the butchers, decided to explore

Reconstruction law, and by the time he was done, there was not much left to it.

Prior to the passage of the Fourteenth Amendment, Miller wrote, there was no "clear and comprehensive definition of citizenship." Now, all of those born in the country could be said to enjoy both state and national citizenship, but these realms were distinct, he said. The protection of nearly all civil rights had to remain with the states, for to "transfer the security and protection [of these rights] from the States to the Federal government" would "radically change the whole theory of the relations of the State and Federal governments to each other and of both these governments to the people." No such radical change was "intended by Congress," Miller insisted. As such, it was up to Louisiana—and not the federal government—to protect the butchers' property rights. The only rights that fell under federal protection, Miller added, were those that could be seen as national in character, such as the right to use navigable waters.

Republicans in Congress who had drafted the amendment, and who had debated for months over the need to make the federal government the protector of the basic rights of all citizens, were stunned. "The American people would say that it was not law and could not be law," fumed Wisconsin senator Timothy Howe. The four dissenting justices saw it the same way, astonished that the majority had so evidently thwarted the will of Congress. The Fourteenth Amendment, they said, was designed to "provide National security against violations by the States of the fundamental rights of the citizen." But now, as a result of this decision, wrote Justice Stephen Field, it could be considered a "vain and idle enactment, which accomplished nothing, and most unnecessarily excited Congress and the people on its passage."

Had only one justice in the majority voted differently, the next hundred years of American history might have been dramatically different, and the suffering of blacks in American society not nearly so great. But the *Slaughterhouse* cases were now precedent law, and with that decision serving as a guide, the Supreme Court quickly tore down the entire edifice of Reconstruction law, brick by brick. In *United States v. Cruikshank* (1876), it effectively gutted the Federal

Enforcement Acts, ruling that the federal government did not have the constitutional authority to prosecute the leaders of a white mob in Colfax, Louisiana, that had murdered more than fifty black men after a disputed gubernatorial election. The court reasoned that while the Fourteenth Amendment barred states from depriving individuals of "life, liberty, or property without due process of law," it did not bar private individuals from doing so. The mob leaders were set free, and whites throughout the South knew what this meant: violence could be used to keep blacks in their place, and those who killed need not worry about going to jail. "When the decision was reached, and the prisoners released," a white attorney in Louisiana said, "there was the utmost joy in Louisiana, and with it a return of confidence which gave best hopes for the future."

Next, in *Reese v. United States* (1876), the Court ruled that although states could not exclude voters on account of race, they could set up standards that would restrict who could vote, and this opened the door to the use of poll taxes and literacy tests to disenfranchise blacks. In *United States v. Harris* (1883), the court expanded on its *Cruikshank* decision, ruling that the federal government could not prosecute whites who had burst into a Tennessee jail, seized four black men awaiting trial, and beaten them so badly that one died. The Court had now given its blessing to lynch mobs who would substitute the hangman's noose for a jury trial. Finally, that same year, the Court ruled that the Civil Rights Act of 1875 was unconstitutional, declaring that while inns, restaurants, and theaters might be public places, they were privately owned and thus had a right to discriminate. The Court even chided blacks for thinking it might be otherwise: "When a man has emerged from slavery and by the aid of beneficent legislation has shaken off the inseparable concomitants of that state, there must be some stage in the progress of his elevation when he takes the rank of a mere citizen, and ceases to be a special favorite of the laws."

The hope and promise of Reconstruction were now gone. As a political reality, Reconstruction had ended in 1877, when the federal government had withdrawn the last of its military troops from the South. This decision marked the burial of Reconstruction law. "A Republican Supreme Court, really a conclave of donkeys, there in Washington declared the whole [Reconstruction] thing null and void, thus leaving the Negro, both those freed and those who were free before, in a condition compared with which the serfs of Russia are lords," raged Bishop Henry McNeil Turner. Other black leaders added their voices to this chorus of protest, and perhaps Frederick Douglass, in a speech a few years later, summed it up best: the "so-called emancipation" could now be considered a "stupendous fraud."

WHILE THE U.S. SUPREME Court may have led the way, the nation as a whole had come to the same decision: the principles of Reconstruction law belonged to a time that was now past. Northern newspapers applauded the Court's voiding of the Civil Rights Act, the *New York Times* editorializing that "the Court has been serving a useful purpose in thus undoing the work of Congress." And with Congress's work undone, Southern states quickly began establishing the legal structure of a Jim Crow society, in which blacks were reminded at every turn of their inferior status. Tennessee became the first to pass a law mandating that railway facilities be segregated, while Mississippi, starting in 1890, pioneered the use of literacy tests and poll taxes to prevent blacks from registering to vote. School boards reduced funding for black schools to a pittance, and as the South set up this separate and unequal society, the Supreme Court provided its blessing every step of the way.

In *Plessy v. Ferguson* (1896), the Court approved state laws requiring segregated railway facilities so long as they were "equal" in kind, turning a blind eye to the fact that Negroes were forced to ride in dirty baggage cars. Next, in *Williams v. Mississippi* (1898), it reasoned that states could use literacy and "understanding" tests to restrict the vote because such laws "reach weak and vicious white men as well as weak and vicious black men." The Court had once again found refuge in rhetorical camouflage, for the justices well knew that such tests were administered by white registrars, who selectively applied the exclusionary rule to blacks. As Mississippi politician James Vardaman put it, the purpose of its voter-registration law was to "eliminate the nigger from politics. Not the ignorant, but the nigger." Finally, in 1899, the Court even retreated from its theoretical "separate but equal" standard, ruling in *Cumming v. Richmond County Board of Education* that if a school district couldn't afford high schools for both races, then it was free to offer such education only to whites. The decision pleased many Southern politicians— "The greatest mistake the white race has ever made was to educate the free Negro," said South Carolina governor Cole Bease—and by 1910, fewer than 3 percent of black youth in the South had the opportunity to attend a public high school.

Meanwhile, lynching became an ever more prominent part of the Southern landscape. By the early 1890s, more than one hundred black men were being killed each year in this way. While many of the victims were accused of having committed murder, rape, assault, or some other crime, others were strung up for violating a social norm, such as "being uppity" or opening a business that competed with a white one. As one Mississippian said, "When there is a row, we feel like killing a nigger whether he has done anything or not." The lynchings also evolved into public spectacles that drew large crowds, with fathers bringing theirs sons to watch as blacks were beaten, shot, and tortured. Newspapers reported how mobs cut off their victims' fingers, ears, and genitals before killing them and burning their bodies on pyres. Photographers even turned their pictures of the lynchings into commemorative postcards, suitable for mailing to family and friends. As one man wrote: "This is the barbecue we had last night my picture is to the left with a cross over it your son Joe."

In 1892, a mob in Texarkana, Arkansas, became one of the first to burn a black man alive at the stake, a crowd of fifteen thousand gathering to watch the "roasting" of Edward Coy. He had been accused of assaulting a white woman, with whom he'd apparently been intimate, and with the pyre ready to be lit, Coy pitifully asked her how she could have him burned alive after they had been "sweethearting" for so long. There were at least twelve other blacks burned alive over the next eight years, and since no one was ever prosecuted for these burnings, Harvard professor Albert Bushnell Hart suggested in 1900 that perhaps the country should drop the pretense and officially sanction them: "If the people of certain states are determined to burn colored men at the stake, those states would better legalize the practice."

The absence of any federal law protecting blacks against white violence was clearly leading the United States to a very dark place, and yet even this did not stir the U.S. Supreme Court, when given the opportunity in 1906, to rethink its *Cruikshank* and *Harris* decisions. On August 17, 1903, a mob in White Hall, Arkansas (about 70 miles west of Elaine), arrived at a sawmill armed with torches and rifles, and demanded that the owner fire all blacks working there and replace them with whites. Federal attorneys in Arkansas dusted off what was left of the Federal Enforcement Acts and convicted three leaders of the mob, with the presiding judge, Jacob Trieber, telling the jury that the case raised "fundamental principles of our government, that of the right of every citizen, be he white or black, to work for a living, to engage in the pursuit of happiness and a livelihood. It is a question of whether right and law should prevail or the unlicensed mob." The U.S. Supreme Court, in *Hodges v. United States,* came down on the side of the mob. It set the three men free, ruling that precedent law was quite settled, and thus it was "vain to contend that the Federal Constitution secures to a citizen of the United States the right to work at a given occupation or particular calling free from injury, oppression, or interference by individual citizens."

There was simply not to be any federal check on white violence. This was a matter for states to handle, and a Mississippi sheriff cheerfully explained how the law now worked in his state: "We have three classes of homicide. If a nigger kills a white man, that's murder. If a white man kills a nigger, that's justifiable homicide. And if a nigger kills another nigger, that's one less nigger."

ON MAY 31, 1909, more than three hundred men and women of both races crowded into the Charity Organization Hall in New York to discuss the deteriorating position of the Negro in American society and what could be done about it. Yet the organizers of the National Negro Conference, which was to lead to the founding of the National Association for the Advancement of Colored People, put none of the obvious wrongs—lynchings, Jim Crow laws, disenfranchisement—at the top of its agenda. Instead, on that first day of the conference, everyone in the audience was asked to look at three brains that had been put on display: one was the brain of a white man, the second of a Negro, and the third of an ape. The purpose of this presentation, wrote W. E. B. Du Bois, the most prominent black scholar in America at the time, was to address a question that he and others believed lay at the heart of the race problem: "From the standpoint of modern science, are Negroes men?"

Despite the Enlightenment rhetoric in the Declaration of Independence that "all men are created equal," this question, of whether Negroes were really part of the human family, had been present in American intellectual circles since the country's founding. Even Thomas Jefferson, author of that ringing phrase in the Declaration of Independence, speculated, in his *Notes on the State of Virginia,* that blacks might, in fact, be "inferior to whites in the endowments both of body and mind." He called for "scientific investigations" into the matter, and in 1821, a Dutch professor of anatomy, Petrus Camper, started such research with a report that the "facial angle" of the Negro was midway between that of an orangutan and that of a European.* Other scientists soon suggested that this progression—from ape to Negro to white European—reflected a "chain of being." In 1839, Dr. Samuel George Morton, a professor of medicine at the University of Pennsylvania, announced that whites had larger skulls than blacks, and argued that this was evidence of their higher intelligence.† Morton speculated that whites and blacks did not in fact

---

* This is the angle formed by two intersecting lines—one drawn horizontally from the ears to the nose, and the other from the upper lip to the forehead.

† As Stephen Jay Gould wrote in *The Mismeasure of Man,* Morton's measurements were badly flawed and led to an erroneous conclusion about the relative size of black and white craniums.

share a common ancestor, but rather had been created separately. His theory of polygenesis had an obvious appeal to pro-slavery advocates, and two Southern physicians, Samuel Cartwright and Josiah Nott, soon claimed that blacks had distinct nervous, circulatory, and pulmonary systems. Most revealing, Cartwright said, was the Negro head, which was "anatomically constructed more after the fashion of the simiadiae," with the lower part of the face "as in the lower animals and monkey tribes."

Morton, Nott, and the others were hailed as having created an American school of ethnology (although Nott called it "niggerology"), and their findings, wrote an editor at the *Richmond Examiner*, led inescapably to the conclusion "that negroes are not *men*, in the sense which that term is used by the Declaration of Independence." This line of research also proved compelling to Louis Agassiz, the famous Swiss biologist who emigrated to the United States in 1846. After he saw Morton's skulls, he became a believer in polygenesis, and for the next twenty-five years he taught his students at Harvard University that blacks were a "separate species." In 1884, one of his students, Nathaniel Southgate Shaler, writing in the *Atlantic Monthly* and other mainstream publications, popularized Agassiz's notion that the Negro skull "closed" at an early age, when the child was only twelve or thirteen years old, which prevented the Negro intellect from developing.

American science had reached a consensus: blacks were inferior in kind to whites, and any number of America's best and brightest, teaching at Harvard and other prestigious schools, expounded on why the Negro's peculiar physiology made the race such a threat to white civilization. Lester Ward, professor of sociology at Brown University, reasoned that a black man was moved to rape a white woman because he realized that mating with a more "advanced being" would "raise his race to a littler higher level." Others said that blacks raped white women because their "regressive, apelike" makeup left them unable to control their lower instincts. And since the Negro skull closed at an early age, it was a mistake to think that education could improve the race. The Negro brain, concluded the editors of *American Medicine* in 1907, "cannot comprehend higher studies any more than a horse can understand the rule of three." Had the nation known these "anatomical facts" at the end of the Civil War, they added, it would not have made the tragic mistake of giving the Negro the right to vote. "Leaders in all political parties now acknowledge the error of human equality," they advised their readers.

Artists, writers, politicians, and the rest of American society all piled on too. Cartoonists drew black characters with simian features and gave them such names as Prince Orang Outan. Professor Charles Carroll's *The Negro a Beast,* published in 1900, proved to be a big hit with readers; in 1905, Thomas Dixon's bestseller *The Clansman* described blacks as "half child, half animal . . . a being who, left to his will, roams at night and sleeps in the day, whose speech knows no word of love, whose passions, once aroused, are as the fury of the tiger." The *Los Angeles Times* published a poem on the "Black Peril" that described the Negro as "the lecherous ape, not human quite," while the New York Zoo put an African man, a pygmy who was from the Chirichiri tribe, on display in its monkey house, an exhibit that caused a stampede of visitors. Meanwhile, black defendants in Alabama were tried by a judge who declared that "there's just as much difference in human nature and Negro nature as there is between the smell of Limburger cheese and a bunch of roses."

Science and art had helped to poison the image of blacks in the white mind, and this was why the organizers of the National Negro Conference opened their meeting with a display of the three brains, and a talk by Livingston Farrand, president of Cornell University, on this subject. The belief in Negro inferiority created a rationale for an unequal society, but with the three brains on display, it was easy for the audience to see that two were of one kind, with pronounced frontal lobes, and the third—the ape's—of another. The belief in an ape-to-Negro-to-Caucasian chain of being could be easily dispelled, and yet, in 1909, theirs was a voice of reason lost in the wilderness of American racism. The notion of blacks as subhuman had taken hold, Negroes were a race that could rightly be viewed with fear and loathing, and this belief was causing Jim Crow policies to spread throughout the country. Baltimore and numerous other cities passed ordinances that restricted blacks to crowded ghettoes. A number of rural towns in the South, in a form of ethnic cleansing, drove them from their communities altogether. Hotels and restaurants in the North discriminated against blacks; hospitals treated them in segregated wards; and the president of Harvard University, Charles Eliot, said all of this made sense. In a democracy, he explained, "civilized white men" didn't want to rub elbows with "barbarous black men." Now and then a lynch mob in the North struck, and in 1911, a mob in Coatesville, Pennsylvania, burned a black man alive.

White hatred toward blacks was sinking ever deeper into the culture, and in 1913 Woodrow Wilson let Jim Crow march into the halls of the federal government. During his campaign, he had promised Negroes "fair dealing," but once he entered the White House he betrayed that promise, standing by as two of his cabinet members segregated the Post Office and Treasury Department. "The federal government has set the colored apart as if mere contact with them were contamination," the NAACP angrily wrote Wilson. "Behind screens and closed doors they now sit as though leprous. How long will it be before the hateful epithets of 'nigger' and 'Jim Crow' are openly applied?" There seemed to be no place in America where blacks were welcome, and then, in 1915, a movie invited all of America to join a lynch mob.

D. W. Griffith's *Birth of a Nation* was a technological masterpiece and, at three hours, by far the longest film ever made. Griffith astounded audiences with his close-ups, his fades, and the epic sweep of his story: the Civil War and Reconstruction. His history, however, was an adaptation of Dixon's *The Clansman,* a narrative told from a Southern gentleman's point of view. The antebellum South was remembered as a near paradise, the slaves picking cotton on plantations happy and carefree, watched over by a protective master. The tragic Civil War brought a lamentable end to state sovereignty, and then came the horrors of Reconstruction, when the South was taken over by corrupt white carpetbaggers and ignorant Negroes who lusted after white women. Black politicians picked at their bare toes during legislative sessions; a black ne'er-do-well named Gus chased a white woman into the woods, where she threw herself off a cliff to avoid his ravenous clutches; and a villainous mulatto politician, Silas Lynch, locked a white woman into a room to force her to marry him. This was the horrific state of things until the Ku Klux Klan finally rode to the rescue, redeeming the South from this black beast. And it was only when Northern whites came to understand this—that blacks were unfit for citizenship and the Klan was to be applauded rather than punished for its activities—that a true "nation" could be born. This became the revisionist history that America was asked to embrace, and Woodrow Wilson, after a personal screening, was reported to have said: "It's like history written with lightning. And my only regret is it is all so terribly true."

GRIFFITH, WHO AS A child had watched his mother sew robes for the Klan, had made *Birth of a Nation* with the hope that it would transform every Northern man "into a Southern partisan for life," and afterward it seemed that he had achieved his goal. The Ku Klux Klan, which had been dormant since the 1870s, sprang back to life, with chapters forming in several Northern states, and the country was wracked by one horrible episode of racial violence after another. In 1917, whites in East St. Louis, upset when blacks were hired as strikebreakers by the Aluminum Ore Co., killed more than forty black men, women, and children and torched three hundred of their homes. The mob ran through the streets yelling "Get a nigger!" and at one point, congressional investigators reported, a white man grabbed a two-year-old running from a burning building and hurled the toddler back into the flames.

Published accounts of lynchings in the South told of similar unimaginable barbarities. In Waco, Texas, fifteen thousand people cheered as a mob mutilated and burned a seventeen-year-old illiterate farmhand, Jesse Washington; the killing process involved dipping him—by means of lowering him from a rope—repeatedly in the fire. In Memphis, a crowd of five thousand shouted "Burn him slow" as a mob doused Ell Persons with gasoline; afterward many grumbled that the burning had taken place too quickly, that "too much gasoline had been used." Their complaint inspired a mob in nearby Dyersburg, Tennessee, to torture thirty-year-old Lation Scott for nearly four hours, the mob jamming a red-hot poker into his eyes and down his throat, and using a clothes iron to burn off his genitals. "It was the biggest thing since Ringling Brothers' Circus came to town," said one observer. Two months later, a mob in Estill Springs, Tennessee, did much the same to its victim, which led the *Nation* to write with astonishment that "the application of red-hot irons is now a regular feature of these tortures."

Nobody was arrested for any of the lynchings, and public tolerance of them was such that, in several instances, the killers wrote letters to area newspapers. "The common people of our state understand that nothing will be done when they lynch a 'Nigger,' " G. C. Brewer told the *Nashville Banner.* "I am one of them. . . . I have had opportunity to see five lynchings in my life." And so, with any threat of prosecution gone, the lynchings went on. A black man in Georgia was tied up, weighed down with rocks, and tossed into a river. A mother and her five sons were shot and killed by a Texas mob. A wealthy black man in South Carolina was lynched for being "not simply insolent once, but generally bumptious." It was open season on blacks, and just when it seemed that nothing a lynch mob did could shock the nation anymore, that surely the hot-iron tortures were the worst that anyone could imagine, a mob near Valdosta, Georgia, proved otherwise. There, in May 1918, whites who had lynched seven sharecroppers grew incensed when the wife of one of the men, a very pregnant Mary Turner, protested that her husband was innocent of any crime and threatened to call federal agents to have them all arrested. They responded by dragging her into the woods, tying her heels together, and hanging her upside down from the limb of an oak tree. After throwing gasoline on her, the mob let her "writhe in agony" for a while—"You ought to have heard the wench howl," one person said—and then "a match was applied." But even then the mob was not done: as the flames engulfed her, a white man stepped forward with a butcher's knife and sliced open her womb. "The infant," it was reported, "gave two feeble cries" as it was thrown to the ground, and then "its head was crushed by a member of the mob with his heel."

This savagery rivaled the worst atrocities of the Belgian Congo, and hundreds of blacks and whites wrote letters of protest to President Wilson and to Attorney General A. Mitchell Palmer, pleading with the federal government to do something. "We are asking that you use all the power of your great office to prevent similar occurrences and punish the perpetrators of this foul deed," the Negro Womanhood of Georgia begged the president. But Wilson turned the letters over to Palmer, and Palmer's office wrote everyone the same stock, cold reply: "The law, as laid down by the Supreme Court of the United States, is to the effect that lynching is a crime which can be dealt with only by the State authorities and over which the Federal Government has no jurisdiction." And then, just to be helpful, the nation's Department of Justice added: "See *Hodges v. United States*."

The Red Summer of 1919

A FEW WEEKS BEFORE the mob in Georgia burned Mary
Turner, a regiment of more than two thousand black American
soldiers dropped into the trenches that marked the front lines of
World War I in France. The 369th Infantry was positioned near the
Aisne River, along a 5-kilometer stretch of land that ran through the
rugged Argonne Forest and had seen some of the heaviest fighting in
the war. As the men stood in the pits, they looked out past an entan-
glement of razor-sharp wire to German lines that were "not more
than 50 yards" away, wrote Captain Hamilton Fish Jr. The soldiers
shared their muddy homes with packs of rats, they were under constant artillery bombardment and needed to have gas masks ever at
the ready, and yet they were proud and even happy to be there. "The
most wonderful thing in the world has happened to this regiment,"
wrote Colonel William Hayward. "A fairy tale has materialized and
a beautiful dream has come true. We are now a combat unit."*

The journey of the 369th Infantry, which was an all-volunteer
unit from New York City, to the front lines had been a long and
difficult one. But now they had reason to hope that their participation in this fight, which Woodrow Wilson had promised was being
waged to "make the world safe for democracy," would bring dramatic changes to their country too.

---

* Both Fish and Hayward were white; however, a number of the field officers of the
369th were black.

. . .

TWO YEARS EARLIER, WHEN it had first become apparent that the United States was going to enter the European war, the U.S. military had turned a cold shoulder to blacks who tried to volunteer. The army rejected most Negroes who sought to enlist, the navy allowed them to serve only as stewards, and the marines banned them altogether. Moreover, War Secretary Newton Baker decreed that blacks joining the army would not be allowed in combat units. Southern whites did not want blacks to become trained in using weapons, while whites throughout the country worried that if black soldiers proved themselves on the battlefield, they would demand equal rights. "Will [the Negro] accept the facts of white supremacy with the same spirit as formerly?" asked the *New Republic.*

But to the NAACP and black leaders, that was precisely the point: "If thousands of American black men do fight in this war," asked the NAACP, "then who can hold from them the freedom that should be theirs in the end?" Indeed, by taking up arms, wrote James Weldon Johnson in the *New York Age,* the Negro would strengthen "his protest for his rights" and fling "a challenge to the white people of this country to rise to his plane of magnanimity and do their duty by him." When the country geared up for a draft in the spring of 1917, Woodrow Wilson and Congress gave in somewhat to these demands: blacks would be drafted and placed in segregated army units, and while most would be assigned to labor battalions, 10 percent of the black soldiers would be trained for combat, with the army creating two new divisions—the 92nd and 93rd—for these troops.

Although the Jim Crow provisions infuriated black leaders, they still called for all eligible black men, ages twenty-one to thirty-one, to register for the draft. Du Bois did so in the *Crisis,* the NAACP's monthly magazine, and so too did black community leaders around the country. "We are not stopping to discuss racial differences now," said John Harrison of the Masonic Lodge in Pine Bluff, Arkansas, "for when a foreign enemy approaches us, we are all one and together we meet him and together we slay him or together we die."

The nation's black men heeded the call. Nearly 2.3 million

registered, and of every 100 called for service, 36 were inducted, versus an induction rate of 25 percent for white men. All told, 368,000 black men were inducted into the military, and as they went off to training camps in the summer and fall of 1917, it seemed that the whole country had come to an understanding. "If the war lasts," the *Chicago Herald* wrote, "America will owe to her Negroes not what she owed in 1863, reparation, but a debt for service, which she will not forget nor seek to evade." Theodore Roosevelt told black audiences that the war would lead to a "juster and fairer treatment in this country of colored people." There could be no mistaking the promise that was being made, and Woodrow Wilson repeated it for all to hear: "Out of this conflict you need expect nothing less than the enjoyment of full citizenship rights—the same as are enjoyed by every other citizen."

Even Du Bois was caught up in the fervor of hope: "The *Crisis* says, *first* your country, *then* your Rights!"

THE 369TH INFANTRY ARRIVED in France on December 27, 1917, only to be immediately snubbed by General John Pershing, head of the American Expeditionary Forces. He put the 369th—and the other three regiments of the 93rd Division (the 370th, 371st, and 372nd)—under French command. "Our great American general simply put the black orphan in a basket, set it on the doorstep of the French, pulled the bell, and went away," wrote Colonel Hayward, the regiment's ranking officer. Yet, in spite of this insult from America's military, the troops clamored to get into battle, so much so that when they dropped into the front lines in mid-April, "God damn, let's go!" became a familiar refrain among the men.

Six weeks later, the 369th gave America its first World War I heroes. On the night of May 13, 1918, Privates Henry Johnson and Needham Roberts crawled past the barbed wire into no-man's-land and slipped into a tiny foxhole—this was the regiment's listening post. The German lines were barely a stone's throw away, and suddenly, as a flare lit up the ground, they spotted a party of twenty Huns rushing forward. Both Johnson and Roberts were wounded in the initial fusillade of shots, and yet, first with their rifles and grenades and then in hand-to-hand combat, they fought off the attack, with Private Johnson burying his bolo knife in several Germans. Both Johnson and Roberts were awarded the French Croix de Guerre, the first American soldiers to be so honored. A trio of U.S. reporters chronicled their exploits, with Irvin Cobb, a Kentucky-born correspondent who was famous for his war dispatches, writing in the *Saturday Evening Post*:

> As a result of what our black soldiers are going to do in this war, a word that has been uttered billions of times in our country, sometimes in derision, sometimes in hate, sometimes in all kindliness—but which I am sure never fell on black ears but it left behind a sting for the heart—is going to have a new meaning for all of us, South and North too, and that hereafter n-i-g-g-e-r will merely be another way of spelling the word American.

The 369th spent 191 days on the front lines, which was longer than any other American unit. In mid-July, the 2,400 men in the regiment repulsed a German attack that lasted four days, and in late September, when the Allied forces launched a final assault against the Germans, they fought for ten days in the bloody Battle of the Meuse-Argonne. In this battle alone, the 369th lost 9 officers and 135 enlisted men, and nearly 1,000 were wounded, suffering from gunshots, gas, artillery concussions, and shell shock. The French so admired the bravery of the 369th Infantry that after the November 11 armistice, they asked the regiment to lead the Allied forces to the Rhine River.

The other three regiments of the 93rd Division—the 370th, 371st, and 372nd—also performed with great distinction. The men of the 93rd were awarded more than four hundred individual decorations for "extraordinary heroism under fire," and three of the regiments were awarded, as a unit, the French Croix de Guerre. And almost everywhere the regiments went, both while the war was waging and after the armistice was signed, they were greeted warmly by French citizens, who referred to the black American soldiers as *les joyeux,* or "the happy ones." The 369th had its own marching band, and it introduced jazz and ragtime to the French, playing the country's national anthem, "La Marseillaise," with a pizzazz that brought wild cheers. "One could not find a soldier more faultless in his bearing, and in his manners more affable or more delicate," a French woman wrote. "We admire their forms, handsome, vigorous and athletic; their intelligent and loyal faces . . . [these] soldiers who arrived among us one clear June day, redolent with the scent of roses, you will always live in our hearts."

The praise and warmth lifted the hopes of the American soldiers. "I am awful proud that I came over to France to fight for my country," wrote Private William Brown of Helena, Arkansas, "for now that we have gone over the top we can go back home with our chests stuck out like a peacock's." Indeed, the troops waiting to return were certain that they would come home to a changed country. "A large faith posses the Negro," reported the *New York Tribune.* "He has such confidence in justice that he believes its flow will yet soften hard hearts."

Black leaders in the United States now spoke optimistically of a second Reconstruction. The country had once again been remade by war, and the promises made to blacks after the Civil War, that they would be welcomed into the body politic as citizens, would finally be realized. "We return from fighting," roared Du Bois. "We return fighting. Make way for Democracy!"

HOWEVER, EVEN AS DU BOIS was sounding that call for democracy, he was publishing an exposé in the May 1919 issue of the *Crisis* that revealed just how unrealistic those hopes were. The country's black soldiers, as Du Bois well knew, had been mistreated throughout the war. At many training camps, they had been given inferior clothing and substandard food, and they were lorded over by white officers who called them "niggers," "coons," "darkies," and "monkeys." When the 369th arrived in France, General Pershing had made it clear that he didn't want to have anything to do with the unit. And then, after Johnson and Roberts's heroics, a member of his staff sent a letter titled "Secret Information Concerning Black American Troops" to the French Military Mission. Du Bois had obtained a copy of the treasonous document, which he shared with the readers of the *Crisis*.

White Americans, Pershing's staff told the French military, did not want the black soldiers to be treated with "familiarity and indulgence." To do so would "inspire in black Americans aspirations which to [whites] appear intolerable . . . the black man is regarded by the white American as an inferior being with whom relations of business or service only are possible." The French were advised that they "must not eat with [blacks], must not shake hands or seek to talk or meet with them outside the requirements of military services." French officers shouldn't "commend" the soldiers too much, as whites in America made it a point to "censure" the black man constantly "for his want of intelligence." The many vices of the Negro were "a constant menace" to American society, which was why they needed to be treated "sternly."

Other black publications soon filled out the picture of how the military had treated black troops in France. In a number of French villages, white American soldiers had posted "Niggers keep out!" signs and advised the locals that "niggers are rapists." In several instances, the U.S. military police had arrested black soldiers who spoke to French women. "The things that happened are of a nature to make one's blood boil and one's feelings to volcanically erupt," wrote the *Crusader,* a black magazine. And with the war now over, the War Department even seemed intent on scrubbing the heroics of the 93rd Division from the historical record. Not one of the 127 Medals of Honor awarded to World War I veterans by the U.S. military went to a black soldier.* The War Department insisted that the

---

* In 1991, President George H. W. Bush posthumously awarded a medal of honor to Corporal Freddie Stowers, a black soldier from the 371st Regiment killed on September 28, 1918, while leading an assault on the Germans. He was the first black soldier from World War I so honored.

French not depict any black Americans in the heroic frieze it had planned for its Panthéon de la Guerre.

The South, meanwhile, was providing its own distinctive welcome-home party for black troops. Although army regulations gave a discharged soldier the right to wear his khaki for three months, Southern leaders had warned the War Department in November 1918 that it didn't want returning Negro soldiers "strutting about in uniform," and that spring of 1919, the white South made good on its threat. Throughout the region, black soldiers arriving back home were harassed, cursed, and, at times, assaulted. In Blakely, Georgia, Private William Little stepped down from a train station in his uniform and was immediately told to strip and walk home in his underwear; he refused and was found beaten to death a few days later. Whites in Norfolk, Virginia, rioted when local blacks tried to hold a parade for returning Negro troops.

The war, blacks were told, had changed nothing. "If the black man will stay where he belongs, act like a Negro should act, talk like a Negro should talk, and study like a Negro should study," the *Shreveport Times* editorialized, "there will be very few riots, fights, or clashes." South Carolina congressman James Byrnes announced that "for any Negro who has become inoculated with the desire for political equality, there is no employment for him in the South, nor is there any room for him in the South. This is a white man's country, and it will always remain a white man's country." The Ku Klux Klan, which boasted that one million Americans now proudly wore the white robes, placed recruitment ads in newspapers that read: "If you wish to make your wives and daughters safe and happy, join the Klan today."

Postwar conditions for blacks quickly turned sour in the North too. In the previous four years, nearly half a million blacks had migrated from the South, and during the war, with so many white men having been drafted, they had been able to find jobs in factories, many of which had geared up to manufacture war supplies. But with the war over, the government canceled these contracts, and with unemployment soaring, blacks were asked to go to the back of the line, the *Chicago News* reporting that "colored soldiers who find employment are given only the most menial and lowest paid jobs." The U.S. Railroad Administration turned that private practice into something of an official policy, cautioning railways not to hire Negroes for any class of work "not heretofore open to them"—the better-paying jobs were to be reserved for whites. Town officials in Coatesville, Pennsylvania, took a more direct approach: they rounded up fifty unemployed blacks, marched them to the edge of town, and ordered them to "head south."

Any hopes that the nation's blacks may have harbored were now gone. Black soldiers had done "their duty at home and abroad, and now they have returned," wrote the *Charleston Messenger,* a black newspaper. "To what have they come? Did they find a grateful country? Instead of the expected 'well done' they confidently and rightfully expected, what greeted them? Let them tell. On every side [the Negro soldier] is met with the statement, 'niggers, as you were.' "

And, of course, lynchings rose. This practice had long been at the heart of social control in the South, and white mobs, in the first months of 1919, resorted to its use again and again, making sure that blacks understood their place. Even the most trivial "social offense" could now stir a lynch mob. In Monroe, Louisiana, George Holden was shot to death after being "accused of writing an insulting note to a white woman." In Star City, Arkansas, World War I veteran Flinton Briggs was told that "niggers get off of the sidewalk down here," and when he failed to do so, he was chained to a tree and shot "forty or fifty" times. A veteran in Woolsey, Georgia, Charles Kelly, was lynched for a similar reason. In Tuscaloosa, Alabama, Cicero Cage was "cut to pieces" for some offense or another, and in Georgia, a seventy-two-year-old black man was strung up after he protected two young black girls from the advances of two drunk white men.

There was also an uptick in the number of blacks burned alive at the stake, with the first such public torture in 1919 occurring on January 20 in Hillsboro, Texas. Next came a burning on March 14 in Castlebury, Florida, then one on May 14 in Vicksburg, Mississippi.

A week later, World War I veteran Frank Livingston was burned alive in Eldorado, Arkansas. The steady eruption of such tortures, which were now occurring with greater frequency than ever before, caused the *Nation* to wonder if America had entered a new Dark Age. The sadistic burnings, it said, surpassed "anything known in ancient Rome or at the inquisition in Torquemada," when people were ripped apart on the wheel. Yet no sooner had this article appeared than a mob in Star City, Arkansas, stripped Clyde Ellison and burned him with flatirons, with his smoldering corpse left to hang from a bridge and draped with a sign that read: "This is how we treat lazy niggers."

Finally, on June 26, the state of Mississippi essentially put an official stamp of approval on this practice. After a sheriff's posse in Ellisville captured John Hartfield, a black man said to have assaulted a white woman, he was brought to a doctor, where his shoulder wound—he had been shot during the hunt—was patched up, the medical care given to ensure that he would survive long enough to be set on fire. The town scheduled the killing for 5:00 P.M., allowing afternoon newspapers to promote the event. "Three Thousand Will Burn Negro—Negro Jerky and Sullen as Burning Hour Nears," shouted the *New Orleans States*. Mississippi governor Theodore Bilbo told the *Jackson Daily News* that he was "powerless" to stop the burning, with the paper assuring readers that it would be done in a proper manner: "A committee of Ellisville citizens has been appointed to make the necessary arrangements for the event, and the mob is pledged to act in conformity with these arrangements." The Reverend L. G. Gates, pastor of the First Baptist Church, would be on hand to "entreat the mob to use discretion," and just as the New Orleans paper had predicted, more than three thousand people poured into Ellisville to watch this "roasting" of a human being.

THE OPTIMISM OF BLACKS at war's end had turned into bitterness and disillusionment, with many swearing that conditions were worse than ever. But while white America had not been changed by the war, black America had, and the bitterness, in April and May, gave way to a growing sense of defiance. "We are demanding our rights," wrote Paul Filton, a soldier back from France, in the *Brooklyn Eagle*. "If that modern Ku Klux Klan thinks that these hard fighting, straight-shooting veterans of the World War are the same timid fieldhands, crouching in terror, they have another 'think' coming. . . . We have helped to gain the Victory for Democracy, and we must share in the fruits." Du Bois and other black writers spoke of how the war had created a "New Negro" who was not going to be pushed around, and a booming black press spread this message of defiance to nearly every black in America.

In 1919, there were an estimated 450 periodicals being published by or for Negroes, including 220 newspapers and at least seven general-interest magazines, and the number of readers for these publications had jumped threefold in the previous five years. "The Negro race," proudly wrote the *Charleston Messenger,* "is united through the colored newspapers that now have a circulation reaching every state and city where there are large numbers of our people." Several—most notably the *Chicago Defender,* a weekly newspaper with a circulation of 150,000, and the *Crisis,* a monthly with a circulation of 100,000—reached a large audience. Together, these publications gave Negroes a national voice and enabled the race "to know itself," wrote black writer Monroe Work.

And what the race learned that spring was that it now found America an impossible place. Negroes in the United States, wrote the *Crusader,* "exist in a Hell on earth, where mob murder, court injustice, inequality, and rank, widespread prejudice are the rule." "The South," sneered the *Challenge,* "is more Hellish than Germany ever was." Woodrow Wilson, the papers said, "stands before the world a discredited man." The *Veteran* wrote of how "Men, Women and Children Writhe under Cruel Peonage System" on cotton plantations, and concluded that "slavery in so many respects could certainly have been no worse." The *New York Age* denounced the white man as "the most damnable hypocrite, scoundrel and savage that the world has ever seen."

By June, there were reports that Negroes in the South were

buying guns and preparing to make a stand. They "have purchased arms in a number of Southern cities, with the intention of defending their lives and the lives of their families," the *Nation* warned. Blacks in the South, several publications noted, were openly talking of warfare between the races. The Associated Press reported similar news: "Negroes are not planning anything, but will defend themselves if attacked." There were a handful of racial skirmishes in various cities around the country in the first weeks of the month, and then came the John Hartfield burning, which pushed blacks to near total revolt.

"Civilization trembles," wrote the *Kansas City Call.* The *Messenger* printed a cartoon of a lynched Negro burning in the flames rising from an American flag, with a caption that sneered, "Oh! Say can you see by the dawn's early light." What option, editors now asked, did blacks have left? "A new Negro is rising who will not surrender or retreat a single step," the *Messenger* wrote, "a Negro with an iron will and an inflexible determination to put down the Hun in America. Law or no law, blood or no blood, lynch law must go." "If we must protect ourselves," said the *Chicago Defender,* "we shall do it with a vengeance." White mobs, wrote the *Veteran,* were "too brutally inhuman to respond to any argument except the argument of cold steel and fire." A correspondent for the *Baltimore Daily Herald,* Reverend William Byrd, was most explicit of all: "The only recourse to safety Negroes have is to arm themselves to the very teeth and to kill every white scoundrel that approaches."

The country appeared headed toward a racial civil war. And white America, trying to make sense of it all, blamed it on the Reds.

SINCE THE BEGINNING OF the year, the nation had experienced perhaps its worst labor turmoil in its history. During the war, inflation had surged while wages for blue-collar workers had stagnated, and on January 21, thousands of shipyard workers in Seattle walked off the job. By the end of May, more than a thousand strikes had roiled the country. Then, on June 2, labor radicals set off bombs in eight cities and dynamited the home of U.S. attorney general A. Mitchell Palmer, the country's top law enforcement officer. The

Reds weren't just coming, they were here, and panic gripped the nation. Communists, it seemed, were on the march worldwide. In late June, the New York state legislature, which had organized a committee that spring to investigate "seditious" groups, announced that they were not just stirring up the nation's workers, they were also undermining the "loyalty of the Negroes."

"Reds Try to Stir Negroes to Revolt," headlines screamed. Negro groups, the country learned, were being "financed from Russia." There was, wrote the *New York Times,* "no use in shutting our eyes to facts . . . Bolshevist agitation has been extended among the Negroes." A few weeks later, the U.S. Post Office added fuel to the fire with a report titled "Radicalism and Sedition Among the Negroes as Reflected in Their Publications." The Negro press, it said, had entered into an "organized alignment with the most destructive forces of our political life today." Many of the publications advocated the "establishment in this country of Bolshevik rule."

The taint of Communism added yet another dose of poison to the image of blacks in the white mind. The public was now being encouraged to view Negroes, particularly those clamoring for change, as traitors. Posters appeared in the South announcing that Bolshevism would lead to "Negro domination," and the U.S. Department of Justice began treating blacks as potential enemies of the state. The department's Bureau of Investigation appointed a young J. Edgar Hoover to monitor the activities of various Negro groups and devise strategies to neutralize them. By early August, Hoover's men were "employing reliable negroes" to snoop on black publications and on "negro lodges and associations."

The chasm between whites and blacks in America had grown larger than ever. While the *Messenger* may have billed itself as a "radical socialist" magazine, and although writers in this magazine and a handful of others—the *Crusader,* the *Challenge*—occasionally spoke of the allure of Bolshevism, black writers and editors, as a whole, were demanding one thing: *democracy.* They wanted blacks to enjoy equal rights and equal opportunities, and they wanted a federal lynch law that would protect them from mobs. They wanted the country to live up to its professed values. Blacks had taken up arms for purposes of self-defense, and only after a long history had made it clear that they had no other option left. The notion that their unrest was due to Communist agitation was so absurd as to deny belief, evidence of how whites were "conveniently blind" when it came to racial injustice. "As long as the Negro submits to lynchings, burnings and oppressions—and says nothing, he is a loyal American citizen," wrote the *Pittsburgh Courier,* with evident bitterness. "But when he decides that lynchings and burnings shall cease even at the cost of some human bloodshed in America, then he is a Bolshevist."

THE FIRST SERIOUS RACIAL clash of 1919 occurred in Charleston, South Carolina, on May 10, when, following an altercation between a black man and a white navy man, U.S. sailors went on a rampage. By riot's end, two blacks were dead and twenty-five more—seventeen blacks and eight whites—had been seriously injured. More than a half dozen racial skirmishes occurred between then and the end of June, and on July 3 five people were shot in a racial clash in Bisbee, Arizona. White gangs in Chicago posted signs on telephone poles that read, "Get all the niggers on July 4," bringing racial tension there to a nerve-racking pitch. Then, on July 10, in Longview, Texas, the Red Summer of 1919 began in earnest.

Three weeks earlier, a mob had lynched a black man, Lemuel Walters, because he had been intimate with a white woman. The mob's presumption was that he had forced himself on her, but the *Chicago Defender,* in its published account, which landed in Longview mailboxes on July 10, quoted the woman as saying that she had "loved" Walters and that they would have married if they had lived in the North. Enraged whites in Longview immediately tracked down the *Defender*'s local correspondent, a teacher named Samuel Jones, and beat him severely. After Jones made it back to his home, his friends joined him there, vowing to defend him from further assault, and when the mob showed up, intent on burning down his house, Jones's friends opened fire. By the time the dust settled in Longview, four white men and one black man were dead, and more than twenty people—white and black—had been wounded.

The nation's capital blew up next. There, the town had been whipped into a frenzy by inflammatory articles in the *Washington Post* and other newspapers about a crime wave sweeping the city, with four white women allegedly having been assaulted by a "negro fiend" during the previous two months. Whites were being primed for violence, and then, on July 19, a Saturday evening, rumors began floating through the bars and pool halls of downtown Washington, D.C., that the wife of a white sailor had been roughed up by blacks. There was a large contingent of white sailors and marines on leave in the city, and they decided to avenge the incident. As they made their way toward the black section of town, they were joined by toughs from a seedy neighborhood called Murder Bay, and armed with clubs, lead pipes, and pieces of lumber, the mob stormed through the black section of town, pummeling black men and women and even climbing aboard streetcars to beat the black passengers. The next day, the *Washington Post,* in a front-page article headlined "Mobilization for Tonight," announced that all servicemen were to gather at Pennsylvania and Seventh Street at 9:00 P.M. for a "clean-up operation," and while the military had issued no such order, the announcement prompted a mob to gather again. However, blacks had read the same article and they spent the day arming and preparing to fight back. Two days of mayhem followed, and by the time two thousand federal troops regained control of the capital, at least six people were dead and hundreds wounded.

The following weekend a Negro boy out for a swim in Lake Michigan drifted over an imaginary line separating the white beach from the black beach, and all of Chicago erupted. The boy was hanging on to a railroad tie as a raft, and whites on the beach, spotting this intruder into their waters, threw stones at him. He slipped from the raft and drowned, and when a white policeman refused to arrest those who had thrown the rocks, Negroes attacked the officer. Fistfights quickly broke out all along the beach, and after night fell, the white gangs who earlier that month had promised to "get all the niggers" went on a rampage, beating and stabbing blacks in "white areas." The following afternoon, they resumed their attacks, thrashing Negroes riding trolleys to and from work, and later that evening, they sped in automobiles through black neighborhoods, shooting randomly at homes. Black snipers returned the fire, and at one point, a black observer wrote, "the Negroes stood in a practically solid line, armed and waiting for attack. Armed white men in automobiles attempted to rush this line, and the discharges of small arms were like a battlefield." Seven regiments of federal troops finally regained control of the city on Thursday, by which time thirty-eight people had been killed and more than five hundred injured.

London newspapers reported that the fighting in the United States had "now assumed the proportions of a race war." The black press saw it in the same light, with magazine after magazine announcing in their August issues that their race had arrived at a moment of truth. "The time for cringing is over," wrote the *Kansas City Call*. Other writers pleaded with black men to take "an eye for an eye, a soul for soul," and the writer Claude McKay rallied black readers with a poem titled "If We Must Die." Even Du Bois, whose usually tried to measure his words, urged blacks to stockpile bricks, clubs, and guns. "If it is to be a Land of Mobs and Lynchers," he wrote in the *Crisis*, "we might as well die today as tomorrow."

Such vows of defiance, however, did not stem the violence by whites. In late August, a mob in Knoxville, Tennessee, stormed a jail in order to lynch a black man accused of murdering a white woman, and when they discovered he'd already been moved to Chattanooga for safekeeping, they stormed into the town's black business district, pillaging hardware stores and pawn shops. The mob's rampage triggered fighting that left six dead and more than a hundred injured. That same week, a pack in Ocmulgee, Georgia, having heard rumors of a Negro uprising, dragged Eli Cooper from his home, shot him, and tossed his body into a church, which it then set on fire. September arrived, and lynchings began occurring every other day. In Oglethorpe, Georgia, a mob burned Obe Cox alive at the stake. In

Bogalusa, Louisiana, whites tied Lucias McCarty, a World War I veteran, to the back of an automobile and tore through the streets, much to the delight of a crowd of five thousand. In Clarksdale, Mississippi, a mob hung L. B. Reed, a veteran who'd served in France, from a bridge. In Montgomery, Alabama, a mob forced its way into a hospital, shoved aside the nurses, and shot John Temple, who had been accused of some crime or another. The turmoil seemed to have no end, and on September 28, a mob in Omaha, Nebraska, burned down a courthouse in order to flush out a black prisoner it wanted to lynch, and when the mayor tried to intervene, the mob strung *him* up, the police able to cut the mayor free only at the last instant.

America was coming undone. "No one who was in the United States in the autumn of 1919," a visiting English journalist wrote, "will forget the feverish condition of the public mind at that time." And with the hindsight of history, it is clear that this was the bitter fruit of a long process, one that had begun nearly fifty years earlier, when the U.S. Supreme Court, in the *Slaughterhouse* case, started tearing down Reconstruction law. If only one of the five majority justices in that case had voted the other way, this horrible summer in American history almost certainly never would have arrived. But the nation's highest court had neutered the Fourteenth Amendment, with its promise of fairness to all, and after that the other causes of America's long decline had lined up like dominoes. America's scientists declared blacks to be inferior in mind and body. Writers and filmmakers told stories about black brutes and honorable whites. Then came the war, the "niggers as you were" welcome home, and the Red Scare. It had all whipped up a cauldron of hate and unchecked violence. And it was precisely at that moment, when the country was in a most feverish state, that the sharecroppers of Phillips County, on the last night of September 1919, met in their humble wooden church. History gave them reason to place a guard at the front door, and history gave them a reason to have men sit out front in a buggy, with shotguns resting in their laps.

Helena

ARLY IN THE EVENING of September 30, most of the business
leaders of Helena—men such as E. C. Hornor, Sebastian Straub,
T. W. Keesee, and E. M. Allen—settled into their seats at the Grand
Opera House. This was opening night for the fall season, the roman-
tic comedy *I Love You* by William LeBaron coming to their stage, direct from the Booth Theatre in New York. All of Helena's leaders
were there, the wealthiest businessmen and their wives sitting in the
fancy boxes that lined the sides of the grand theater, which had been
built in 1887 and ever since had hosted road shows of the finest sort.

These men had reason to be content. They ran the town's banks
and its political affairs, and they had their hands in nearly every aspect of the cotton trade, and cotton prices were just going up and up.
They furnished supplies to the plantation commissaries, stored the
cotton once it was brought to Helena, and sold the compressed bales
on the commodities market. They all owned large plantations as
well. Edward Chaffin Hornor, the county's most prominent businessman and president of the Bank of Helena, had cleared 12,000 acres
in the Hoop Spur area in the early 1900s. Thomas Woodfin Keesee,
owner of the Helena Compress Company and president of the Helena Cotton Exchange, had cotton ripe for picking on 2,000 acres.
Edward Mort Allen, president of the Helena Business Men's League,
owned the entire townsite of Elaine. They were all rich men, and
with the price of cotton soaring, they were about to become much
richer.

In February, the Helena planters had set up a committee to devise an "infallible plan" for raising the price that cotton would fetch that year. With the war over, international trade was certain to boom, and that meant a growing demand for cotton. The Helena group met with Mississippi planters, and together they concluded that they needed to reduce the number of acres planted in cotton, as this would help create a shortage and drive up the price. The difficulty with implementing this plan was that every individual planter wanted to increase the number of acres *he* planted, and it was while the Helena committee was trying to overcome that stumbling block that the market began cooperating on its own. The futures price for cotton on the nation's commodity markets, which the *Helena World* tracked daily on its front page, began to rise, with the paper announcing in May that "cotton prices may be high" in the fall. After that, the news for the Helena planters just kept getting better. A wet spring was followed by hot June weather, leading the *Helena World* to predict that the season was going to bring a "bumper crop." The boll weevil stayed away from their fields that summer, and yet it destroyed much of the crop in Georgia, Florida, Mississippi, and Alabama, such that by August the U.S. Department of Agriculture was forecasting that the cotton harvest that year would be only 11.3 million bales, which was 62 percent of normal. International demand for cotton was going to be strong, the national supply was going to be below normal, and their own fields were producing a bountiful crop—that was a combination that made for a perfect market for planters in the Arkansas Delta. The Helena businessmen expected more than 150,000 bales to flow through their warehouses, and at 50 cents a pound, that represented a $37 million market. Individual planters would enjoy a crop worth $250 per acre—the *Arkansas Democrat* jubilantly calculated that it might even be higher than that, "a single acre of land" likely to produce "$300 worth of cotton" that fall—and if the sharecroppers were given just a pittance of that, as was the custom, anyone who had even a few hundred acres in cotton stood to make a small fortune. Keesee, with his 2,000 acres, could hope to gross more than five hundred thousand dollars, and this at a time when a fancy automobile, such as the Chandler Touring Car, could be bought in Helena for $1,795.

There was only one thing nettling them: the union. The sharecroppers in the southern part of the county were holding a meeting that very night in Hoop Spur, and the Negro detective they'd hired to spy on the union, a Detective Scarbrough, had told them serious trouble was brewing. As Charles Young, publisher of the *Helena World,* later recalled, he'd "reported that the niggers was fixin' to uprise." Hornor, Straub, Keesee, and a handful of others had run this town for some time, and they liked to keep everything nice and orderly, which meant that blacks knew their place. And what was really getting on their nerves, irritating them until they were just about ready to burst, was that every day as they walked down Cherry Street, which was where they all had their offices, they had to pass by a building where the law firm of Bratton and Casey had hung out a shingle. That would be *Ulysses Simpson* Bratton, as in *Ulysses Simpson* Grant, who had dared to come into their town, and while it was G. P. Casey who staffed the office, there was still the Bratton name on the office door, and every time the men who ran Helena saw a black person go into that office they had to grit their teeth. "Bratton," sneered Keesee, "was an old carpetbag Republican."

And if you knew anything about the town's long and proud history, you could be certain that those were fighting words.

THE CLEARING OF LAND on this site began in 1800, when the Arkansas Delta was mostly a gloomy swamp. Everywhere else up and down the delta the terrain was flat, rising barely a few feet above the Mississippi, such that it was impossible to imagine how the swamplands could ever be drained, but here the banks sloped upward to 200-foot hills, which were the southern terminus of an unusual geographical formation known as Crowley's Ridge. The ridge, which runs 200 miles north into Missouri and is only a few miles in width, is composed of fine silt soils blown in from the west. Springs flowed from the bottom of the hills, which were about 400 yards from the river, and so the settlers had fresh water and an elevated place they could retreat to when the spring floods came.

The first to arrive planted cotton, and soon other settlers began clearing land to the west of the ridge, bringing their cotton here for shipment to New Orleans. This clearly was going to become a transportation hub, and in 1820 Sylvanus Phillips plotted out a mile-square townsite, even drawing up a grid of streets. He named the fledgling community Helena after his two-year-old daughter.

Arkansas was the new frontier, and men seeking their fortune began arriving from Louisiana, Tennessee, Mississippi, Virginia, and North Carolina—all the Old South states. William B. R. Hornor, who was from a prominent Virginia family, arrived in 1811, and his nephew John Sidney Hornor came in 1836. Not long after that the county boasted among its residents a Straub, a Moore, a Burke, a Tappan, a Keesee, and a Pillow—the family names that would dominate the town for the next hundred years.

Like most Mississippi River towns, Helena in the 1830s and 1840s was a wild, cantankerous place. Hucksters and adventurers of every stripe drifted into town, eager to make their fortune. The town filled with prophets, gamblers, thugs, saloonkeepers, and prostitutes. Helena's notoriety was such that George Featherstonhaugh, an English geologist traveling through the South, was warned that it was a "sink of crime and infamy," a place where "negur runners, counterfeiters, horsestealers, murderes and sich like took shelter again the law." Killings and shooting scrapes were a common occurrence, and yet so too were evangelical revivals. Methodist ministers regularly came to town to preach the virtues of piety, harmony, and self-control. Churches rose on nearly every corner, and in 1835, several of the "finer" families in Helena formed an anti-gambling society, intent on making their town into a more proper place.

The first large plantations in Phillips County began to appear in the 1840s, mostly to the west and north of Helena, and then, from 1850 to 1860, plantation life took hold. By the end of that decade, there were 113 planters in the county who owned more than 20 slaves, and these men, on average, farmed 1,315 acres. John Sidney Hornor and his sons owned 49 slaves who worked their large plantation six miles north of Helena. Thomas Keesee Sr. owned 39, James C. Tappan 55, and Gideon Pillow 139. More than 6,000 slaves were brought into Phillips County in the 1850s, such that by 1860 its population consisted of 5,931 whites, 8,941 slaves, and 4 free blacks. Helena, with a total population of about 1,500, had 500 blacks living in slave quarters.

The town, in its appearance and culture, took on some of the trappings of the Old South. Several of the more prosperous planters built large mansions in Helena, most notably James Tappan and Robert C. Moore. Both of their homes featured Greek Revival architecture, and Moore's, which was built on the first step of Crowley's Ridge, was distinguished by 16-foot ceilings, intricate molded plasterwork, a long sweeping stairway, and a fireplace in every room. A frontier town had turned into an antebellum one, with the wealthy devoted to graceful Southern living. The young men of Helena played sports and went sailing on the river, and in the early evenings, carriages discharged women in hoop skirts and men in frock coats to the Moore home or to Tappan's for a festive night of dinner and refined conversation.

This prosperous time was brought to a quick and traumatic end by the Civil War. Arkansas seceded from the Union on May 6, 1861, and within weeks, Tappan and another prominent planter, Thomas Hindman, had recruited enough men to fill a regiment in the newly formed Confederate Army. In June, the people of Helena gave a rousing send-off to the hundreds of fathers and sons marching gloriously off to war; a year later, Union troops marched into Helena, arriving from the west, and the town fell without a fight, as no Confederate soldiers were stationed there. By the fall of 1862, Helena had grown into a garrison for twenty thousand Union troops, with thirty-six hundred freedmen crowded into the town as well. Malaria, yellow fever, and other diseases broke out, turning Helena into the deadliest town on the Mississippi, the Union soldiers rechristening it "Hell-in-Arkansas." That winter, starvation haunted the town, and Union troops scoured the countryside for food. "Everywhere they are devouring and laying waste the labor of man's land," wrote Helena minister William Barksdale. "Some of my dear brethren are stripped of nearly everything by these northern invaders."

Many Helena residents and plantation owners fled, and yet enough Southern whites stayed on their farms that when eight thousand Confederate troops, in the first days of July 1863, began marching on Helena from the west, they were greeted by wild cheers. "The people through here are true and loyal to us," one Confederate soldier wrote. "Hundreds of them flock to the roadside to see us as we pass, cheering us with their smiles, waving their handkerchiefs, and giving demonstrations of joy in every way, shape and form." The Confederates launched their assault on Helena at 3:00 A.M. on July 4, the Rebel soldiers heroically charging up Crowley's Ridge, intent on dislodging the Union forces from the hilltops. They were quickly mowed down. "The ridges and ravines," wrote one Union soldier, are "thickly strewn with ghastly corpses covered with gore—hands, arms, legs shot away." One hundred sixty-nine Rebel soldiers had been killed, and another 1,463 were wounded or missing. There was to be no liberating of Helena, and news soon came that Vicksburg had surrendered to Grant. The South was lost, and as the war's end neared in early 1865, Susan Cook, who lived on a plantation outside Helena, summed up the fears of Southerners everywhere. "My God! What is to become of us? From present prospects we will be subjugated. Oh, how gladly would I welcome Death, in preference to such."

DEATH, LOSS, *HUMILIATION*—THE trauma of the Civil War settled deeply into the psyche of the white men of Phillips County. Theirs was now an occupied land, the future looked so bleak, and yet once Tennessee's Andrew Johnson assumed the presidency upon Lincoln's assassination, their prospects began looking up. Johnson issued his Proclamation of Amnesty, which returned land in the South to the antebellum owners, and all across Phillips County, freedmen who had been working abandoned plantations were told to gather their things and go. By the spring of 1866, 99 of the 128 planters in Phillips County who had owned twenty or more slaves in 1860 were seeding their fields with cotton once again. Gideon Pillow, who had been the largest slaveholder in the county prior to the war and had served as a Confederate general, was back, as was John Sidney Hornor. While Hornor's sons had all joined the Confederate cause, John Sidney had fled with his slaves to Texas during the conflict, and now he returned with them in tow—they may have been "free," but they were back working the same fields. "With proper energy and industry on my part I shall be able to make a comfortable living for my family," Hornor wrote. "We may ere long get the old order of things properly resumed."

Sharecropping proved to be an arrangement that helped the plantation owners restore the old economic order. The freedmen, who at war's end had hoped there would be a land redistribution program (a desire expressed in the phrase "forty acres and a mule"), wanted to become independent farmers rather than fieldhands. Beginning in the spring of 1867, the Freedmen's Bureau, which the federal government had set up to protect and help the emancipated slaves, pushed sharecropping as a solution. The plantation owner would provide the land and supplies, black families the labor, and together they would "share" in the profit from this capitalistic enterprise. While plantation owners had no interest in divvying up the yearly profits, they quickly embraced this arrangement, as they could see that since they would be the ones who "settled" the account at the end of the year, they would have all the power in this relationship. "The nigger," one Delta planter boasted, "is going to be made a serf, sure as you live."

That fall his prediction was borne out, as the freedmen besieged the Freedmen's Bureau with complaints. "They take all the cotton we raise, all the hogs, corn, everything," said Cora Gillam, who was working a farm outside Helena. "We was just about where we was in slave days." In their reports, bureau agents regularly described how "the colored people are being swindled out of their year's work," and how, "when the settlement takes place, the [plantation owners] persist in trying to defraud the freedmen in every conceivable way."

Hornor, Pillow, and the others had their land back, and, remarkably, their labor cost was now much *cheaper* than it had been before the war. An adult slave in 1860 had cost $1,000 to $5,000 to buy, and of course slaves had to be housed and fed. But now? There was no purchase price, the sharecroppers' cabins didn't have to be any nicer than the old slave quarters, and the sharecroppers could plant a small garden and feed themselves.

All that the Helena planters had to do now was regain control of town and county politics, but, much to their dismay, they were for a time stymied in this effort. After the South balked at ratifying the Fourteenth Amendment, Congress passed the Military Reconstruction Act of 1867, which enfranchised blacks and disenfranchised many ex–Confederate civil and military leaders, and for the next six years, Republicans in Arkansas, a party composed of blacks, Northern carpetbaggers, and scalawags—Arkansas whites who'd remained loyal to the Union—ruled the state. In Phillips County, there were only a handful of carpetbaggers and no scalawags, and so it was blacks who dominated the Republican party. From 1868 to 1874, Phillips County elected blacks to the state legislature in twelve different contests, and numerous blacks were elected to county posts, including the sheriff's office. However, by the 1874 election, all ex-Confederates had been reenfranchised, and the Helena Democrats, even though whites were outnumbered three to one by blacks in Phillips County, negotiated a "fusion" agreement with the town's black leaders that allowed for a sharing of power. The Democrats were led by two ex–Confederate officers—Major John J. Hornor (son of John Sidney Hornor) and General James Tappan—and in 1878 they grew tired of this power-sharing arrangement. The U.S. Supreme Court had recently ruled in its *Cruikshank* decision that the federal government couldn't protect black voters from white violence, and so Hornor and Tappan organized their followers into a local militia, who rode about on horseback. They also brought a train into town with two small cannons mounted on a flatbed. Blacks in Helena were warned to wear Democratic ribbons in their buttonholes or else they would be killed. Whites in the county, wrote one correspondent to the *Helena World,* a daily newspaper that the Democrats had founded in 1871, had suffered a "long dismal period of persecution and torture," and so it was time for fusion politics to end. As voting day neared, Helena was "full of armed men" who "strongly reminded of warlike times," and the Democrats swept the elections, as few blacks dared to vote.

Over the next fourteen years, blacks in Phillips County struggled to retain a voice in county politics, electing a Republican to office now and then, including a black to the state legislature in 1886. Fusion politics did not entirely disappear, and for the Democrats the fact that blacks could still vote—and thus retain some semblance of political power—was the one last nagging leftover from the Reconstruction era. Finally, in 1892 Arkansas passed a poll tax that disenfranchised most blacks, and when Democrats in the Delta counties swept all races in the ensuing elections, white newspapers celebrated the results as a great day for "democracy." "Except for that dark period when Phillips County was represented by sons of the African race, her legislators have been good men and true," the *Helena World* gloated. "It is a fact that neither in town, municipal, or state affairs will the colored ever [again] be permitted to administer affairs."

In so many ways, the mores of an antebellum society had been restored in Helena and Phillips County. In the 1890s, the price of cotton dropped to 6 cents a pound, and yet wealth still flowed in such quantities to the clique of planters and businessmen who ran Helena that several built "mail-order mansions" designed by famed architect George Barber. Their grand Victorian homes featured parquet floors, stained-glass windows, and carved ceilings, and none was more fanciful than Jerome Pillow's home, which had so many turrets that many thought it resembled a "castle on the Rhine." And with this restoration of the old ways, the personal histories of these men and their families was almost mythic in kind: their ancestors had carved Helena out of the wilderness and grown prosperous by the eve of the Civil War, then had come tragedy and suffering, and out of that loss came—and there was no other word for it—*redemption.* In the long run, the Hornors, Tappans, Moores, and others had prevailed, and by the turn of the century, one Arkansas historian wrote, the planters and business leaders of Delta towns were ruling over their communities "in a manner reminiscent of a medieval lord. The town was their kingdom."

THE TRANSFORMATION OF THE southern part of Phillips County, from swamplands into cotton fields, began in the early 1900s. This is where Elaine and Hoop Spur were located, and the story of that process occupies a prominent chapter in the county's history, for it involved many of the wealthiest families of Helena, and a few rich industrialists from outside the state, most notably Gerard Lambert. The wealth it generated also ushered in a period when the town reached its heyday, the 1910s later remembered with a palpable nostalgia by Helena's upper class.

Southern Phillips County is shaped somewhat like an inverted triangle, with the White River angling in toward the Mississippi from the west and joining with the Arkansas River shortly before it enters the Mississippi. With both the White and the Mississippi regularly overflowing each spring, the land in between was long thought to be doomed to be a hopeless swampland, a wilderness where hunters could come to shoot panthers, bears, wild turkeys, and deer. However, around 1890 a wealthy banker from Fort Smith, Arkansas, Harry Kelley, traveled through the bottomlands with state geologist George Brannon, who told him that the White River dropped lime on the rich silt deposited by the Mississippi, a combination that created "a soil more fertile than any land in the Nile Valley." Kelley bought 35,000 acres, paying 10 to 40 cents an acre, and then bided his time during the 1890s while a levee was constructed along the Mississippi. Once that was done, he knew it would be possible to drain the land.

Kelley had paid pennies for one of the last great stands of virgin hardwood forest in the country. Out of this rich soil rose sweetgum, water tupelo, bald cypress, ash, sycamore, cottonwood, hickory, bitter pecan, and a number of oaks, with some of the trees seven, eight, and even nine feet in diameter. The timber could be harvested and the cleared lands planted in cotton, and after Kelley, in 1903, negotiated a deal with the railroad to bring tracks through here, many of the county's wealthiest families jumped at the financial opportunity that was now so obviously present. Lafe and Joseph Solomon bought thousands of acres in the southernmost part of the county, around what was to become Ratio. J. N. Moore purchased a large tract near the area that was to become Elaine, while Richard Burke and E. C. Hornor bought 12,000 acres east of Elaine, adjacent to the Mississippi River. The Hornor estate also gobbled up thousands of acres in the Hoop Spur area, and a few miles to the north, Greenfield Quarles, John Thomas Moore, and T. W. Keesee bought land near Old Town Lake. Once the railroad was up and running in 1906, timber camps sprouted up all along the line, with short "dummy lines" built every few miles into the woods to where the crews were working.

In 1906, Kelley formed a partnership with E. M. Allen to develop part of the land he owned into the town of Elaine. Allen lived for a time in the railroad depot there while streets were graded, wooden sidewalks laid, and an artesian well drilled, with the first lots sold in January 1911. Hoop Spur already had a post office by them, as did Wabash at Old Town Lake, but Elaine became the commercial hub because it was developed specifically for that purpose by Kelley and Allen. It quickly became a place for loggers, most of whom were Negroes, to work off steam on Saturday nights, which gave the town a reputation as a rough-edged place.*

Young Gerard Lambert arrived in 1912, and he later wrote in detail about his grand adventure. As he was quick to admit, he had led

---

* In 1916, eight-year-old Richard Wright, later to achieve fame as a writer, came with his mother to live in Elaine. His uncle Silas Hoskins owned a tavern that was frequented by black sawmill workers. Whites who coveted the business often threatened Hoskins, warning him that he would be killed if he didn't leave town. In his autobiography *Black Boy*, Wright described how when Hoskins was finally murdered, his family was warned not to investigate. Wright's family fled to Helena, where the young Richard struggled to make sense of their reaction to his uncle's murder. "Why had we not fought back, I asked my mother, and the fear that was in her made her slap me into silence."

a very privileged life. His father was Jordan Wheat Lambert, the inventor of Listerine, a mouthwash that generated millions in profits for his Lambert Pharmacal Company. However, both of Gerard's parents died while he was still a child, and so he was raised by wealthy relatives, passing his summers at a family estate in Virginia, where, he remembered fondly, there were lots of black servants. "Little colored boys hurried back and forth from the kitchen to the basement and hoisted the food up the dumb-waiter to the dining room," he wrote in his autobiography, *All Out of Step*. "In the dining room on hot days there were always two little colored girls, in bright dresses of gay tints, whose duty it was to waft the flies from us with enormous peacock feathers." Best of all, he had his "own little colored companion. My boy was named George Washington."

At Princeton, Lambert lived in a five-room apartment by himself and was chauffeured around in a Peerless limousine. At times, he would have his chauffer drive him "from my rooms to chapel, a mere few hundred yards," an affectation, he said, that gave him "great delight." After graduating, he married, took a grand tour of Europe, bought a yacht, and then threw himself into building a mansion in New Jersey modeled after Mount Vernon, complete with a bowling green out front. He was twenty-six years old, his time devoted mostly to living the life of a wealthy man, when his father-in-law, Arthur H. Lowe, a former president of the Southern Cotton Manufacturers' Association, told him about the rich soil being cleared in southern Phillips County. This prompted Lambert to buy 21,000 acres of virgin timber six miles to the west of Elaine, with the land now going for $25 an acre, nearly a hundred times what it had fetched twenty years earlier. He asked a friend from New York, Harry Holbrook, to run the operations, which he named Lambrook, taking one syllable from his name and the other from Harry's.

After running a rail spur from Elaine to Lambrook, Lambert's workers cleared 1,200 acres of timber within eight months. They cut the forest at such a furious pace that they shipped 180,000 feet of hardwood a day to the Chicago Mill and Lumber Company in Helena, which had to build a second mill to process the logs. As the land was cleared, Lambert recruited Negro families as sharecroppers, each family given 20 acres to work and a cabin to live in. "They preferred small houses, and I found they liked to line them inside with newspapers," Lambert wrote, apparently unaware that his tenants were using the newspapers to cover cracks in the walls. And here, in this remote part of the Delta, he found that race relations were different than they had been in Virginia, where Negroes such as George Washington "were nearer to us than members of our family. We trusted them and loved them." But at Lambrook, he confessed, they "held no such position in our affections."

This conversion of swampy hardwood forests into cotton plantations stirred a manufacturing boom in Helena. With carloads of timber arriving in Helena each day, E. C. Hornor, who was the son of Major John Hornor, and his cousin bought an old plantation on the west flank of Crowley's Ridge and plotted out an industrial town, which they named West Helena. By 1910, the two Helenas were home to more than sixty manufacturing companies that turned the logs into furniture, doors, flooring, brooms, and boats. The Helena Business Men's League, which E. C. Hornor founded, recruited new manufacturers with a brochure that touted Helena as a "land of opportunity where your capital can earn you more money than in any other section" of the country. With its many mansions and beautiful homes, the Business Men's League added, Helena resembled "a panoramic scene of fairyland, the atmosphere redolent with the perfume of the magnolia and the Southern rose."

There was so much for Helena's elite to do. An amusement park went up in West Helena, and the Helena Country Club, high up on Crowley's Ridge, boasted a golf course "that would put a sparkle of delight in the eye of President Taft." On warm summer evenings, the Hornors and Tappans and the rest of the town's elite would gather on the clubhouse's veranda to listen to music in the moonlight. Nearby was the Beech Crest Theatre, which featured "high-class vaudeville" and dramatic plays during its summer season. Young men raced their cars at Sportsman's Park, baseball fans cheered local teams at a tidy ballpark, and everyone could enjoy a ride on the electric trolley that connected West Helena to Helena. As it cut through Crowley's Ridge, the air freshened and the eye feasted on a wooded landscape so beautiful, the Business Men's League boasted, that this fifteen-minute ride, which cost a nickel, was the most "picturesque route in existence." And social life in Helena was a regular whirl. There were summer barbecues and candy pullings to attend, movies at the Jewel Theatre and musicals at the Grand Opera House, and—one Hornor remembered—a stream of "fabulous parties and gala events."

Cherry Street was the commercial center of the town, and it was a lively, fun place. A trolley ran down the middle of the street, the sidewalks were almost always crowded, and in the four blocks between the train station and the courthouse, there were two billiard parlors, a dance hall, the Jewel Theatre, two hotels, several dozen retail stores, and a couple of barber shops. The sign for the shop owned by "Whittle and Fazio" boasted "Our Service Excels and We Don't Mean Maybe." Of the many cafes and restaurants, Habib's— which a Syrian immigrant, Habib Etoch, had opened in 1888—was the most popular, with a sirloin steak selling for 35 cents in 1917. Across the street, Habib ran a private zoo, which housed deer, a pelican, wildcats, and monkeys, and whenever the latter escaped, running around the street "snatching fruits and purses," the "entire population of the city turned out for the round up." Perhaps the most popular event of the summer on Cherry Street was Merchants' Day, when the lucky winner of a drawing might walk away with a new car, and the town fathers would gather atop the Solomon Building, a five-story "skyscraper" at the corner of Cherry and Elm, and throw chickens to the shoppers below.

This, of course, was a whites-only world. Helena had its colored neighborhood, and the surrounding cotton fields were dotted with sharecroppers' cabins, but whites in Helena didn't think much about the lives those folks led, even though the image of the Negro occupied a prominent place in their minds. Indeed, laughing at blacks and their presumed follies was a popular pastime. All of the great minstrel men of the era appeared at the Grand Opera House, including

Lee "Lasses" White, Primrose, and George "Honeyboy" Evans, their shows, recalled county engineer L. R. Parmelee, always "good for a turnout of Helena's best." The white actors blackened their faces, dressed in outlandish costumes, performed Negro dances and songs, and put on skits in which they mangled the language and got into mischief. The minstrel show was an art form with its roots deep in the antebellum South, ever since Thomas "Daddy" Rice, in 1828, played Jim Crow on stage. The *Helena World* advised patrons coming to see the Jolly Jokers, a minstrel group that would be performing "all the latest coon and sentimental songs of the day," to bring a doctor, "for you will laugh until it hurts."

Whites in Helena loved the harmless Negro, but they also feared the Negro as brute, and not surprisingly, when *The Birth of a Nation* came to their town, playing at the Grand Opera House on May 9 and 10, 1917, it created a sensation. The *Helena World* promo declared it to be "The Most Stupendous Dramatic Spectacle the Brain of Man Has Yet Visioned and Revealed." This was *their* history in all its details, a tale of an idyllic antebellum era, when slaves loved their masters, followed by the horrors of Reconstruction, when apelike blacks and corrupt carpetbaggers ran their town, and then came the Redemption of their society by honorable ex-Confederates. The lingering image from that film was of the black man as rapist, and on the morning of May 11, with the movie so fresh in the minds of Helena's whites, Mrs. Pat Parham reported that while out in the woods searching for hen's eggs, a black man had chased her and thrown her to the ground, running off only when she screamed. It was as though the film's climactic scene, in which a black man chased a virginal white woman through the woods, had been re-created in their town. A hapless black, Will Dial, was quickly rounded up and thrown in jail, a mob forming to lynch him, although Sheriff Frank Kitchens and his deputies were able to hold them at bay. At a trial held four days later, Dial denied ever having gone near Mrs. Parham, but who could possibly believe that? The town had just experienced what *Birth of a Nation* told them was true, and Judge Jimason Jackson tossed Dial into prison for twenty-one years.

All of this, from the white point of view, spoke of a well-ordered society. E. C. Hornor, E. M. Allen, Sheriff Kitchens, and a handful of other businessmen kept tight control over Helena and the rest of Phillips County, and while there was an occasional problem with a Negro such as Will Dial, judicial punishment was swift and sure. The Helena Business Men's League even liked to boast that there had never been a lynching in Phillips County. While that claim wasn't actually true, it did reflect the fact that, by Arkansas Delta standards, public lynchings had been a rarity here. Since 1888, there had been ninety-three black men lynched in the Arkansas Delta, but only three of those lynchings had occurred in Phillips County, with none having been reported since 1890. Theirs was a relatively peaceful county, black laborers knew their place, and the town fathers made sure that no outside agitators disturbed that peace.* A pair of union organizers who dared to venture into Phillips County in 1917 were tarred and feathered; a second pair who showed up a few months later were arrested and sent to jail for twelve months. "In the present crisis of the country," said municipal court judge J. Graham Burke, "it was a most unpropitious time for creating dissension in the ranks of labor." Even the U.S. government, in 1917, backed down when confronted by the Helena Business Men's League. That summer the U.S. Army hired blacks from Phillips County to build Camp Pike near Little Rock, but the Business Men's League, upset over this poaching of their labor, complained and got the federal government to fire the men. "Helena Negroes now employed in this work will be released and told to return home," said R. B. Keating, an official with the U.S. Labor Department. The country may have been gearing up for war, but the planters had exacted a promise from the government that their interests would come first.

Now and then, however, a murmur of racial discontent intruded into this idealized world. In 1914, the *Crisis* reported that Negro

---

* In 1904, there was a mass killing of thirteen black men in St. Charles, 20 miles west of Elaine. The catalyst was a fistfight between two black men and a white man, with papers reporting that the black men who were lynched had a "threatening attitude."

girls in the Phillips County jail were being "stripped and beaten unmercifully," a news item that irritated many whites in town, as the *Crisis* circulated nationally. Two years later, a traveling evangelist, the Reverend Burke Culpepper, dared to tell those gathered under his tent that there was a "spiritual wickedness in high places in this community, in the unfair treatment of labor, especially of colored farm labor, on the part of those whose positions as financial and social leaders should make them above such practices." This was not the sort of thing that a visitor was supposed to say in Helena; it was a peek into a world that was supposed to remain out of sight and out of mind. As the war neared, Helena's businessmen also became increasingly concerned about the stream of Negro publications—most notably the *Crisis* and the *Chicago Defender*—that had begun to circulate widely throughout the Mississippi Delta, with the *Defender* even having a correspondent in Helena. These "radical" publications, with their reports of blacks being burned alive and their calls for equal rights, could clearly cause trouble, and the U.S. Bureau of Justice shared this worry. "This is bad literature for the negroes of the South," agent E. J. Kerwin told his superiors. "It is not intended to promote peace, or even activity in behalf of the war, but borders on a spirit that begets hatred and an inner feeling of getting even." Kerwin advised in 1917 and again in 1918 that the black publications, which came to include the *Messenger,* needed to be suppressed, but they continued arriving, month after month, in post offices throughout Phillips County.*

In early 1919, with discharged soldiers filtering back into the county, E. C. Hornor, Sebastian Straub, E. M. Allen, T. W. Keesee, Sheriff Kitchens, and three others formed a "citizens committee" to keep an eye on the racial situation. Nothing in particular happened that spring, and yet the signs piled up that something was brewing. There were whispers here and there that French women were writing love letters to black veterans in Helena, urging them to demand

---

* According to shipping lists, the area within a 90-mile radius of Phillips County had among the highest number of subscribers anywhere in the South. "My people," said one *Defender* reader, "grab it like a mule grabs a mouthful of fine fodder."

equal rights. There were rumors of unrest on the plantations, and even the *Helena World* suggested that perhaps plantation owners should treat their sharecroppers better. The Negro "is an asset which the community can ill afford to lose or abuse or neglect," the paper editorialized. "He is a producer, and occupies a place in our economic life which cannot be easily filled by others." The planters apparently had reason to be nervous, and remarkably, the *Memphis Commercial Appeal*, which had an unquestioned pro-planter pedigree and was regularly filled with white-supremacist sentiment, printed a letter to the editor from a "white Southerner" that dared to suggest that the Negro, who "has again demonstrated his patriotism and trustworthiness in war," was not going to stand much longer for the mistreatment that everyone in the Delta knew was routine:

In certain parts of the south men who consider themselves men of honor and who would exact a bloody expiation of one who should characterize them as common cheats do not hesitate to boast that they rob the Negroes by purchasing their cotton at prices that are larcenous, by selling goods to them at extortionate figures and even by padding their accounts with a view of keeping them always in debt. Men of this stripe have been known to lament that in the last two years the negroes have been so prosperous that it has not been possible to filch from them all they make. A protest from a negro against tactics of this kind is met with a threat of force. Justice at the hands of a white jury in sections where this practice obtains is inconceivable. Even an attempt to carry the matter into the court is usually provocative of violence.

This was quite a crack in the facade of Mississippi Delta society, and it reflected the fact that tensions were rising throughout the region. Everyone had reason to be nervous, and Gerard Lambert, on one of his visits to Lambrook, sensed that "racial hatred" there was reaching a flashpoint. "Here," he said, "we had a tinderbox to be set off by the slightest spark." Racial fighting erupted in several cities across the country, the federal government warned that Communists were stirring up the nation's blacks, and in June a printer in the Arkansas Delta told local and federal officials that a Negro named Robert Hill had hired him to print incendiary literature for a sharecroppers union. "Even a blind man could see the dangerous character of the pamphlets and when I found that thousands of copies of them were being printed, the matter immediately began to look serious to me," he said. Not long after that, Helena's Citizens Committee sent Sebastian Straub and his fourteen-year-old son Charles to Chicago, where Straub hired a detective "to find out just what the union plans were." The detective, young Charles said, was told "to join the union and report to my father."

The blacks of Phillips County, it seemed, were rising up. They were daring to organize, even though they knew that such a thing was not going to be tolerated. And it was right about then, in July 1919, that E. C. Hornor and the others began to notice an unusual number of blacks entering the offices of Bratton and Casey. The previous fall the two attorneys had rented office space at 427½ Cherry Street, less than two blocks from the county courthouse, and Bratton had even initiated a lawsuit—on behalf of a sharecropper in Mellwood—against a plantation owner. Now it seemed as though Bratton might be taking on new clients, and this was perhaps the most alarming development of all, for Ulysses Simpson Bratton had a long history of tangling with planters in the Mississippi Delta.

ALTHOUGH T. W. KEESEE may have sneered that Bratton was a "carpetbag Republican," he was in fact—in the derogatory terms of a Democrat—a "scalawag." His family hailed from Wiley's Cove, a small town in northwest Arkansas, and his father and two uncles had fought with the Union Army during the Civil War. Young Ulysses, born in 1868, had grown up listening to his father tell of how he and his brothers had daringly crossed Confederate lines to join the Union troops, at one point "hiding out and covering themselves with snow." General Ulysses Simpson Grant was a hero in the Bratton household, and in 1895, there was still enough of this scalawag sentiment in Bratton's home county of Searcy that he was able to win election to the state legislature as a Republican. Bratton immediately introduced a bill designed to lessen the disenfranchisement effects of the state's poll tax, an obviously doomed effort that brought jeers and catcalls from the Democrats. "My Dad was a man of top courage," his son Ulysses junior remembered many years later. "No one could frighten him. If he thought something was right, he would stand up for it, no matter what the cost. We felt that all people, regardless of the color of their skin, were human beings and should be treated fairly." In 1897, President William McKinley appointed Bratton assistant U.S. attorney for the eastern district of Arkansas, and it was while he was in that position that he took on the planters. He sought to send them to prison for violating a federal peonage law, a prosecutorial effort that conjured up for planters all the worst horrors of Reconstruction.

The peonage system that had developed in Phillips County and the rest of the country's Cotton Belt was fairly straightforward. A landowner would advance a sharecropper a small sum of money to recruit him to his plantation, and then, under the local law, the sharecropper would not be allowed to leave until he'd worked off that debt, and since the landowner kept the books, that day would never come. If the black farmer tried to flee, he would be arrested, fined, and sent back to the employer, and the fine would be added to the amount the sharecropper had to work off. A market even developed where one landowner would buy the "debt" from another, with the sharecropper then having to go to work for that person. His labor was being bought and sold, much as it had been before the war. However, an 1867 Reconstruction law prohibited such debt servitude, and in 1898, the U.S. Justice Department, which previously had made no effort to enforce the statute, began to investigate peonage cases throughout the South. After a few test cases, the bureau, in early 1905, told Bratton and his boss, William Whipple, that "it is the practice of the department to break up this practice where it exists."

Whipple, who in fact was a carpetbagger, as he had come to

Little Rock from Connecticut in 1868, was as fierce as Bratton, and within weeks, they were hot on the trail of a man named M. Z. Cook, who had kidnapped a carload of Negroes and put them to work on cotton plantations. Cook, vowed Bratton, was going to end up "in the penitentiary, where he belongs." Peonage, Bratton concluded, was "nothing more than slavery." In April 1905, Whipple and Bratton made their first arrests, charging nine men from Portland, Arkansas, with peonage. Remarkably, seven of the men pled guilty, telling the federal judge that they "did not know that they were violating the law." At trial, Whipple and Bratton convicted one of the other two. These "were the first cases of the kind ever known in Arkansas," the *Arkansas Gazette* reported, adding that Whipple and Bratton had also brought "charges against a number of other prominent planters."*

Bratton left the U.S. Justice Department in 1907, but the federal government's investigation into peonage still had a ways to run, and both E. C. Hornor and Orley R. Lilly, who was a Helena town alderman in 1919, were soon to come under its glare. The Hornors owned a plantation and a cotton mill in Barton, 12 miles west of Helena, and a federal investigation into the holding of Italian immigrants in peonage, which was led by a New York attorney, Mary Quackenbos, identified their operations as an example of this sort of abuse. While blacks worked in the cotton fields at Barton, Italian immigrants labored for thirteen hours a day in the mill, and since they were paid but a few cents an hour and were forced to buy high-priced goods at the plantation commissary, they always remained in debt. Overseers regularly beat the workers, including children who didn't work fast

---

* Whipple and Bratton were the federal prosecutors in the *Hodges v. United States* case. In 1904, they indicted three white men in Whitehall, Arkansas, who, as leaders of a mob, forced a sawmill owner to fire his black workers. Since the U.S. Supreme Court had previously ruled that it was up to the states to protect blacks from white violence, Whipple and Bratton, in order to prosecute the men under federal law, made the novel argument that the right to work was constitutionally guaranteed under the Thirteenth Amendment (which abolished slavery). As was noted in Chapter 2, the U.S. Supreme Court threw out the convictions, a decision that allowed white violence against blacks to go unchecked.

enough, and anyone attempting to escape was brought back to the commissary, fined by a justice of the peace, and sent back to work. In Arkansas, Quackenbos concluded, "slavery not only exists but state laws protect slavery—laws which allow arrests for debts, the honesty and existence of which have rarely been proven."

However, the Hornors were not prosecuted, or at least there is no record of such an effort. Peonage continued, and in 1912 Whipple made one last effort to curb it by prosecuting Orley Lilly and two others who ran a plantation near Marked Tree, 80 miles north of Helena. The plantation was worked by thirty-six Negro families whom labor agents had recruited from Mississippi. Other blacks in the area, in a letter to a federal judge, Jacob Trieber, detailed the conditions there:

> These people are held in confinement on the said farm. They are worked by overseers armed with guns and pistols. They are worked in the mud, in rain, in snow, in the severest weather and on Sunday. They are not allowed at any time to leave the farm and the only way from the farm is to steal away at night. Some men have run away at night. They have afterwards sent for their families but those whom they sent were clubbed and driven away while their families were held and are now so held.

At the trial at a federal court in Jonesboro, Whipple was able to prove that Lilly's overseers promised to kill anyone who tried to escape. The blacks lived in tents during the cold winter, and many were so impoverished they went barefoot in the snow. The jury, however, acquitted Lilly by a vote of 10 to 2. "The sympathy was with the planters [and] there was a feeling that if they were convicted in this case, it would demoralize the negro help," Whipple told his superiors in Washington, D.C. "The [local] press severely criticized the trial, and really was guilty of contempt of court. The mayor of the town declared the trial an outrage. It is easy to perceive that the environment was very unfavorable to a conviction."

After that, federal attempts to prosecute planters in the Arkansas Delta ceased. Quackenbos's investigation had prompted Delta planters to let their Italian workers go, which meant they were back now to only treating blacks in this way, and with Woodrow Wilson the president and racial scorn toward blacks sweeping the country, the plight of sharecroppers in the Arkansas Delta was once again put out of mind. The Arkansas planters had triumphed again, and they all were able to enjoy the news that Bratton, in 1915, was forced to declare bankruptcy. After the peonage investigations, he had been able to get few whites as clients, as most dismissed him as a "coon" lawyer. Yet Bratton was persistent, if nothing else, and in 1918 he sued several Arkansas planters for cheating sharecroppers in their settlements. "I am glad to be able to say that with but one exception," Bratton wrote, "I recovered the judgment against the offending landlord." These suits, he confessed, "resulted in arousing the animosity of the Southern Planters who were thus being interfered with in their nefarious practices." Indeed, to the planters, Bratton was like a pest that wouldn't go away—he was a "degenerate white man" and a "shyster," is how *Helena World* publisher Charles Young put it—and now here he was, pursuing a case in Phillips County Court against a Mellwood planter, with more blacks coming into his office every day, and this was happening even as the Red Summer of 1919 was erupting in full force.

IN ITS REPORT ON the Chicago riots, the *Helena World* told of an astonishing spectacle. The paper informed its readers that 200,000 had fought in Chicago, with white mobs raging through the streets shouting "Kill the Coons!" and black snipers picking off whites.* The paper called it a "race war," and even as that news shook up the town, whites in southern Phillips County told Hornor and his

---

* Similar headlines appeared in other Southern newspapers as well, which led several Southerners to argue that in the South mobs only killed individual Negroes, who were thought to be guilty of crimes, whereas in the North mobs were now attacking Negroes indiscriminately. As one paper wrote, with an evident sense of moral superiority, white mobs in the South might "shout 'Kill the coon!' but never 'the coons.' "

committee that they had passed Negro churches where "guards [were] sitting on the steps with shotguns, or rifles." All of Arkansas was in a panic over the Red Scare too, one paper editorializing that it was the duty of all good citizens to "slay" the Bolsheviks, and the Red Scare came to Helena on August 6, when forty shopmen at the Iron Mountain Railroad struck for higher wages. The Business Men's League immediately placed an ad in the *Helena World* warning of impending "famine" because of the shutdown of the railroad line—the same hysteria that had overtaken the country was now loose in Phillips County. The sharecroppers were arming, workers were going on strike, and Hornor and his committee prepared to put down any uprising that might develop, purchasing $5,000 worth of shotguns and ammunition. They stored the weapons in the courthouse.

A few days later, the *Helena World* urged all whites in the county—and only whites—to come to the fairgrounds to celebrate the founding of a local American Legion post, which was to be named after Sheriff Kitchens's son Richard, who had died in the Great War. "It is expected that every white person that is able to walk, ride, or propel themselves by any means will be there," the newspaper wrote. The Legion, it noted, would seek "to maintain law and order, to foster and perpetuate a 100 percent Americanism." Everyone understood what those words meant: this was the organization that would put down any rebellion by blacks, and at the August 14 barbecue, town leaders cornered the guest of honor, U.S. Army major general S. D. Sturgis, commander of Camp Pike. Their county had a population of 32,929 blacks and only 11,601 whites, they reminded Sturgis. The whites might need help, but Sturgis only partially allayed their fears. The army, he said, "could provide troops to quell domestic violence, but only in an extreme emergency."

September arrived, and "rumors upon rumors" ran rampant. Black men were reported to be going around Helena telling other blacks to demand their rights, while discharged white soldiers returning to Phillips County were advised to keep their guns loaded and "to get ready for trouble," recalled J. W. Butts, whose father owned a plantation near Elaine. Detective Scarbrough filed his report, and word spread that the sharecroppers in Elaine and Ratio were planning their uprising for "early October." In several instances, maids and other plantation servants passed on information about Hill and his union to their white employers, including E. M. Allen. "Hill," Allen reasoned, "had the ability of rousing the spark of savagery lying dormant in every negro's heart." Thanks to this tattling by a "few darkies," added Lynn Smith, who ran a plantation near Ratio, they knew the names of the union leaders. Everyone's nerves were on edge, and in Elaine, even Negro women were reported to be acting impudently, pointedly addressing each other as "Mrs." when in the company of whites. *Mr.* and *Mrs.* were terms of respect to be reserved for whites only, and this sort of behavior, Smith said, was "a thing unheard of previously." The planters' world seemed to be in danger of falling apart, and then the September issue of the *Messenger* arrived at Phillips County post offices, with an editorial urging sharecroppers to rise up in "revolution" against the capitalist system. "Strike!" the *Messenger* shouted. "Southern white capitalists know the Negro can bring the white bourbon South to its knees by one strike at the source of production. So, go to it!"

With the end of September drawing near, Sheriff Kitchens and the citizens committee made plans for organizing armed posses to put down any Negro insurrection. Elaine's telephone operator was told to phone Helena at the first sign of trouble, the Helena operators already having been given a list of "designated citizens" to call—this was the start of a phone tree that would prompt hundreds of men to report to the sheriff's office. There was little more that could be done now: There were guns and ammunition in the courthouse, the American Legion could quickly assemble a posse of World War I veterans, and Sturgis had promised that, if necessary, military troops would come to their aid. All of the necessary preparations had been made, and on a number of plantations, sharecroppers were warned what to expect should they dare to strike. "They realized," Gerard Lambert said, "that if they got out of line, there would be no compromise with sudden death."

On Thursday, September 25, Ed Ware and the other Hoop Spur farmers gathered in Elaine for a union meeting. The warnings had not caused them to back down, and after darkness fell, two white men—twenty-eight-year-old Henry Bernard and a friend—circled through a cotton patch to approach the church from the rear. "We crawled through the cotton, and got under the church to see what was going on," Bernard said. It was hard to hear, there was a lot of stamping of feet, and yet they were certain—much to their surprise—that it was a *white man* who was leading the meeting. And then they heard this: blacks were telling each other *"to get rid of the boss man."* Bernard and his friend exchanged hurried glances—this could only mean that "each boss man was to be killed by somebody that lived on the place"—and they raced to alert local plantation owners, in particular Will Cragg and K. P. Alderman.

"This," Cragg replied firmly, "won't do."

AND SO HELENA AND the rest of Phillips County arrived at that fateful evening of September 30, 1919. E. C. Hornor and the other prominent men and women of the town settled into their seats at the Grand Opera House, and while they were waiting for the curtain to rise, deputy sheriff Charles Pratt walked from the courthouse to the Cleburne Hotel, a distance of only one block, where he called on T. K. Jones, head of security for the Missouri-Pacific Railroad in this part of Arkansas. Pratt had been in Elaine and Ratio earlier that day, talking to plantation owners, and now he asked Jones whether either of his two agents, H. F. Smiddy or W. A. Adkins, could go with him to Elaine to arrest a white bootlegger, John Clem. Clem had been causing trouble ever since the weekend, shooting off his gun in the colored part of town, and according to Pratt, he was drunk and on the rampage again. Smiddy begged off—"I was too sleepy and tired," he said—but Adkins agreed to go as soon as he finished his meal with Smiddy.

A little after 9:00 P.M., Pratt and Adkins climbed into a Model T Ford parked at the courthouse. Kid Collins, a Negro prisoner from the county jail, whom the deputy sheriffs "trusted" to help out, hopped in the back. Collins was serving time for a murder rap, and yet Pratt gave him a .32-30 revolver to carry, along with a full complement of bullets. Pratt said they needed "to get some whiskey," and since Arkansas's Bone-Dry Law had closed Helena's many saloons, they headed over to a friend's house where they could get some moonshine.* Perhaps they stayed there thirty minutes, perhaps a little longer, and then they headed south on Route 44. It was a miserable dirt road with potholes, making it impossible to drive more than 10 or 15 miles an hour, and so it wasn't until a little after 11:00 P.M. that they spotted the Hoop Spur church, which Pratt had passed twice that day. They could see that the meeting was still in progress, a soft beam of yellow light pouring out from the church windows, and just before they came to a small bridge, about 40 yards north of the church, Adkins pulled off to the side of the road and cut his engine. They waited for five or six minutes, their headlights off, and then all three men stepped from the car.

---

* Arkansas passed a state prohibition law in 1917. The Eighteenth Amendment to the Constitution, prohibiting the sale of liquor, was ratified in 1919 but didn't go into effect until January 1920.

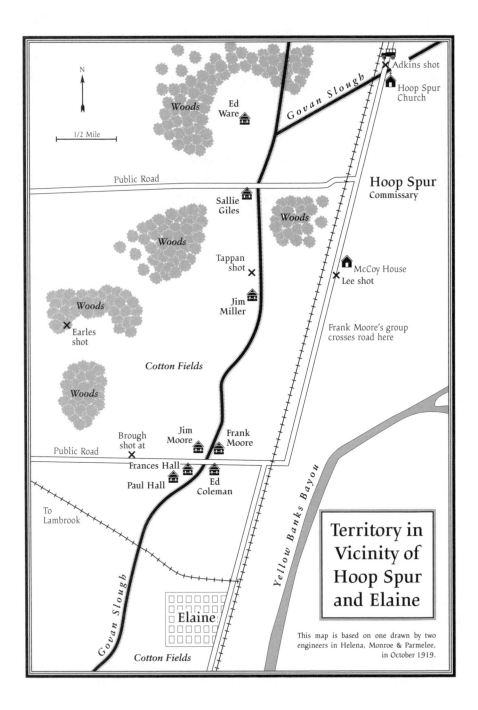

N

1/2 Mile

Woods

Ed
Ware

Govan Slough

Adkins shot

Hoop Spur
Church

Public Road

Hoop Spur
Commissary

Sallie
Giles

Woods

Woods

Tappan
shot ✕

McCoy House
Lee shot ✕

Jim
Miller

Woods

✕ Earles
shot

Frank Moore's group
crosses road here

Cotton Fields

Woods

Brough
shot at ✕

Jim
Moore

Frank
Moore

Public Road

Frances Hall

Paul Hall

Ed
Coleman

To
Lambrook

Yellow Banks Bayou

Govan Slough

Elaine

Cotton Fields

Territory in Vicinity of Hoop Spur and Elaine

This map is based on one drawn by two
engineers in Helena, Monroe & Parmelee,
in October 1919.

The Killing Fields

STANDING BY THE CHURCH door, Lit Simmons watched as the three men got out of the car. None of the guards had known what to do when the auto sat there for long minutes in the darkness, but now they did. "Come on," the Beco brothers said, "let's go." As they approached the car, the man who'd stepped from the driver's side clicked on a flashlight, and then, a few seconds later, there was the flash of gunfire.

"It was a white man that fired the first three shots," Simmons said. "I saw by the flashlight, and the light of the pistol. He fired very rapidly—from an automatic pistol. He was about 21 or 22 yards from the church."

Nearby, John Ratliff saw the same sequences of events: as the Beco brothers and other guards walked toward the car, the "firing commenced. The first shots, about three, were one right after the other . . . As near as I could see, the first shooting came from the back end of the car, and was ranging toward the church."

Inside, pandemonium reigned. An instant earlier, Ed Ware had stood up and begun walking toward the pulpit, where Jim Miller was speaking, when "a bullet came right across my face," he said. "Someone shot right into the window and knocked the glass all over me. Frank Moore fell right across me; then bullets just kept raining through the house and I could hear the glass fall there, and I was lying on the floor." Moore and Ware had fallen together in a heap, knocking down Joe Mershon and his wife. They "piled down on my wife's leg and hurt it," Mershon remembered later.

It was pitch black in the church. One of the first shots had struck a lamp, and then somebody had cried out, "Blow out the lights, women get on the floor," and Lizzie Wright, Sallie Giles, Vina Mason, and all of the other women and their children had taken cover behind upturned benches. "The first shots came in at the northwest window, a couple of shots were made, and then I could hear them raining all over," said Wright. Added Giles: "We were falling around there, begging the Lord, getting under benches and everything else."

The shooting stopped for a moment, perhaps for as long as two or three minutes, and then a second car pulled up out front. "It got closer than the first car did," said Will Wordlow, one of the guards. "I don't know how many shots were fired—[it was] like popcorn popping." This round of shooting went on much longer, and down on the church floor, Vina Mason was desperately trying to shield her child from the furious rain of bullets. "The house was packed and jammed, and I got down with the baby in my arms. The men, women and children were scuffling, and I raised up, and got shot in my arm. When the shooting ceased, people were jumping out the windows. I made it to the door, walking over people, but lost my hat and the baby's. When I got out, my husband took the baby, and told me to run for the house."

They fled in whatever way they could. Some made a mad dash for the front door, while others broke the windows on the south side of the church, away from where the bullets had come, and clambered out that way. They ran mostly to the south, some into a nearby alfalfa field and others into a sorghum patch, while a few took cover in the brush by the side of the road and hid, waiting to see if any other cars were going to pull up to the church. But mostly they ran. There was Henry Mason clutching his baby and urging Vina to keep up, and old man Charlie Robinson limping along on a gimpy leg as fast as he could, and Sallie Giles wondering as she raced home whether her sons were safe—a rush of nearly two hundred men, women, and children fleeing the church, and all of them stumbling along the rough ground in the dark. They had nowhere to go but to their cabins, and what with the white men having shot up their church, which they all knew was a warning that they were not to meet anymore, they thought that perhaps morning would come and all would be okay. They could go back to picking cotton and the white men would leave them alone, as long as they didn't hire that attorney. They could go back to their cabins, and they would be safe.

AROUND 2:00 A.M., T. K. Jones was awakened by a call from deputy sheriff Dick Dalzell. "There was some shooting" at Hoop Spur, Dalzell said. "Our men might be hurt." Jones woke up Henry Smiddy, whose room in the Cleburne Hotel was directly across from his, and by 3:00 A.M., the two Missouri Pacific special agents were on their way to investigate, with Dalzell filling them in about what he knew as he drove. Pratt had been shot in the knee, but he had managed to crawl away from the car to the nearby railroad tracks and flag a passing freight train, which had taken him to Wabash, a few miles north of Hoop Spur. There, Pratt had phoned Sheriff Kitchens. A second man, W. K. Monroe, had also phoned Kitchens. While passing by the Hoop Spur church around midnight, on his way from Helena to Elaine, he'd been fired upon and wounded by men hiding in the brush. A final call had come from Kid Collins, the Negro trustee, who'd walked to Wabash.

Amos Jarman was in the car with Dalzell, Smiddy, and Jones, and a second car with five more men—Helena police chief Sam Austin, deputy U.S. marshal Will Molitor, circuit court clerk A. G. Burke, and two others—was right behind. Except for Smiddy and Jones, all of the men were part of the ruling clique of Democrats that ran Phillips County. Jarman owned cotton fields, as did one or two of the others, and most could tell of fathers, uncles, and grandfathers who had helped build Helena. Jarman and Burke, in particular, were regulars at the Helena Country Club.

Jones and Smiddy got along well with the Helena crew, but they were not part of that ruling clique and never would be. In Helena, the Cleburne Hotel was their home away from home—their families lived in Memphis. Jones, forty years old, had worked for the Missouri Pacific Railroad for four years, supervising the special agents who tried to keep thieves out of the railroad's freight yards in eastern Arkansas. Smiddy, who worked for Jones, was thirty years old, with a twenty-six-year-old wife, Maude, and three children: four-year-old Jessie, two-year-old Henry F. Smiddy Jr., and a baby girl. Jones and Smiddy were Tennessee men, but what separated them most from the Helena group was class. Neither was the sort who socialized with wealthy planters at a country club. Both were lower-class working-men, literate but not well schooled.

At around 4:00 A.M., they spotted a Model T Ford parked on the side of the road, next to a bridge that crossed the Govan Slough. Jones was the first to reach the body lying next to the rear wheel. "He's dead," he muttered, and then he and Smiddy turned the body over. Adkins had been shot in the stomach "with a load of buckshot," Smiddy observed, and "through the neck with a rifle or pistol."

Burke, meanwhile, had been examining the car. "It's all shot to pieces—there must be 15 or 20 bullet holes all through it," he said.

They drove to Elaine to phone Kitchens with the news that Adkins had been killed, and then, a short while later, they came back to examine the church, arriving just as dawn broke. Everyone saw the same thing. "The last people who had been in the church had left there hurriedly," Smiddy said. "Benches were turned over, window lights broken out on all sides of the church, glass scattered all over the floor, women's and men's hats and coats scattered around over the floor and every evidence of a stampede." They gathered up the union literature scattered about—blank applications, membership cards, and circulars. This last piece of material, someone sneered, read: "We battle for the rights of our race."

Back outside, Jones and Smiddy walked around the wooden building. "The church," Smiddy discovered, "had been shot into from the north side." A shed just north of the church, Jones noticed, also "appeared to have been shot into." A gun battle of a furious sort had apparently broken out here, and even as they were trying to imagine the scene, Kid Collins suddenly showed up.

"He told me they came down there for the purpose of breaking up the meeting," Smiddy said. "They stopped there in the road and Mr. Adkins begun shooting. The Negroes returned the fire and shooting became general."

After that, the men broke into two groups. Jones and Sam Austin went down the road a short piece to the Hoop Spur commissary, a store where sharecroppers could buy supplies, with plans to arrest any Negroes who came by there armed. Smiddy, Dalzell, and the others started knocking on the doors of nearby cabins and arresting those inside. All went peacefully, and none was "found armed," Smiddy said. A white law enforcement officer was dead, there had been a shootout at the Hoop Spur church the previous night, and yet, for the moment, it seemed that calmer minds might prevail.

FRANK KITCHENS HAD BEEN ill for some time, but early that Wednesday morning he hurried to the courthouse, where members of the Richard Kitchens Post of the American Legion were already gathering. The town's telephone tree had worked well, and Kitchens and Sebastian Straub immediately began handing 20-gauge Winchester shotguns to the one hundred or so men assembled there. They also made certain that everyone had an ample supply of ammunition.

There were few men more powerful in Phillips County than Frank Kitchens, and perhaps none more feared by blacks. Born on a plantation in 1869, Kitchens had first been elected sheriff in 1900, and except for a period of two years, 1910–12, when he'd served a term as county treasurer, he'd manned the post ever since. And while he was known through eastern Arkansas as Sheriff Kitchens, he also owned a sizable plantation. A 1912 book on prominent people in the state, the *Historical Review of Arkansas,* described him as a "substantial and prosperous agriculturalist" who had "met with well-deserved success as a cultivator of the soil." He, E. C. Hornor, and Straub went way back, and at the moment, he and Amos Jarman jointly owned the Phillips County Real Estate Company, a business that for the past decade had helped wealthy planters consolidate their holdings. Since 1910, the average size of an overseer-run plantation in Phillips

County had increased from 671 to 999 acres, and Kitchens, while wearing his businessman's hat, had helped make this possible.

A big man with wavy hair and dark eyebrows, Sheriff Kitchens kept tight control of Helena and the rest of the county, and he didn't particularly care for anyone outside the area telling him what to do. Phillips County was part of the First Judicial Circuit in Arkansas, and in 1918, when the newly elected district attorney for the district, John Miller, had tried to prosecute several Helena men for running a gambling den, Kitchens and other county Democrats—as Miller later recalled—told him to knock it off. "We have ways of doing things down here that you don't have in White and other counties," they said. "We've decided to ask you to let us run the internal affairs of the county where we live and you prosecute what indictments we return."

Every Negro who lived in Helena, or came to town to shop, knew to mind Sheriff Kitchens's rules. There were certain hours that Negroes were allowed on Cherry Street and other times when they were not, and every black man knew that if he was walking down the sidewalk and a white man or woman came toward him, he had damn well better step out of the way, either by flattening himself up against the building or by stepping off the curb, and that if he didn't and this was brought to the attention of Sheriff Kitchens, there would be hell to pay, most likely in the form of a good whipping. It was the little things like that that kept order in Helena, and what with Adkins dead, it was fairly easy for those who knew Kitchens to imagine what was on his mind. "Nothing," a friend of his said a few days later, "could have suited Frank better than to be given free hand to hunt Mr. Nigger in his lair."

Kitchens cleared his throat. Pratt and Adkins, he said, had been "ambushed" the night before, while stopping "to repair a punctured tire." It was just as the town had feared—the Negroes were rising up "against the white residents of the southern part of Phillips County." Kitchens deputized the men, and since he was too sick to go with them, he appointed Sebastian Straub acting sheriff. Straub would direct the posses in the field, and Herbert Thompson, who had been a captain in the American Expeditionary Forces in World War I, would be second in command. Kitchens, the *Arkansas Gazette* reported, since he was "unable to direct the attack," would remain in his courthouse office, overseeing operations from there.

By 8:30 A.M., the posses were ready to move out. Many of the men were discharged World War I veterans, and they were a tough-looking group: most wore felt hats, with the front brims turned down, and nearly everyone had a cigarette between his lips. The men checked and rechecked their shotguns, made sure they were loaded and ready to go, and then piled into a long line of cars, which kicked up a cloud of dust as they sped out of town.

MOST OF THE SHARECROPPERS who'd fled the Hoop Spur church the night before weren't aware that the guards outside had returned the fire and killed a white man. They'd made it safely back to their cabins and had gone to sleep. Around 4:00 A.M., however, Paul Hall and a handful of others who lived three miles south of the church—and were aware that there was a white man's body lying in the road—began knocking on the doors of union members in that area, telling them to go to Frank Moore's house. A dead white man meant more trouble was coming their way.

By dawn, more than fifty people had gathered at Moore's, and most of the men had brought shotguns and pistols. Several hours passed, and then around 10:30 A.M., they heard gunshots coming from the north, up near the center of Hoop Spur. Everyone exchanged frightened glances, and soon a small boy came running frantically down the road. "He told us some white people were coming and said they were going to kill everything that was big enough to die," Nina Jenkins said.

THE HELENA POSSES HAD barely paused when they'd reached Adkins's car and the Hoop Spur church. They'd stopped just long enough to take in the sight of that shattered auto, and then they'd raced on to the Hoop Spur commissary, where they'd turned west along a small dirt road. This was where they'd first fired their guns,

100 yards or so west of that small store, and now blacks living along this road were scurrying ahead of the men from Helena. The sharecroppers made it to Sallie Giles's cabin, and so too did Ed Ware, although he had come from a different direction, from the north.

"I asked what was the matter," Ware later recalled. "They said a gang of white people had killed a little fellow they called Lemon, and were coming to kill me and every Negro they saw. I got afraid, got stirred up, and started back home. I looked up toward Hoop Spur, and saw in the big road about three automobiles coming abreast, about a quarter of a mile away from my place, [and] a gang of white gentlemen with guns, walking about four or five abreast."

Ware raced home to get his gun, and even as he was inside loading it, the pack marched across his cotton fields, led by none other than Kid Collins, the Negro trustee. "Come out that house nigger," Collins shouted. "Come straight to me." Ware's wife, Lulu, raced outside to confront—and stop—the men.

"What are you going to do with us women?" she asked.

"Nothing, if there are no men in the house."

"There are none."

"There better not be."

At that instant, Ware slipped out the back door and began to run. Charlie Robinson, who had been watching all this from his cabin, also took off—or tried to. He gimped along, his body flailing from side to side with every painful step, but he only made it a short distance before a bullet sliced into his back. "They started on to my house," Lulu Ware said, "and commenced shooting about the left of it, and that old man, Charles Robinson, was killed, and put in my bed. They took me then, and put me in jail."*

Ed Ware was now in flight, and so too were Albert and Milligan Giles, and everyone else who had been at Giles's cabin. A number of women, thinking that there was no way to outrun the gang of white men now bearing down on them, fled into the nearby Govan Slough, a thicket of brush and trees maybe 40 feet wide, with a ditch in the

---

* For a map of the killing fields, see the Appendix.

middle. The Giles brothers, along with Joe Fox, hurried one-half mile south to Jim Miller's place. A handful of other men—Alf Banks Jr., Arthur Washington, and one other—had also raced to Miller's, and Miller, who was president of the Hoop Spur union, ordered everyone into the slough. "We heard the shooting at Ed Ware's house," Banks said. "We was hiding to protect ourselves." Banks and several of the others had guns, and as they flattened themselves against the wet ground, Miller "told us if they didn't bother us, don't bother them," Fox said. The men remained as quiet as they could, holding their breath for ten, fifteen minutes. "Lay close and if they pass on by, let them pass," Miller whispered, their panic rising when they heard a flurry of shotgun blasts. "The white people," the men figured, must have been shooting "at the women, who were about 200 yards above us, in the thicket."

THERE WERE FIFTY OR so men making their way south toward Jim Miller and the other sharecroppers, and this group consisted of both Herbert Thompson's posse and a second one from Elaine. They had met up about fifteen minutes before, the Elaine posse having chased a "big gang" of blacks into the woods earlier that morning, said Henry Bernard, the man who, following his spying expedition under the Elaine church the previous Thursday, had alerted everyone to the sharecroppers' plans "to get rid of the boss man." Both groups had seen the blacks running into the slough to hide, and Thompson had ordered the men to get on both sides of the ditch so that there would be no chance that the blacks could escape. Thompson was carrying an arrest warrant for Miller, but Smiddy, who earlier had helped arrest Negroes, understood that their orders had now changed.

"When we started down that thicket," he said, "it was the understanding with all of us that we would shoot the negroes as we came to them."

As they followed the slough southwest, five or six blacks came "out unarmed, holding up their hands and some of them running and trying to get away," Smiddy said. "They were shot down and killed." The posse members walked steadily along the sides of the brush, apparently unconcerned that Negroes hiding there might dare to shoot, and as they neared Miller's house, Smiddy spotted a figure—a teenage boy, it seemed—crouched behind a bush. "When I shot him," Smiddy said, "he was not trying to shoot anybody and didn't have a gun." Smiddy and five or six others then looked to see "if there were any more negroes in there," and they found the boy "shot through the chin and the bullet lodged in the back of his neck." Bernard was also keeping a loose count of the number of Negroes shot: "I saw some six or eight bodies in there, dead ones," he said. The posse moved on, the frenzy of fire coming from the two sides of the slough such that Smiddy and Dalzell were struck by stray shotgun pellets. "Look out, we are shooting our own men," someone cried out, and it was at that moment that James Tappan was struck full in the face by a "load of buckshot." As Smiddy and others rushed to his side, two black men burst from the brush, making a desperate run for it.

Posse members quickly carried Tappan back to where they'd left the cars, on the road near Giles's cabin, and ferried him over to Finis McCoy's house, which was a mile or so away on the main road. Late-arriving Helena posses had begun using his home as a staging area; there were now a number of cars parked in his front yard. Everyone there was stunned by this sudden turn in the "fighting."

This wasn't any ordinary Helena citizen who'd been shot. Tappan, thirty years old, had been a first lieutenant in the war and was known as one of the most dashing figures in town—he'd turned his 1917 Buick into a racing car, and regularly won sulky horse races at area tracks. Plus, he was a *Tappan*. Elaine was located in Tappan township, and there was nobody more revered in Helena history than James C. Tappan, the rich planter who'd served as a brigadier general in the Confederate Army during the Civil War. In 1861, while still a colonel, Tappan had led the 13th Arkansas Volunteers regiment at the Battle of Belmont in Missouri, where, according to Southern accounts of the fight, he won a great victory over Ulysses Grant. While young James was not a direct descendant of the famous

Helena general, he did belong to the larger Tappan clan, and now he lay dying in McCoy's bedroom. The fact that he may have been shot by others in the posse was not, to most of the men, at all relevant. The tally of whites killed in this Negro "insurrection" was about to reach two, and as one Arkansas newspaperman wrote a few years later, "the fact that even ONE WHITE MAN had to lose his life in the riot is cause for deep regret."

SEVEN MEN WHO'D BEEN at Jim Miller's house had gone into the slough, and it was Alf Banks Jr. and Joe Fox who'd burst out when Tappan was shot. Arthur Washington and one other share-cropper—a discharged army veteran—were dead, and most likely Miller was too, as he had been "shot in the head," Banks said.* Fifteen-year-old Milligan Giles was the teenager who'd been shot by Smiddy; he lay in the mud with a bullet in the back of his neck, unconscious but breathing. His older brother Albert was in a similar state. He'd been shot five times, with one bullet passing through his skull and exiting near his left ear.

Farther to the south, the sharecroppers who'd spent the morning at Frank Moore's were on the move. They'd heard the shooting up at Miller's place, and now they were heading off in three different directions. Many of the women and children, along with some of the men, were fleeing west into the woods. Another group of men had mounted horses and were racing to the south to warn everyone that white people had come "to kill all the Negroes they could find." Moore and a dozen or so others—including Ed and Frank Hicks, the leaders of the Elaine chapter of the Progressive Farmers and Household Union—were heading *north,* toward Miller's house. Moore, a thirty-one-year-old army veteran, told them: "Don't you all hear that shooting? Come on, let's go help them people out."

As they headed through the cotton fields, they walked along two by two, almost as though they were in a military formation. They had not gone far before a gang of white men off to the northwest

* There is conflicting evidence as to whether Miller died in the Govan Slough or escaped to the woods and was killed there later in the day.

spotted them. They "tried to cut us off," Moore said. "They were shooting at us all the time." Moore and the others hurriedly turned east, crossing the railroad tracks and emerging onto Route 44 about one-quarter mile south of McCoy's house.

At some point during this journey—and it's not clear when this happened—somebody in Moore's group fired his gun. "It was only two shots made from we colored men," said Ed Coleman. Perhaps one of the sharecroppers shot back at the white gangs that had cut them off, or perhaps, as they crossed Route 44, someone took aim at the men gathered out front of McCoy's and squeezed off two rounds. Either way, Moore and the others did not get any closer to McCoy's than that, for they all quickly disappeared into a cornfield east of the road and headed south, their thoughts about taking on the posses having already dissipated.

"I slipped back through the field to save my mother and little children," Moore said, and the others did the same, returning to their cabins to scoop up wives and children and to head to the woods to hide. Few dared any longer to stay at home.

UP AT MCCOY'S, NOBODY seemed to know where the bullet had come from. Perhaps someone's gun had accidentally discharged, several suggested. Others had seen a band of Negroes off in the distance scurry across the road, and someone said it looked like one or two in the pack had kneeled down, and then there was the sound of a gun being shot, and suddenly a bullet had sliced through the left rear door of a car turning around in the road, striking twenty-two-year-old Clinton "Buddie" Lee under the left arm. "I am hit," Lee had cried out, and five minutes later, Dr. Parker, who had been tending to Tappan's wounds, pronounced Lee dead.

This shooting, with the bullet having come out of nowhere, like sniper fire, caused the posses to regroup. Tappan was dying, Lee was dead, and one other posse member—Ira Proctor—had been seriously wounded while chasing Negroes into the woods. It seemed that they were truly in a fight now, and Negroes greatly outnumbered whites in this part of the county. "After the shooting of Lee," Smiddy said, "we thought the Negroes that had crossed the road were going to make an attack on the McCoy house, and we scattered out around the house and up and down the lane." They needed reinforcements, and once this message reached Helena, Sheriff Kitchens and other town officials immediately wired Governor Charles Brough in Little Rock. "Circuit and county judges, sheriff, mayor and leading private citizens urgently request immediate dispatch of 500 troops with machine guns to Elaine. Situation intense . . . Presence of troops is earnestly desired on account of the moral effect."

Kitchens also briefed reporters in Helena on the dire situation. The Negroes in Hoop Spur, he said, "were assembling in large numbers and had begun promiscuous firing on white persons." More than a thousand were now gathered in the woods north of Elaine, and all were "armed with high-powered rifles."

At McCoy's, Henry Bernard and others prepared for the assault. "I got in this corn crib, with Jim Austin and Isey Bernard, but my rifle barrel wouldn't go between the logs, and I took my knife and whittled out a place," Bernard said. Several Negroes "got in this corn patch, and when one would show himself, one of us would get him, but they never did attack us from there."

An hour and then two passed in this way, Bernard and the others occasionally picking off a Negro moving about the corn patch, and then at 3:00 P.M. the rumor arose that a Negro assault on Elaine was imminent. A train had been dispatched from Helena to go to the aid of whites there, and the posses at McCoy's house, which still included T. K. Jones and Henry Smiddy, boarded it at Hoop Spur for the short trek to Elaine, Route 44 having been deemed too dangerous for travel.

TUMULTUOUS EVENTS HAD ALSO been unfolding in points farther south that day. At 9:00 A.M., Ulysses Bratton's oldest son, Ocier, accompanied by Robert Hill, had stepped off the train in Ratio, the two men having come from McGehee. Just as Hill had promised at the union meeting in Elaine the previous Thursday, he was back with someone who could help them press their complaints against the plantation owners. The twenty-five to fifty black farmers waiting for them at the station, none of whom knew about the shooting at Hoop Spur the previous night, were all from Theo Fathauer's plantation, and for the next half hour Bratton met with them one by one, taking their statements and having them sign contracts. Most of the share-croppers were able to give him only $5 or so for an initial retainer, with Bratton having collected a total of $167 when eight "heavily armed" white men rode up.

"I guess you will have to adjourn your little meeting," they said.

"If you insist. You seem to be in the majority."

As Fathauer's overseers circled about Bratton, angrily asking "what he meant by keeping their niggers out of the fields," the share-croppers hid Hill, enabling him to slip away unnoticed. Fathauer's men decided to drive Bratton to Elaine, where an angry mob began debating whether to hang him "from a telegraph pole." He was then "conducted to a brick store" and chained to two Negroes, the lynch-ing sentiment rising with every tick of the clock.

"Isn't he a pretty-looking son of a bitch?" a voice cried out.

"You had better tell it all before we break your neck," said another, waving a copy of a union contract that had been taken from him.

"Get ready to die," said a third.

A call from E. C. Hornor in Helena finally quieted such talk. "Mr. E. C. Hornor advised that there be no violence at Elaine," said J. W. Butts. "For that reason, Bratton was not killed by the members of the armed forces. . . . Had we not listened to Mr. Hornor's advice he would certainly have had violence because we all felt that he was to blame for the insurrection."

What took place next in Elaine is only sketchily documented. At around 1:00 P.M., the town's telephone operator phoned Helena, screaming hysterically that "fighting was in progress in the streets." She must have been hearing gunfire close by, and the *Arkansas Gazette*, in its first report of the day's events, said that by early after-noon, the "negroes had been driven from Elaine," and that posse members who'd returned to Helena had counted "at least 15 negroes lying in the streets and outskirts of town." However, in the following days, whites from Elaine swore that the sequence of events described by the *Arkansas Gazette* had never happened. There had been no fighting in their town, they insisted, and such remained the public record until 1927, when Bessie Ferguson, who interviewed both whites and blacks to write a master's thesis about the "riot," concluded that killings had indeed taken place there: "Barbarism such as cutting off the ears or toes of dead negroes for souvenirs and the dragging of their bodies through the streets of Elaine are told by witnesses. Authorities who were honestly trying to quiet the trouble were at the same time endeavoring to stop such atrocities."*

At around 4:00 P.M., Bratton and fifteen Negro "prisoners" were placed on a train to Helena, along with most of the white women and children of Elaine, who were being evacuated for safety reasons. Bratton was still chained to two black men, and upon the train's arrival in Helena, he was paraded down Cherry Street, a spectacle that provided the seed for lynching sentiment to form there, particularly after Kitchens and his committee told newspaper reporters that a "white man" had been in the Hoop Spur church on Tuesday evening. "It is alleged that Bratton has been connected with activities of propagandists in this county who have been preaching the doctrine of social equality to the negroes," the *Arkansas Gazette* reported. Bratton, the Helena authorities said, would be charged with "first degree murder."

T. K. JONES STAYED IN Elaine that day until 7:00 P.M., waiting for an attack by the large force of Negroes that was said to have assembled nearby. But none ever materialized, and during his three hours there, he—like Henry Smiddy—grew ever more skeptical about the official story, which was that Pratt and Adkins had been ambushed at Hoop Spur. He'd seen the bullet holes in the shed by the church,

---

* She wrote from a pro-planter perspective, which adds to the credibility of her report.

and as he stood on the crowded streets of Elaine, he overheard this conversation:

"My negroes don't belong to that goddamn union," one of the men said.

"How in the hell do you know they don't?"

"I told my negroes about two weeks ago that if they joined that goddamn union I would kill every one of them."

On Jones's way back to Helena, the train passed Hoop Spur and he was not at all surprised by what he saw: the church, with its telltale bullet holes, had been burned to the ground.

SMIDDY DECIDED TO REMAIN in Elaine for the night. White men, more than five hundred in all, were flooding into the town. These late arrivals were from places such as Marianna, Clarendon, and Marvell, in eastern Arkansas, and from Tunica, Lulu, Friars Point, and Clarksdale, in Mississippi, and they had come rushing into Phillips County in the early afternoon, all of them drawn by news of a "nigger uprising." They were a boisterous lot, with stories to tell.

These men, while making their way to the "battle" scene earlier that afternoon, had come to Helena and headed south. As they'd driven toward Hoop Spur, they'd spotted sharecroppers in the fields. While black farmers living between Helena and Wabash must have seen cars speeding south earlier that day, they apparently hadn't been told of the nature of the trouble at Hoop Spur, and so they were out picking cotton. Men, women, and children were in the fields, but by late afternoon, when a Mississippi contingent accompanied by a *Memphis Press* reporter headed south from Helena, nobody was moving anymore, and all the Mississippi men could do was engage in a little target practice. "Dead bodies were lying in the road a few miles outside the city," the *Press* reported. "Enraged citizens fired at the bodies of the dead negroes as they rode out of Helena toward Elaine."

Like the killings in Elaine, the gunning down of blacks along this 20-mile stretch of road, between Helena and Wabash, is only sparsely documented. Some of the men from the outside posses returned to Helena that evening, and when asked about the number of blacks that had been killed, they simply replied: "Plenty of them." One of the dead Negroes, the *Memphis Commercial Appeal* was told, had been "struck by 26 bullets." However, most of the men from Mississippi and other outside areas went to Elaine that night, where Smiddy was, and later he summed up what he'd learned from them: "During that afternoon, October 1, 1919, a crowd of men came from Mississippi and began the indiscriminate hunting down, shooting and killing of Negroes. They shot and killed men, women and children without regard to whether they were guilty or innocent of any connection with the killing of anybody, or whether members of the union or not. Negroes were killed time and time again out in the fields picking cotton, harming nobody."

No Arkansas paper reported on this killing field. The *Arkansas Democrat* wrote that the outside posses had "numerous clashes with negroes," and then said no more. The Memphis papers provided a few nuggets of information about what they did that first day, but then they too clammed up, and a veil of public silence descended. It was to become part of the oral history of the riot, documented mostly by stories told to others rather than by direct confessions from those involved. Bessie Ferguson heard all about it in 1927, with blacks telling her of how "armed bands of whites from neighboring counties and from Mississippi rushed to the scene of trouble and began, particularly the posse from Mississippi, a more indiscriminate slaughter, killing both men and women." One particularly brutal party of "twelve men from Mississippi equipped with eleven guns and an ax created havoc wherever they went."

That story of slaughter, related to Smiddy on that afternoon of October 1 and later repeated to Ferguson, was also told to district attorney John Miller. The real killing, he said, began "when that damn Mississippi contingent came over. They started the marauding." The men from across the river, Miller said, had come with "blood in their eyes."

NIGHT FELL, A DAY of killing was coming to an end, and the white posses in Elaine hunkered down. "We formed a cordon around the town to repel any invasion which might come from the woods around, where we knew a world of negroes were," Butts said. Every white growing up in the Delta harbored fears about the brutish Negro, and on this night, the darkness was filled with such ghosts. Butts was so scared that "when several cows came wandering through the cotton patch," he barely "resisted the impulse to shoot."

"The quiet, however, holds the tenseness of waiting," the *Arkansas Gazette* told its readers. "At dawn, the posses are expected to begin a hunt for the disaffected negroes of the southern part of the county, who are said to be waiting for them in the canebrakes."

And out in the those canebrakes, both in the woods west of town and in the Yellow Banks Bayou east of Route 44, hundreds of men, women, and children settled down for the long night. The rivercane was 20 to 25 feet in height, so dense in spots that the sharecroppers had to turn sideways to squeeze through the bamboo-like cane stems. It was wet in there, mud giving way to swamp, and this was where Nina Jenkins and her family had come. So too Ed and Frank Hicks, and John Martin and Alf Banks, and Will Wordlow. "I had eight women and children with me to hide, keep them from getting killed," Wordlow said. Ed Coleman, seventy-eight years old, was out in the canebrake, worried sick that his wife, who was too frail to have come with him, might already be dead. And this was where Frank Moore had come with his mother, his wife, Mary, and their small children, all of them stumbling along in the darkness until they reached a spot where the cane was a little less thick. This was where they would pass the night, their backs resting against the cane.

Less than ten months earlier, Moore—a big-shouldered man, about 5 feet 8 inches tall—had been a soldier in the U.S. Army, stationed at Camp Pike. He'd worn his private's uniform proudly, and he knew by heart his serial number: 3848337. Like all the other black soldiers, he'd been told that at war's end Negroes would be treated in a "juster and fairer" manner, that America would change. He'd been honorably discharged on December 22, 1918, and he and his father had planted 51 acres of cotton that spring, and the cotton had come up high, and then he'd joined the union, become a leader in it, thinking that this year he would get his fair share of proceeds from the crop. Yet now here he was in this rivercane, his arms wrapped around his children, telling them not to cry, that everything was going to be all right, all the while knowing that when dawn came, the posses were certain to be up and about, and the "nigger hunt" would begin again.

They Shot Them Down Like Rabbits

THE FIRST CALL FOR help from Phillips County authorities to Arkansas governor Charles Hillman Brough had come at 12:30 P.M. on Wednesday, and within a few minutes the governor had wired U.S. war secretary Newton Baker. "Four whites said to be killed; negroes said to be massing for attack," he wrote. "Request authorization commanding general Camp Pike be authorized to send such United States troops as may be necessary and called for by me." Brough was intent on personally taking charge of the situation, and he was, as anyone familiar with his academic writings could attest, of firm and certain mind about what needed to be done.

Brough was, in so many ways, a paradox. He was known in political circles, both locally and nationally, as a progressive Southern leader, which reflected his background as an academic. Yet he was also a staunch white supremacist, his racial beliefs reflecting the fact that while he may have been the son of a blue-blooded Yankee, he was Mississippi born and raised.

Brough's father, Charles Milton, was from Pennsylvania and had been a captain in the Union Army during the Civil War. Afterward, he married Flora Maria Thompson, who had moved from Maine to Mississippi as a young girl, and they settled in Clinton, Mississippi, where Charles was born on July 9, 1876. His parents then moved to Utah, but because of a lack of schools in the territory, Charles remained in Clinton with his aunt and uncle, Walter and Adelia Hillman. They too were transplanted New Englanders, his aunt the prin-

cipal of the Hillman College for women and his uncle the president
of Mississippi College, which taught students from the primary grades
through college. This was where Charles was schooled, and although
his aunt and uncle may have had liberal sensibilities, he soaked up
from his peers a sweet nostalgia for the Confederate South. He hailed
Robert E. Lee as the "only person in human history without a per-
ceptible flaw," and championed Mississippi as a "land ennobled by
having cradled some of the most magnificent statesmen, matchless
orators, and noblest women" to be found anywhere.

After earning a doctoral degree at the tender age of twenty-one
from Johns Hopkins University, Brough took a job teaching at Mississippi College, and for one of his first papers, he wrote a treatise on
the Clinton Riot of 1875, which had helped bring Reconstruction to
an end. At that time, Republicans in Mississippi still held the reins of
government, and as the fall elections neared, armed whites, vowing
to redeem their state, regularly broke up Republican meetings and
warned blacks not to vote. In response, on September 4 hundreds of
blacks in Clinton brought guns to a political rally, and when whites
arrived to break it up, fighting broke out. "Kill the damned whites,
run over them, God damn them, run over them," the blacks yelled.
White militia from Vicksburg joined the fray, chasing the blacks into
the swamps and killing more than twenty Negro men. As this massacre was but one part of a statewide campaign of terror by whites,
Republican governor Adelbert Ames begged President Ulysses Grant
to send federal troops to protect blacks and their right to vote in the
coming elections. However, the president refused, stating that the
country was tired of these "autumnal outbreaks." The president had
adopted a noninterference policy, and a few months later the U.S.
Supreme Court ruled in *Cruikshank* that federal authorities couldn't
prosecute whites who killed blacks trying to exercise their right to
vote, putting the court's stamp of approval on his decree.

In his 1902 paper, which was published by the Mississippi Historical Society, Brough made clear his partisan feelings. He called
Governor Ames a "Carpet-bag Charlatan," described Republicans as
a party of "mongrelism, ignorance and depravity," and compared the

blacks who had fought in the Clinton Riot to "barbarians at the sack of Rome." The Vicksburg militia, he said, had done "valiant and vigorous work for the protection of life." Most important of all, Brough wrote, the "terrorized negroes" never did successfully "return to municipal, county and State politics."

> This opportunity for home-rule granted by the President sounded the deathknell of reconstruction rule in Mississippi and thus the Clinton riot of September 4, 1875, indirectly made possible the glorious triumph of Democracy at the polls in 1876. . . . This lesson of Anglo-Saxon supremacy, written in letters of blood, will ever remain the most important of the many lessons taught in the modest college town of Clinton to the rising young manhood of a proud and untrammeled Commonwealth.

Brough moved to Fayetteville, Arkansas, in 1903 to chair the economics department at the University of Arkansas, and soon he added lecturer on the Chautauqua circuit to his resume. Each summer, he'd leave his academic post to join musicians, magicians, and actors at their traveling tent shows, which were meant to both entertain and educate. In his talks, Brough touted education as a solution to society's ills, and this progressive message led, in 1912, to his being named chairman of the newly formed University Commission on Southern Race Questions. The group's stated goal was to help Negroes make educational and economic progress, and in his role as chairman, Brough now spoke out for Negro rights. "As an American citizen the Negro is entitled to life, liberty, and the pursuit of happiness, and the equal protection of our laws for the safeguarding of these inalienable rights."

Not surprisingly, such pronouncements came back to haunt him when he ran for governor in 1916. His opponent in the Democratic primary, Earl Hodges, pointed to them as evidence that Brough was, in the vernacular of the times, a "nigger lover." With his political future at stake, Brough responded by taking out newspaper ads assuring

Arkansans that he was no such thing. "I am not in favor of negroes serving on juries, I am not in favor of negroes holding political office in the South," he declared. He was against "the enfranchisement of the inferior race," and promised that, as governor, he would pursue policies that maintained the "everlasting superiority of the white race."

Brough's white-supremacist protestations proved convincing to the planters of Phillips County, with J. L. Hornor, John Moore, C. A. Wooten, and Elaine mayor Sid Stoaks all pledging him their support. "Congratulations from Phillips County," Stoaks wrote on April 2, 1916, after Brough won the Democratic primary. Elaine, he said, gave "you the biggest majority in the county." At his inauguration, Brough tipped his hat to his supporters in Phillips County, praising General James Tappan as the "only Confederate General who ever had the honor of whipping the great and magnanimous Grant," and on September 7, 1918, Democrats in Helena filled every seat at the Grand Opera House to hear him speak.

GIVEN THE LAW REGULATING federal intervention in a state civil emergency, Brough's call to Newton Baker was a bit premature. The U.S. Supreme Court, of course, had ruled that federal authorities, acting on their own, could not send troops to prevent mob violence, even when it took such extreme form as burning a Negro alive at the stake. State authorities had to request such federal intervention, and even then, the War Department had concluded, the law permitted "use of federal troops only if the civil emergency is beyond control of state authorities after it has exhausted its means, including civil officials and National Guard." Brough had bypassed this intermediate step of calling out the Arkansas National Guard. Asking for federal troops so quickly also seemed to go against his belief in home rule, but this emergency was apparently different. Several whites were dead and armed Negroes were reportedly massing for an attack, and shortly after midnight, 583 white officers and troops from Camp Pike, along with Governor Brough, departed Little Rock by train, the War Department having given its okay.

The commander of the Camp Pike force, which included five

hundred men from rifle companies and fifty troops from a machine gun squad, was Colonel Isaac Jenks, a West Point graduate. Equipment loaded onto the train included six liberty trucks, two ambulances, two motorcycles with sidecars, and twelve machine guns, along with "a sufficient supply of ammunition to quiet the situation no matter how serious." Many of the soldiers had served in France as part of the American Expeditionary Force, and as the train chugged through the dark night, the men, anticipating what morning would bring, dubbed themselves the "Phillips County Expeditionary Forces." Theirs was to be a heroic venture, Phillips County was to be saved, and as *Arkansas Gazette* reporter William Wilson circulated among them, he sensed their excitement. "Every one of the 500 troops," he wrote, "appeared anxious to get into battle with the blacks—not because they wanted to kill them but because they realized the negroes who had armed themselves and who were bent upon 'cleaning up the country' should be stopped before women and children and more white men should be murdered."*

"The machine guns," Wilson added, "are expected to have a powerful moral effect upon the rioters."

THAT WEDNESDAY NIGHT RACIAL tension crackled throughout Phillips County. In Mellwood, three miles south of Ratio, two Negroes "paraded the streets at a late hour, making remarks about the whites and the race trouble at Elaine," and "were instantly killed by officers and residents of the town," the *Arkansas Democrat* reported. In Helena, where fifty Negroes and Ocier Bratton were jailed, emotions were "above fever heat," with no black daring to venture from his home. White men, including many from the surrounding counties

---

* During the war, there were a number of problems that arose between black and white soldiers at Camp Pike. The disdain that most of the camp's white officers felt toward blacks was so pronounced that on April 1, 1918, Captain E. C. Rowan refused an order to line up his brigade next to a Negro company, stating that it would "embarrass" his men and "violate" their "self-respect." Six months later, an army investigator who visited the camp observed that "it seems to be an established rule or custom in this camp for white officers and noncommissioned officers to address colored soldiers as 'you niggers.' "

and Mississippi, patrolled the streets, while "a small army waited at the Phillips County Courthouse to respond to emergency calls." And in Elaine, few of the posse members slept. Perhaps as many as one thousand men, the newspapers noted, would be heading out at the crack of dawn, and they would be searching in particular for four ringleaders: Robert Hill, Ed Hicks, Jim Miller, and Frank Moore.* "They are known personally to most of the possemen here," the *Arkansas Democrat* wrote, and "they will be killed on sight, it is believed, if possemen catch them."

Shortly after 6:00 A.M., the posses headed out, with the crew of twelve Mississippi men, "equipped with 11 guns and an ax," at the head of the line. They strode up Route 44 for about a mile, the adjacent fields empty and quiet, and then turned west along the small dirt road that led to Frank Moore's place. At the first cabin they came to, the Mississippi men barged in and dragged Lula Black outside.

Did she belong to the union?

"Yes," she said.

"Why?"

"It will better the condition of the colored people."

At that point, the mob "knocked her down, beat her over the head with their pistols, [and] kicked her all over the body," a black journalist later reported. The posses continued on to Frank Moore's house, which was empty, and then, a little ways further, they stopped at Frances Hall's cabin. Paul Hall's mother was known to all as a "crazy old woman," and as the mob of white men neared, she came out and stood on the front step of her home, screaming at the men to leave. She screeched and screeched, her arms flailing wildly about, and so the men decided to have a bit of fun with her, "tying her clothes over her head." Still she squawked, and finally one of the men raised his rifle and shot her in the throat, the old woman tumbling down the steps, landing facedown in the dirt. Then the posses moved on, continuing on west toward the woods where the Negro

---

* Miller had been killed the day before. However, since the bodies in the Govan Slough (and in other areas) were left lying there, Helena authorities didn't know of his death.

men were thought to be hiding, and by 7:00 A.M., people in Elaine could hear "heavy firing" coming from the "scene of engagement" to the northwest of their town.

A second day of killing was under way.

AS BROUGH AND THE troops entered southern Phillips County, arriving via McGehee, they passed by stations in Mellwood and Ratio where "small groups of white people armed with shotguns, pistols, and rifles" had gathered, observed Captain Edward Passailiague. "They appeared tired and very much excited." When their train pulled into Elaine at 8:15 A.M., Mayor Sid Stoaks and other local authorities—county treasurer Amos Jarman, Helena town councilman Orley Lilly, and Joseph Meyers, a plantation owner who was also a major in the Arkansas Guard—provided Jenks and Passailiague with an update.

"We were met by a committee of civilians who explained that the negroes of the surrounding country had assembled and were killing the whites whenever they ventured out to their farms," Passailiague wrote. "The white population had armed themselves as best they could and were assembled at Elaine. The negroes were holding the woods around the town and prevented them from getting out."

The Negro leaders of the uprising, thought to be at least fifteen in number, had "sent notice that they will not surrender," Jenks and Passailiague were informed. They were "desperate characters," and several were "discharged soldiers" who had urged other blacks to "battle for their race." The fighting that morning had begun around 7:00 A.M., and gunfire could be heard even at that moment. "The engagement in progress," Jenks concluded, was "three miles north, northwest of the town."

Jenks quickly established field headquarters in the telephone building on Elaine's main street. The situation, he surmised, was just as Brough had said—the whites in Elaine were surrounded, and out on the plantations blacks were indiscriminately shooting whites. Jenks set up a machine gun atop the town's tallest building, and from that perch he peered through binoculars at the battle scene off in the distance. His soldiers might need some help, he thought, and after he came down from the rooftop, the town's hardware merchants gave "shotguns, rifles and revolvers" to the Camp Pike officers, "who turned them over to the possemen," Wilson wrote in a dispatch for the *Arkansas Gazette.* A number of the deputized men would accompany the troops as they marched into battle.

There was no time, Jenks decided, for the troops to eat breakfast. He ordered a small detachment of men, under the command of Major Baxter, to remain in Elaine to protect the people there. Baxter was told to disarm all of the residents, white and black. The rest of the Camp Pike troops—more than four hundred riflemen and the machine squad—were ordered to gather their weapons. Out in the field, they would be commanded by Major Nathaniel Callen, who was battle-hardened from his service in France. Brough and Chaplain E. C. Sliney would ride in a car at the rear, with Jenks by their side. Wilson and Paul Grabiel from the *Arkansas Democrat,* along with a *Democrat* photographer, were allowed to tag along.

At 9:15 A.M., the soldiers began their march north, and both reporters noticed that there was no mistaking Jenks's orders. "The troops," Grabiel wrote, "are all under orders to kill any negro who refuses to surrender immediately."

THAT MORNING, FRANK MOORE and the others hiding in the woods east of Route 44 had heard the gunfire come from Paul Hall's place, and they had listened carefully as the sound grew fainter, the posses continuing to head west, toward the woods and canebrakes on the far side of the Hoop Spur cotton fields. Moore and the others crept forward to the edge of the canebrake where they had spent the night, and at the sight of the army troops coming up the road, Moore—who had gone to the canebrake the day before to "save my mother and little children"—stepped out into the road, thankful that his family was going to be rescued. "I took the children and women and made it to the soldier men," he said. "Then they took us and carried us to Elaine village and put us in the white schoolhouse."

Others from the union did the same. Nina Jenkins made it safely to the troops, as did John Martin and Alfred Banks. "I stayed in the bushes until the soldiers came," Banks said. "We came right out to the soldiers." Will Wordlow had spent the night in the woods with eight women and children, and they were all safe now. "I stayed [in the woods] until the soldiers came," he said. "Then I came to them." What surprised the troops, a reporter for the *Memphis Press* observed, was that "hardly any had guns or ammunition. The soldiers are of the opinion that the blacks had hidden their weapons."

Up around Hoop Spur, black men, women, and children gathered on Route 44 in ever growing numbers, emerging from the woods or their cabins, all of them frightened and waiting for the troops to rescue them. *Helena World* publisher Charles Young, driving from Helena to Elaine with two reporters, reached Hoop Spur around 10:00 A.M. "I saw several hundred niggers along side the road. I didn't know what they were doing or who they were, so I put my foot on the gas and got over the road as soon as possible. . . . Later I found out that the niggers gathered there were innocent and scared of their lives too."

As the black families came to the road, they were walked in long lines to Elaine, a handful of soldiers dispatched for this task. "Gangs of them were brought in at a time," Wilson wrote. "Vacant buildings in Elaine were used as temporary guard homes and they soon were full. Then the basement of the public school building, a new structure, was opened. It was there that all negroes arrested were taken." Many "Negro women and children," he noted, "were among the number" who'd been "captured."

The reporter for the *Little Rock Daily News* thought that the trouble had come to an end. "With the arrival of the soldiers," he wrote, "rioting died out."

EVEN AS SHARECROPPERS WERE being led back to Elaine, however, Jenks and the bulk of the troops were headed west, following in the footsteps of the posses. "On route" to the woods, Jenks wrote in his report, "about a mile and a half from town we found a negro woman lying in front of her doorstep and barely alive, shot through the neck several hours before. Medical attention was given to her but she died shortly afterwards." In addition to Frances Hall, the posses had killed at least four other blacks along this road, and most likely—given that the shooting had been going on for several hours—many more as they'd chased blacks into the woods. The sharecroppers in this area had spent the morning being attacked, such that none were stepping forward to surrender, and when four men were flushed from a small copse of trees, they frantically fired off a couple of shots as they fled down the road. Although the bullets whizzed harmlessly by, the troops—and the governor, riding in a car—had now been shot at. "Major Callen deployed the battalion as skirmished, and started forward," Passailiague said. "One company was held in reserve and followed two hundred yards in rear of front line in squad columns. Jenks took his position in rear of the center of the formation."

Every man with a rifle had his finger on the trigger. Posse members advised the troops that there were perhaps 150 Negroes in the woods, and that many were "ex-soldiers." The patch of trees and rivercane they were approaching was about 200 yards thick, east to west, and ran for a half mile to the north. *Shoot to kill* at the first sign of resistance, that was what they had been ordered to do, and as the troops came to a stretch of barbed wire that fronted the canebrake, someone hiding *in there,* in that darkness, shot twenty-nine-year-old Sergeant Pearl Gay in the chest. His was only a flesh wound, but neither Jenks nor Callen had to say anything more. "The soldiers," said posse member J. W. Butts, "immediately laid down a field of fire."

For the next hour, the troops moved through the swampy woods, the rat-a-tat-tat of their machine guns and the blasts from their rifles shattering the Mississippi Delta morning. The sound of the gunfire, it was said, could be heard for miles. The soldiers moved methodically ahead, stepping over fallen trees and poking their guns into the brush, on the alert for any Negroes who might be crouched there. "I saw many persons fired upon," wrote the *Memphis Press* reporter. "The soldiers used their machine guns on one group of negroes. When they fired the powerful rapid-fire gun two negroes were killed outright and the rest threw up their arms and surrendered."

The troops cleared the first patch of woods, crossed a small field, and entered a second patch, a little further to the north. "This terrain was uncleared, covered with dense cane brake and nearly impenetrable," Jenks wrote, describing it as a "jungle." There was little resistance, the soldiers fired and then the Negroes who were hiding fell or jumped to their feet and ran deeper into the woods, and then this was repeated over and over. The officers "gave them orders to shoot everything that showed up," Brough told Young later that afternoon, "and they took machine guns out there and let 'em have it."* This went on until about noon—they "were shooting them down like rabbits," a soldier was later heard to boast—and it all went without incident for the troops until Corporal Luther Earles stepped on a fallen log where a scared sharecropper was hiding. The black farmer leapt to his feet, shooting the soldier in the face, the blast "tearing away part of Earles' jaw," Wilson wrote.

One killed and one wounded—such were the casualties suffered by the Camp Pike troops in this "battle," and by noon the woods had been emptied. "We captured several prisoners," Jenks wrote. "All the rest of the colored outlaws had disappeared." He did not estimate the number of dead Negroes, but the *Memphis Press* reported that "many negroes" had been "killed by the soldiers," and that seemed about right to J. W. Butts, one of the posse members. They "killed many negroes who were resisting them."

By 12:15 P.M., Jenks and the troops were headed back to Elaine. "Situation quiet and orderly, situation well in hand," Jenks would tell Camp Pike headquarters when he got there, and on their way back, they came to a plantation house where more than fifty white women and children were holed up, protected by a handful of men. For the Camp Pike soldiers, this sight was a vivid reminder of why they had rushed to Phillips County, and Jenks immediately ordered a dozen soldiers to stay with them. "This group of helpless people was

---

* Twenty-eight years later, Young was at a U.S. State Department function in Vienna when a high-ranking military officer introduced himself as a "veteran of the battle of Elaine," and recounted the same thing: "He told me that when the niggers fired on them, they gave them orders to fire on anything they saw," Young said.

guarded throughout Wednesday night by ten white men armed with shot guns," Passailiague said. "Their situation had been desperate. It was about two miles from Elaine and had troops not arrived, the fate of that party would have been disastrous." Blacks outnumbered whites by a ratio of five to one, the captain figured, and thus, "had troops not been sent to quell the disorder, the negroes would have succeeded in carrying out their murderous plans."

THERE WAS ONE OTHER shooting from that morning of October 2 that made headlines, and that drama began around 9:30 A.M., moments after the troops marched out of Elaine. Orley Lilly, Amos Jarman, W. H. Molitor, and Joseph Meyers had stayed behind, as they wanted to wait for a passenger train that was due to arrive from Ratio at any minute. They had been informed that a Negro they had been searching for, D. A. E. Johnston, would be on it.

David Augustine Elihue Johnston, forty years old, was an unlikely person to be involved—or suspected of being involved—in an uprising by sharecroppers. Raised in Pine Bluff by parents who were educators, he was a graduate of the Chicago Dental School and had set up shop in Helena in 1910, the year he married Maria Miller, the daughter of Helena minister Abraham Miller. The Millers were Helena's most prominent black family. Abraham Miller, although born a slave in 1851, had served in the state legislature during Reconstruction and had subsequently earned, one Arkansas historian wrote, a "sizeable fortune through money lending and real estate investments." The Millers were the very class of people that local whites referred to as the "better type of coloreds," and D. A. E. Johnston had followed in his father-in-law's footsteps, building up a "splendid practice" in Helena and investing in real estate. In 1919, he owned a three-story building on Walnut Street, which was the business street for blacks in town, a steady stream of customers going in and out of his drugstore. Johnston had two daughters, and his two younger brothers, Leroy and Gibson, also lived with him, as both had been recently discharged from the army and were busily getting an automobile dealership established. Both of the men had come home from the war bona fide heroes. Leroy had rushed off to New York City prior to the war to join the fabled 369th Infantry, while Gibson had been wounded in the trenches of France, shot and gassed in the Battle of Château-Thierry.

The Johnstons' credentials as true-blue Americans seemed impeccable and yet, in the last heated weeks of September, the Citizens Committee had begun keeping its eye on David and his two brothers, particularly after rumors circulated that a band of men was going door-to-door in the colored section of town, urging blacks to stand up for their rights. Trouble was brewing not only on the plantations but in Helena too, and the Committee suspected that the Johnstons might be behind it. They were "very prominent niggers," Young said, and "that building had been watched for some time because they knew that the niggers were meeting there." Young and his managing editor, J. P. Burks, in the last days of September began checking up on the Johnstons nightly, strolling by David's drugstore. "We'd take a look and see if there was anything going on. We knew there was something in the air."

On Tuesday, September 30, the three Johnston brothers, along with their eldest brother, Dr. Louis Johnston, a physician who was visiting from Coweta, Oklahoma, took off for a hunting trip in the swamplands near the confluence of the Arkansas and Mississippi rivers. Sheriff Kitchens and others soon realized that they'd left town the very day that the "uprising" had occurred—yet more evidence that D. A. E. Johnston was tied up with the sharecroppers' union. It was believed, the *Memphis Commercial Appeal* wrote, that he was "instrumental in getting plantation Negroes to quit their work and arm themselves."

The four brothers started back from their hunting trip early Thursday, their car loaded with game, but when they reached Ratio, they were warned that racial fighting had broken out ahead and that it was too dangerous to drive to Helena. They left their car behind and boarded the train, but when they reached Elaine at 9:30 A.M., Lilly and the others arrested them, charging them with "distributing ammunition to the insurrectionists." The white men chained the four brothers together, and—as Bessie Ferguson concluded a few years later after interviewing witnesses to this arrest—"securely fastened" their hands as well. After shoving the Johnstons into the back of Lilly's "big old Hudson," Molitor and Jarman hopped into the front seat, next to Lilly's Negro chauffeur, while Lilly, armed with a pistol, sat on a collapsible seat in the back. Meyers and and other posse members trailed behind in a second car.

Lilly, forty-one years old, had apparently quarreled with D. A. E. Johnston the week before, and he loathed the Brattons, as he'd never forgotten how U. S. Bratton's old "carpetbag" partner, William Whipple, had tried to send him to prison, the Republicans presenting him to the press as a modern-day slave owner. Now the Brattons were stirring up things again, and Johnston, it seemed, was the Negro "ringleader" of the entire affair.

There is no black eyewitness version of what happened next. The only eyewitness account that history offers is the one told by Amos Jarman to the *Helena World*. In his telling, the Johnston brothers were not handcuffed at all:

> We met a car coming from Helena. It contained some boys from Helena and Elaine, and it looked to me like their car was in trouble. I told Jim [the chauffeur] to stop our car. . . . I stepped out and asked the boys in the other machine if they needed any help. They said no. At that moment, I heard a commotion behind me, and looking around saw the larger of the Johnston brothers reach over and snatch Lilly's pistol from its scabbard and begin shooting. Molitor, who saw the movement also, wheeled around in his seat to bring his pistol into action and we both began firing about the same time. Johnston had emptied Lilly's pistol into Lilly's body before we could stop him. The shots brought the men from the other car on the run, and the Johnstons were riddled where they sat.

Lilly was dead. As for the four Johnston brothers, Jarman and the others dumped their bodies onto the road. A short while later,

Young—on his way to Elaine with the reporters—came to this spot, which was just north of the Hoop Spur church, and he found the four men still chained together, all in a heap in the dirt. This proved to be an inconvenience to the *Helena World* publisher: "We had to go off the side of the road into a ditch to go around those four niggers," he said.

ALTHOUGH JENKINS HAD INFORMED his superiors at Camp Pike in his 12:15 P.M. report that the situation was "quiet and orderly," in truth it was anything but. After Elaine residents fed his soldiers—the "lunches and coffee furnished free to everyone," the *Arkansas Gazette* reported—Jenks divided them into small squads, sending them to trouble spots around the county. Armed whites in Helena were said to be gathering at the courthouse, with many threats having "been made to lynch certain prisoners," and so Jenks ordered a hundred men there by train. He established a machine gun outpost on the outskirts of Elaine and another at Hoop Spur, and dispatched "half a company" to Mellwood, where three more blacks had been killed that morning. He ordered the bulk of his troops, more than three hundred in number, back out to the Hoop Spur cotton fields, with orders to search every cabin for weapons and for "records and all other obtainable evidence" that might document the sharecroppers' criminal intentions. Finally, he sent a squad of twenty-five to the Lambrook plantation, where he'd been told there were "several malcontents and ringleaders."

Ever since the "fighting" had broken out the day before, whites in Elaine had worried about Lambrook. Gerard Lambert had more than seven hundred Negroes working on his land, either cutting timber or growing cotton under sharecropper contracts, and the previous afternoon, a handful of blacks, having been told of the Govan Slough shootings, had ridden on horses toward Elaine, only to back off. The Negroes there seemed like an army in waiting, and early Thursday morning posse members had hauled a "steel gondola back and forth on the railroad track" that led to Lambrook, and while hiding behind "the steel walls of the car," they had established control over this

The *Arkansas Democrat* identified this building as the church where the Hoop Spur sharecroppers met. *Courtesy of the Arkansas History Commission.*

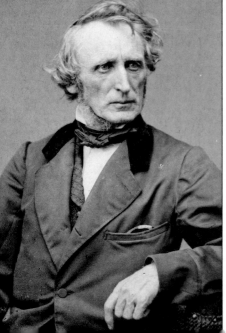

A sharecropper's cabin in the Mississippi Delta. *Library of Congress.*

Ohio congressman John Bingham drafted the Fourteenth Amendment, which Congress believed would protect the rights of blacks in the South. *Library of Congress.*

In 1867, newly enfranchised blacks lined up to vote (*Harper's Weekly*, Nov. 16, 1867). *Library of Congress.*

By the mid 1870s, the triumph of the Ku Klux Klan and other white terrorist groups left blacks in the South in a condition "worse than slavery" (*Harper's Weekly*, Oct. 24, 1874). *Library of Congress.*

Thousands gathered in Waco, Texas, on May 15, 1916, to watch 17-year-old Jesse Washington be tortured and burned alive. His corpse can be seen smoldering beneath the tree. *Visual materials from the NAACP records; Library of Congress.*

THE FUNNY PAGE

In 1918, lynch mobs knew that the Constitution, as interpreted by the U.S. Supreme Court, didn't provide blacks with protection from mob violence (*The Crisis*, March 1918).

Black infantrymen on the front lines in France. Black troops hoped that by fighting in the war to make the "world safe for democracy," they would gain democracy at home. Photo published in *Scott's Official History of the American Negro in the World War*.

The first American heroes of World War I were two black soldiers, Henry Johnson (left) and Needham Roberts, who routed a German raiding party. *National Archives, American Unofficial Collection of World War I Photographs.*

The NAACP collected headlines from newspapers announcing that John Hartfield, at 5 P.M. on the afternoon of June 26, 1919, would be burned alive (*The Crisis*, August 1919).

In its September 1919 issue, the *Messenger* celebrated blacks who fought back against white mobs.

In the 1890s, Helena veterans of the Confederate Army formed the Sam Corley Camp. In Helena, as was true throughout much of the South, the war was increasingly remembered as a noble fight for states' rights, as opposed to a fight to preserve slavery. *Courtesy of the Phillips County Historical Museum.*

Starting around 1905, the virgin hardwood forests in southern Phillips County were cut, and cotton was planted in the cleared land. This photo was taken near Wabash, a few miles north of Hoop Spur. *Courtesy of the Department of Arkansas Heritage, Delta Cultural Center Archives, Howe Collection.*

Helena planter Jerome Pillow built this spectacular home in 1896. *Courtesy of the Arkansas History Commission.*

Edward Chaffin Hornor, Helena's most prominent businessman, owned thousands of acres in southern Phillips County. Photo published in *Annals of Arkansas* by the Historical Record Association, Little Rock.

Helena in 1915. The town's "skyscraper," the Solomon Building, is on the right. *Courtesy of the Butler Center for Arkansas Studies.*

Opposite bottom: By late afternoon on Wednesday, hundreds of white men from neighboring counties and from across the river in Mississippi had flooded into the Hoop Spur area to "assist" the local posses. *Courtesy of the Arkansas History Commission.*

The Model T driven by W. A. Adkins, its windshield shattered by gunfire. *Courtesy of the Arkansas History Commission.*

Early Wednesday morning, Helena posses headed toward Hoop Spur to put down the Negro "insurrection." *Courtesy of the Arkansas History Commission.*

Arkansas governor Charles Brough.
Library of Congress.

Shortly after arriving in Elaine on Thursday morning, Governor Brough spoke to the town's white residents. *Courtesy of the Arkansas History Commission.*

Left: Governor Brough accompanied Colonel Isaac Jenks and his troops as they headed toward the woods north-west of Elaine, where blacks were said to have fought with posses earlier that morning. *Courtesy of the Arkansas History Commission.*

route into town, firing away whenever they spotted blacks scurrying about, running from one cabin to another. "Several blacks," Lambert reported, "had been picked off in this way."

When the squad of Camp Pike soldiers reached Lambrook, probably around 2:00 P.M., they immediately rounded up one of the "colored ringleaders." In his autobiography *All Out of Step,* Lambert described what happened next:

> Troopers brought him to our company store and tied him with stout cord to one of the wooden columns on the outer porch. He had been extremely insolent, and the troopers, enraged by the loss of two of their men that day in the woods, had pressed him with questions.* He continued his arrogance, and one white man, hoping to make him speak up, poured a can of kerosene over him. As he was clearly unwilling to talk, a man suddenly tossed a lighted match at him. The colored man went up like a torch and, in a moment of supreme agony, burst his bounds. Before he could get but a few feet he was riddled with bullets.

Lambert was told of this burning on Saturday, October 4, which was when he arrived in Elaine. His superintendent, he wrote, "told me with some pleasure that they had to use our fire hose to put him out."

THAT AFTERNOON OF OCTOBER 2, the soldiers sent out to search the sharecroppers' cabins confiscated "about 400 guns and 200 pistols," which was not surprising, as it was a rare sharecropper who didn't own a firearm. They began this assignment by fanning out along the road that ran west from Route 44 past Frances Hall's cabin, and then they moved steadily north, this methodical search triggering a new rush to the woods by the sharecroppers. What began as a search turned into a chase, and it produced yet another killing field, although there are conflicting accounts of its extent.

---

* Lambert is referring to Sergeant Pearl Gay and Corporal Luther Earles. While Earles died, Gay had suffered only a minor wound.

In his 1925 book *What a Preacher Saw Through a Keyhole*, L. Sharpe Dunaway, who was remembered at his death as "the best known newspaperman in Arkansas," claimed that the soldiers, while moving from cabin to cabin, killed many unarmed blacks. He was not a writer predisposed to being sympathetic toward blacks—he was an ardent white supremacist—and he believed that the killing of blacks in the Govan Slough area on the first day was justified, the actions of a "chivalrous white citizenship" rightly "avenging" the deaths of Adkins and Tappan. Yet, after he conducted his interviews for the book, he became convinced that the federal troops, in concert with the posses, went on a "march of death," leaving behind "a path strewn with orphans and widows."

> The thing that "stumps" us, however, is by what authority did a coterie of Federal soldiers, aided and abetted by a collection of low-lived creatures who call themselves WHITE MEN, march down among the ramshackle homes of good old innocent, hard-working Darkeys, and then and there unlimber their guns on those poor old servants of the rebellion, finally snuffing out their lives before passing on to the next house, where the same cruel scene was enacted, thus leaving a path strewn with aching hearts and besprinkled with the red blood of innocent humanity.

The soldiers, Dunaway concluded, "committed one murder after another with all the calm and deliberation in the world."

Old Ed Coleman, who, unlike Moore and many of the others, hadn't come in from the woods east of Route 44 early that morning, snuck back to his cabin late in the afternoon in search of his wife, and later told of that precise scene. "When I got there," he said, "the white men had went and shot and killed some of the women and children." Yet Coleman lived next to Frank Moore and Paul Hall, and so perhaps the killings that he was talking about had been done by the posses that morning, rather than by the soldiers. During their search, at least some of the soldiers, in fact, provided aid to injured sharecroppers. The troops who found Albert Giles, who by that time was lying in Joe Mershon's cabin, dressed his wound. "They put a board under my arm and wrapped it up and carried me away and brought me to the hospital," Giles said. His brother Milligan was also cared for by the soldiers, although it is unclear whether they discovered him—miraculously still alive—while searching Govan Slough or in a cabin. There was at least that touch of humanity during that afternoon, and so it may simply be that with the troops moving across a cotton field 2 miles wide, there were instances that afternoon of both "blood-thirsty" murder, as Dunaway put it, and of decency.

As the troops moved north through the fields, however, many sharecroppers—and this part is certain—scurried away before they arrived. By 3:00 P.M., there were at least a hundred blacks—and perhaps as many as four hundred, according to newspaper reports—trapped in the canebrakes west of the Hoop Spur fields. The soldiers moved methodically forward into the wetlands, and once again, the sound of constant gunfire could be heard from miles away.

"The riots are raging with renewed ferocity and it is expected that the troops will bring machine guns to play on the rioters," the *Little Rock Daily News* reporter said in a 3:10 P.M. telephone call to his editors. "A lull in the rioting this morning was followed by intense shooting and rioting and it is estimated that the number of dead and injured will be nearly one hundred people." The *Memphis Press* reporter was equally apocalyptic: "The negroes are surrounded in the woods near Elaine by nearly 500 soldiers and have refused to surrender. A battle to the finish is expected. The negroes are well drilled and armed. The soldiers have trained machine guns on them. Constant fighting is now in progress."

No soldier was wounded in that late afternoon "battle," and reporters did not give any further accounts of what happened to the trapped Negroes. Nor did Jenks or any of the other Camp Pike officers describe that afternoon's fighting in their reports. The shooting apparently went on for more than an hour, though, and there is no report of any Negro emerging alive from those woods. "There can be no correct estimate of the number of negroes killed and wounded, as no bodies have been brought here," Paul Grabiel wrote in his evening report for the *Arkansas Democrat*. "The negroes in the surrounding country have the bodies of the dead negroes, or they are still lying where they fell."

The blacks who collected those bodies did so anonymously—no reporter came to ask them what they found. Yet their whispers naturally spread to blacks in neighboring communities, and soon an ex-soldier who lived in nearby Marvell wrote in a letter to Howard University: "It was a good many of Negroes down their killed and the white Peoples called for the troops from Little Rock and they went down their and killed Negroes like they wont nothen but dogs." His was as accurate a description of that day as any, and as Henry Smiddy headed back to Helena that Thursday night, his thoughts were not so different. He passed the Hoop Spur church where it had all started, and like T. K. Jones, he noticed "that it had been burned down."* He had been at Govan Slough, and he had spent all of Thursday in the field with the posses and the troops, and the scenes of the many killing fields ultimately all ran together into the montage of a massacre. "I do not know how many negroes were killed in all," he said later, "but I do know that there were between two and three hundred negroes killed that I saw with my own eyes."

WHILE THE KILLING DIDN'T come to a certain and final end until the following Monday, October 6, Jenks and the Camp Pike troops, beginning on Friday morning, began directing most of their attention to processing Negroes who had been "arrested." There were, by that time, 225 men and women crammed into the basement of the Elaine schoolhouse—a number suffering from wounds, the *Memphis Commercial Appeal* noted—and 60 in the Helena jail.

---

* There are conflicting accounts of whether the church was burned by posses on October 1, which is when T. K. Jones said it was, or on October 2. However, Jones didn't return to the Hoop Spur area after October 1, and he remembered seeing it in ashes as he went back to Helena that day, so it seems likely that posses torched it that first day.

Hundreds more were on their way, Jenks that morning having ordered a roundup of all Negroes within "a radius of several miles of Hoop Spur and Elaine." This, he said, would allow them to "be questioned as to their connection with the Progressive Farmers and Household Union."

Jenks was joined by the local plantation owners for these inter-rogations, which were held on the school's second floor. J. O. Crow, K. P. Alderman, C. W. L. Armour, J. M. Countiss, Sid Stoaks, and E. M. Allen were all there, with Gerard Lambert joining them on Sat-urday. "Here, in a large bare room, an examination of suspects was going on," Lambert said. "There were several troops, my superinten-dent, and an officer seated at a small pine desk. One by one the col-ored men were brought from an adjoining room, questioned, and either held or released. It was cotton-picking time, and everyone was anxious to get the men back to work."

The criteria applied by Allen, Lambert's superintendent, and the others were quite simple. "Those found to be interested in the union which started the uprising last Tuesday are being held," the *Memphis Commercial Appeal* reported, "while those who prove their inno-cence [of having been in the union] are being released with passes, pending good behavior." The pass was a stay-out-of-jail card, with Jenks deciding on Friday that all Negroes in the vicinity would need to have one, signed by an army officer, "before they would be al-lowed to appear upon the streets or to work in the fields," the *Arkansas Gazette* wrote, adding that passes were being "issued only when the negroes' employers would vouch for them." Negroes could then show this pass to whites, as it would prove "that they were law abiding and reliable," Jenks said.

By Saturday, the *Arkansas Democrat* reported, more than eight hundred Negroes had been detained and were going through this culling process, and it took Jenks and the planters nearly a week to complete this task. Alfred Banks remained in the Elaine schoolhouse for six days and Will Wordlow seven, but one by one all of the union members were transferred to the county jail in Helena. All told, about three hundred black men and a handful of black women were sent to Helena for criminal prosecution, with the union leaders expected to be charged with first-degree murder. While Hill and Ed Ware had escaped and remained "at large," state authorities also arrested the leaders of the Progressive Farmers and Household Union in Winchester, including its president, T. L. Duker, and of course Dr. V. E. Powell.

The killings that went on during these days were scattered events, and the worst episodes occurred on Friday, October 3. Around 3:00 A.M., a guard at the outpost on the outskirts of Elaine spotted four Negroes making their way to the river, and when they refused his command to stop, he opened fire with his machine gun. "One negro's body was almost cut in two. Another black was killed, one received a shot in the head and was captured, and the other escaped," the *Arkansas Gazette* reported, noting that two of the four were "former soldiers" who "had on their khaki." A few hours later, with heavy rain coming down, a squad of seventy-five soldiers began clearing the woods and canebrakes east of Route 44, and by noon, they had "cornered" fifty or so Negroes in a bayou 3 miles east of Elaine, with newspapers reporting that "heavy fire" could be heard there throughout the early afternoon. Fifteen Negroes were "captured" and brought back alive to Elaine, and one of those was Ed Hicks, the president of the Elaine lodge. He was found sitting in the mud, trying to get his shoes on, dazed from a head wound. His rebellion had led to a "badly warped head," the *Arkansas Democrat* gloated, adding that once the other blacks in the schoolhouse saw his injury, they were sure to understand that "the torch of liberty which leads to rights and privileges"—the union's slogan—was in fact "a will-of-the-wisp that leads to sorrow." None of the newspapers said anything about the remaining thirty-five Negroes who'd been surrounded in the bayou, but presumably many and perhaps all had been killed, as the soldiers had been ordered, once the gunfire began, to "shoot on sight." By Friday's end, there were reports of more killings at Lambrook too, the "machine gun squad and squad of infantry" operating there said to have shot "four or five negroes." Given that this squad had begun its "cleanup" operations by burning one of the sharecroppers alive, it seems likely that the Friday toll at that plantation was actually much higher.

OVER THE WEEKEND, THERE were reports of a Negro shot in West Helena, one in Post Elle, and one way south in Snow Lake, and at some point, troops in Elaine gunned down a Negro named Isaiah Murphy who was trying to escape from the schoolhouse. "Two men calmly picked up the man's body and carried it to a spot where the others were confined," Lambert said. "As they dropped it on the ground they looked up at the staring faces of the Negroes in the window and told them this should be a lesson to them." With Robert Hill and Ed Ware still on the loose, the troops mounted an extensive manhunt on Sunday and Monday, cordoning off 25 square miles of woods and swamps between Route 44 and the Mississippi River. It was possible that Negroes were being killed "in the course of the drive through the canebrakes now in progress," newspapers reported, but the manhunt ended with the arrest of thirty-five Negroes, who were said to have surrendered peacefully, and so perhaps that last roundup ended without any more deaths.

"Order restored and work of troops completed," General Sturgis informed the War Department on October 7. "Troops to return to this camp Thursday [the] ninth."

THERE ARE LIMITS TO the narrative of these events that can be constructed today, and in particular, it is impossible to come up with a good estimate of the number of blacks killed. The best that can be done is a mapping of the killing fields, locating them in space and time, and identifying whether it was the local posses, the outside posses, or the Camp Pike troops that were doing the shooting. (See Appendix.) That provides documentation for twenty-two killing sites, but there is no way to know how many blacks were slaughtered in the largest killing fields, such as the woods west of Elaine, where hundreds were reported hiding—and surrounded—by the troops.

Beyond the twenty-two sites that can be mapped out, there were two other killing fields remembered by Dunaway and John Miller, the prosecutor for the First Judicial Circuit. In his 1925 book, Dunaway stated that sixteen Negroes were hung from a bridge four miles south of Helena, and he claimed it was the troops who did it. However, it is hard to identify a time when the troops might have done this, and there is no mention of such lynchings to be found elsewhere. If such hangings did occur, most likely it was the outside posses who rode into the county on Wednesday afternoon, rather than the troops, who were the perpetrators. Miller, meanwhile, was told that at some point a large group of Negroes on horseback rode up to a train with troops on it, and, thinking that the army had come to rescue them, fired shots "in celebration of the army being there." The troops, Miller said, then "fired on them and they must have killed 100 niggers right there."*

There are scraps of information that suggest something like that might have occurred. In November 1919, Clair Kenamore of the *New York World* wrote that on Thursday, October 2, the Negroes believed that the troops, when they arrived, were "coming to aid them against the whites. They were soon undeceived." That seems to suggest that the troops, at one moment or another, may have killed some of the sharecroppers who came to them for safety. That basic scenario is also remembered today in the form of a rumor, one recounted by Arkansas historian Tom Dillard, that the soldiers mounted a machine gun on a flat car and shot "people who had their hands in the air coming out of canebrakes, looking upon the troops as saviors." Finally, there is a time and place when the "slaughter," as remembered by Miller, could have happened: Thursday afternoon, on the railroad spur to Lambrook. The squad of twenty-five men sent to the plantation most likely traveled by train, and given that they had just come from the woods west of Elaine, where machine guns had been used, it is almost certain that if a large group of blacks

---

* Miller recalled this killing field in an interview with Arkansas historian Walter Brown on March 18, 1976. In it, he referred to both army troops and the National Guard being sent in to restore order, and said that it was the National Guard who fired on the sharecroppers from a train. But the Arkansas National Guard was not called out, and so if this occurred, it would have been the Camp Pike troops who did the shooting.

had come riding up to the train firing guns in the air—and the Negroes at Lambrook had been reported traveling about on horses—the soldiers would have responded by shooting to kill.

Dunaway, for his part, concluded that 856 Negroes were killed, a number that is certainly much too high, yet reflects his findings that a massacre occurred. Miller spoke of well more than 100 killed, as did Smiddy, and in Pine City, a small town 30 miles west of Helena, George Washington Davis, grand secretary of Pythian and Masonic lodge, a black fraternal order, said that he paid death benefits for 103 Negroes, and that his group "knew personally" of 73 more blacks who had been killed. Three of his sons, two of whom had served in the army, were among those who died, Davis said.*

What so many remembered, however, was simply the sight of corpses strewn about everywhere. "The militia would kill these colored rioters in the road, ditch, or any place they happened to be," recalled H. M. "Tip" Sullivan, a posse member from the nearby town of Wynne. "They would then leave the bodies lying where they had fallen for a couple of days before allowing them to be buried. They did this to show the other colored people what would happen if they ever started another riot."† Dunaway told of twenty-eight bodies that were "thrown into a pit and burned," and there were whispers too of mass graves. "The stench of dead bodies," it was said, "could be smelled for two miles." A white man many years later remembered how "dead niggers were stretched out as far as you can see."

Given all this—the killing fields that can be plotted, and the various testimonies that tell of a massacre—even a very conservative estimate today would put the number of blacks killed at well over one hundred, and perhaps the real toll was two or three times that many.

---

* Davis made this statement on November 30, 1920. It appears that his three sons were sharecroppers on a plantation "a mile and a half southeast of Elaine." However, he also claims that there were a high number of whites killed, and so there is reason to question his death count for blacks.

† The *Arkansas Democrat* made the same point in its report on the killing of the Johnston brothers. The bodies of the four brothers lying on the side of the road, with D. A. E. Johnston having "two bullet holes through his forehead," served "as an object lesson to the negroes who pass," Paul Grabiel wrote.

What is known for certain is that the killing fields of Phillips County stretched nearly 50 miles, from Helena south to Snow Lake in Desha County, and those gunned down included at least a few women and children, and a number of discharged soldiers. It is also possible today to at least record the names of fourteen who were killed: Lemon and Charlie Robinson on the road west of Hoop Spur; Arthur Washington in the Govan Slough; Jim Miller in the Govan Slough or later that day in the woods; Frances Hall next to the steps of her cabin; the four Johnston brothers on the road near the Hoop Spur church; Joe, Boisy, and Ransom Beco, these brothers most likely killed in the woods west of Elaine on Thursday; Dan Dixon, cut down by machine-gun fire at 3:00 A.M. on Friday; and Isaiah Murphy, out in front of the Elaine schoolhouse.

The Red Summer of 1919 had come to an end. There were three more black men burned alive at the stake in the United States during the next three months, including one in Arkansas, but this massacre in the Mississippi Delta marked the moment that America reached the nadir of that horrible time, a fall that had been fifty years in the making. In 1868, the country had approved an amendment that made blacks citizens and promised all citizens equality under the law, but instead of following that path of fairness, the country had gone down another, and while there were many reasons that it did, one stands out above all the rest. First came the *Slaughterhouse* decision, then *Cruikshank,* then all the decisions enabling Jim Crow policies, and then the *Hodges* decision, the U.S. Supreme Court reaffirming in 1905 that there would be no federal check on white mob violence, even though it was being used to keep "blacks in their place"—this was the erection of a body of national law that had led America to this very dark place. The black farmers had dared to dream of getting a fair share of the cotton crop, but that was not something they were supposed to do, and now more than one hundred were dead and three hundred were in jail. The union had been crushed, and its members—those who had survived—would soon experience the brutal sting of American justice.

Whitewash

THE FEDERAL TROOPS HAD begun their mass roundup of blacks on Thursday, October 2, and that was also the day that the planters, in essence, began their prosecution of the sharecroppers, for it was on that morning that Arkansas newspapers and the Associated Press ran their first coherent accounts of the shooting of Adkins at Hoop Spur. The articles that had appeared on Wednesday afternoon, in their descriptions of that initial moment, had been rather confused, but by Wednesday evening Helena's town fathers had established firm control over the Hoop Spur narrative, and after that there were no further glitches in the story told to the public.

In its initial report on the "outbreak" at Elaine, the *Arkansas Democrat* informed its readers that Pratt and Adkins had been ambushed the night before by "two white men and one negro." The bootleggers, the paper added, made "their escape after the shooting in a touring car, which was standing by." Pratt, it seemed, was the source for this account, but it presented an obvious problem for the planters, for it didn't logically explain why, earlier that morning, Helena posses had set out to arrest Negro farmers. The *Helena World* only added to the confusion with its Wednesday edition. James Tappan, it said, had been shot "when his party was surrounded and fired upon by alleged bootleggers." A few hours later, Clinton Lee was killed "when his gun accidentally discharged."

However, even as those afternoon newspapers were hitting the streets, the telephone and telegraph wires from Hoop Spur and

Elaine to outside communities were being cut. Unnamed officials in Helena now became the source for most of the news, and starting on Thursday morning, a coherent account of the blacks' criminal actions began to emerge. The planters turned Henry Bernard's report from his spying adventure beneath the Elaine church—of his having heard a white man in there, with the sharecroppers boasting that they needed to get rid of the "boss man"—into a most startling tale.

Pratt and Adkins, the papers said, had been on their way to Elaine on Tuesday night to arrest a bootlegger when they pulled off the road near Hoop Spur to "repair a punctured tire." They knew "nothing of the negro meeting in progress" at the nearby church, explained the *Arkansas Democrat,* and while the two law enforcement officers were tending to their flat tire they were "fired upon from the church." Pratt and Adkins had been "ambushed" by an "organized band of negroes."

On Wednesday morning, Helena posses drove out to arrest the Negroes who'd "murdered" Adkins. When they arrived, they were met by a "force of armed negroes," who were "dug into a trench." The black outlaws all had "high-powered rifles" and began "promiscuous firing on white persons." The blacks "greatly outnumbered" the whites, and they gunned down Tappan while he was "crossing a field." A little while later, they shot Clinton Lee in the "back," the bullet so accurate and deadly that it was best described as a "missile."

On Wednesday afternoon, hundreds of "brave men" from Mississippi and neighboring Arkansas rushed to the aid of the beleaguered white posses. These outside posses had "numerous clashes with Negroes" that day.* Late Wednesday evening, fifteen hundred Negroes massed for an attack on Elaine, with the whites holed up there bravely preparing to defend the women and children who had yet to be evacuated. The Negro forces, the *Arkansas Democrat* informed its readers, were committing "wholesale killings."

Some of the information that had been reported earlier, the newspapers said, had been in error. "It has been established since yester-

---

* The *Memphis Press,* with its descriptions of posses shooting at the bodies of dead Negroes, was the only paper to provide any specific details of those "clashes."

day," the *Helena World* explained, "that none of the [white] men killed and wounded were victims of accidents, as was believed yesterday." The papers also informed readers that the instigator of the entire affair was a white man: Ocier Bratton.

Bratton, the papers explained, had been coming to the sharecroppers' "secret meetings" for some time, distributing "propaganda" that urged the Negroes to "fight for their rights." The young Bratton advocated "social equality for the races," which readers everywhere understood meant interracial sex, and he and his entire family were apparently Reds, for Helena police announced that they had confiscated "socialistic literature, including some written by Emma Goldman," from Bratton and Casey's law office. Young Bratton had urged the sharecroppers to demand "50 cents a pound" for their cotton crop and to strike "unless their wage demands were met." He had been in the Hoop Spur church on Tuesday evening, with the Negro "sentries" posted outside killing Adkins because "they believed that their plan had been discovered."

"Vicious Blacks Were Planning a Great Uprising," an *Arkansas Gazette* headline screamed. Explained the *New York Times*: "Trouble Traced to Socialist Agitators."

On Friday, the newspapers finished their coverage of the first two days of "fighting." Governor Brough and the Camp Pike troops, they said, arrived in Elaine early Thursday morning in order to put down this "Negro insurrection." On the way to the fields west of town, a group of Negro men jumped out from behind a bush and tried to "assassinate" Governor Brough, who "narrowly escaped death." Moments later, Negroes hiding in the woods fired upon Sergeant Gay, which was when the troops—having been given shoot-to-kill orders if fired upon—turned the canebrakes into a war zone. Most of the soldiers were World War I veterans, and readers learned that the fighting here was as perilous as what they'd known in France. "Fallen cane, dense vine and undergrowth add to the difficulties of the dragnet process, veterans of the Meuse-Argonne campaign in the war asserting the Mississippi lows are more inaccessible even than the Argonne forest," Grabiel wrote.

Together, the newspaper accounts published on October 2 and October 3 told of Negroes doing the unthinkable. They were waging a "war" on whites. They had killed Adkins for no reason; they had gunned down Tappan and Lee; and they had lain in wait for the governor and nearly killed him too. There were even reports on Thursday that blacks had hidden in trees the day before and fired at a special train bringing "women and children from Elaine" to Helena. By the grace of God, however, "none of the refugees was hit," the *Helena World* reported.

A LYNCH MOB FIRST formed outside the Phillips County Courthouse around noon on Thursday. The news that Ocier Bratton had urged the sharecroppers to arm themselves and go on strike had further incensed a population already boiling with rage, and with a crowd of armed men converging on the jail where Bratton and fifty or so blacks were locked up, suddenly Helena authorities had a new problem on their hands. They urgently called Colonel Jenks in Elaine for help, but since it would take several hours to get a train down to Elaine to pick up a squad of soldiers to guard the jail, the mob still had to be "dissuaded" from acting. Precisely how the authorities did so is unclear, but after a short while the mob agreed that it would be better—as a jailer later informed Bratton—to "wait until night" to storm the place. The crowd temporarily dispersed, many lining Cherry Street for Tappan's funeral that afternoon, holding their hats over their hearts as his cortege filed past, and then around 6:00 P.M., with twilight descending, they once again gathered outside the courthouse, the men undeterred even by the presence of the one hundred Camp Pike troops that had arrived with machine guns. At last, E. M. Allen and other town leaders beckoned them inside the courthouse to discuss, the *Arkansas Gazette* reported, a "threatened lynching."

Whatever their personal thoughts about lynching may have been, Allen and the others had practical reasons for wanting to stay the mob. They had long sought to paint Helena as a "progressive" Southern town, one where Northern industrialists would feel at home, and a mass lynching would surely spoil that image. Even more important, they were already worried that the killing that had gone on in Hoop Spur would cause blacks throughout the county to flee. The planters, Allen said, were "very anxious to reassure Negroes in the quiet section of the county" that it was safe "so there may be no danger of an exodus." If the mob stormed the jail and strung up dozens of blacks, their cotton fields were not going to get picked this year, and perhaps not for many years to come.

The doors to the courthouse were now locked, preventing anyone from leaving, and Allen raised his arms for the crowd to quiet. The Camp Pike troops, he shouted, had "machine guns and would shoot" if they stormed the jail. Besides, there was a better way to handle this: he and the other town leaders would make certain that the Negroes were prosecuted for murder and electrocuted. As posse leader Herbert Thompson later explained: "A solemn promise was given that if these guilty parties were not lynched, and [the crowd] let the law take its course, that justice would be done and the majesty of the law upheld."

Although it took hours for this promise to quiet the mob's desire for revenge, at last, around midnight, the men agreed to go home. Sheriff Kitchens let them out in groups of "ten and fifteen," as this staggered exit, he figured, would keep the mob from forming anew.

THE FIRST CREAKY MACHINATIONS of the law were now in motion, and Governor Brough, before leaving Helena on Friday morning, appointed a "Committee of Seven," composed of the town's "leading businessmen," to investigate the Negro revolt and decide who should be prosecuted. Later that day he arrived back in Little Rock, where he assured reporters that the committee, who for the time being would have to remain nameless, would be fair in its deliberations, unaffected by any racial bias: "All parties, both white and black, who are said to be behind the Progressive Farmers Household Union of America, the order which proclaims equality of rights in connection with getting a minimum price of 50 cents a pound for cotton, will be treated absolutely fairly and will be dealt with by the law."

Brough let the Little Rock reporters see for themselves some of the damning evidence that Helena authorities had already gathered. He held up the steel jacket of a .32-40 bullet—this was the type of lethal ammunition that the Negroes had used—and he passed around a union circular that, as the newspapers alarmingly noted the next day, called for "equality of rights." In the deaths of Tappan, Adkins, and Lilly, Brough added—and here his voice cracked—the county had lost some of its most "prominent and promising citizens." Lilly, he said, was a man who "enjoyed the esteem and confidence of everyone who knew him." The governor, "worn and fatigued from the strenuous trip," had but one last word for the press. "The white citizens of the county deserve unstinted praise for their action in preventing mob violence," he said. "The Citizens' Committee at Helena and Elaine cooperated with Colonel Jenks and the federal troops to maintain law and order."

With Brough back in the capital, it was evident that the crisis had passed, and over the weekend, Arkansas newspapers wrapped up their coverage of the "rioting" in Elaine. On Friday morning, troops cornered renegade blacks in a bayou east of Elaine, a battle that came to an end, the *Arkansas Democrat* reported, when Sergeant Major Louis Lorber, a "determined little fellow in khaki," single-handedly captured Ed Hicks, the "big powerful acknowledged leader of his race." This knocked "the principal prop out from under the revolution," and thus, at last, "peace" had been restored. "The Negro uprising is now considered to be history," the *Helena World* wrote, and Arkansas newspapers assured all blacks—other than those connected with the "uprising"—that it was safe for them to return to their cotton fields. Indeed, Kitchens and others said that the initial accounts of the fighting had been "terribly exaggerated." There had been no blacks killed in Elaine or at Lambrook, and by Sunday evening, the official tally of black casualties was down to "14 dead and eight wounded."

The uprising, concluded the *Arkansas Democrat,* had been "nipped in the bud by prompt and vigorous action, which does credit to Phillips county, both for its efficiency and its notable self-restraint. In spite of some very aggravating circumstances, absolutely no violence has been done to law-abiding negroes or to negroes who showed a willingness to surrender their arms without bloodshed."

ALTHOUGH BROUGH HADN'T NAMED the members of the Committee of Seven, the newspapers reported that the group was an offshoot of an eight-man Citizens Committee that had formed earlier that year to monitor the racial situation, and everybody in Helena knew who those men were. Sebastian Straub was officially made chairman of the group; the other members were Kitchens, Helena mayor J. G. Knight, county judge H. D. Moore, T. W. Keesee, E. C. Hornor, and E. M. Allen.* All of these men, as their friend Greenfield Quarles confided in a private letter, were "large landowners," and Allen's connection to the sharecroppers in the Hoop Spur area was the most intimate of all: not only did he own the townsite of Elaine and large swaths of surrounding lands, he was the treasurer for the Lambrook plantation. But that information—that Brough had left it up to the planters to decide whom to prosecute—was never revealed by any Arkansas newspaper.

Straub and the rest of the committee, however, did find themselves with a bit of a dilemma. They had promised the mob that the union leaders would be electrocuted, and while it was clear that many blacks could be prosecuted for murder in connection with the deaths of Adkins, Tappan, and Lee, it wasn't so clear what the union, as an organization, had done that was *illegal.* Certainly the sharecroppers had been engaged in an insurrection—organizing to battle for equal rights, contemplating a strike, and hiring an attorney to sue plantation owners was not the sort of behavior tolerated in the Mississippi River Delta in 1919—but none of those actions was against *written* law. There were three hundred union members locked up in jail, but for what crime?

The committee leaked its answer to that question to the Associated Press on Sunday, and the following day, Allen and others met

---

* Most likely, Orley Lilly had been the eighth member of the Citizens Committee.

with reporters to tell of the committee's findings. Theirs was a story that astonished the nation.

The union, the committee explained, had been "established for the purpose of banding negroes together for the killing of white people." It had been started by Robert Hill, a scheming Negro who "saw in it an opportunity for making easy money" in the form of dues. He told the other "darkies" that the federal government was supporting the union's plan to kill Southern whites and was even "erecting at Winchester three huge storehouses where arms, ammunition and trained soldiers would be ready for instant use." Hill, Allen explained, "simply played upon the ignorance and superstitions of a race of children, most of whom neither read nor write."

The union had set October 6 as the day they would launch their killing spree. Early that morning, union members planned to present a bale of cotton to twenty-one planters and demand a settlement based on a price of 50 cents a pound. Then, "without awaiting a reply, the whites were to have been shot down and the general uprising thus launched," the *Helena World* reported. "All white people were to be slain and the Negroes were to have taken over the land." The union had appointed certain members as "Paul Reveres" to "ride into all parts of the territory" and cry out, "We've just begun," thereby summoning the "members to arms" to complete this coup. Even the sharecroppers' wives, in anticipation of this uprising, had been hiding "automatic revolvers in their stockings."

This was the nefarious plot that the Hoop Spur farmers had been discussing in their church on Tuesday, September 30, when Adkins's car broke down. Fearing that their plans had been discovered, they murdered Adkins and began their uprising "prematurely." The next morning, the union members hid in the weeds next to Route 44 "waiting for Hill's Army to materialize." The only reason they held their fire as posses drove by was because "they wished to wait for Hill's Army in order to clean up in one fell swoop."

Nor could there be any doubt about the Negroes' guilt. "I have cross-examined and talked to at least one hundred prisoners at Elaine," Allen said. "The stories they tell are almost identical." The sharecroppers had even drawn up a list of twenty-one planters to be killed, a smoking-gun document that the Committee of Seven had obtained. All of the committee members, the *Arkansas Gazette* reported, "expressed amazement at the definiteness with which the coup had been planned and organized."

Allen told the reporters that he had been as surprised as they were to learn of this plot. He knew many of these Negroes personally. He cared for them, even called them by their first names, and yet his own name had been on the list of twenty-one planters to be killed. This was a story of betrayal too, and as the newspapers later wrote, the planters felt mostly "hurt," rather than angered, by the entire affair. Many of the ringleaders of the uprising, Allen explained, were among "the oldest and most reliable of the negroes we have known for the past 15 years." These were families who "own mules, horses, cattle and automobiles, and clear money every year on their crops, after expenses are paid."

The next day, the Citizens Committee posted a circular on all the telephone poles in town. Blacks were told to "go to work!" and to "stop talking!" "No innocent negro" had been arrested, and what was needed now was for blacks to go back to the cotton fields, and "remain at work just as if nothing had happened." There was nothing more to be said about the Elaine "insurrection."

THIS NEWS CAME AT the end of a traumatic week in the United States. All week long, it had seemed that the country was on the verge of falling apart. The previous four months had been one of the worst periods in the nation's history: racial fighting in twenty-five cities, horrific lynchings, hundreds of labor strikes, and panic that the Reds were coming. Then on October 1 readers opened their papers to learn that a mob in Omaha had nearly lynched the mayor. The next day there were reports of a racial outbreak in Elaine, Arkansas, and then on October 3 the nation learned that President Wilson had suffered a severe stroke and might be permanently incapacitated. Police in Pittsburgh, Pennsylvania, and Gary, Indiana, fought with striking workers; racial clashes broke out at a cement plant in Indiana; and a mob in Georgia lynched a Negro and made plans to hang five more. Everywhere the nation looked it seemed as though the bonds that kept a society together were breaking, and now *this:* hundreds of Negro farmers in the Mississippi Delta, apparently led awry by Socialists, had conspired to commit *mass murder.*

"Massacre of Whites Planned by Negroes," screamed the *Dallas Morning News.* "Negroes Seized in Arkansas Riots Confess to Widespread Plot; Planned Massacre of Whites Today," shouted the *New York Times.* This was monstrous evil of a new sort: "The mind is chilled," the *Seattle Times* said. Or as the *Shreveport Weekly Caucasian* put it: "This is the first attempt to massacre white people in the United States since the insurrection at Harper's Ferry."

And like E. M. Allen, many of the nation's editorial writers struggled to understand why blacks would hatch such a malicious plot. "Arkansas negroes are in all material respects in better condition than they have been in years," reasoned the *Nashville Banner.* "They should be exceptionally well contented." The *Portland Oregonian* concluded that the rebellion was proof of the hopeless "ignorance" of Negroes, as otherwise how could they have believed Hill's wild fantasy about a government-supported plan to kill the plantation owners? The *St. Louis Post-Dispatch* wondered how it was that Negroes could be so easily led astray by Communists. On and on the speculation went, the one theme common to all such writings a sense of bewilderment: who could make sense of the Negro mind? "The unusual thing about this whole prepared black uprising is that the investigators can find no generally applied reason for such a move," wrote the Arkansas *Hot Springs Sentinel Record.* "The negroes who have been caught and are making the confessions know all about what was to be done, but they don't know why."

If there was one thing that most whites in America could understand, however, it was that all of the white parties involved deserved to be lauded. Those who had died—Adkins, Tappan, Lee, Lilly, and U.S. Army corporal Luther Earles—were eulogized as "heroes" who'd died in the "line of duty," while congratulatory messages from around the country poured into Governor Brough's office. "The people of Southeast Arkansas are to a man loud in your praise," wrote one correspondent, and Brough's well-wishers inevitably commented on his "splendid courage" for having survived the "dastardly attempt" on his life.* As for the Camp Pike troops, they were feted for their gallantry and remarkable neutrality. "The behavior of the troops was excellent throughout," Colonel Jenks told his superiors in Washington, and Brough seconded this thought in a letter to War Secretary Newton Baker, citing the soldiers for having been "tireless in their apprehension of the leaders of the race disturbances." Baker in turn bragged to a Cleveland audience that the nation—as evidenced by the Elaine riot—could rest assured that when federal troops were called to quell a civil emergency, "they are not partisans in any dispute except one, and that is the dispute between those who want order and those who try to create disorder in America. As between those two contestants, they are on the side of order."

The thank-you notes, mutual-admiration letters, and public resolutions of praise, all of which generated headlines in Helena and Little Rock, reached something of a crescendo toward the end of the second week of October. Elaine mayor Sid Stoaks and the "citizens of Elaine" publicly expressed their gratitude to Brough, the Camp Pike troops, and the "citizens of Helena and the neighboring towns" who so "promptly came to their aid." The troops in turn thanked the people of Elaine and Helena for all their "hospitality, friendliness and hearty cooperation," their time in Phillips County so pleasant that it had been like a "furlough." The Helena American Legion passed a resolution citing James Tappan and Clinton Lee for their "courage and bravery" in "preserving order in county and state," and then the state chapter of the American Legion praised all of the members of the Helena post for their heroic actions. The *Arkansas*

---

* Brough turned the letters and newspaper clippings into a scrapbook, the legend of his "narrow escape" growing and growing until, many years later, a biographer wrote of how the bullets "had gone through his hat."

Gazette, in an editorial titled "The Law and No Mob," summed up what the entire nation could learn from this affair:

> When negroes in Phillips county, Arkansas killed one officer and wounded another, there was no indiscriminate war upon negroes, even though evidence developed to show that negroes had been misled into organizing and providing themselves with high-powered rifles and supplies of ammunition. . . . A number of negroes were killed but only because they resisted lawful authority. Many negroes were arrested, but violence was not visited upon a single one of them. The newspapers the length and breadth of the United States, and especially north of the Mason and Dixon line, should not fail to remark this outstanding feature of the trouble in Phillips county, that through it all the law, as represented by local authorities and by federal troops, was in control. There was no bursting of all restraints and no uncontrollable disorder like that disorder which reigned in Washington and Omaha and Chicago.

The praise for whites seemed to have no end, and then the director of the Mississippi Welfare League, Jack Wilson, added a new theme, complimenting the white people of Phillips County for their "absence of race hatred." This theme was expanded on by many newspapers and also by Brough, who told audiences that the "white people of the South are the negroes' best friends." The Southern white man, added the *Arkansas Democrat,* "does not hate the negro. Long years of association have taught him to love him with a love which Northern agitators and theorists cannot understand or comprehend." Finally, the self-congratulation reached such a pitch that the *Helena World* editorialized that it wasn't just the nation that should take notice of the exemplary behavior of whites in Phillips County—no, their behavior deserved wider renown. "We have set the good example, and thus challenge the world to set a higher mark than ours."

The first draft of history was now complete. And while it was a story of the moment, of a Negro insurrection in the Mississippi Delta that had been "nipped in the bud," it was one that, in fact, fit with the larger narrative that the country had been telling itself ever since the end of Reconstruction. It was a tale of honorable whites having to deal with Negroes who were at once childish and savage, and that was a story that fit with what Harvard University anthropologist Louis Agassiz had to say about the Negro brain, and with what Charles Carroll wrote in his bestseller *The Negro a Beast*, and with what D. W. Griffith portrayed in his epic film *Birth of a Nation*. It was just as the president of Harvard had once said, America was populated by two types, "civilized" whites and "barbarous" Negroes, and so it made sense for the nation to learn, in those first two weeks of October, that vicious black sharecroppers in the Mississippi Delta had wanted to murder kindhearted whites for no reason at all.

THERE WAS, AT THIS moment, an official in Washington, D.C., who could have pricked a hole in this narrative: Frank Burke, chief of the Justice Department's Bureau of Investigation. While the nation's newspapers had been telling of a Negro plot to kill whites, he'd been receiving confidential reports from four of his agents— McElveen, Walser, Maxey, and Kerwin—that painted a much different picture. The murder plot, it seemed, was either a figment of the planters' imagination or—and this was even worse—a calculated lie.

Burke's men had arrived in Helena on October 3. They'd spent a week there, and during that time they had interviewed Deputy Sheriff Dick Dalzell, the Committee of Seven, and Edwin Pipkin, the assistant prosecuting attorney for the First Judicial Circuit. Although they hadn't spoken to any Hoop Spur sharecroppers, they had reviewed the various documents that had been gathered by the Committee of Seven, and they'd also done a little snooping of their own, checking out in particular Ocier Bratton's alibi. In total, Burke had received nine reports from his field agents, along with a copy of the union's bylaws.

According to Dalzell, the agents said, Pratt and Adkins had been on their way to Elaine to arrest a bootlegger when they "stopped their car" near the church. The two men got out, and "as they approached the church and [were] about thirty or thirty-five yards distant from it, they were fired upon by Negro outposts." In the subsequent "exchange of shots," McElveen wrote, "special agent Adkins was killed."

Ocier Bratton had not been in the church that night. Nor, apparently, had any other white man been there. Ocier, the agents learned, had left Little Rock on Tuesday morning, bound by train for Ratio. He'd stopped off that night in McGehee, "where according to the hotel register he spent the night," Walser and Maxey said. "He could not therefore have been at Hoop Spur when Adkins was killed."

The contracts Bratton was having the Ratio sharecroppers sign when he'd been "arrested" were straightforward, the agents noted. The documents stated that for a fee of $50, Ulysses Bratton would represent the black farmers "in an upcoming settlement with Mr. Theo Fairthy [Fathauer], or his agent, Mr. J. J. Pedro, relative to the proper accounting, division and settlement of the proceeds of this year's crops raised by us as sharecroppers on the land of the above-named landlord." The sharecroppers could pay Bratton either with cash or with Liberty Bonds they'd bought to support the war effort.

"The contract Bratton had with these negroes indicates nothing more than the relationship of the attorney and client," McElveen concluded. Added Walser and Maxey: "It does not appear that he was engaged in the furtherance of any illegal enterprise."

The agents weren't able to get a firm grip on the number of blacks killed. Walser and Maxey relayed the various estimates that appeared in the newspapers, while McElveen compiled his own estimate. Captain Passailiague had stated in his report that the soldiers had killed "about 20 negroes for refusing to halt when so ordered for resisting arrest," and this number, McElveen knew, was greater than the official tally. The posses had obviously killed blacks too, and even whites in Helena were whispering of a much higher death count. "Anywhere from fifty to eighty negroes were killed," McElveen informed Burke.

As for the interrogation of the sharecroppers, there were problems there too. Pipkin, the assistant prosecuting attorney, had arrived in Elaine late on Friday, October 3, the agents said. However, by that time, Colonel Jenks, E. M. Allen, and other local officials had already interrogated "more than one hundred negroes," and they had been "over zealous" in their questioning of the sharecroppers. As Pipkin delicately explained to the federal agents: "Some information has been secured which we will never be able to use in court because obtained by duress." Pipkin then personally interviewed the imprisoned blacks and examined the various union documents, expecting to find evidence of the Negroes' conspiracy to kill whites, but found nothing. "Pipkin advised that he had been unable to develop testimony bearing out this conclusion [of a planned slaughter] beyond developing that the leaders, Robert Hill and V. E. Powell of Winchester, Arkansas had cautioned the members of this lodge to keep their racks full, meaning of course to be fully armed," McElveen told Burke on October 5.

Rattled by this information, McElveen tried to find out for himself whether the Hoop Spur farmers had planned to commit mass murder. There was, he discovered, no written list with the names of twenty-one planters to be killed. Nor did the union literature tell of a government-backed plan to "seize" the land of whites. Instead, the union's constitution declared that the "Grand Lodge" would "levy special taxes on subordinate Lodges for the purpose of purchasing land," and that it would do so once it had "accumulated $2,000." *Purchase,* not *seize.* Even the reports that the union had large caches of weapons had been greatly exaggerated. "Rioters had small amount ammunition; no large quantities found [in] Helena," McElveen wrote.

In cables to his boss on October 7 and October 9, McElveen emphasized the bottom line: "Only evidence of intended murder [of] whites is that leader advises members to keep your racks full and fight for your rights."

Although the four agents hadn't tried to put together their own narrative of events, there was, in their reports, the clear outline of one. The black farmers had been planning to hire an attorney to represent them at settlement. Pratt and Adkins had then stopped their car for unexplained reasons late at night near the Hoop Spur church and there had been an "exchange of shots." Whites had killed fifty to eighty Negroes over the next couple of days. And now county authorities were moving ahead with the prosecution of three hundred imprisoned blacks on a charge that they conspired to commit mass murder, even though there was no evidence to support it.

There was a time in the nation's history when Burke might have been expected to do something with this information. In 1870, Congress had created the Justice Department with the expectation that it would prosecute whites who terrorized blacks and that it would also protect blacks from unfair prosecution in the South. But then had come the Supreme Court decisions—*Cruikshank, Harris,* and *Hodges*—that had stripped the Justice Department of its power to intervene, and that Reconstruction mandate had faded away. The Justice Department had other concerns now. At the moment, Burke's boss, U.S. attorney general A. Mitchell Palmer, was polishing a report on the radical black press and how it was stirring blacks to seditious acts. That was the narrative that the Justice Department was invested in now, and so Burke quietly filed the reports away in a desk drawer.

Agents McElveen, Walser, and Maxey also said nothing publicly about their findings. The only agent who said anything to the press was E. J. Kerwin, and the *Pine Bluff Daily Graphic* was only too happy to report Kerwin's summation of the evidence: "Every piece of literature which has been found, Judge Kerwin said, was used for the purpose of getting the negroes together, after which the organizers, officers, and other agitators connected with the society, deliberately and maliciously told the members lies, and otherwise incited them to uprise against the white people."

And then Judge Kerwin had one last nugget of wisdom for the public: "The people of Helena deserve much credit for the masterly manner in which they have handled the situation."

KERWIN'S ANNOUNCEMENT SERVED TO put an exclamation point on the Citizens Committee's report—the story of a black conspiracy to murder whites had been confirmed by the U.S. Justice Department. The black farmers were clearly guilty as charged, and faced with this astonishing outbreak of criminal behavior, newspapers in Arkansas and neighboring states now issued a word of advice to all Negroes: they had better behave, because next time, whites might not be so nice.

"The United States will not countenance sedition and lawlessness," the *Helena World* editorialized. "If the negro didn't know it before, he knows it now, and for him common sense ought to dictate a course entirely opposite to that which he has been pursuing." Indeed, should blacks dare to rise up again, the *Arkansas Gazette* warned, it would likely lead to the "annihilation of the Negroes in the affected district." Brough sounded a similar message, telling Negro audiences that "they would be protected [from white violence] as long as they were law-abiding citizens."

The warning was loud and clear—who could forget the machine guns?—and cowed blacks in a number of communities held meetings to attest to their law-abiding intentions and to distance themselves publicly from the Hoop Spur farmers. In Forrest City, Arkansas, blacks presented whites with a signed petition stating that they did thereby "unanimously reaffirm our friendship and goodwill toward the white citizens of our county and state." A coalition of leading blacks in Clarion, Mississippi, declared that "there are no Bolshevists, I.W.W.s, Seditionists, Clans or any other kind of people who connive at opposition to constituted authority among our people in the state of Mississippi." Their "white friends" could rest assured that "we are living in the blessed sunshine of good will towards all." Black Baptists and educators meeting in Chattanooga, Tennessee, similarly announced: "We urge that the race as a whole be not held responsible for the actions of individual members of the race. As ministers and members of this convention, our full influence must be thrown on the side of law and order." In Hot Springs, Arkansas, a Negro preacher told his flock that no black needed to keep a gun, as the sharecroppers in Phillips County had done, because in this "civilized country" prayer alone would keep them well. This was the restoration of normalcy that white authorities wanted to see, and finally blacks in Mississippi County, Arkansas, which was about 100 miles north of Helena, explicitly condemned their colored brethren in Phillips County. "There have been seditious and riotous acts committed against organized law and society which we greatly deplore and we feel that it is the duty of every law-abiding and law-loving citizen of our race to pledge himself to stand by our white friends, to maintain that good will which has existed for years."

The Hoop Spur farmers were now about as isolated as a group of people could ever be. Their side of the story had gone completely untold—no reporter had interviewed a single sharecropper—and now other blacks were publicly shunning them. They had nobody left on their side, or so it surely seemed, and even many of those who'd been released when Colonel Jenks and the planters had culled through the "rioters" were now on the run. Although the *Helena World,* which was eager to tell of harmony restored, reported on October 8 that "negroes are returning to their work," few of the sharecroppers stayed long. Instead, they scattered to distant spots throughout the Delta. On October 15, the *Greenwood Commonwealth* newspaper in Mississippi, after interviewing a visitor from Elaine, reported that the fields in southern Phillips County remained unpicked. "Few negroes," the paper explained, "can be secured to gather the cotton crop."

The women from Hoop Spur who'd been arrested were released from the Helena jail during that second week of October, and they too were desperate to leave the county. Yet they needed to stay close by—their husbands and sons were still locked up. There was only one thing they could do, and so, with their children in tow, they headed back to their cabins. Mary Moore went back, as did Lulu Ware and Edna Martin, but as they walked from the railroad stop in Hoop Spur through the cotton fields, they all saw the same thing. Their hogs and chickens were gone; their homes had been stripped bare. Household goods were missing, their "clothes burned."

"Everything was gone," said Mary Moore, and when she went to her landlord's place to complain—her landlord was Billy Archdale, who'd been trying to run them off even before the "riot"—he quickly chased her away. "He told me that if I didn't get out and stay out, he would kill me, burn me up, and no one would know where I was."

As for Lulu Ware, she found that the mob had "broken open trunks and drawers" in her home, "shot into the mirrors," and stolen the family's safe. Their two mules, horse, cow, eight hogs, 135 chickens, and Ford car were nowhere to be seen. John Martin's wife counted up the same loss: chickens, hogs, household goods, and clothes—"everything" had been taken away or burned. Landlords told these Hoop Spur women, who had belonged to the union, that they had to go. Katie Knox and her three children were driven off, and even old Ed Coleman's wife was "run from home."

It had all gone so wrong so fast. A few weeks earlier, they had dreamed of hiring an attorney to represent them at settlement, and with the price of cotton so high, they had hoped to earn several thousand dollars that year. And now this: the Hoop Spur women and their children, a black visitor soon wrote, were "penniless, ragged and starving."

The Longest Train Ride Ever

O N THE EVENING OF October 7, when the nation was still trying to digest the startling news of a Negro conspiracy to commit mass murder, a small twenty-six-year-old man with blond hair and blue eyes—and the slightest hint of color in his skin— boarded a train in New York City bound for Memphis. His name was Walter White, and a few days earlier, when the first reports of the Arkansas riots had appeared in the New York City newspapers, he'd immediately wired NAACP branch offices in the South, asking if they knew anything about the Johnstons or what might be the real story of this uprising. "The propaganda published in the press about 'Negroes being armed to kill all the white people and take their farms away from them' is too ridiculous to be given any thought," replied Robert Church Jr., leader of the NAACP branch in Memphis. "The real issue was the dispute over the price of cotton between the tenants and planters."

White planned to meet briefly with Church, and then go to Little Rock and—if he dared—to Helena. He would present himself in Arkansas as a reporter for the *Chicago Daily News,* as the editor of that paper, Charles Dennis, had agreed to give him an assignment to write about the riot. White knew that this would be the most danger-ous investigation he'd ever made for the NAACP, and that if his cover was blown in Arkansas, he almost certainly would be beaten and very possibly lynched.

Everybody at the NAACP was still shaken by what had happened to Secretary John Shillady in August. He had gone to Austin, Texas, to talk to elected officials about their efforts to shut down the NAACP's branch office in that city, and shortly after he arrived, a gang of men grabbed him outside his hotel and beat him severely, even whipping him publicly in the street. A county judge and a local constable were among his assailants, and not only were none of his attackers arrested, they were publicly praised by many, one Southern newspaper calling them "heroes" for their "devotion to law and order." "Shillady," crowed an Austin deputy sheriff, had been "received by red-blooded white men" who did not want "negro-loving white men" in Texas. Even Texas governor William Hobby had given his blessing to the attack, telling the NAACP that Shillady had been properly "punished." "Your organization," Hobby wrote, "can contribute more to the advancement of both races by keeping your representatives and their propaganda out of this State than in any other way." Now White was heading into the heart of the Mississippi Delta, where the entire white population was enraged over a plan by Negroes to massacre whites, and he would be passing himself off as a white newspaper reporter investigating that plot, even though in truth he worked for the NAACP and had grandparents who were slaves.

Although Shillady had come back to work, he was no longer the same man. "His great gaiety and warm smile had disappeared," White thought, and prior to leaving for Memphis, he hadn't conferred with his boss, certain that Shillady would try to talk him out of going. "In view of the critical situation which existed in Arkansas during the past week, it appears to me that this is a matter which needs careful investigation," White had written in a memo to Shillady moments before he'd left the office. "I am exceedingly anxious to make the investigation personally and I do so with full realization of the past, and am assuming complete responsibility for any personal consequences which may possibly arise."

With darkness enveloping the train, White let his eyelids close. In a couple of days, he would arrive in the part of the country that the NAACP had come to call "the American Congo."

THIS UNUSUAL MAN, WALTER Francis White, had been born to a family prominent in Atlanta's black community on July 1, 1893. His mother, Madeline, was a teacher, while his father, George, was a postal carrier and a deacon in the First Congregational Church, which was the religious home for the city's affluent blacks. Both of his parents were very light-skinned, with Walter and his six siblings so fair that the 1900 census enumerator mistakenly marked the family down as white. "The traits of my race," Walter White often said, "are nowhere visible upon me."

This mix of African American heritage and white skin put Walter and his siblings into a netherworld in Atlanta's Jim Crow society. Black and white were supposed to be sharply defined, but where did they fit? If they sat in the black section of a street trolley, whites would glare at them and blacks who didn't know them would wonder what they could possibly be trying to prove. Yet if they sat up front with the whites, blacks who knew them would taunt them for trying to pass, and if they were unmasked as Negroes, which legally they were given the drop-of-blood standard of the day, whites would give them a thorough beating. "There is magic in a white skin," White wrote, while "there is tragedy, loneliness, exile in a black skin," and he and his siblings moved uncomfortably between these two worlds.

The defining moment for White, in terms of fixing his racial identity, came in 1906, when whites in Atlanta, enraged over inflammatory headlines in the Atlanta newspapers about alleged rapes committed by Negroes, went on a rampage, setting black businesses on fire and pulling blacks from streetcars and beating them. At one point, a torch-carrying mob marched down the street where White's family lived. "I knew then who I was," White said. "I was a Negro, a human being with an invisible pigmentation which marked me a person to be hunted, hanged, abused, discriminated against, kept in poverty and ignorance." After that evening, he added, "I never wanted to be a white man. I was glad that I was not one of those who hated."

The seed for White's career as an undercover investigator for the NAACP was sown in the summer of 1915, prior to his final year at Atlanta University. He worked for three months as a salesman for Standard Life Insurance, a black-owned business, and as he traveled around rural Georgia he discovered that he could move about both racial worlds like a chameleon. The blacks he called on accepted him as a very light-skinned Negro. Yet if he dropped into a white diner, nobody would bat an eye, and soon he found that he could get the other customers to speak freely to him about their feelings toward Negroes, including their thoughts about lynchings in the news.

After that, it was only a matter of time before he went to work for the NAACP. After graduating from Atlanta University, he took a position with Standard Life but put his energies into establishing an NAACP branch office in Atlanta, he and the other "race men" immediately launching a protest against a plan by Atlanta's school board to eliminate the seventh grade from the city's black schools. "We have got to show these white people that we aren't going to stand being pushed around any longer," White shouted at one rally. "As Patrick Henry said, só must we say, 'Give me liberty, or give me death!' " They won that battle, the seventh grade remained open, and their success caught the attention of the NAACP's national office. White moved to New York City on January 31, 1918, to work as an "assistant secretary."

Less than two weeks later, a mob of a thousand in Estill Springs, Tennessee, burned Jim McIlherron alive at the stake, and White volunteered to investigate the lynching firsthand. Although the NAACP had occasionally investigated such killings before, with someone traveling to the scene to interview blacks, White convinced Shillady that he could go to Estill Springs and get the whites to tell him what they knew. He casually dropped into a general store, telling the "good old boys" that he was a salesman of hair products. "The first few times the conversation veered toward the lynching I purposely exhibited eagerness to talk about politics or the weather or cotton raising," White wrote. "My studied indifference and apparent ignorance of the fact that there had been any trouble began to become highly irritating to them. Even when they boasted and began to reveal more than they realized as to the actual participants I deliberately intimated that I had known of much more exciting lynchings than that of McIlherron. When local pride had thus been sufficiently disparaged, the facts came tumbling forth."

White's report in the *Crisis* on McIlherron's burning bared the horrors—and sadism—of lynching to the American public in a way that had rarely been done before. The mob in Tennessee had chained McIlherron to a tree, poked and tortured him with red-hot irons, and burned off his penis before setting him on fire. McIlherron's "crime" was that he had killed a young white man, but the white men in the country store—besides filling in the graphic details of the lynching—admitted that McIlherron had done so because the young man and two of his friends, some days earlier, had pelted him with rocks for no reason. Throwing rocks at Negroes was just something that younger men in Estill Springs did to pass the time, and apparently they were about to toss stones at McIlherron again when he shot the young man. It was self-defense of a sort, but even so, lynching McIlherron had been necessary, the men in the general store told White, because "any time a nigger hits a white man, he's gotta be handled or else all the niggers will get out of hand."

White returned to the scene of numerous lynchings in 1918, his vivid reports triggering a surge in the NAACP's membership rolls and in readers for the *Crisis*, with its circulation topping one hundred thousand in 1919. The entire country was being made to face up to the shame of lynching, and in the spring of 1919, the NAACP published *Thirty Years of Lynching in the United States, 1889–1918*, which revealed, among other things, that fewer than 20 percent of the 2,522 blacks lynched during that period had been accused of rape, the crime that had long been used to justify lynching in the white mind.

White's own understanding of racial violence continued to deepen as well. In the fall of 1918, he'd traveled to Arkansas and throughout the South to investigate "work or fight" laws that states had passed to conscript Negro labor during the wartime emergency. Under the statutes, draft boards could require men of military age who did not end up in the army to work at jobs deemed essential. States had also passed vagrancy laws to put Negro women to work, and White found that blacks were being forced to labor in cotton fields or as domestics for little or no pay. His report, published in the *New Republic,* gave him new credibility as a writer on the economic exploitation of blacks. More recently, in August, he'd investigated the Chicago riot and come away with a story of how competition between whites and blacks for jobs and housing had fueled the fighting. "What I learned there caused me more than ever before to understand the economic factors in race prejudice," he said.

As his train neared Memphis, White made some last-minute preparations for his excursion into Arkansas. He wrote U.S. attorney general A. Mitchell Palmer, advising him that he expected to learn "certain facts" that he would like to make known to the Justice Department upon his return to New York. He also wired NAACP field secretary James Weldon Johnson, asking if Johnson could find out about the "credit ratings" of the "Committee of Seven" in Helena. "I want these facts so that I may know the character of these men with reference to the treatment of Negro labor and whether they are connected in the exploitation of Negro labor," White explained. The story was already forming in his head, and he was growing confident that he could get in and out of Arkansas alive. "I have pretty well mapped out my plans for going into the community where the trouble occurred, and I believe I can secure the information I want," he told Johnson, and then he optimistically cabled Dennis for a bit of last-second editorial direction. Should he file his story from Little Rock, or did the paper "want a complete article on the whole situation on [his] return to New York?"

BASED ON HIS CORRESPONDENCE, it appears that White reached Little Rock on Saturday, October 11. There, White said, he "read the leading Arkansas newspapers," which provided him with a number of telling facts about the riot, such as how posses had "rushed into Elaine and Helena armed to the teeth." He also managed to run down a Hoop Spur sharecropper to interview, a woman who'd arrived in the capital only a few days earlier. The white sheriffs, she said, had "fired into the church without provocation," with the union guards then firing back. This was a detail, he knew, that helped frame the story in an entirely different light.

Early Monday morning, White called on Governor Brough. They talked for fifteen minutes or so—"I purposely led him to believe that I had little knowledge of the Negro question and was open-minded to whatever facts he, as chief executive of the state, cared to give me," White wrote—and then White got Brough talking about the NAACP. The NAACP had been haranguing Brough all summer about the five lynchings that had taken place in Arkansas that year, writing on September 4 to ask whether he approved of "unpunished murder," and the governor, invited to take a swing at the NAACP, took the bait. "The entire trouble" in Phillips County, he told White, "was caused by publications such as the *Crisis,* the organ of the National Association for the Advancement of Colored People in New York, and the *Chicago Defender.*" The Negro press and "Northern agitators," he said, were to blame for the "lawlessness."

While White reveled in this sort of comment, as it revealed so much about the speaker's character, it didn't add anything to his understanding of the riot and its causes, and Brough was unwilling to say much about what had happened in Hoop Spur other than to repeat the official version. This had been a Negro uprising put down by whites with "remarkable restraint and kindness," he explained. Finally, Brough pulled an autographed picture of himself from his drawer and handed it to White—this was a little memento the fine reporter could take back to Chicago.

Next stop was Ulysses S. Bratton's office. Once again, White presented himself as a representative of the *Chicago Daily News,* and while Bratton immediately made time for him, he too proved reluctant to talk about what had happened. White quickly came to understand Bratton's dilemma: talking about this matter with a reporter put him into an impossible spot.

Publicly, in an effort to save his son Ocier, Bratton had maintained that the violence at Hoop Spur had nothing to do with his taking on the Ratio sharecroppers as clients. Ocier, he'd told reporters, "knew nothing of the affair [in Hoop Spur] and was not in the county at the time that the trouble started." It was essential that the two become disconnected in the public mind—his son's life depended upon it. Privately, he'd confided that the two were related. "The Negroes at Elaine," Bratton wrote in a letter to the U.S. Justice Department, had "probably" gathered at Hoop Spur "to take up the matter of employing us." The planters had undoubtedly learned of their intentions, and Pratt and Adkins had shot up the church to "interfere with this. It was probably not intended to kill anybody but merely to deter, but by reason of some of the Negroes being armed and fighting back, the white man was killed and thus the trouble originated." Such was Bratton's dilemma: If he told the truth, he would put his family—and thus his imprisoned son Ocier—at the center of a very real "insurrection." But if he didn't, and he let the story of the Negroes organizing in order to seek a fair settlement go untold, he would be betraying the sharecroppers.

White and Bratton, in the manner that a reporter and a confidential source may do, settled on a middle path. White asked Bratton about peonage, and once Bratton understood that his name would not be mentioned in the article, he filled in all the details. He told White about how the plantation owners regularly refused to give their tenants itemized statements and how they charged them outrageous prices at their commissaries, and he even provided White with specific examples. As Bratton later related to Burke, "I have bills in my possession which show that they are charged the most outrageous and exorbitant prices imaginable." He explained too how this was all part of a process that kept the sharecroppers continually in debt and under the landlord's control, the entire system a kind of "slavery," Bratton said.

That was all White really needed from Bratton. The story was just as Church had said, and before White left Little Rock, he obtained copies of the union's printed materials. Although he never revealed who provided him with the documents, most likely it was Thomas Price, an attorney who, in August 1918, had helped found a Little Rock branch of the NAACP, and who had also provided legal services to Hill's union. Early Monday afternoon, White cabled the home office. "Everything favorable," he wrote.*

WHITE EXPECTED TO UNCOVER the details of what happened during the riot—the number of blacks killed, descriptions of the fighting that went on—in Helena. He planned to interview Sheriff Kitchens and see if Kitchens would let him talk to the jailed sharecroppers. He also figured that he could talk to blacks in Helena who could tell the Negro side of the story. But as he traveled by train to Phillips County, via the same route that Ocier had, coming through McGehee and then passing through Mellwood, Ratio, and Elaine, he became increasingly worried. Murderous passions, he knew, still ruled the town. Bratton's son Guy had gone to Helena the previous week to visit Ocier, and authorities had needed to spirit him out of town, lest a mob form. And Bratton himself had been warned that Helena planters had placed a $1,000 bounty on his head. "I was advised by numerous friends that if I dared to go to Phillips County to take any steps whatever for [Ocier's] release that it would mean my being shot down without any ceremony whatever," Bratton said. White was traveling deep into America's heart of darkness, and perhaps on that train ride he thought back to what had happened to Shillady in Austin, or back to some of the lynchings he'd covered— his mind had much to fret about. Even as he stepped from the train in Helena, he anxiously looked around. The "crowd of men," he said, "closely watched" his every step. Could they have been forewarned about his coming? Several people in the station asked why he had come to Helena, and as he made his way north from the train

---

* He signed the telegram "Francis," his middle name. He apparently feared that if he signed it Walter White, his identity might be exposed.

station along Cherry Street, on his way to the courthouse to interview Kitchens, he lost his nerve altogether. "We did not know whom to trust," he wrote a short while later. "We wanted to get the news, the whole truth, not to be lynched. For in the present state of mind of the white people of Phillips County, any Negro is good as dead if he be even suspected of writing for a northern Negro publication."

Going to see Kitchens was now out of the question. But even speaking to blacks seemed perilous. White had read about how they had been warned to "stop talking," and after he quietly tried to strike up a couple of conversations, he gave up. "Negroes here," White wrote, "live in fear and terror, afraid to even discuss the subject except in whispers and to well-known friends." All that was left for him to do now was to wander around the town, and in that way he "overheard the conversations of many whites." Perhaps he had lunch at Habib's—he'd arrived in Helena on the morning train—and the eavesdropping did provide him with snippets of additional information. "Several white men" told him "that more than one hundred Negroes were killed," and in one manner or another, he came to understand that "Negroes who did not know any trouble was brewing were shot and killed on the highways." At one point, he gathered the nerve to strike up a conversation with several planters, who "brazenly admitted" that they made certain that their sharecroppers stayed indebted to them. "If niggers had gotten all they earned," one laughed, "they would own the Delta by now."

This was the type of conversation, White knew, that could give his article some punch. Yet he couldn't shake the feeling that he was being watched, and once he turned back toward the train station, having decided not to linger in Helena, he practically broke into a run. "It is dangerous to life and limb even to attempt to discuss rationally the rioting and its causes," he wrote in his *Chicago Daily News* article.

Even after he was on the train, White had trouble controlling his panic. Helena, he wrote a few days later, was "the most dangerous situation in which I have been." The train moved slowly across the Mississippi River on a barge, White worrying that a mob might be waiting on the other side. "No matter what the distance, I shall never take as long a train ride as that one seemed to be," White said, and perhaps even then, as the train headed toward Memphis, his mind began transforming that fear into the fanciful anecdote that would appear many years later in his autobiography, *A Man Called White*. He had narrowly escaped being lynched in Helena, he wrote in 1948, a mob forming to get the "damned yaller nigger" even as he stepped on the train. While nothing like that had happened, it was nevertheless a story that accurately reflected his feeling, on that October day in 1919, that he'd been lucky to escape the town alive.*

WHITE'S ARTICLE FOR THE *Chicago Daily News* was published on October 18. That same day, the NAACP held a press conference to announce his findings. In some ways, his report was a disappointment. In his previous investigations of lynchings, he'd always returned with a blow-by-blow account of the killing. The graphic details were what grabbed readers' attention and sparked their outrage. But this time, his fears had chased him out of Helena before he could secure such information. On his trip, he had spoken to only one Hoop Spur sharecropper, and he hadn't interviewed any posse members or anyone from the Committee of Seven. As a result, the best he could do in his article—in terms of providing information about the riot—was to drop hints that there was a black side of the story waiting to be told. It seemed that Adkins and Pratt may have

---

* White first wrote about nearly being lynched in Helena in a 1929 magazine piece titled "I Investigate Lynchings" and then elaborated on that scene in his 1948 autobiography. He wrote that as he walked on Cherry Street toward the jail, where he had arranged to interview the sheriff, a tall Negro pulled him aside and told him that people in town were planning to do him harm. White then scrambled back to the train station, with the conductor asking him why he was in such a hurry given that the "fun" was just about to start. The "boys" in town, the conductor told White, were getting ready to lynch a "damned yaller nigger," and when they got through with him, "he won't pass for white no more!" However, in his correspondence in the fall of 1919, White reported that while he had found Helena to be dangerous and feared for his life while he was there, nobody had seen through his "guise." Had it not been for this, he wrote upon his return to New York, "I do not think I would have gotten out safely."

fired into the church, and it seemed that perhaps as many as one hundred Negroes had been killed, and there was a possibility that mobs had shot blacks who had nothing to do with the union. Such were the whispers he had overheard. However, he did provide a very detailed report on peonage in the Arkansas Delta and of the plan by the Phillips County sharecroppers to sue their landlords. The riot in Arkansas, White wrote, was about "debt-slavery" and the "systematic robbery of tenant farmers and sharecroppers." His was an account of the economic exploitation of blacks, and this provided a powerful counternarrative to the white story of a Negro uprising. Thanks to his interview with Bratton, White got the big picture right.

"Exploiting of Tenant Farmers Causes Ill Feeling," read the *Chicago Daily News* headline over White's story, and while most other mainstream papers ignored the NAACP release, or gave it little play, the black press turned it into four-inch headlines. "Riots Caused by Profiteering; White Owners Swindled Tenants of Thousands of Dollars," screamed the *Afro-American*. "Arkansas Land Owners Defraud Tenants," reported the *New York Age*. Wrote the *Chicago Defender*: "Expose Arkansas Peonage System: Truth Comes to Light When Unprejudiced Report Is Given." Editors at these publications and other black newspapers now began to write of the Arkansas "massacre," or described it as a "pogrom," and demanded a "Congressional investigation into the awful butchery of Negroes and their disarmament by United States soldiers." This was a story, wrote the *Boston Chronicle*, of "bloodthirsty mobs" and U.S. soldiers working together to "crush the human desire and the new hope of its Colored peons for becoming freer."

The battle had been joined. There were now two narratives for the nation to ponder, and both spoke not just of the moment in Arkansas but of a larger history. There was the white story of civilized whites and savage blacks, and the black story of economic exploitation and white violence used to keep them down. These were dueling themes that dated back to the Reconstruction era, and it seemed that if the "facts" of the Arkansas riot could be settled, one or the other of these narratives would be revealed as "true."

Not surprisingly, whites in Phillips Country and the rest of Arkansas were outraged. "Considerable indignation at the reported assertion was expressed here," the *Helena World* wrote. The state, editorialized the *Arkansas Gazette,* should not suffer such "slings and arrows" in silence, but rather answer "each and every publication that fails to give a true account of the recent troubles." Whites in Helena and Little Rock demanded that U.S. Postmaster General A. S. Burleson declare the *Defender* and the *Crisis* seditious and thus "unmailable." These reports in the black press, said Helena postmaster W. L. Jarman, are "far from the truth and the real facts in the case." Arkansas senator Joe Robinson joined in calling for government suppression of the Negro press, and Brough may have been the most furious of all. "I personally and officially most emphatically protest to the Post Office Department that Arkansas has no peonage system," he wrote. "Our negroes are kindly and justly treated." And then the governor, without mincing any words, explained to Burleson why it was so essential that the black version of events be suppressed: "It is highly imperative that both races live in harmony but it can never be disputed that all ideas of complete equality must be permanently dismissed and that the white race must ever be supreme."

The struggle for America's soul—and its future—was under way.

A Lesson Made Plain

THE PHILLIPS COUNTY COURTHOUSE in Helena is a handsome red brick building, and in 1919 it was a source of much local pride, having been built four years earlier at a cost of $300,000. Massive Corinthian columns grace the north and west facades, and visitors, after climbing the stone stairway in front, enter through doors crowned by stone cartouches. In 1919, the offices of the deputy sheriffs were in the basement, while sheriff Frank Kitchens and county judge H. D. Moore—two members of the Committee of Seven—had theirs on the first floor. The second floor was given over to two courtrooms, one for circuit court, which handled criminal cases, and one for chancery court, which handled civil matters, and both had balconies where blacks were allowed to sit. The second floor also had private offices for circuit court judge Jimason Jackson and prosecuting attorney John Miller, as well as jury and witness rooms, and a small stenographer's office.

The county jail was attached to the rear of the building. When it opened, the *Helena World* boasted that it had "18 tool-proof apartments," meaning that the cells were escape-proof. There were six cells to a floor, and each cell had four bunks, with a commode in between. The jailing of the Hoop Spur sharecroppers began on Wednesday, October 1, and quickly the cells overflowed, with six, eight, and even ten men crammed into a single cell. The farmers were packed so tightly into the cells that many had to sleep each night sitting upright on the concrete floor. As the number of imprisoned sharecroppers topped two hundred and then three hundred, Helena authorities found that it was impossible to cram them all into the eighteen cells, and they were forced to create a makeshift jail in a nearby grocer's warehouse.

All of the union leaders, however, remained in the courthouse. Frank Moore, Preacher Joe Knox, Will Wordlow, John Martin, Frank Hicks, John Ratliff, and Alf Banks were all here, as were Mary Moore and Lulu Ware—there were a handful of women who'd been arrested. Several of those who'd been shot—Albert Giles, Milligan Giles, Ed Hicks, and Paul Hall—were initially taken to the hospital, and then transferred to the jail once their wounds had at least somewhat healed. The jailed farmers were not allowed any change of clothes, and so most of them remained dressed in overalls caked with mud from the time they'd spent hiding in the canebrakes, and no visitors were allowed to see them. "There were a great many negroes, more than a hundred, in the same jail with me," said twenty-two-year-old Wordlow. "I was not permitted to see my friends, talk with them, or do anything towards preparing any defense." However, as Wordlow and all the other prisoners could attest, the prosecution was busily preparing its case.

The Committee of Seven had begun its interrogation of prisoners on Saturday, October 4. After it issued its report on October 6, it began the chore of sifting through the three hundred men to decide which of them should be remanded to the grand jury and indicted for murder, with municipal court judge J. Graham Burke presiding over this process. The Committee of Seven expanded during this period as well, as it was twelve men who signed the circular on Tuesday, October 7, telling the Negroes to "stop talking," and it is likely that several of the additional men—in particular, attorneys John Ike Moore and Edwin Bevens—sat in on the interrogations. There even seemed to be an open invitation for any planter to drop in, with Gerard Lambert one of those who pulled up a chair in Burke's office.

The interrogations began in earnest on Tuesday, October 7, with Henry Smiddy or deputy sheriff Dick Dalzell coming to the jail every thirty minutes or so to fetch a prisoner. At first, the sharecroppers did not tell the planters what they wanted to hear. "In no instance so far as I remember did a Negro give the committee any information they wanted on first examination," Smiddy said. "Different members of the committee would say to the Negro, 'Don't you know so and so,' and the Negro would answer, 'No sir.' Somebody else would say, 'You know you are lying about it, you know so and so is true, and you got to tell it.' The Negro would answer, 'I don't know, sir.' Different members of the committee would curse and abuse the Negro."

After that, Smiddy or one of the deputy sheriffs would take the prisoner to a small room on the top floor of the jail. There the sharecropper would be stripped, blindfolded, and made to lie facedown on the concrete floor, with four Negroes—men held in the Helena jail on charges not related to the riot—pinning down the man's arms and legs. All of the sharecroppers knew what was coming. The whipping of blacks was rooted deep in the Southern culture, as it had been the principal mode of punishing slaves, and as the men were held down, spread-eagled on the floor, Smiddy or one of the other men in the room—T. K. Jones, Dalzell, posse members Louis Anselman and Charley Gist,* and the Negro trustee Kid Collins—would begin the lashing, the whip a seven-pound leather strap.

"A short time after I had been in jail they told me that I had to testify against Frank Moore, Frank Hicks and these other men," said thirty-five-year-old Walter Ward. "I told them I didn't know anything against these men. They told me that I did and that I had to tell it. I refused to tell a lie on these men and they sent me back to jail where they stripped me and whipped me with a rubber strap that had lead or copper placed in it that cut me. Every lick he would hit me would cut the blood out. I do not know how many licks I was hit, but I do know that they nearly killed me."

Added Wordlow: "I was frequently taken from the cell, blindfolded, whipped and tortured to make me tell things I did not know, and furnish false information, and testify against other of the negroes. They whipped and tortured all or nearly all of the negroes in

---

* Anselman was with the Helena police department; Gist was a Phillips County deputy sheriff.

the same manner and for the same purpose . . . the officers would tell me that I knew things I did not know, and that I had to tell it or they would kill me."

The securing of desired testimony was done in a systematic way, Smiddy said. "We wanted them to tell facts that would convict themselves and others under arrest. We would have before us in writing the statements [the prisoner] made to the committee. We would whip them a while and then read to them what they had said to the committee and ask them if that was false. If the Negro didn't say yes, we would whip him some more. Then we would ask him if he is not certain other things are true, which would reflect upon himself and others, and if he didn't answer they were true we would whip him again."

As the whipping went on, one of the deputy sheriffs would bend down near the prisoner's head and stuff a "strangling drug"—most likely a cloth dipped in formaldehyde—into his nose, as this would cause him to think that he was being suffocated. After the whipping finally ended, the blindfolded man, often bleeding profusely, would be picked up and plunked down into an "electric chair," the sheriffs having rigged it so they could gradually ramp up the current until "the pain became unbearable." This was done, explained T. K. Jones, "to further frighten and torture them."

Twenty-nine-year-old Alf Banks Jr. got this treatment and more. "I was frequently whipped with great severity, and was also put into an electric chair and shocked, and strangling drugs would be put to my nose to make me tell things against others, that they had killed or shot at some of the white people and to force me to testify against them. I had not seen anything of the kind, and so told them at first, but they kept on and tortured me so that I finally told falsely that what they wanted me to say was true and that I would testify to it. They would have me blindfolded when torturing me. Once, they took me upstairs, put a rope around my neck, having me blindfolded, pulled on the rope, and one of them said, 'Don't knock the trick out yet, we can make him tell,' or words to that effect."

The torture session would last thirty minutes to an hour, and by then, T. K. Jones said, the prisoner usually "was unable to walk back to his cell and was dragged back and his clothes were thrown in after him. They were whipped so brutally and unmercifully that a physician had to be called in to take care of them afterwards." Jones estimated that he personally whipped "two dozen" prisoners; Smiddy said that he "personally administered the lash and saw others do it time and time again to a great many Negroes." A number of the sharecroppers had to be whipped two or three times before they agreed to give false testimony. "The lash," Smiddy explained, "was applied on the old sores made at the first whipping and usually the second whipping would get the Negro to say what was wanted if he had refused in the first instance."

Walter Ward made it through two torture sessions before he crumbled. "The third time they took me out I agreed to testify to anything they wanted me to say. They had it all written out what they had said others had testified to and told me that I knew it and that I had to tell it. So in order to save further punishment I agreed to testify against Frank Moore and the others."

Alf Banks, Wordlow, and five or six others similarly agreed to testify for the state. While Banks and Wordlow were both tortured, there were a few sharecroppers who agreed to testify without having been beaten. All day long, they would hear the cries coming from the room on the third floor, and their imaginations got the better of them. "We could hear the licks as they whipped [a man], and when they would bring the man back, blood would be running from him," said twenty-seven-year-old George Green. "Knowing that if I did not do what they told me to do that I would be punished as they were, and in order to avoid such punishment, I finally agreed to testify to anything they wanted me to say."

Said twenty-eight-year-old John Jefferson: "I could hear the licks and when they came back bleeding and unable to walk and all whipped to pieces, some of them were so badly beaten up that they had to crawl for several days. . . . They took me out of jail three times and talked to me about my testimony, told me that I had to testify against Frank Hicks and Frank Moore and these other men, and that if I didn't testify against them they would do me like they did the others and beat me up."

The imprisoned farmers were cracking, and the planters were getting the testimony they desired. A number of the prisoners escorted into Burke's office, Smiddy said, simply declared: "White folks, what do you want me to say? I will tell you anything you want." However, one man never did break: Frank Moore.

Thirty-one years old, Moore could read and write, and perhaps it was during his service in the army that he developed the extraordinary willpower it took to bear such torture, or perhaps it simply had always been part of his character. "I was whipped nearly to death to make me tell stories on the others, to say we killed the white people when at the church that night I did not have a gun whatever," Moore said. "Also, while whipping us men, they put something in our nose to strangle us. Also we was put in an electric chair and shocked to make us lie on each other." Moore knew that his wife, one of the few women arrested, was being whipped too, and still he refused to give in.

"Frank Moore," Smiddy said, "was whipped at least three times to try to compel him to give evidence against himself and the other petitioners, which he never did do. He stated that he would rather die in this manner than to tell something on himself or others that was not true."

Most of the needed testimony was secured by the middle of October, and so the whipping and torture, as a regular daily feature, ended at that point. The committee had its witnesses lined up, and yet the planters were still a little nervous about handing over the case to prosecutor John Miller. This outsider, they realized, was not totally on board with them.

MILLER, THIRTY-ONE, HAD BEEN tied up in court in nearby Marianna for the first two weeks of October, and his arrival in Helena in the middle of the month made for a rather farcical moment, as a handful of white men, thinking that he was Ulysses Bratton, briefly chased him. Miller was finally able to mollify the small mob, which included a deputy sheriff, by convincing them that he was there to prosecute the sharecroppers, not to help them.

Miller, who had graduated from Kentucky State University of Law in 1912, harbored big-time political ambitions. His first step up this ladder had come in 1918, when he'd defeated Helena attorney P. R. Andrews in the election for First Circuit Court prosecutor. Andrews had been the incumbent, and although Miller received almost no votes in Phillips County—a grand total of eleven, by his count—he carried the other four counties in the district. Now he was in charge of a case that was certain to make him known throughout Arkansas, and possibly the country. The problem, as he explained in an interview years later, was that once he got to "the bottom" of the case, he knew that there had been no Negro conspiracy to commit mass murder.

Southern Phillips County, he said, was "as near a feudal state as ever existed. Those farms down there, five or six thousand acres of land, were owned usually by a corporation or a combination of men or now and then an individual, [and] never was a bigger fraud perpetrated on any set of people than was perpetrated on those sharecroppers . . . [the owners] got all the money." Robert Hill, Miller concluded, was a "reformer fellow" who "started organizing the sharecroppers down there and the purpose of the organization was legitimate. The purpose of the organization was to have an accounting settlement with all the land owners on what they were entitled to." But then Adkins had been killed, and "when that boy was killed, the planters decided to crush it."

Having been chased upon his arrival in Helena, Miller also knew firsthand that a mob mentality was at work in the county. Tension in Phillips County was so high, he told Guy Bratton, that he would have to indict Ocier on a charge of barratry, an obscure statute that prohibited an attorney from stirring up strife, as he needed to "appease the mob." He would then have Ocier released on bail and whisked out of town, and he would never bother to pursue the charges. Miller, Guy Bratton informed his father, "said that he knew the conditions [of the sharecroppers] and the reason [the planters] were so mad at us, but that he was not going to allow himself to be made a party to such an outrage by further persecuting us."

Miller had other facts nagging at his conscience too. The whites from Mississippi, he knew, had come over with "blood in their eyes." Together with the troops, the outside posses had killed more than "100 niggers." There had been a "real slaughter down there," he thought. His deputy, Edwin Pipkin, had told him that county authorities had been "over zealous" in their interviewing techniques. Soon the sharecroppers were telling him about the whipping room.

"I turned loose four or five niggers that they had whipped down there trying to make them confess," Miller said. "I remember one great big nigger [who] said they were whipping him all the time. I just stopped and I said, 'Were whipping you? Were leaving scars?' I said, 'Pull your shirt off.' By God, they'd whipped the hell out of him."

Conflicted as he was, Miller decided to take what he considered a middle course. He released about 150 of the men in the Phillips County jail, as well as all of the women who'd been locked up, and then assured Helena authorities that he would prosecute most of the remaining 150 men for first-degree murder. Blacks had shot whites, and thus Miller reasoned that the union members, although they may have had quite the "provocation," were still "guilty all right, technically."

In his own mind, Miller had found a way to proceed in a manner that he believed was at least somewhat ethically correct: "I went in there," he said, "and tried to uphold the law."

WHITE CONTROL OF THE criminal justice system in Arkansas began with the election of white circuit court judges, as they appointed the jury commissioners for each term of court, and the commissioners in turn selected men of "good character, approved integrity, and sound judgment" to serve on the grand and petit juries. In Phillips County, prominent planters regularly served as jury commissioners—James Tappan, E. C. Hornor, Greenfield Quarles, Amos

Jarman, and E. M. Allen had all taken a turn—and they had made certain that no black had served on a jury for more than thirty years. And with the sharecroppers' trials looming, Helena's town fathers knew that the criminal justice system was in safe hands, for in 1918 they had elected their good friend Jimason Jackson as First Judicial Circuit Court judge.

Jackson, born in Helena in 1881, moved in the same social circle as the Hornors, Moores, and Tappans. "His friends in Helena are legion, most of them having known him since boyhood," an Arkansas historian wrote in 1922. One of Jackson's grandfathers had been a Confederate soldier, and his maternal grandfather was John P. Moore, who in the late 1800s was one of the most prosperous planters in the entire Mississippi Delta. Jackson had served in the Arkansas state legislature from 1909 to 1913, and like most Democrats from the Delta, he was proud of his white supremacist beliefs. "Judge Jackson," said one observer, "has always given his political endorsement to the Democratic party and the principles for which it stands."

The sixteen-person grand jury that convened in the Phillips County Courthouse on Monday, October 27, was filled with familiar names. Two from the Committee of Seven—Sebastian Straub and T. W. Keesee—were on it. So too was J. J. Petro, manager of the Theo Fathauer plantation in Ratio; it was his men who had nearly lynched Ocier Bratton. Plantation owners on the grand jury included C. L. Bernard from Elaine, James H. Pillow, C. L. Moore Jr., and C. A. Wooten. Moore and Wooten were also prominent cotton factors, meaning that they lent money and provided supplies to plantation owners during the growing season. This grand jury would be mulling over "evidence" of a Negro plot to kill whites that "is very strong," Arkansas newspapers reported.

Miller brought only a handful of black witnesses before the panel—"They heard mostly from posse members," the *Helena World* reported—and then the grand jury basically divided the sharecroppers into two groups. Those who were members of the Elaine and Hoop Spur lodges were indicted for first-degree murder or for assault with intent to commit murder, while the men from the Lambrook plantation who had ridden at some point toward Hoop Spur—summoned there by "Paul Reveres," according to the Committee of Seven—were indicted either for "intent to commit murder" or on night-riding charges.* Miller had held 143 men over for the grand jury, and by the end of the week it had indicted seventy-three men for first-degree murder and forty-nine on the lesser charges. The jury let twenty-one sharecroppers go free for "insufficient evidence." It also indicted Ocier Bratton and G. P. Casey for barratry, Casey having been captured a few days earlier in Kansas.

"The indictments," E. M. Allen told the *Arkansas Gazette,* "were based entirely on voluntary confessions and upon evidence of the negroes who were involved. This evidence has been carefully transcribed and verified by the negroes themselves. No hearsay or circumstantial evidence was considered. No innocent negro was permitted to suffer."

Most of the murder indictments were served on Wednesday, October 29, with Judge Jackson announcing on Friday that the trials of the 122 men would begin the following Monday. The trials promised to be speedy, with the Arkansas newspapers predicting—given the strong evidence and the confessions—that it would take only a month for all 122 men to be tried.

AS PART OF THEIR pretrial preparations, Helena's town fathers had also taken care of one final critical matter: they had put together their own roster of attorneys. They did not totally trust Miller or Pipkin, and so, with the consent of Judge Jackson and Miller, they had retained two prosecutors of their own: P. R. Andrews, who'd been defeated by Miller in the 1918 election, and J. D. Mosby, who'd led one of the posses during the "fighting." At the same time, Jack-

---

* Night-riding laws had been enacted by Southern states to prevent whites from riding around at night and terrorizing blacks in order to drive them from the land. Plantation owners pushed for the statutes in order to protect their supply of cheap black labor, as otherwise they would have needed to rely on poor whites as tenants, who were in a better position to demand a fair share of the crop.

son had appointed six or seven Helena attorneys to serve as the sharecroppers' defense counsel.

Nearly all Helena lawyers had their offices in the Solomon Building, at the corner of Elm and Cherry. This was the town's skyscraper, a five-story building with an elevator, and the attorneys who would be handling the trials—both for the prosecution and the defense—were a close-knit group, their offices next to one another on the fourth and fifth floors. John Ike Moore and Greenfield Quarles, the elder statesmen of the Helena bar, would be heading up the "defense" team.

Born in 1856, Moore had studied law in the offices of Major John J. Hornor and General James C. Tappan, the men who, with the assistance of a cannon, had "redeemed" Phillips County in the 1870s. Moore soon rose to great prominence in the Democratic party, and by the time he retired from the state legislature in 1913, he had served as Speaker of the House of Representatives, president of the Senate, and, for a brief period in 1907, acting governor. In 1918, he and his old friend E. C. Hornor were Phillips County's two delegates to the state's constitutional convention.

Like Hornor, Moore was involved in a number of business enterprises. He was vice president of the Wooten-Agee Company, a plantation-supply company, and he, Greenfield Quarles, and E. M. Allen jointly owned the People's Savings Bank. In August, he had helped found the town's American Legion post, and in the wake of the "riot," he had authored the post's resolutions deploring the deaths of James Tappan and Clinton Lee, writing with great emotion how everyone in town had "loved them."* Most likely, he had been one of the "businessmen" who had promised the lynch mob at the courthouse on October 2 that the union leaders would be put to death in the electric chair. A few days later, he had signed the circular that urged Negroes to stop talking, the *Helena World* listing him as a member of the expanded Committee of Seven. His law partner was J. D. Mosby, who would help prosecute the sharecroppers.

---

* Although Moore was not a veteran of World War I, he'd headed up the Citizens Committee that helped organize the post.

Greenfield Quarles's credentials as a man of the Old South were, if possible, even more polished. A native of Kentucky, he'd joined the Confederate Army in 1862 at fifteen years of age, serving under his uncle, Brigadier General William A. Quarles. Young Greenfield had been wounded twice during the war, the second time at the battle of Franklin, Tennessee, on November 30, 1864, where he was taken prisoner. Even though he was now seventy-two years old, he still liked to dress up in a Confederate uniform for camp meetings of the United Confederate Veterans in Helena. He was the group's commander and he very much looked the part of a Civil War officer, as he had a fine white goatee. "His interest in the comrades of those days has never abated and he is distinguished as quite one of the youngest of those brave wearers of the gray and blue who participated in the struggle between the states," an Arkansas historian wrote in 1912. Like Moore, Quarles had studied for law in the offices of Major Hornor and General Tappan, and was then elected to a number of political posts, serving in the state legislature from 1879 to 1883 and again from 1895 to 1899. "A Democrat in politics, he has ever been passionately devoted to the interests and principles of his party, always ready to do anything, to go anywhere, to proclaim its ideas," one writer noted. Quarles owned a large plantation, and earlier that year had helped organize the planters' meeting where they discussed devising an "infallible" plan for raising cotton prices. The sharecroppers, he believed, had "committed one of the greatest crimes on record."

The other defense attorneys were also solidly Democratic in their politics. Edwin Bevens was a planter who, as chairman of the Phillips County Council of Defense, had commanded the posses the night they'd bivouacked in Elaine. R. B. Campbell was a business partner of Sebastian Straub and E. M. Allen, the men having jointly founded an oil-drilling company in June. At first glance, the one outlier in this group of attorneys was Jacob Fink, as he was Jewish. His family had come to Helena in 1868, when he was six years old, but Fink, an Arkansas writer observed in 1912, was a Democrat through and through, "giving his heart and hand to the men and measure of that party." His white-supremacist credentials were such that he'd been elected mayor of Helena in 1907, and he jointly owned the Interstate National Bank with members of the Tappan and Wooten families.

The sharecroppers, as would be noted later in court proceedings, were represented by eminent men. Judge Jackson had assigned the black farmers the best lawyers that Helena had to offer.

A FEW MINUTES BEFORE 1:00 P.M. on Monday, November 3, the circuit courtroom began to fill with spectators, with at least a few blacks daring to enter, taking seats upstairs in the gallery. Fink and Quarles hovered about the defense table, and in the jury box, as Smiddy and others observed, sat several men—such as Charlie Afflick, treasurer of the American Legion post—who had been "in the posses that went to Elaine." Even Louis Anselman, the Helena police deputy who'd helped whip the defendants, had been picked for the jury earlier that morning. Everyone rose as Judge Jackson entered, he gaveled the court to order, and then Deputy Sheriff Dalzell led Frank Hicks into the courtroom, the thirty-seven-year-old sharecropper, as the newspaper reporters noted, "dressed in ragged overalls and a dirty overcoat."

Hicks certainly stood out, in his dress, from everyone else in the front of the courtroom. The attorneys wore starched white shirts and suits, and the twelve jurors were similarly clad, whereas Hicks was wearing the same clothes he'd had on when arrested. His jailers hadn't provided him with a clean change of clothes for this trial, nor had they allowed anyone to visit and bring him some clothes, and so now he stood before the bench looking "visibly frightened" and wearing those stinking overalls, which clearly marked him, in the eyes of the whites in the court, as a "field negro," or, as one Arkansas newspaper wrote, as an example of the "ignorant plantation negro." Deputy court clerk L. E. Bernard read the indictment out loud, the state charging that Hicks "willfully, feloniously and with malice aforethought and after deliberation and premeditation did kill and murder one Clinton Lee," and all the while Hicks shifted from one foot to another, his fingers anxiously "clinching the seams of his overalls."

"Not guilty," he muttered, and then he sat down, about as alone as a defendant in a courtroom could ever be.

There was nothing in Hicks's life, or even his immediate past, that had prepared him for this moment. He was married, a Methodist who attended church regularly, and he'd never been in criminal court before. A month ago he'd been arrested, and then there had been the weeks of whippings and torture, and all the while he had not been allowed to speak to anyone from the outside. Nor had he been told what he was being charged with. The previous Wednesday someone had finally tossed a piece of paper at him in his cell, but he couldn't read it, as he had never been to school. Perhaps Frank Moore or one of the other literate sharecroppers had read it for him, and so he might have learned then that he was being charged with first-degree murder, but nobody had come to the jail to talk to him about his defense. Now here he was in this courtroom, his attorneys Jacob Fink and Greenfield Quarles still hadn't spoken one word to him, and yet already his trial was under way, prosecutor P. R. Andrews telling the jury that the sharecroppers had formed the Progressive Farmers and Household Union in order "to kill planters," the insurrection erupting prematurely when Adkins was gunned down.

Fink pushed back his chair and half stood up—"I ask for a fair, impartial trial," he said—and then sat back down. The defense's opening argument was now over too.

The trial unfolded with dizzying speed. A witness would be called to the stand, raise his right hand, swear to tell the truth, and then five minutes later he'd be done. Posse member R. L. Brooks, who'd been with Lee when he was shot, testified that Lee had been seated in the rear of the car, and that although he'd heard the "whistle" of two bullets, he didn't know where they had come from. Next Dr. O. Parker testified that Lee had been brought to the McCoy house, where he was tending to James Tappan, and had died within a few minutes. Parker had been too busy with Tappan to examine Lee and thus had no idea where the bullet had struck him. Another posse member, Tom Faulkner, said that the two shots had come from the south, and that he'd seen three or so Negroes cross the road there, with one of the Negroes "crouching" down to shoot. Finally, George Green and John Jefferson, the state's two black witnesses, fingered Hicks for the killing. The Thursday before the shooting, they said, they had gone to the union meeting in Elaine, where Frank Hicks and nearly everyone else had guns. Although neither Green nor Jefferson had been at the Hoop Spur church on that Tuesday night, both had been awakened around four the following morning and told to go to Frank Moore's. By 11:00 A.M., there were about seventy-five share-croppers at Moore's place and, once again, they all "had guns." They heard shooting up the road, and then Frank Moore said, "Come on, let's go help them people out." Moore lined everyone up two by two, marching them toward McCoy's house. Along the way, Ed Hicks and Preacher Joe Knox also gave orders to the group, which prosecutor Andrews referred to as an "army." As Moore and the others crossed the road, they spotted "some white gentlemen up the road in an au-tomobile," Jefferson said, and that's when Frank Hicks, armed with a .45-70 rifle, fired two shots.

Although Andrews may have told the jury in his opening argu-ment that this was a case about a Negro plot to kill whites, he had not, to that point, provided one bit of evidence to support it. There was even some uneasy stirring in the courtroom. Where was the hit list of twenty-one planters? All of the spectators had been waiting to see that. Nor had there been any testimony about the sharecroppers plotting to seize the planters' land. The only testimony that had been elicited so far was that Frank Hicks—part of a group of three, if posse member Faulkner was to be believed, or part of an army of seventy-five, if Green and Jefferson were understood to be telling the truth—had fired off two shots, one of which presumably killed Lee. But Jefferson was still on the witness stand, it was the defense's turn to question him, and suddenly Fink was asking him why he had brought a gun to union meetings.

"Just told to bring it, because they was looking for [whites] to break this up, looking for them to come down there and break the meeting up," Jefferson said.

"Who told you that?"

"This fellow Hill."

"He told you to arm yourselves because they were coming there to break up the meeting?"

"Yes sir."

"What did you all understand your union was going to do?"

"Give us legal rights and everything, and we would have justice in the law and everything."

"Was that the way you were going to get it—with your guns and pistols?"

"No sir. [Hill] said we all was going to have our rights, we was going to get along better in this world, but it might cause trouble."

"And then, if you had any trouble, you wanted to have your guns with you?"

"Yes sir. He told everybody to come and bring their guns to the meeting."

As Fink sat down, Quarles nodded slightly. Although Jefferson may have denied that the union had planned to kill whites, Fink had nevertheless done what the prosecution had failed to do: he had reminded everyone in the courtroom of the bigger picture, of blacks *organizing* and of coming to their meetings *armed,* in anticipation that there might be *trouble.* That at least proved their readiness to shoot at whites, that they had prepared for it, and that provided evidence—at least to the whites in the courtroom—that their killing of Adkins, Lee, and Tappan had been premeditated. The jury now had at least some legal cover for convicting Hicks of first-degree murder.

Elaine mayor Sid Stoaks was the state's final witness. He testified that Frank Hicks had confessed to killing Clinton Lee. "He said when he got to the road he thought he would just take a shot into the crowd and maybe get some of them," Stoaks said. Hicks's confession, he added, was freely made—he had not been "whipped or threatened."

Everyone in the courtroom now looked at Finks and Quarles. Nobody expected them to call any defense witnesses, but certainly Frank Hicks—and the more than one hundred blacks sitting up in the gallery—hoped that they would. There was the sharecroppers' side of the story waiting to be told. There were witnesses who could testify that their Hoop Spur church had been shot up, and that the next morning posses had gunned down Lemon and Charlie Robinson, the white men shooting the old man in the back as he tried to run away. There were witnesses who could testify that the Helena legionnaires, including that man in the jury box, Charlie Afflick, had methodically walked down both sides of Govan Slough and shot the Negroes hiding there, and that it was only then that Moore and the others had headed toward McCoy's. Everyone in the courtroom knew that there was another version of events, this was the big elephant in that room, and for just a moment, all eyes turned toward Fink and Quarles. It had been only fifteen seconds or so since the prosecution had rested, but it seemed much longer than that, then Fink cleared his throat and said in a loud, clear voice: "The defense has no witnesses, Your Honor."

After Judge Jackson charged the jury—neither Fink nor Quarles made a closing argument on Hicks's behalf—the newspaper reporters in the front row all looked at their watches: 2:24 P.M. The trial had taken eighty-four minutes, and the big question now was how quickly the jury would be back in the courtroom. Eight minutes later, the reporters had their answer. "Record time was made in returning the verdict," the *Helena World* wrote, and this seemed to set up the biggest drama in the trials to come: could the other juries beat this time?

LATER, THERE WOULD BE claims that an angry mob milled around the courthouse on Monday and packed the courtroom, but, in fact, there was never any serious threat of mob violence that day, or during any of the subsequent trials, for the simple reason that a deal had already been struck. All of the white spectators knew that the sharecroppers were to be found guilty and sentenced to die. That was what had been promised to the mob that had gathered outside the courthouse on Thursday, October 2, and the instant the spectators entered the courtroom, and saw that Jacob Fink and Greenfield Quarles were acting as the defense attorneys, and that men such as Charlie Afflick and Louis Anselman were on the jury, they knew that there was no chance of any other outcome. The second trial featured John Moore and Quarles as the defense attorneys, with E. C. Hornor's son Tully and posse member John Miles in the jury box. It was more like a theater show, rather than a trial with an uncertain outcome, that the white spectators had come to watch. On Tuesday, the courtroom was once again filled, and although Judge Jackson occasionally had to gavel for quiet, it was not because of outbursts of anger. Instead, the Marianna *Courier Index* reported, it was because of outbursts of "laughter," the white audience amused at something or other that one of the black witnesses said. Blacks continued to fill the balcony as well, although they remained solemn-faced throughout the proceedings.

All of the other trials that were held basically followed the same blueprint. There was a brief bit of testimony from white witnesses, and then one or two blacks would slightly incriminate the defendant, either by stating that he saw him fire a gun, or saw him with a gun, or saw him near someone who fired a gun, and that this all happened at a time when a white person was shot and killed. After that, a person of authority—either Stoaks, municipal court judge J. Graham Burke, or circuit court clerk A. G. Burke—would swear that the defendant had confessed or made some sort of damning admission, and had done so voluntarily, without having been whipped or threatened. Each jury then raced the clock, the mark for returning to the court with a guilty verdict falling to seven minutes, then five minutes and thirty seconds, until the last jury made it back in two minutes, which perhaps still stands today as some sort of national record for the fastest verdict ever in a capital case. Five such trials were completed by the end of Tuesday, with eleven men having been found guilty of first-degree murder. The proceedings in the last one, in which Will Wordlow was convicted of murdering Adkins, took about an hour, and that included impaneling the jury.

Even so, the trials had their revealing moments. The state never made any serious attempt to prove that the sharecroppers had plotted to kill whites. The prosecution never produced a list of the twenty-one planters to be killed, even though the Committee of

Seven, in its report, had pointed to its existence as "concrete proof" that the Negroes had hatched such a plot. In the course of the five trials, the best that the state could do in this regard was get two blacks to testify to the sharecroppers' malevolent intentions. One of the two was Dave Archer, who worked for Sid Stoaks. He said that the union sharecroppers "captured" him on Wednesday morning, took him to Frank Moore's, and forced him to join their army. Before they left the house for McCoy's, he said, both Moore and Frank Hicks boasted that they were "going to kill the white people." The other testimony of this kind came from Alf Banks, who had been a guard outside the Hoop Spur church. He said that Ed Ware, just before the meeting started, told him "not to let nobody pass unless they give the password," and that if they didn't have the password, "just to kill them." Banks was one of the sharecroppers who'd been whipped, shocked in the electric chair, and nearly suffocated with formaldehyde, and as he'd been escorted to the courtroom that day, the deputy sheriffs had reminded him of that torture. "They told me if I changed my testimony or did not testify as I had said, when they took me back [to the jail], they would skin me alive," Banks later said. "I testified [in court] in the same way they had made me tell."

Lacking any evidence of a conspiracy to kill whites, the state, in the five trials, focused on prosecuting the union leaders and a handful of others for killing Lee, Adkins, and Tappan. After Frank Hicks's trial ended, Frank Moore and four others—Ed Hicks, Joe Knox, Paul Hall, and Ed Coleman—were jointly tried for murdering Lee. The one revealing moment during this trial came when R. L. Brooks said that Lee had been shot "under his left arm." This raised an obvious question: was this a wound that was consistent with his having been shot by someone one-quarter of a mile away? Or was it consistent with a self-inflicted wound, which is what the other posse members had initially thought had happened? Miller quickly dropped the point, and of course neither Moore nor Quarles explored it, but perhaps it did explain why Dr. Parker, an Elaine plantation owner, had failed to notice where Lee had been shot.

There were three sharecroppers convicted of killing Adkins: Banks, John Martin, and Wordlow. Here too there was a revealing moment, and it came when Charles Pratt testified that he and Adkins stopped near the Hoop Spur church in order to "take a leak." Pratt had apparently forgotten the original excuse, that they had stopped to repair a punctured tire, and his testimony was so transparently devastating to the narrative of white innocence that reporters for the Arkansas newspapers simply covered for him, writing that the law enforcement officers had pulled to the side of the road because "something went wrong with their car." None of the reporters dared to write that the deputy sheriff had a new excuse, one never heard before, for coming to a halt outside the Hoop Spur church that night.

The three men were tried in two trials, as the prosecution needed to have Banks, once he'd been convicted, testify against Wordlow. The basic story that emerged during the trials, in terms of how Adkins was killed, went like this: After Adkins, Pratt, and Kid Collins stepped from the car to take a leak, a number of sharecroppers—perhaps "eight to twelve"—surrounded them. Adkins shone a flashlight on Alf Banks and then, noticing that the black men were all armed, said, "Going coon hunting, boys?" The blacks responded with a volley of gunfire, the bullets coming from all directions, "north, south, east and west," Pratt said, with "50 or 75 shots, possibly 100" in total. One shotgun blast hit Adkins in the stomach; a bullet tore into his throat. Pratt was wounded in the knee, while Kid Collins escaped unscathed—all of the other five dozen or so bullets fired at close range apparently missed their mark. John Ratliff, one of the guards, testified for the state that he'd seen Banks and the Beco brothers shoot, and that he'd also seen a flash of gunfire come from under a nearby railroad trestle, and that this was where John Martin had been hiding. Thus, Ratliff fingered Banks and Martin for the murder, and then Banks testified in the second trial that Wordlow had opened fire with an automatic pistol. Witnesses in both trials agreed that after the shooting died down, Martin stepped forward and turned Adkins over with his foot to see who it was they'd killed.

In the other trial held on Tuesday, Albert Giles and Joe Fox were convicted of murdering James Tappan. Posse leader Herbert Thompson was the prosecution's main witness. He described how the posses had surrounded the Govan Slough thicket, and testified that he'd shouted to the sharecroppers that "if they would come out they would not be hurt." His voice, he said, easily could have been heard "125 yards" away, but the Negroes hiding in the thicket, rather than come out with their hands up, answered in the form of a "shot from a rifle." The posse began moving down the sides of the thicket and then, "five to fifteen minutes later," Tappan was hit in the face with buckshot; he may have been hit with a slug from a pistol or rifle as well.

What distinguished this trial from the others was that Giles and Fox insisted on taking the witness stand in their own defense. The two men were represented by Quarles and Edwin Bevens, and Quarles, forced to accede to his clients' request, immediately invited Giles, with his first question, to confess: "You are charged with murder in the first degree," he said. "Just go ahead and tell the jury if you helped to shoot anyone, and all about it." But Fox and Giles told the story they wanted to tell. Jim Miller, they said, told them to lie low and let the posses go by. Only then the "white people started shooting before they got to us," Fox said. They'd never heard Thompson telling them that they could come out and not be harmed. Theirs was testimony of being *hunted,* and it was hard for the white jury to miss that point while Albert Giles was on the stand. He had been shot multiple times. His arm was wrapped in a splint, and he also had "a bullet hole in each side of his head," the *Helena World* reported. Giles had some trouble speaking, but he was able to point out for the jurors where a slug had entered the right side of his skull and exited "near the left ear."

By Tuesday's end, Giles and ten other sharecroppers had been convicted of murder. All of them were expected to die in the electric chair, and with Miller advising newspaper reporters that he anticipated wrapping up the remaining 111 cases within a week or so, the defendants began pleading en masse to lesser charges. Most of this pleading was finished by Friday, and by the time it was all over, thirteen men had pled guilty to second-degree murder and been sentenced to twenty-one years in prison, twenty-seven had pled guilty to either second-degree murder or assault to kill and been sentenced to five or six years, and eighteen more—mostly the men from Lambrook, who'd ridden toward Hoop Spur—had pled guilty to night riding and been sentenced to one year.* Three more were found guilty at trial of night riding and sentenced to three years. Fifteen-year-old Milligan Giles, whom Smiddy had shot in the face, pleaded guilty to both second-degree murder and assault to kill, and was sentenced to ten years.

In total, there were seventy-three sharecroppers by the end of that first week who had been convicted or pled guilty, and a few days later Ed Ware, who'd escaped to New Orleans, having survived for four days in the woods by eating persimmons, was captured and brought to Helena. He was convicted of first-degree murder in a matter of days, the state suddenly developing testimony that Ware shot Adkins while hiding behind a log, his shots apparently part of the cascade of bullets that erupted all at once. The jury took four minutes to decide his fate.† Meanwhile, Dave Archer—the sharecropper who'd testified that he had been "captured" by Frank Moore and the others—went free. So too did Kid Collins: by December, his murder sentence had been commuted and he was living in Memphis with his family.

---

* The variable sentences for those who pled guilty to second-degree murder depended on two things: whether they'd cooperated with authorities and the timing of their pleas. Most of those who'd testified for the state, including John Jefferson, George Green, and Walter Ward, were given five-year sentences, and a number of others who pled guilty on Wednesday, November 6, got five-year sentences as well. However, at the end of that day, Miller and others complained to Judge Jackson that he was being too lenient, and so the rest of those who pled guilty to second-degree murder got twenty-one-year sentences.

† After Ware's conviction, forty-nine sharecroppers still remained in jail. Of that group, thirteen pled guilty at a subsequent term of court, and Miller chose not to prosecute thirty-five others. There was one black charged with night riding who won at trial, Judge Jackson dismissing the charges for lack of evidence. Thus, the final tally: seventy-five were sentenced to prison terms, and twelve more to die in the electric chair.

There was no one tried for killing U.S. Army corporal Luther Earles, and today that provides some insight into how many black farmers may have been killed by the Camp Pike troops in the woods that Thursday morning. There was one sharecropper, Sam Wilson, who'd been indicted for first-degree murder in regard to Earles's death, but he'd been allowed to plead to second-degree murder, the newspapers reporting that this was necessary because of an "absence of witnesses" to testify against him. There apparently were no other blacks who could attest to Wilson having been armed and in those woods, and no other blacks to be charged for Earles's death. The posses that morning had told the Camp Pike soldiers that there were perhaps 150 Negroes in that copse of trees, which the troops, acting on shoot-to-kill orders, cleared with their machine guns and rifles. Wilson, it would seem, was the only black farmer to have emerged alive from those woods.

On Tuesday, November 11, Judge Jackson sentenced Frank Moore and the others convicted at trial the previous week. They were brought into court as a group, Albert Giles noticeably "nervous and ill at ease," while Moore "kept his eyes directed toward the floor," the *Arkansas Gazette* reported. The remaining nine men "listened to the steady voice of Judge Jackson without sign of interest and appeared to accept their fates as a matter of course." Jackson told them they had been convicted at fair trials—"Frank Moore," he said, "you have been convicted by a jury of your own choosing"— and then he gave them a short lecture about their cold-blooded ways, scolding them for having shown their victims no mercy. Frank Moore and his four co-defendants would go to the electric chair on December 27, the other six on January 2. They were, Jackson said, to be electrocuted until they were "dead, dead, dead."

THERE WAS OTHER NEWS during those first two weeks of November that made headlines in Arkansas and the rest of the country. The price of cotton topped 50 cents a pound, with one Helena broker selling bales for 70 cents a pound. Apparently the sharecroppers had been right in thinking that cotton prices were going to reach stratospheric heights that fall. In Magnolia, Arkansas, a cheering mob of several hundred burned a fifty-year-old black man, Jordan Jameson, alive at the stake in the town's main square, with authorities standing by as the "funeral pyre" was built. And the U.S. Bureau of Justice, which had remained silent during the prosecution of the Helena farmers, issued its report on the "radical Negro press," U.S. attorney general A. Mitchell Palmer blaming the Negro publications for sowing racial hatred. They were, Palmer said, creating a race consciousness that is "antagonistic to the white race, and openly, defiantly assertive of its own equality."

The news that Palmer deemed fit to be printed could be found in mainstream newspapers such as the *New York Sun,* which on November 16 published a long article by Clair Kenamore on the trials in Helena. Of the three hundred Negroes arrested in the case, Kenamore reported, all could have been "indicted for first-degree murder." However, the white people of Phillips County, he said, "earnestly tried to administer a fairer justice," and indicted only about one hundred men. The accused were then ably defended by the "best lawyers" in the county, most of the attorneys choosing not to allow their clients to testify because "the story they had to tell made the cases worse for the defendants." The evidence against the sharecroppers, Kenamore concluded, was so strong that "it would have convicted the men in any court in the country." Arkansas senator Thaddeus Caraway introduced the article into the *Congressional Record,* telling his colleagues that the Negroes had "admitted the organization of a plot and their intention to assassinate the landowners." They were, he said, "given a fair trial in a court of justice."

On Friday afternoon, November 21, Frank Kitchens and eleven other guards shackled the seventy-four prisoners two by two to a long chain and marched them to a waiting train. First stop was Cummins State Farm, a state-owned penal plantation 75 miles southwest of Helena. There, the sixty-two men who'd received prison terms would be put to work growing cotton, guarded by men on horses who employed the whip liberally to keep inmates in line. The train with the twelve condemned men—Ed Ware had been sentenced a few days earlier—pulled into Little Rock's Union Station on Saturday morning. As they had not been told why they were being moved from the Helena jail, they feared, as they stepped from the train, that their execution dates had been changed and that they were now going directly to the electric chair. "Their black faces were ashen and their knees trembled in terror," the *Arkansas Democrat* wrote. Even though the train had arrived at 6:30 A.M., a huge crowd had gathered at the station, and as the twelve farmers—all chained together—shuffled by, the blacks in the audience "stood in hushed silence." No one could mistake the sight: this, the paper said, quoting Rudyard Kipling, was "the price of a white man slain," and "thus was the lesson plain."

The Walls, as the state prison was called, was located 5 miles to the southwest of the city, and upon their arrival, the guards lined the men up at the front gate so that an *Arkansas Democrat* reporter could snap their picture. Ed Hicks stood at one end and Will Wordlow at the other, and most of the condemned men, the paper noted, still had on "the clothes they have worn since their arrest." They were, the *Arkansas Gazette* wrote, "shaggy, slovenly creatures, not far removed from the primitive days of savagery." The paper's reporter marveled in particular at the sight of seventy-eight-year-old Ed Coleman. He was a small man—he weighed only 125 pounds and was barely 5 feet 5 inches tall—and yet inside apparently beat the heart of a monster. Most ex-slaves, the reporter explained, had remained "faithful" to their "white friends and loyal to the trust imposed in them, whereas old man Coleman"—and this truly was the wonder of it all—"had planned to murder them in their sleep."

Frank Moore and the other eleven men were taken to the "death house," the two cells having been newly painted for them, and here they were to remain, the newspapers noted, for the next six weeks or so. Then they would be escorted one by one into the adjoining room and strapped into the high-backed oaken chair, which naturally was nicknamed "Old Sparky" by the guards. Yet Moore and the others now understood that their date with the electric chair was still a few weeks off, which was a relief, and before they were locked into the death house cells, they were allowed to bathe. Since condemned men didn't wear stripes, they were given "new underclothing, a cap and a new suit of brown denim overalls" to wear. This was the first touch of humanity they'd known for a long, long time, and on Sunday, when more than a thousand white people from Little Rock descended on the prison, hoping to get a peek at the "shaggy, slovenly" Helena Negroes, officials wouldn't let them in. The Walls suddenly felt like a bit of a refuge, and all in all, their mood lightened. "Considerable hope up," Coleman said.

And it was then, at that late and desperate hour, that an extraordinary man named Scipio Africanus Jones went to work.

Scipio Africanus Jones

O N MOST MORNINGS, SCIPIO Africanus Jones could be found in his office at 402 West Markham Street in downtown Little Rock, sitting at a large oak desk, the glass top crowded with papers. He worked with his suit coat on, dressed in a starched white shirt and bow tie, and if he needed to know the time, he would pull a gold watch from his pocket. His office was but a few steps from the Pulaski County Courthouse, and on his way out, he would always grab his Panama hat. He was short, perhaps 5 feet 5 inches tall, and a bit portly. The downtown streets would be filled with people he knew—white politicians, businessmen, and attorneys—and as he passed them by, many would nod and greet him with evident friend-liness. "Judge Jones," they'd say, and now and then one of the men would even touch the brim of his hat. This was a sign of respect nor-mally reserved for whites, and what was most remarkable about this moment of grace in 1919 America was that for the past thirty years no man in Arkansas had done more to fight for the rights of blacks than Scipio Africanus Jones. "His whole professional career," noted one black educator at the time, "has been altruistically devoted to the protection of the inalienable rights of his own people."

The arrival of the twelve condemned men from Phillips County on November 22 had caused quite a stir in Little Rock, and every-one in town knew what to expect next. Scipio Jones would be the man who would mount an appeal to save them. "He is," confessed

Pulaski circuit court judge Albert Lea, "the best and most worthy Negro lawyer I've ever known."

SCIPIO JONES NEVER LIKED to talk about his youth, even to his closest friends, and thus the details of his boyhood remain a bit obscure. His mother, Jemmima, was owned by a planter named Adolphus Jones, and upon his death in 1858, she and the other slaves were given in trust to his brother-in-law, Dr. Sanford Reamey. Jemmima, thirteen years old in 1858, labored as a maid in Reamey's house in Tulip, Arkansas. Five years later, with federal troops making forays into Arkansas, Reamey fled with his slaves to Texas, traveling there in a covered wagon. Jemmima gave birth during this flight, most likely in late 1863, either while they were in Texas or returning to Arkansas. Given the baby's light skin, the father almost certainly was Sanford Reamey.

The name that Jemmima bestowed on her boy—Scipio Africanus—was one that was popular among blacks and a trigger for taunts by whites. Prior to the Civil War, slaves had often named their children after famous Romans, and there were few Romans more famous than Scipio Africanus, who defeated Hannibal at Zama in 202 B.C. and thus was celebrated for having conquered Africa. To blacks, this was a name that spoke of high aspirations and future greatness, and perhaps Jemmima, at this hour of emancipation, was filled with such hopes for her son. However, minstrels had mocked that aspiration since the mid-1830s with a stock character named "Zip Coon," Zip being a nickname for Scipio. They portrayed Zip Coon as an urban dandy who fancied himself the equal of whites, forever mangling the King's English as he tried to impress others with his use of big words. Zip Coon and Jim Crow were the two characters that white minstrel audiences loved to laugh at, and young Scipio was sure to have heard minstrel-inspired jibes as he grew up.

With the Civil War having ended, Jemmima and another of Reamey's former slaves, Horace Jones, settled in Tulip. Horace picked cotton while Jemmima labored as a domestic, and by 1870 they were raising four boys, the family living in a shack and in a cotton-growing area where many antebellum mannerisms were still observed. "I used to say master myself," recalled Joseph Badgett, a sharecropper who was born in Tulip in 1864. "We had to do that 'til after '69 or '70. I remember the time when I couldn't go nowhere without asking the white folks. I wasn't a slave then but I couldn't go off without asking the white people."

In 1868, the Reconstruction government in Arkansas established public schools for blacks, and young Scipio—his friends called him "Sippi"—attended classes three or four months a year. "I went to school a little," said Evans Warrior, who grew up in Tulip with Scipio. "Didn't get far enough to read and write . . . Kept me in the field all the time." While none of Scipio's brothers learned to read, he did, the only member of the Jones household listed as literate in the 1870 census.

A decade later, Scipio was still living in Tulip and working in the fields, as were his four brothers and two sisters. At age seventeen, he could see his fate stretching out for him: a Negro farmhand could expect a life of hard labor and poverty. Sixty miles to the north, however, Little Rock beckoned as a place of hope, and sometime between 1880 and 1883, Scipio moved there. Although he could only find work as a farmhand, the planter who hired him, James Lawson, evidently liked him, as he allowed young Scipio to stay in the rear of his home at 802 Rock Street. This was only a few blocks away from the heart of Little Rock's black community, at West Ninth and Broadway, and in the 1880s, there was no better place in the South for an ambitious young black person to be.

Although Reconstruction in Arkansas had been a violent affair, the Democrats, after redeeming the state in 1874, had chosen to govern in a relatively benign manner. The reason for this was demographics: in Arkansas, whites outnumbered blacks three to one, and thus once ex-Confederates were reenfranchised prior to the 1874 elections, they had no fear—at a state level—of "Negro domination." Whites could control politics through the ballot box. Black voters, in some ways, simply became a minority to be placated, and the Democratic governor elected in 1874, Augustus Garland, did not try to roll back all of the gains that blacks had made under Reconstruction. The state funded segregated schools and established Branch Normal College at Pine Bluff as an institution for training black teachers, and it passed a civil rights law. Blacks could still vote, and they elected dozens of representatives to the state legislature in the 1870s and 1880s. There was even a fair amount of race mixing in Little Rock, a visiting reporter for *Harper's New Monthly* magazine remarking in 1888 that everywhere he went, the "intercourse between the two races was friendly."

In comparison to the rest of the South, Arkansas and its capital seemed to be a welcoming place, so much so that it came to be viewed, during the 1870s and 1880s, as something of a "promised land" for blacks. "The meager prejudice compared to some states, and opportunity to acquire wealth, all conspire to make it inviting to the colored man," said Bishop Henry Turner of the African Methodist Episcopal Church. "This is the state for colored men who wish to live by their merits."

The West Ninth Street neighborhood, which had originated as a log shantytown constructed by the Union Army in 1864 to house freed slaves, was the heart of this colored man's El Dorado. In the 1880s, one could find here the stirrings of a black middle class. There were black-owned groceries, clothing stores, and restaurants along West Ninth, and black tailors and barbers provided services here too. Bethel African Methodist Episcopal Church anchored one corner of Broadway and West Ninth, and across from it were the offices of the Mosaic Templars, which was destined to become one of the most successful black-owned businesses in the country. Two men who'd been born slaves, John Bush and Chester Keatts, had founded the lodge in 1882 in order to provide burial insurance to blacks, and within a few years the lodge was also operating a moneylending association that helped blacks purchase their own homes. Bush and Keatts and other prosperous blacks built fashionable houses in an area southwest of Broadway and West Ninth, creating what came to be known as the Dunbar neighborhood. The Methodists established

Philander Smith College in this neighborhood, the school providing instruction for all ages, including college classes.

This was the world of opportunity now at Scipio's doorstep. Little Rock offered him the chance to reinvent himself, and perhaps because he was embarrassed by the thought of entering Philander Smith's college preparatory course at such a relatively late age (twenty or so), he began this process of reinvention by shaving five years off his birthday, telling people he'd been born on August 7, 1868. While Scipio apparently received some money from Sanford Reamey to help with his schooling, he was still just a poor migrant from the country, and there were times, during his first years in Little Rock, that he was nearly homeless. "We slept on pool tables many a time when we didn't have no other place to sleep," recalled R. B. Anderson, his friend at the time. "He was poor when he was a boy and glad to get hold of a dime or a nickel."

Scipio took only three years, instead of the usual four, to finish the college preparatory course, and in 1885, he began teaching school in Sweet Home, five miles to the south of Little Rock, earning $50 a month. For the next two years, he also took classes at Shorter College in North Little Rock, graduating in 1887. Teaching was a well-respected career, but Scipio had his sights set on becoming an attorney, and that same year he applied to the law department at the University of Arkansas. This was his first show of civil rights bravado, as there were no black students at the university. After being summarily turned down, he volunteered to work for free as a janitor, thinking that such proximity to the law classes might enable him to "pick up crumbs of learning." When the university said no to that, he knocked on the office door of three prominent Little Rock attorneys and asked if he could read for the law under their tutelage. This was an outrageous request, as white lawyers were not at all inclined to mentor a young black man in the law, and yet Scipio's charm and evident intelligence won them over. "He was exceptionally friendly, very polite and courteous, very astute," recalled his friend Louis Tarlowski. Scipio passed his oral bar exams before a trio of white attorneys on June 15, 1889.

At that moment, Scipio Jones could look back and see in his own experience that America could be a land of opportunity. In less than a decade, he'd made the leap from cotton picker to educated professional. While there were a handful of other black attorneys in the city, most were men who'd been free before the war and had migrated here, or men who were the sons of white fathers who'd paid for them to be educated at a Northern law school that accepted black students. But Scipio—like Chester Keatts and John Bush—had pulled himself up by his own bootstraps. He had reason to love Little Rock and the great state of Arkansas, and also reason to love, as he would often say, this "great nation of ours."

Attorney Jones soon married twenty-year-old Carrie Edwards, and in 1891, they had a daughter, Hazel. Four years later, Bush and Keatts asked Jones to be the Mosaic Templars' national attorney. Scipio, they reasoned, approached the law "devoid of any mercenary motives, but inspired with an exalted ideal of service to his fellow man." Jones was now on his way to becoming the most prominent Negro attorney in Arkansas, having linked up with two other self-made men who, like himself, were imbued with a spirit of optimism and a desire, as they often said, "to lift up their race."

SCIPIO JONES ENTERED THIS world of black leadership at the very moment that whites in Arkansas—and the rest of the South—began setting up their Jim Crow society. Arkansas passed literacy and poll tax laws in 1891 and 1892 to disenfranchise blacks, and it segregated its railroad cars and waiting rooms at the same time. In 1900, gubernatorial candidate Jeff Davis made white supremacy the center of his campaign, calling a black who voted an "ever-present eating, cantankerous sore." He publicly embraced lynching, boasting that in his state, "when we have no doubt about a Negro's guilt, we do not give him a trial, we mob him and that ends it." Arkansas, which during the 1870s and 1880s had been heralded as a "promised land" for blacks, turned into a lyncher's paradise. It was here in 1892 that Edward Coy was roasted alive, and from 1889 to

1918, 182 blacks were strung up by white Arkansans, with none of the perpetrators ever sent to jail.

At a national level, Booker T. Washington and W. E. B. Du Bois offered conflicting visions for how blacks should respond to Jim Crow and this flowering of white-supremacist law. Washington advised blacks to be patient, to accept segregation and loss of voting rights for the moment, and instead prove themselves worthy of citizenship by becoming better educated and by prospering economically. His National Negro Business League encouraged blacks to raise themselves up by owning stores and shops. Black leaders, he advised, should cultivate good relations with white leaders. However, Du Bois denounced Washington's accommodationist policies, thundering that "manly self-respect is worth more than lands and houses, and that a people who surrender voluntarily such respect, or cease striving for it, are not worth civilizing." Those two responses seemed diametrically opposed, and yet Scipio Jones—and this was the curious part of the man—personally adopted both.

Bush, Keatts, and Jones all saw their Mosaic Templars fraternal order as the embodiment of Washington's ideals. Their organization came to publish a weekly paper, operate a hospital and a school for nurses, and provide clerical jobs to hundreds of black women. By 1917, it had eighty thousand members and more than two thousand lodges operating in twenty-six states, Central America, and the West Indies. Bush, Keatts, and Jones all became personal friends of Booker T. Washington, Jones serving on the executive committee of his National Negro Business League. In 1909, Jones helped organize the National Negro Bar Association as an auxiliary to the business league.

Jones prospered on a personal level as well. By 1907, he lived in a comfortable house in the Dunbar neighborhood and owned ten or so other houses and lots, his net worth estimated to be between $15,000 and $20,000. At some point, he became wealthy enough to have a live-in housekeeper and travel around town in a chauffeured Cadillac. He also was tireless in his efforts to build up Little Rock's black community: he served as the attorney for at least six fraternal organizations, raised funds for United Charities, helped found a home for the elderly and orphans, and was a trustee at both Shorter College and Bethel A.M.E. Church, where he also directed the Sunday school. In 1907, he told the editor of a Negro society book that his "highest ambition" was to remain in Arkansas, practice law, help the members of his race better themselves, and "assist in establishing and maintaining a friendly relation between the races." He had closely followed the Booker T. Washington philosophy and achieved success.

Yet, in politics and in the courtroom, Jones waged the battles that Du Bois urged. This part of his career began in 1891, when he and another black attorney, John Hibbler, joined forces to try to defeat the railroad segregation law. They lost, of course, but Jones emerged from the struggle as a leader in the black wing of the state's Republican party, and when lily-whitism reared its ugly head in the party during the 1890s (the lily-whites argued that since Jim Crow laws disenfranchised most black voters, it was a mistake for the party to continue agitating for black rights), Jones began a lifelong career of fighting that evil. In 1900, he organized a separate slate of black delegates from Pulaski County to the state Republican convention. Two years later, he created the Independent Political League, which fielded black candidates for all county offices. He personally ran for the Little Rock school board in 1903, and while he was crushed, the vote tally was beside the point. By running for office, he and other blacks were refusing to retreat from the political arena, as the lily-white Republicans and Democrats would have preferred. In 1908, Jones joined forces with a handful of white Republicans who'd remained true to the party's abolitionist roots, most notably William Whipple and Ulysses Bratton, and together this "black and tan" faction successfully elected Jones as Pulaski County's delegate to the Republican National Convention. On and on his fights with the lily-whites went: in 1916, when the lily-whites in Pulaski County prevented blacks from participating in the Republican convention by holding it in a segregated hotel, Jones responded with a blistering speech to the Black Republican League, urging them to deliver a "death blow" to the "contemptible lily whites" by voting against their candidates in an upcoming election. "Win a glorious victory for Negro manhood, Negro honor, Negro representation and true Republicanism!" he shouted.

Jones's most notable political triumph occurred in 1911. That year, the Democrats proposed a "grandfather clause" amendment to Arkansas's state constitution. Jones and a small number of blacks were still voting, and this amendment, said Governor George Donaghey, was designed "to eliminate the Negro from politics."* Jones organized a state suffrage league to oppose it, and his group rallied blacks to pay their poll taxes and also cultivated enough white support that they sent the proposal down—as Jones rejoiced—to a "crushing defeat."

Jones's career in the courtroom was of the same bold stripe. During this period, 1890 to 1919, most black attorneys in Little Rock resigned themselves to non-trial work, as they were not particularly welcome in the courtroom. In some Arkansas counties, it was an unwritten rule that a black lawyer could appear before the bench only if accompanied by a white attorney, and in criminal proceedings, any black defendant with money typically hired a white lawyer, as he reasoned it was the only hope he had of getting anything close to a fair shake. Black attorneys mostly prepared contracts and wills, arranged adoptions, and filed civil lawsuits between black parties. Jones accepted none of those limitations. He turned himself into an accomplished trial attorney who did not hesitate to appeal a lower court's decision to the Arkansas Supreme Court. He was the first black attorney in the state to create such an appellate record, and by 1919 he had argued before the state's highest court seventeen times, with a record on appeal of eight wins, eight losses, and a tie.

His style in the courtroom, at least during criminal trials, was admittedly pure Booker T. Washington. He would be "humble in

---

* The proposed amendment stiffened literacy requirements for voting but exempted all descendants of those who could vote before 1865—in other words, whites—from the onerous requirements.

appearing before white juries trying black clients," explained his friend Louis Tarlowski. Jones, said J. H. Carmichael, dean of the University of Arkansas Law School, always conducted "himself in such a way as not to offend the sensibilities of the white jurors, the white judges, and the white attorneys appearing in the cases." Yet, behind this aw-shucks exterior, Jones's keen mind was always at work, "his vigilant eye detecting every silent movement of the most sagacious opposing counselor," wrote one courtroom observer. Circuit court judge Robert Lea thought that he was "the finest cross-examiner of Negro witnesses" of any attorney he'd ever had in his courtroom. Jones even won his share of criminal cases, at least when his client was on trial for a relatively minor offense. "Scipio," said Reverend Joseph Crenchaw, "could get them released in a way nobody else could do."

In 1901, Jones became the first attorney in Arkansas to argue that a criminal conviction of a black defendant should be overturned because of the exclusion of blacks from the grand and petit juries. This, Jones told the Arkansas Supreme Court, violated his client's Fourteenth Amendment right to due process. He lost that case *(Eastling v. State),* but it was an argument that he continued to revisit during his career. And in many other legal battles, he emerged victorious. He successfully sued a planter in federal court for abusing the convicts leased to him by the state; he bested the Arkansas State Insurance Commission when it sought to put the Negro Grand Lodge of the Arkansas Knights of Pythias out of business; and he successfully defended black Shriners in a suit in which white Shriners tried to prevent them from using the Shriners name.

All of this made Jones a hero to blacks in Little Rock and Arkansas. "It is hard to find language and thought sufficient to do justice to the ability and record of this brilliant and talented young lawyer," wrote D. B. Gaines in his 1898 book *Racial Possibilities as Indicated by the Negroes of Arkansas.* The *Blue Book of Little Rock* in 1907 called Jones the most "successful and unpretentious jurist of African descent in the state." A number of parents named their children after Scipio and held him up as a role model. "He was an inspiration, even to the little children," remembered William Pickens, who had grown up in Arkansas and in 1919 was dean of Morgan College in Baltimore. "Our sister, then a tiny girl, used to take her position in the middle of the floor, raise her hands forensically, use big and solemn words, and conclude by exclaiming, 'I'm Scipio Jones!' "

Jones's success did bring a few white barbs his way. Governor Davis once derided him as that "Nigger lawyer, an insignificant personage," and the *Arkansas Democrat* regularly baited him, writing in 1906 that he handled a lot of divorce cases, evidence that he "had nothing else better to do." In 1909, the *Arkansas Gazette* ran a front-page article titled "Scipio Jones Buys a Mule," the article mocking him for allegedly failing to notice—unlike everybody else at the auction—that the animal's front legs were crippled. Apparently the great Negro lawyer didn't have the intelligence to do so, the paper gleefully reporting that Jones was now the "sad possessor of a perfectly wuthless animule." But Jones shrugged off such attacks. He had many white friends, and he was so comfortable with municipal court judge Will Sheppard that after Arkansas passed its Bone Dry Law in 1917, he discreetly left "four quarts of 18-year-old whiskey" in a desk drawer for Sheppard, who had an admitted fondness for such drink. "This," Sheppard later laughed, "had some influence upon me when Scipio had a client in my court." And in 1916, white attorneys in Little Rock showed their respect for Jones in a novel manner. A municipal court judge, Fred Isgrig, had to recuse himself from a case involving two Negro parties, and the attorneys in the court that day, required by law to select one of their own to serve in his stead, unanimously picked Jones. That meant that suddenly there was the spectacle of a Negro *presiding* over the court, and it so outraged a visiting Mississippi lawyer that he came to blows with city attorney Harry Hale, who had nominated Jones for the job. "I suppose all the white lawyers thought as I did," Isgrig explained to newspaper reporters. This was done "in recognition of [Jones's] reputation and standing in the community and in the bar of Little Rock."

After that day, Jones became known to all of his friends, black and white, as "Judge Jones." Many whites—aware that they could never call him Mr. Jones, as that was too great a breach of protocol—were grateful to have a moniker they could use to show their respect. Jones's election to his one-day stint as a judge, said one black newspaper, proved that "there are white men in Little Rock who will recognize a man for his character, worth and ability rather than for his color."

Jones's wife, Carrie, died young, sometime between 1907 and 1910, and in 1917, he married Lillie Jackson, from Pine Bluff. He visited Tulip twice a year, where Jemmima and Horace continued to live, neither of them ever having learned to read. This was an ongoing part of his world too, and University of Arkansas Law School dean J. H. Carmichael saw this firsthand on a train trip that he and Jones took together to Texas: while Carmichael traveled in a sleeper, Jones "had only a chair and a pillow during the night, and, of course, slept very little." Although it would have been impossible for Jones to obtain sleeper accommodations, as they were reserved for whites, he might have negotiated something more comfortable than a chair and a pillow. "He said that he didn't want to have any privileges above his own people," Carmichael explained, "and wanted to meet them on a common ground."

THE FIRST PUBLIC RESPONSE by Jones and other black leaders in Little Rock to the "Elaine riots" was, at first glance, rather baffling. After the *Chicago Defender* and the NAACP published their reports on the "massacre" that so infuriated Governor Brough, Jones, Bishop J. M. Conner of Bethel A.M.E. Church, and others jumped to the governor's defense. "You put down the riot, you stopped the mob, you restored order, thus saving many lives in both races and much destruction of property," they wrote in a letter that Brough quickly made public. "We know what you have done and wish to again assure you that the best colored people of the state of Arkansas endorse your stand and stand shoulder to shoulder with you in all things that tend to bring peace and good will between the races and for the uplift of Arkansas."

Not surprisingly, many blacks in Little Rock felt—as Little Rock resident Gwendolyn Floyd said—"betrayed" by this letter. It seemed that even Scipio Jones, the attorney who had always fought for black rights, had sided this time "with the whites." But Jones and the other men had their reasons, both sincere and political, for writing it. At that time Arkansas newspapers were still reporting that only a few blacks had been killed after Brough and the federal troops arrived. The shoot-to-kill orders apparently had not led to any great number of additional deaths. The troops had also prevented a lynch mob from storming the county jail on Thursday, October 2, and so, based on that information, it did seem that Brough and the federal troops had "stopped the mob." Furthermore, Jones and other black leaders knew that in the weeks and months ahead, as they moved to help the hundreds of imprisoned Elaine sharecroppers, it would not serve anyone to alienate Governor Brough, given that he had the power to issue pardons.

A few days after the Helena trials ended, Jones, Conner, and three black attorneys—John Hibbler, Thomas Price, and Joseph R. Booker—quietly met to form a defense committee for the sharecroppers. Price's presence made for a delicate situation for them all: a former law partner of Jones, he'd served as an attorney to the Progressive Farmers and Household Union, Hill even having written to him on October 27 from his hideout in Boley, Oklahoma. If Price's participation in this fledgling defense effort became known, the public might conclude that they—like Ulysses Bratton—had been involved with the union prior to the "insurrection."

"Scipio," Conner said, "you take charge of the case. Employ whatever other counsel that will be needed."

All three attorneys knew what Conner meant by that: there would have to be a front man for the appeal, a white lawyer who, simply by agreeing to take on the case, would lend it some legitimacy. Ideally, that would mean finding a Democrat who was nevertheless sympathetic to the Negro cause, and those requirements quickly narrowed Jones's list of candidates to one: Colonel George W. Murphy.

Jones and Murphy had known each other for more than twenty years and had squared off in the courtroom several times between 1901 and 1905, when Murphy had been state attorney general. Jones, in fact, had bested him once or twice in appeals to the Arkansas Supreme Court. Murphy's credentials for the job at hand—an attorney who was a member of Arkansas's ruling class, known to all as a perfect Southern gentleman—were impeccable. Born in Tennessee in 1841, Murphy had been wounded twice during the Civil War, at the battles of Shiloh and Murfreesboro. With his gimpy leg, droopy gray moustache, and sleepy eyes, Murphy looked the ex-Confederate as much as Greenfield Quarles did, and the colonel was known, one courtroom observer said, "to exaggerate his limp to gain sympathy for his clients." Although he was a Democrat, he believed that the law should strive to be fair.

Jones and the others kept quiet about their plans while the Elaine sharecroppers were locked up in Phillips County, fearful that if whites in Helena discovered that black attorneys in Little Rock intended to mount an appeal, a mob might storm the jail and the black farmers would "suffer bodily harm," Hibbler said. They quickly raised $1,500 among themselves as seed money for the defense fund, with the understanding that Jones and Murphy together would be paid a total of $12,000. On the very day that the prisoners were transferred to Cummins Farm and The Walls, they began their fundraising, firing off letters to Robert Church and other black leaders in the South. On November 26, Price wrote to Walter White:

Mr. Scipio A. Jones and myself are attempting to do what we can to save those 12 unfortunate Negroes convicted at Elaine from the chair. . . . We plan to lay the foundation to carry the cases to the United States Supreme Court if need be. We are now engaged in making up a record of all 12 cases. This work is very expensive and we need money, as all this work must be done rapidly in view of the time set for the executions. The firm of Murphy & McHaney [white] are in the case with the understanding that a fee can be raised. Both are Democrats and have only stood square on the Negro. We need about $10,000. Can your society assist? Any substantial amount will help. Please be confidential, give the matter no publicity for the present until the work is well under way and we get the time for the executions stayed.

That, surprisingly enough, was not a letter the NAACP was happy to receive.

The Constitutional Rights of a Race

WHILE JONES AND HIS group in Little Rock may have been content to work quietly as they laid plans to save the twelve condemned men, that was not true of blacks nationwide. The guilty verdicts provoked a storm of protest in the Negro press and from various black organizations, including the NAACP, and although this national pressure was surely appreciated by Jones and the others, it briefly complicated their efforts to get an appeal under way.

Blacks, of course, saw the trials as part of a larger history, and their bitterness was palpable. "If there is one infamy more damning than another," editorialized the *Baltimore Daily Herald,* "it is the infamy of the Elaine trials in excess of the infamy of the Elaine butchery of Negroes." The *New York Age* denounced the trials as nothing more than a "judicial lynching, equivalent to cold-blooded murder," while *Favorite* magazine called the Helena juries "enemies of humanity." Meanwhile, the *Crusader* reasoned that "the contemplated murder of these men constitute the most brutal notice the Negro has yet had from the American dominant race that democracy or even simple justice is not for him." The magazine asked its readers: "To this brutal notice, what answer will the Negro make?"

In Chicago, Ida B. Wells-Barnett, the great anti-lynching crusader, stirred blacks to immediate action. Three groups—the Equal Rights League, the People's Movement, and the Negro Fellowship League—warned Governor Brough, by letter, that if the men were electrocuted, they "would immediately take steps to see that thousands more of our people who had enriched the South by their labor would leave Arkansas, never to return." Blacks in Boston similarly petitioned Brough to pardon the men, writing that "their only crime was defending their property and their manhood rights." The *Messenger* editorialized that "nationwide protests should be held" in order to "save the lives of these men," and across the country, a number of blacks mailed Brough angry letters, with a few anonymous ones threatening that he would be "assassinated" and "Helena burned" if he went ahead with the executions.

Although the published articles and protest meetings served as a powerful national cry for racial justice, they did not have the desired effect on Governor Brough. "I was on the ground during that insurrection and I know what transpired, and I am therefore a better judge of the situation than somebody in New York," he told reporters on November 15. "Some of those negroes I know deserved electrocution and this office will not interfere with the decisions of a court that knows what it is about and is dispensing justice." If anything, Brough now seemed intent on rushing the executions so that no appellate review could be had. However, blacks in Arkansas were also up in arms, and on November 24, Brough organized an interracial conference in Little Rock to try to defuse racial tensions, and at the end of the day the conference delegates, in response to a motion by Bishop Conner and others, passed a resolution expressing their "willingness" to have the trials reviewed by the Arkansas Supreme Court. The governor was asked to sign off on that resolution, and it was easy, at that moment, to see the political foresight that Jones, Conner, and others had shown in their October 19 letter to the governor. They had praised Brough for being a leader who fostered goodwill between the races, and now he had to play the part, the governor grudgingly agreeing to stay the electrocutions so there would "be no doubt as to [the sharecroppers'] guilt."

Little Rock's black leaders had things under control. There was now time for an appeal to be perfected, and they would soon officially organize a Citizens Defense Fund Commission to raise the full $12,000 needed to fund this effort. And that's where things stood when Thomas Price received a reply, quite curious in kind, from Walter White. "I have your letter of November 26th and beg to advise that we are now in the process of arranging for defense for the twelve men now under sentence of death as well as of those who are in jail. I shall write you in a day or two giving you in detail the facts regarding this defense."

IN ITS TEN-YEAR HISTORY, the NAACP had never tried to help criminal defendants at this early stage of the appeals process, when the case was still solely in the hands of state courts. The organization, which had only a handful of employees and constantly struggled with its finances, was primarily devoted to publicizing all the ways that American society unjustly treated blacks, with the hope that such publicity (and its own lobbying in Congress) would spur change. However, Ulysses Bratton had suddenly shown up at the NAACP's Manhattan office on October 30, and he had his own ideas about what the NAACP should do in this case.

Like White and other NAACP leaders, Bratton wanted Congress to launch an investigation of the riot, and the very next day, October 31, he and White traveled to Washington, D.C., to meet with members of Congress and Frank Burke at the Justice Department. Both Kansas senator Charles Curtis and Missouri representative Leonidas Dyer, who were leading the effort within Congress to make lynching a federal crime, said they were "thoroughly astonished" by what Bratton told them about peonage and the riot, and promised they would seek congressional hearings. Even more encouraging, Burke confessed that the Justice Department's own "investigation showed no grounds for belief that any massacre of whites was planned." As White later explained to the NAACP's board, Burke understood that the union "sought through legal means to test the methods by which landowners, their agents and merchants exploited Negro sharecroppers."

After he and White returned to New York, Bratton laid out for the NAACP the second part of his agenda. Once the trials in Helena were over, he wanted the NAACP to "secure counsel for the colored people." This was a case that would put the entire American justice system under a national microscope, he said, and the NAACP board was immediately intrigued. Bratton "is a man of attractive personality who tells a wonderful story of the Negro's wrong," said board chairwoman Mary White Ovington, and over the course of the next two weeks, she had Bratton speak at several parlor meetings for NAACP supporters in New York and Boston. "We have never yet, and we have known of many terrible happenings North and South, been so impressed with the unjust methods practiced against the Negro as in this case," Ovington said.

The NAACP's decision on whether to fund an appeal was soon given a push by Congress and the Justice Department. Curtis reported that he could not get the Senate Judiciary Committee interested in holding hearings on the Arkansas "riot," and on November 16, the NAACP learned that the House wasn't interested either. Next, the Justice Department informed the NAACP that it would not be making any public statements about the case because its investigation had "not yet been completed." The federal government was simply turning its back on the entire affair, and it was at that gloomy moment, when the NAACP knew that it had to do *something,* that Bratton reported that he had found the perfect lawyer for the NAACP to hire: Colonel George Murphy. "He is one of the most courageous and noble men I have ever known," he said.

On November 24, the NAACP board took the leap. Murphy would be paid $3,000 to represent all of the imprisoned sharecroppers and to appeal the death sentences of the twelve condemned men, with the understanding that there would be an additional fee if the cases ever made it to the U.S. Supreme Court. "There would have been no probing into the Arkansas situation and no effort made to save the lives of these twelve men if we had not been fortunate enough to come in contact with a white lawyer of Little Rock," Ovington confided to a friend.

Ovington took charge of the fund-raising effort, which was made difficult by the fact that the NAACP knew that it had to keep its involvement secret. "It would queer the case if a northern organization was known to be financing it," she wrote in one of her letters. Meanwhile, White worried that if Arkansans learned that Bratton had urged the NAACP to take this step, there would be the "very grave danger of Mr. Bratton being subjected to mob violence." Ovington and other NAACP officers quietly solicited donations from wealthy individuals who'd supported the NAACP in the past, most notably Julius Rosenwald, president of Sears & Roebuck, and asked that every NAACP branch contribute at least $10 to the defense fund. The $3,000 was quickly raised, with branches quietly praising the NAACP for this "noble work."

THE FACT THAT BOTH the NAACP and Jones's group in Little Rock had stepped forward to represent the twelve condemned men, and had done so simultaneously, should not have been a problem. Once the NAACP received Price's letter requesting financial help, it was in a position—given that both groups had chosen the same *white* attorney—to easily resolve the confusion. The NAACP and the Arkansas group could work together to fund and mount an appeal. Yet the NAACP utterly bungled the situation, primarily because its leaders were burdened by their own stereotypes of Southern blacks as Uncle Toms. They simply didn't think that Thomas Price and Scipio Jones could possibly be up to the task. Privately, Ovington wondered whether the Little Rock blacks, given their evident friendliness with Governor Brough, might be "bootlickers," while board member John Milholland said that organizing one mass protest meeting "would do more to save these poor unfortunate men from death and imprisonment than all the local lawyers you can get together in a 10-acre lot." White revealed his feelings in a letter informing a friend that the NAACP had hired an attorney for the case: "A white one, of course," he said.

On December 2, NAACP field secretary James Weldon Johnson wrote board member Robert Church Jr. in Memphis, asking that he go to Little Rock and politely inform Price and Jones that they were to take a backseat to Murphy, or perhaps bow out of the case altogether. "We do not want Mr. Price to gum up the case," Johnson explained. "We do not know how good a lawyer he is. But if Colonel

Murphy wishes Price, or any other lawyer to associate with him in the case, that is all right with us. You can see that there is a possibility of some colored lawyers going off on a tangent to raise money and, of course, to figure in the cases, thereby messing up the whole matter. We want to avoid that just now."

Church, however, never passed on this message to Jones and Price, perhaps because it was so transparently insulting. Nor did the two men take to heart White's cryptic letter stating that the NAACP was going to take charge of the case. Jones and his group soldiered on unaware that the NAACP had hired Murphy, and for some reason, Murphy didn't inform Jones about this. The effort to save the twelve men was off to a rocky start, and ultimately this confusion would lead to a miswriting of the early history of the case by the NAACP, but it did not cause any real problems for Jones and Murphy, as they were quite clear about the division of labor. Jones would be the one to interview the sharecroppers, secure transcripts of the trial records, write at least the first drafts of the briefs, and file papers with the court. Murphy would speak to the press and step forward onstage during the courtroom proceedings. As Murphy confessed in early December to newspaper reporters: "I am not yet fully informed about the case." Attorney Jones, he added, "is making an effort to raise the necessary funds and gather such information as may be necessary to ask for an appeal."

In short, this was Jones's case. He would be the one doing all the heavy lifting, and during the first two weeks of December, he repeatedly visited Frank Moore and the other eleven men in the death house. The sharecroppers finally had someone to tell their story to— "I first told my lawyer, lawyer Jones, in the penitentiary at Little Rock how it was," said John Martin—and Jones quickly put together a motion for a new trial for each of the men.

The narrative that Jones wrote made for a compelling argument that the trials had been hideously unfair. He detailed how the imprisoned men had been tortured and whipped so that they would either confess or falsely testify against others; how they'd never been given an opportunity to consult with friends or seek counsel of their own before their trials; and how, at best, they'd been served with indictments on October 29, only five days before the trials. The twelve condemned men, Jones added, had "never been at a trial in court before and had no definite idea of their rights," and thus couldn't have been expected to raise timely protests to preserve those rights. Both Alf Banks and Will Wordlow provided affidavits describing the whippings and their utter lack of an opportunity to prepare a defense. Jones also noted that only whites had served on petit and grand juries in Phillips County for more than thirty years, and that the defendants' court-appointed attorneys hadn't sought a change of venue, allowing the trials to take place in a town where there was a decided "bitterness of feeling among the Whites against the Negroes." Nor had the defendants' attorneys ever consulted with them prior to their trials, and they had called no witnesses on their behalf. The twelve men condemned to die, Jones and Murphy concluded, had been deprived of "their rights under the Constitution, and especially the 14th Amendment," which promised all men "equal protection of the law."

On December 20, Judge Jackson denied the motions, but he gave the sharecroppers sixty days to perfect their appeals to the Arkansas Supreme Court. Within three weeks, Jones had completed this task, and he busily wrote to several of his more prominent friends, asking if they would contribute to the Citizens Defense Fund. "I would have written you sooner, but was waiting the results of my effort to perfect the appeal for the 12 condemned men before doing so," Jones told Monroe Work, a prominent scholar at Tuskegee Institute. "I succeeded at great expense in securing the records and yesterday the appeals were granted to the Supreme Court, which automatically stays execution until the cases are disposed of. . . . As the Constitutional rights of the race are involved I hope you will feel justified in assisting us to raise a reasonable defense fund. Anything you may be able to do along this line will be deeply appreciated by at least every Negro in Arkansas."

At last, the "most important case of its kind in the history of America," as the NAACP would come to call this appeal, had officially begun.

I Wring My Hands and Cry

WITH THE ELECTROCUTIONS HAVING been stayed, Frank Moore and the other condemned men settled into a daily routine at the state penitentiary, where, they said, they were treated well. Each morning, Joe Knox would lead them in prayer, and most afternoons they would gather and sing, mostly the old spirituals they'd always sung in church, although they also sang a tune newly composed by Ed Ware. "I Stand and Wring My Hands and Cry" told of the despair they'd felt in the Phillips County jail and still occasionally experienced, for they knew that if the Arkansas Supreme Court upheld their convictions, it was almost certain that they would be put to death.

They were, in almost every way, an ordinary group of men. Will Wordlow and Joe Fox were the youngest at twenty-two years of age, and of course Ed Coleman at seventy-eight was the oldest—he, in fact, was the oldest man ever to have been on Arkansas's death row—and most of the others were in their thirties or forties. Nine of the men were married and many had children—Ed Hicks and his wife, Arreita, had three girls; John Martin and his wife, Edna, had three boys and two girls; Joe Knox and his wife, Katie, had one boy and two girls. Coleman was a grandfather several times over. Nearly all of the men belonged to a Baptist or Methodist church, six were literate, and none had been in trouble before. Their penitentiary admission forms, which listed their height, weight, and age, and provided such personal details as scars and missing teeth, noted that the men had "no previous convictions."

Jones and the Citizens Defense Fund Commission had provided funds for their families to move to Little Rock, and so at least their wives were now nearby. The story these women told, Bratton informed the NAACP, "was heart rending to say the least. All relatives claim to be completely stranded and their part of crops taken from them." Every Sunday, the women would come to the penitentiary to visit their husbands, and on one such occasion they brought a copy of the December 13 edition of the *Chicago Defender,* which contained a story detailing how Ida B. Wells-Barnett had championed their cause before a rally in Chicago of more than a thousand people. "The principle at stake," she said, "involves every one of us—the right to organize for our own protection."

This outpouring of support was heartening news, and on December 30, Ed Ware wrote Wells-Barnett a letter:

> This is one of the 12 mens which is sentenced to death speaking to you on this day and thanking you for your great speach you made throughout the country in the Chicago Defender paper. So I am thanking you to the very highest and hope you will do all you can for your collord race. Because we are innercent men, we was not handle with justice at all in Phillips County court. It is prejidice that the white people had agence we Negroes. So I thank God that thro you, our Negroes are looking into this truble, and thank the city of Chicago for what it did to start things and hopen to hear from you all soon . . . So, I will close with much love from all to Chicago, Ill. Please pray for us. I am a Christian man. Please Chicago, let us hear from you at enny time.

A few weeks later, Frank Moore's wife, Mary, arrived at the state prison accompanied by a short black woman, her gray hair bundled atop her head, and as they neared the two death house cells, Mrs. Moore said quite loudly: "Boys, come and shake hands with my cousin who has come from St. Louis to see me." The guard, who was sitting fifty feet away, briefly looked up from his Sunday paper and then went back to his reading, and once he had, Mary Moore put her finger to her lips and whispered to the men: "This is Mrs. Barnett from Chicago."

Their eyes, Wells-Barnett recalled later, lit up. And then, as she extended her arm through the bars and shook hands with each of the men, "an expression of joy spread over their faces."

This was the first time that Wells-Barnett had traveled to her native South in nearly thirty years. In 1892, after she published a scathing account of a Memphis lynching in a small newspaper she co-owned, the *Free Speech and Headlight,* a mob burned her press and threatened to lynch her too, if only she could be found. She was traveling in the North when the article appeared, and so she simply never returned to Memphis, and she had not dared to venture into the South again until this moment. "I made myself look as inconspicuous as possible, and thus had no trouble whatsoever in gaining entrance to the prison," she said.

With a guard so close by, Wells-Barnett turned her chair so that her back was to him. One by one each of the sharecroppers drew near and whispered his story, Wells-Barnett scribbling notes on a small pad of paper. They told her how many acres they'd been working and how many chickens and hogs they'd owned, and they described how the planters had shot up their church, and how, the next day, posses had descended upon them with a fury. It took Wells-Barnett a couple of hours to complete her interviews, and as she put away her notepad, Mary Moore said: "Boys, don't you want to sing for my cousin?"

The men formed a semicircle, and after Ed Ware hummed a note so they could harmonize their voices, they launched into the song he'd composed:

I used to have some loving friends to walk and talk with me
But now I am in trouble, they have turned their backs on me
They just laugh me to scorn and will not come nigh
And I just stand and wring my hands and cry.

Then came the chorus:

> And I just stand and wring my hands and cry,
> And I just stand and wring my hands and cry, Oh Lord!
> Sometimes I feel like I ain't got no friends at all
> And I just stand and wring my hands and cry.

Ware had composed a number of refrains for this lonely song, and so they sang for some time until they came to the final one:

> My heart is overwhelmed with sorrow
> My eyes are melted down in tears
> But I have called to the God of Heaven,
> And I know He always hears.

"They sang in the most mournful tones ever heard," Wells-Barnett said, their song so haunting that the guard put down his paper and turned toward the men. Soon even the warden, John Burkett, appeared. He and his wife had been entertaining guests when this heartbreaking sound reached their dinner table, and now they had all come to the death house to hear some more. For the next hour, the twelve men "sang and prayed together and were so grateful to the warden for his kind treatment of them," Wells-Barnett wrote. "They exhorted each other to be faithful to the end, expressed their innocence of wrongdoing and readiness to die if it was God's will they should do so."

As she took her leave, Wells-Barnett told the men to have faith: "I have been listening to you for nearly two hours. You have talked and sung and prayed about dying, and forgiving your enemies, and of feeling sure that you are going to be received in the New Jerusalem because your God knows that you are innocent of the offense for which you expect to be electrocuted. But why don't you pray to live and ask to be freed? The God you serve is the God of Paul and Silas who opened their prison gates, and if you have all the faith you say you have, you ought to believe that He will open your prison doors too. If you do believe that, let all your songs and prayers hereafter be songs of faith and hope that God will set you free; that the judges who have to pass on your cases will be given the wisdom and courage to decide in your behalf. . . . Pray to live and believe you are going to get out."

During her time in Little Rock, Wells-Barnett obtained copies of the trial transcripts and other documents from Jones. "He was extremely kind and generous in assisting me," she wrote in a short article published in the *Chicago Defender.* Wells-Barnett also raised money to print a 62-page pamphlet titled *The Arkansas Race Riot.* Hers was the only piece of journalism ever published that told about the personal lives of the sharecroppers and provided their eyewitness accounts of the Hoop Spur shootout, but it attracted no attention in the nation's newspapers, and thus their stories remained quite unheard.

BEFORE HE WROTE THE briefs for the appeals, Jones decided that he should go to Helena, as he wanted to interview some of the Hoop Spur women who were still there, and naturally he wondered whether he could do this safely. Other blacks had decided that it could not be done. Monroe Work, who had traveled to Arkansas in early January at the NAACP's request and met with the prisoners at The Walls, reported that it was "unsafe to visit" Phillips County. Jones, however, confronted this problem in his usual straightforward manner: he spoke to Sheriff Kitchens and had him promise that he "would be protected" while he was in Helena, and soon Bratton told the NAACP that Jones had "mingled freely with the people and claims to have gained all information desired."

This was encouraging, and upon his return to Little Rock, Jones wrote to Work. "We are hard at work on the briefs and hope to have them ready for the printer in the next ten days," he said, adding that "some of the condemned men asked me the other day when I was at penitentiary what I had learned from you and to request you not to forget them." Jones was always the optimist, and this sentiment, via letters written by Bratton, filtered back to the NAACP in New York.

"The report from Arkansas is quite wonderful," Ovington told a friend. "It seems strange to speak of being encouraged when conditions are so terrible, but it looks as though we might get really extraordinary results from these Elaine cases, and if we can get the facts not only before this country but before the world, we may hope for some improvement."

Yet such hope rose from the heart, not the head, and Jones knew this better than anyone. The truth was that the chance of getting these verdicts overturned was a long shot at best. He and Murphy may have stated in their motions for new trials that their clients' constitutional rights had been violated, but that was a very problematic argument, for the Constitution, as interpreted by the U.S. Supreme Court, did not in fact guarantee a fair trial for criminal defendants tried in state courts, and that was particularly true if the defendants were black.

THE FIFTH AND SIXTH Amendments to the Constitution detail what James Madison and the other authors of the Bill of Rights thought were the essential elements of a fair trial. The Fifth requires those accused of a capital crime to be indicted by a grand jury, and states that the defendant cannot be required to testify against himself. The Sixth says that the accused shall enjoy a speedy and public trial by an impartial jury, and that he has the right to confront witnesses against him and call witnesses in his favor, and to have the assistance of counsel. In 1833, however, the U.S. Supreme Court ruled in *Barron v. Baltimore* that the Bill of Rights did not limit the states, and that meant that there was no federal guarantee of a fair trial. It was up to the states to protect the rights of the accused.

Ohio congressman John Bingham and the others who drafted the Fourteenth Amendment believed that they were fixing this defect in constitutional law. But then the Supreme Court, in its *Slaughterhouse* and *Cruikshank* decisions, decreed that it was the state, rather than the federal government, that was the guardian of a citizen's civil rights, and that precedent subsequently led the Court to rule, in *Hurtado v. California* (1884), that an indictment by a grand jury in a murder case was not necessary in a state criminal proceeding. "The 14th Amendment," the Court wrote, "does not profess to secure to all persons in the United States the benefit of the same laws and the same remedies. Great diversities in these respects may exist in two States separated only by an imaginary line. On one side of the line there may be a right of trial by jury, and on the other side no such right. Each State prescribes its own modes of judicial proceeding."

With this decision, the U.S. Supreme Court had revived the *Barron v. Baltimore* precedent. The Bill of Rights did not limit the states, and in a number of subsequent rulings the Court reiterated that point. In *Maxwell v. Dow* (1900), it determined that trial by a twelve-person jury was not, in fact, a federally guaranteed right. In *West v. Louisiana* (1904), the Court wrote that "the Sixth Amendment does not apply to proceedings in state courts," and thus a defendant did not necessarily have the right to confront witnesses. And in *Twining v. New Jersey* (1908), the Court ruled that if a defendant refused to take the stand, the jury could take that as evidence of his guilt.

The *Twining* decision gutted the Fifth Amendment's protection against self-incrimination, and when writing up the majority opinion, Justice William Moody reviewed the legal history that had brought the Court to this astonishing point. Moody acknowledged that in English law the right not to testify against oneself had long been regarded "as a privilege of great value, a protection to the innocent though a shelter to the guilty, and a safeguard against heedless, unfounded or tyrannical prosecutions." Moody also admitted that the Court's *Slaughterhouse* decision, which had so neutered the Fourteenth Amendment, "undoubtedly gave much less effect to the Fourteenth Amendment than some of the public men active in framing it intended." Nevertheless, he said, ever since the *Slaughterhouse* decision, "the distinction between National and state citizenship and their respective privileges there drawn has come to be firmly established," and as such, the "Fourteenth Amendment did not forbid the States to abridge the personal rights enumerated in the first eight Amendments." Finally—and this really was the bottom line—the federal courts were not to worry about whether state criminal proceedings were fair: "We are not invested with the jurisdiction to pass upon the expedience, wisdom or justice of the laws of the states as declared by their courts, but only to determine their conformity with the Federal Constitution."

Although most state constitutions guaranteed the due-process protections articulated in the Bill of Rights, state courts still needed to see to it that all citizens, both white and black, enjoyed those protections, and by and large, they had failed in that task. As a result, by 1920 the nation's criminal justice system had devolved to the point that it was anything but fair. Defendants were given little time to prepare a defense; poor defendants had no right to effective counsel; and police routinely beat defendants to coerce confessions, a practice known as giving them the third degree. Such tactics, the American Bar Association concluded around this time, were "in use almost everywhere" in the United States. In the South, police routinely whipped black defendants, and in Phillips County, the electric chair was at least somewhat frequently used. In 1929, after a black defendant in Helena complained that deputy sheriffs had strapped him into an electric chair and tortured him, the judge ordered the chair brought into the courtroom. County sheriff J. C. Barlow, when asked about its use, testified that he had "inherited" the chair "from a long line of former county sheriffs."

Yet, as unfair as the due-process abuses and coerced confessions were, the much bigger problem for black defendants in the South was the systematic exclusion of their peers from juries. This discriminatory practice ensured that they would be convicted if the alleged victims were white.

After the Civil War ended, blacks put the right to testify in court and the right to serve on juries at the top of their wish list, even above the right to vote, and the Radical Republicans in Congress agreed that such rights were essential. "Where would be the virtue of declaring that a colored man should have equal rights of trial by jury and equal rights of judgment by his peers, if you are to say that the jurors are to be composed of the Ku Klux?" asked Vermont Republican senator George Edmunds. "You are to put him into the hands of his enemies for trial."

The Fourteenth Amendment guaranteed the right of blacks to serve on juries, and the 1875 Civil Rights Law declared that any jury commissioner who discriminated against blacks was guilty of a misdemeanor and could be fined up to $5,000. And during the early 1870s, when Reconstruction governments were in power, blacks did serve on juries in many Southern states, and these mixed-race juries proved their merit. The presence of blacks on juries enabled federal prosecutors to convict more than seven hundred white terrorists, and modern research has shown that mixed-race juries in state criminal trials during this period handed down "remarkably similar sentences" to blacks and whites convicted of felonies. However, as Southern Democrats redeemed their states, they quickly moved to exclude blacks from the jury box. This was an essential component of white supremacy, and in 1880, the U.S. Supreme Court, in *Strauder v. West Virginia,* gave whites the okay to do just that. While the Court ruled that a state could not pass a law that explicitly barred Negroes from jury service, it could "prescribe the qualifications of its jurors, and in so doing make discriminations." The Court also happened to note that whites were a race with "superior intelligence," and Southern states did not have any difficulty deciphering the Court's message: they passed laws requiring jurors to be "honest and intelligent," with jury commissioners thus able to exclude all blacks because they theoretically lacked such qualifications.

The *Strauder* case—and subsequent decisions by the U.S. Supreme Court that further approved the use of such exclusionary "qualifications"—turned jury selection in Southern courtrooms into a wink-wink charade. If a black defendant challenged the absence of Negroes on a jury, the jury commissioner would be called into court to testify that the jury selection process wasn't race-based, but rather a process that placed only the names of male voters who were "honest and intelligent" into the jury box. Everyone in the courtroom, including the judge, would know that the jury commissioner was lying, but this was the charade that the U.S. Supreme Court had mandated, and it meant that perjury became an integral part of Southern justice.

The Supreme Court—and the rest of the country's legal establishment—also understood that this exclusion of Negroes from juries turned the Southern courtroom into an instrument of social control, rather than a forum where a semblance of justice might be had. "I have defended Negroes in Georgia, Alabama and Florida, and where a white man and a Negro are on opposite sides of a case in these states it is impossible for the Negro to get a fair trial," said John Cooper, a white Georgia lawyer, in 1916. "The Fourteenth Amendment was supposed to have been passed for the uplift of the Negro race, but it is used for the benefit of the railroads. The Negroes do not benefit by it." In 1918, a Mississippi lawyer spoke in an even blunter manner: "A Negro accused of a crime during the days of slavery was dealt with more justly than he is today."

Such was the system of "justice" that the U.S. Supreme Court had given its blessing to, and thus Jones had little reason to expect that the Arkansas Supreme Court would be sympathetic to the sharecroppers' appeals. All of the judges on the court were Democrats, which meant that they'd been elected by voters devoted to white supremacy. Jones, in fact, had lost all four murder cases he'd previously appealed to the Arkansas Supreme Court, and as he reviewed the transcripts from the Helena trials, he couldn't find any due-process errors that, as a matter of Arkansas law, would justify a reversal. Although a defendant in a capital case was supposed to be served with an indictment at least forty-eight hours before trial, once he appeared in court and announced through an attorney that he was "ready for trial," he was said to have waived that right. Similarly, while a defendant could challenge the exclusion of blacks from a jury, he needed to do it when the jury was selected. The Elaine sharecroppers had been assigned counsel, and it would be difficult to argue that John Moore and Greenfield Quarles—two Democrats known throughout the state—were not capable lawyers. The "confessions" too would stand up on appeal; Jones could see from the transcript that Moore and the other defense attorneys had made sure of that. Every time Sid Stoaks or one of the other Helena authorities had been called by the prosecution to testify to such a confession, one of the defense attorneys had jumped to his feet and asked whether the confession had been coerced. If Moore and Quarles had been interested in bringing out the fact that the sharecroppers had been tortured, they would have called them to the witness stand. Instead, their questions to Stoaks and the others were designed to elicit testimony that the confessions had been freely given.

The trials may have been hideously unfair, but they did not appear to have been conducted in a manner that violated Arkansas due-process standards. However, once Jones reviewed the *wording* of the verdicts, his spirits jumped. The six men who'd been convicted of killing Adkins or Tappan were almost certain to get new trials. In those cases, the juries had been in such a rush that they'd failed to state whether they were finding the defendants guilty of first-degree or second-degree murder, and Arkansas law required juries to make that distinction.

Jones had the briefs ready for the printers by the end of February. "Colonel Murphy," he advised the NAACP, "assisted" him with this work. The Arkansas Supreme Court set March 22 for oral arguments.

DURING THE EARLY PART of 1920, the NAACP continued to make this legal fight a celebrated cause. Du Bois wrote about it in the *Crisis,* while Walter White penned articles that appeared in the *Nation* and in the *Survey.* Several NAACP leaders also appeared before House and Senate committees that were considering making lynching a federal crime. This wasn't the congressional investigation of the Elaine riot they had wanted, but still, it gave them a forum for talking about it, and Ulysses Bratton joined them in their appearance before the Senate subcommittee, expounding on the evils of peonage. In their presentations, the NAACP officials put the massacre and farcical trials into a historical context: there was, they noted, the long history of exploiting black labor in the South, the long record of white violence against blacks going unpunished, and the many devastating Supreme Court decisions. "The Supreme Court," said NAACP board member Neval Thomas, "has always been able to sidestep an issue when it means justice to black men."

The NAACP representatives told a powerful story—the Arkansas trials were "one of the worst miscarriages of justice that has ever disgraced any civilized country in the world," Archibald Grimké told the House Judiciary Committee—and yet, after each appearance, they returned to New York disheartened. Only two members of the Senate subcommittee had even bothered to come hear them speak, while the House Judiciary Committee was mostly concerned about whether it could draft an anti-lynching bill that would be constitutional, and didn't find the massacre of black farmers in Arkansas particularly germane to that topic.

However, the newspaper reports of the two congressional hearings, along with the continued outcry in the black press about the "Elaine massacre" and the "judicial lynchings," did produce a subtle shift in the white narrative of the "riot." The basic story that had been told up to that point was that white posses, in the first two days, had killed a dozen or so blacks, and that the Camp Pike troops had then restored order without any further great loss of life. But the black press and the NAACP were now telling of how white mobs had killed scores of blacks, and that of course raised the question of why they had not been prosecuted. The shift in the narrative took care of that question. "The killing of Negroes that followed [the insurrection] was not a lynching and not the result of a mob, but was done very largely by soldiers of the United States under the command of their officers and in obedience to orders issued by the War Department," said Arkansas congressman Thaddeus Caraway, who was a member of the House Judiciary Committee. "To call that a mob is such a perversion of the truth that one can have but little choice in language in which to denounce it." This theme was soon repeated by Arkansas attorney general John Arbuckle—"The colored people that were killed in the Elaine riot were killed by the soldiers," he said—and finally the *Helena World* rewrote its own history of the "insurrection." In an article recapping the events of the previous October, it didn't mention anything about posses having killed any blacks, but said of the Camp Pike soldiers: "The troops used machine guns with telling effect, sweeping the canebrakes and clearing them of insurrectionists. They were under order to shoot every Negro who failed to halt when ordered to do so, and they obeyed orders."

As could be expected, Bratton's appearance before the Senate subcommittee infuriated Governor Brough and Arkansas newspapers, as they insisted there was no peonage in their state, and public animosity toward Bratton flared up once more. There were new death threats, and finally Bratton and his family threw in the towel. "It has been made evident that unless conditions are remedied that one who dares to stand for the interests of the colored man can not afford to remain" in Arkansas, Bratton wrote on February 21 to Vermont senator William Dillingham, who earlier had listened to him speak about peonage. "I have given up the fight and located in St. Louis, but hope that some way may be found to correct those terrible conditions [in the Mississippi Delta], where hundreds of thousands of people are held in a condition of slavery."

THERE REMAINED, DURING THESE first months of 1920, much confusion in the minds of the NAACP leaders over the working relationship between Murphy and Jones, so much so that NAACP secretary John Shillady asked Monroe Work to please explain "just where Mr. Scipio A. Jones gets off at or comes in at, as the case may be." The organization was worried that the Arkansas blacks would claim "credit" if the appeals were successful, even though such claims might "not be justified." While Work quickly set the NAACP straight—"Mr. Jones is an able lawyer and is the heart and center of the defense," he replied rather testily—it became evident, in the aftermath of Robert Hill's arrest, that the NAACP and Jones had disparate aims and legal strategies.

Hill was arrested on January 21 at a restaurant in Topeka, Kansas, where he'd secretly gone to rendezvous with his wife. Arkansas authorities immediately asked Kansas governor Henry Allen to extradite him, a request that was usually granted by another state as a matter of course, but the NAACP, acting through attorneys in Topeka, asked him to deny it. Hill, the NAACP said, would probably be lynched if he were sent to Arkansas, and even if that didn't occur, he certainly couldn't expect a fair trial. When Allen agreed to investigate the matter, white Arkansans were of course outraged, and Brough turned to his Commission on Race Relations, which had formed in the wake of his interracial conference, for support. The commission assured Allen that the trial would be moved from Phillips County and that Hill would be given every opportunity to prove himself innocent, and what gave the letter such weight was that three of the commission's black members—Bishop Conner, J. M. Cox, president of Philander Smith College, and Joseph A. Booker, president of Arkansas Baptist College—had signed it.

These three men were raising money for the Citizens Defense Fund, and yet at first glimpse it seemed that they had utterly betrayed Hill, their actions the behavior of cowardly Uncle Toms. "Henceforth," the *Chicago Defender* wrote, "they should be shunned as a pestilence and hated as traitors of a type that would have made Benedict Arnold blush with shame." Even Bratton privately referred to Conner as a "Judas," a sentiment that summed up the thoughts of the NAACP leadership. William Pickens, who'd recently left Morgan College to work for the NAACP, told Conner: "You and I know that under present conditions there is small chance for Hill in an Arkansas court. These are no times for colored people to work at any cross purposes." But what none of the critics knew was that the three men had signed the letter only after consulting with Jones. And they all saw in Hill's extradition an *opportunity* to save the twelve condemned men.

In a February 13 reply to Pickens, Cox laid out their legal strategy:

Last Saturday [we] three Negroes who signed the petition held conferences with some of Little Rock's leading Negroes, and with just two exceptions, all approved our course. Attorney T. J. Price, who knows as much about Mr. Hill's order as any other man in the state and who is Mr. Hill's representative, thinks it best for him to return. Attorney S. A. Jones, who is making the appeal to the Supreme Court for a new trial for the condemned men, believes Hill should return. We all believe he will be acquitted. We all further believe that Hill's trial will do more than anything else to show the innocence of the other men.

This letter somewhat mollified the NAACP leaders in New York, and yet it was now clear that the two groups had different agendas. The NAACP saw this struggle for justice as part of its larger effort to reform the nation. If Governor Allen refused to extradite Hill, his decision could be seen as proof that blacks could not expect justice in Southern courts. Scipio Jones and his group had a more limited objective. They were focused first and foremost on simply saving the condemned men and getting the other seventy-five men released from Cummins. They also believed in their own skills and were confident that they could turn Hill's trial into a showcase affair. This would enable them to make the sharecroppers' story known, and by doing so they hoped to achieve a victory that would prod Arkansas—which was their *home,* a state they ultimately *loved*—to reform its ways. "If we believed, as some other Negroes believe, that Arkansas is a regular hell and that nowhere in the state can the Negro get justice in the courts, we would be the biggest fools possible to remain here," Cox explained.

On March 22, the same day that Jones and Murphy argued the sharecroppers' appeal before the Arkansas Supreme Court, Governor Allen held a public hearing on Arkansas's extradition request. He examined the union's literature, listened to Hill testify, and reviewed affidavits from Hoop Spur sharecroppers describing how they'd been tortured. Arkansas attorney general John Arbuckle then slowly rose to his feet and started speaking about the "uprising of the niggers," a phrase that drew gasps from the blacks who had packed the Topeka courtroom, and any lingering doubts Allen may have had about what to do were removed when he reread the many threatening letters he'd received from white Arkansans demanding that he send Hill back. "You Kansas nigger lover," one Helena correspondent wrote, "it is too bad you were not at Elaine on October 1, 1919 and had your nasty white liver shot out by some of your beloved brethren."

Such letters, Allen confided, convinced him "that the temper of that community made it impossible for anyone to guarantee a fair trial."

Hill was home free, or so it seemed. However, the instant Allen announced that he would not extradite Hill, federal prosecutors swept in and arrested him for having "impersonated a federal officer." Hill, the *Helena World* explained, "is alleged to have represented himself as a United States detective [to the sharecroppers] and to have worn a large tin star bearing the initials U.S.," which he had "obtained from a correspondence course for detectives." Federal agents in Arkansas also arrested V. E. Powell on a similar charge, as he had signed his name above a line on a union membership form— a form the union had apparently copied from another organization—that said "Employed in the United States Service."

The U.S. Department of Justice, which for so long had remained silent in this case, had at last found reason to act.

THE ARKANSAS SUPREME COURT handed down its decision on March 29, and it was just as expected. "Everybody knew before the verdicts were rendered just what they would be," Murphy said. New trials were ordered for Ed Ware and five others because the verdicts in those cases were "fatally defective" as a matter of statutory law, the court wrote. However, the court found that Frank Moore and the five others convicted of killing Clinton Lee had received a "fair and impartial trial." Arkansas's highest court noted that "eminent counsel was appointed to defend appellants," and concluded that there was no evidence that "the trial was an empty ceremony, conducted for the purpose only of appearing to comply with the requirements of the law." Moreover, the mere fact that Frank Moore and the others had left his house armed, the judges unanimously agreed, was proof of a "conspiracy previously formed, which contemplated violence, and the possible killing of white men."

The next month proved to be a whirlwind for Jones. He had to prepare filings to delay the setting of a new execution date for Moore and the others whose convictions had been affirmed; he had to prepare to defend Dr. Powell in federal court; and he had to prepare for the retrials of the Ware six in Phillips County Circuit Court. This last task required, among other things, traveling to Helena to line up as witnesses some of the women who'd belonged to the union. Finally, he had to do all this legal work while fighting his customary election-year battle with the lily-whites in Arkansas's Republican Party, and this year Jones turned it into a full-scale civil rights protest.

In January, Jones had warned the Pulaski County Republicans not to hold their April 13 convention in a segregated hotel in order to keep black Republicans from attending. In his letter, Jones had reminded the lily-whites that during the war blacks in Little Rock had "cheerfully complied with every call of the government, from the giving of their sons on the battlefield to the purchase of bonds," and as such, they were intent on being "treated as citizens and granted the right of representation." But the lily-whites went ahead and booked the segregated Marion Hotel, and so, on April 13, Jones and more than a hundred followers boldly defied Jim Crow law and marched into the Marion. When the lily-whites decamped to another segregated hotel, Jones's group stayed where they were and proceeded to elect a slate of black delegates to the state convention, although they had to finish this business in the dark, as the hotel turned off the lights to get them to leave. Two weeks later, Jones and the other black delegates demanded to be seated at the state convention, and when the lily-whites threw them out, they held their own convention in the Mosaic Templars building, nominating a black man for governor and electing their own delegates to the national convention. Theirs was a revolt, they proudly declared, that would "overthrow lily-whiteism in this state."

Jones wrapped up that historic protest on Friday, April 30. Three days later, at 9:00 A.M., he and Murphy took their places at the defense table in the Phillips County Courthouse. Jones was neatly dressed in a dark suit, his gold watch hanging from a vest pocket, and he appeared, as always, quite calm and even cheerful. He was not at all ruffled by the fact that, at this second round of trials, there was considerable tension in the air, with angry white men filling the seats on the main floor and blacks tightly packed into the gallery.

IT WAS COLONEL MURPHY'S job to play the role of lead attorney, and for the first two days he did just that, an ex-Confederate who, at seventy-nine years of age, still appeared full of vigor and wit. But early Wednesday, just as the second trial was getting under way, he suddenly clutched his chest and collapsed to the floor, and even as he was carried from the courtroom whispers arose that he'd been "poisoned."

Jones now had to carry on alone, and his first challenge, once the proceedings that day were done, was to find a safe place to sleep. Precisely how he did so, however, is not certain, for those who knew him gave somewhat conflicting accounts of how he spent his nights. According to J. H. Carmichael, Jones "had to shift his lodging place every night to keep those who wanted the Negroes punished from killing him. Sometimes he would go out into the country four or five miles to spend the night." Mary White Ovington later recounted a similar story. "When the day at court was over, he would enter a drug store in the colored section, and there talk to the men who dropped in. As it came time to go to bed, he went out, and walking to a colored home, knocked at the door. Though he was not expected, the door always opened and the home sheltered him. He slept and left early the next morning. No two nights were spent in the same house. No one knew where Scipio Jones put up." But Jones, who was always quite reticent to talk about himself in his letters, never wrote about those nights, and it is possible there is a bit of an exaggeration in the remembrances by Carmichael and Ovington, their accounts the type of lore that develops in the aftermath of an act of bravery. Prosecutor John Miller swore that while Jones, fearing for his life, did spend a couple of nights moving from home to home, he then came to him and asked for protection, with Miller ordering Sheriff Kitchens to find him a safe house and "detail a deputy sheriff to guard that place."

Regardless of the precise details, the accounts all attest to the threatening atmosphere that Jones now faced, and what can be known for certain today is that every morning he would suddenly appear on the courthouse sidewalk looking as calm and collected as he always did, ready for that day's work. He was not about to sneak in via a back door, and he would make his way up the front steps and climb the stairs to the second-floor courtroom, politely nodding to the officers of the court with that gentle, reserved smile of his. Every black in the gallery would be inspired by the presence of this fifty-six-year-old man on the floor below, and then for the next eight or ten hours he would wage a most vigorous fight to save his clients, poking holes in the testimony of the white witnesses whom Miller called to the stand and, when it was his turn, calling a steady stream of black witnesses to testify. Many of those defense witnesses were scared to be there, yet Jones would gently coax them to tell their story, and as he did so, he surely knew that their words were increasing the desire of the white spectators to see him dead.

By the time that Jones stepped to the fore, John Martin had already been found guilty of first-degree murder, and in each of the next five trials, Jones pursued the same aggressive legal strategy. First, he would ask the court to move the trial to another county, and once Judge Jackson denied this motion, he would move to have the trial transferred to federal court, and after Jackson denied that motion, he would ask that the jury pool be set aside because of the exclusion of blacks and request that the "jury commissioners who selected the juries be summoned to testify upon this motion." With this last motion, Jones was setting up Judge Jackson to make a reversible mistake, and each time Jackson fell into his trap. U.S. Supreme Court law required the trial court to call the commissioners into court so that they could swear that the absence of blacks from the jury pool was not due to racial discrimination, but each time Jackson failed to do so. Even before the first witness in each of the trials was called, Jones had reason to believe that any guilty verdict rendered would not stand. As he told the NAACP: "I made a good record and took all the proper exceptions for appeals."

With Jones in charge of the defense, the trials proved rather humiliating to all white Arkansans, so much so that the *Helena World* and the Little Rock newspapers quickly curbed their coverage and published only cursory reports of the proceedings. The prosecution's problems began with Charles Pratt, whose story, after Jones finished his cross-examination, seemed flimsier than it had at the first round of trials. According to Pratt, they stopped near the Hoop Spur church to take a leak and got out of the car, and then a "few minutes" later a group of blacks gathered around, one of them saying, "What's the matter, is your car broke?" By Pratt's own admission, he snapped back: "Is this any of your business?" As he did so, he noticed that one of the Negroes was putting his shotgun together. Pratt pointed his finger at him and said, "Don't do that, son," and then "the lights in the church went out and the thing started, the shooting started, by those [black] parties."

Now this was a scene, as Jones noted in one of his arguments, in which the Negroes approached Pratt and asked a question that "was a civil one, and indicated a desire to help." And by the time Pratt stepped down from the witness stand, he'd admitted under Jones's cross-examination that he'd driven by the church earlier in the day, that a second car had come along that night and been involved in some shooting, that the church had been subsequently burned down, and that Kid Collins was now out of jail.

Miller then brought Amos Jarman and Henry Smiddy to the stand, and both testified that they'd found the church in disarray, with benches turned over and hats and clothing left behind. "It looked like [the Negroes] had gone away hurriedly; quite a number of the windows were broken out, it looked like they had jumped through them in the back end," Jarman said. While this was accurate, Smiddy then swore that "there were no bullet holes at all in the church," and so the prosecution's story now seemed to be that the blacks inside the church had jumped through the windows to flee even though their church had not been fired upon, a rather paradoxical reaction. Then, when the prosecution called Kid Collins, Jones got him to contradict Pratt's claim that they had not fired their guns. "I had a .32-30 revolver and fired four shots," Collins said.

In the first round of trials, Miller and the other prosecutors had relied on the testimony of John Ratliff, Sykes Fox, and other union members to finger Ware and others for Adkins's murder, but this time, when Miller brought them back for a repeat performance, they all swore that they had lied at the earlier trials because they'd been brutally whipped or tortured in an electric chair, or that they had at least been threatened with such torture. Several of the men offered to show the juries their scars, and Will Wordlow dared Miller to ask him to take off his shirt. "If you don't believe I have any scars on me, I will let my clothes down and let you see it." Faced with this recantation, the prosecution, as the *Helena World* admitted, was forced "to rely on the former statements of the witnesses," their earlier testimony read into the record.

That was the core of the prosecution's case in the four trials in which John Martin, Will Wordlow, Alf Banks, and Ed Ware were tried for killing Adkins.* The only other evidence offered by the prosecution came from W. K. Monroe. He testified that perhaps thirty minutes after Adkins was killed he'd been driving down the road when he spotted a coat in the middle of it, and after stopping to investigate, he was fired upon and struck in the arm and nose by two small pellets before he made his getaway.

Then it was the defense's turn to call witnesses, and in each trial Jones put the defendant on the stand and also had a number of the sharecroppers' wives testify. Together, they told a story of how they'd organized their union to better themselves and "care for one another," and how prior to the Tuesday meeting at Hoop Spur they'd been threatened by the planters. One after another they described how a volley of bullets had shattered their church and how all of them had stumbled over each other in the darkness after the lights were put out. Jones saved Vina Mason as his star witness; she testified that she was clutching her baby when a bullet sliced through her shoulder—a bullet, in fact, that was *still in her.* All told, Jones

---

* In Ed Ware's trial, the prosecution also introduced a black witness, Suggs Bondsman, who testified that at the Thursday night meeting in Elaine, Ware had drawn up a list of planters to be killed. However, Jones got Bondsman to admit that he couldn't name any of the other union members who'd been at that meeting, and Jones also called to the stand several rebuttal witnesses who testified that no such talk had taken place.

elicited testimony of this sort from nine witnesses, and they also described how they'd hurriedly fled from the church, breaking out the windows on the south side in order to escape, and how there had been gunfire from a second car that drove by.

And so the juries in those four cases could weigh the evidence: Did they have reason to doubt the prosecution's claim that the church had not been fired upon? And if the church had been shot up, couldn't the sharecroppers be said to have acted in self-defense?

The stories put forth by the prosecution and the defense in the other two trials, in which Albert Giles and Joe Fox were retried for killing James Tappan, were not all that different. Lulu Ware and a number of black witnesses testified that the morning after the Hoop Spur shooting they heard that white men were coming to kill them all, and that as soon as the first posses arrived, they gunned down "a little fellow, Lemon" and an old crippled man, Charles Robinson. Banks and Giles then testified that they and five or six others fled into the Govan Slough to hide, with Jim Miller telling them to lie low and let the posses pass. When the posses were still several hundred yards away, they heard them start shooting and figured that they were killing women hiding in the upper part of the Govan Slough. Then the posses came and shot at them, and while they were under attack they heard some of the white men holler, "Look out, we are killing our own men." The prosecution didn't dispute that the posses had already killed Lemon and Robinson before Tappan was shot. Rather, its case rested on posse commander Herbert Thompson's claim that he had hollered for blacks hiding in the slough to come out, that they wouldn't be harmed if they did, and that after he shouted his warning someone in the slough fired at them. However, he admitted on cross-examination that posse members were on both sides of the thicket, and that they had been firing away for a "few minutes"—and perhaps nearly as long as fifteen minutes—before Tappan was shot. "I don't know how many persons were killed before Mr. Tappan was killed," he admitted on cross-examination. "I have an idea, but won't attempt to say, because there may have been more in the thicket than I saw."

The critical evidence in these trials seemed quite consistent: white posses had already gunned down blacks before Tappan was killed.

All in all, Jones, in his handling of the trials, had turned the tables on the prosecution. The six juries had heard a narrative that ultimately told not of a Negro uprising but of white violence and murder, and even much of the testimony by the prosecution's witnesses supported that conclusion. As Ovington later wrote, Jones's cross-examination of the witnesses had been "masterly." At each trial, Jones had also introduced into evidence the union documents, which showed that the farmers had organized to better themselves and to "fight for their rights," and even the white jurors must have wondered what had happened to the famous list of twenty-one planters to be killed. "Is it not striking," Jones wrote in a follow-up court proceeding, "that not a single incriminating paper was offered or introduced into evidence?"

Jones had come into the lion's den of Phillips County and waged a most vigorous defense, and while the all-white juries found all six men guilty of first-degree murder, Miller, the prosecutor, understood well what Jones had achieved. "Scipio Jones," he said, "his skin was black but by God he was a good man. He was honorable in every way, shape, form and fashion. And smart, too."

WARE AND THE OTHER five men returned to the death house later that week, and all twelve men were quickly given a new execution date of July 23. Jones, however, told them that this legal struggle had a ways to go, and the sharecroppers gladly put their faith in him, and in God. "We feel that they never convict us if prejudice was left aside," Ware told the *Arkansas Gazette* on May 17. "We also think that the Lord will never let us die, for we are innocent. . . . All we can do is to read the scriptures, pray to the Lord and sing, and time passes on."

And then the other eleven men on Death Row whispered in unison: "Amen."

All Hope Gone

ALTHOUGH THE TWELVE MEN were back together in the death house, the two groups were now at very different risk of being electrocuted. Jones and Murphy—the colonel hadn't been poisoned after all, but rather had suffered a mild heart attack—quickly appealed the verdicts from the Ware retrials, and they knew that the Arkansas Supreme Court, if it followed the law set down by the U.S. Supreme Court regarding the exclusion of blacks from juries, would have to rule in their favor. Judge Jackson had refused to hear evidence on whether blacks were being excluded from juries because of their race, and that was clearly a reversible error. But Jones and Murphy had little reason to believe that the six men convicted of killing Clinton Lee could be saved by an appeal to the U.S. Supreme Court. On May 21, Jones mailed a petition for a writ of certiorari to the United States Supreme Court, asking that it review the cases, and yet he and Murphy were unable to point to any precedent law to support their argument that the trials had violated the sharecroppers' due process rights under the Fourteenth Amendment. The nation's highest court had never set aside a verdict in a state criminal trial because a defendant or a witness had been tortured. There was no precedent requiring states to provide defendants in a murder trial with an attorney. The Court had given its blessing to the exclusion of blacks from juries as long as state courts pretended that it wasn't being done because of their race. All Jones and Murphy could do in their petitions was relate once again the story of what had happened—the massacre of black farmers, the near lynching of prisoners at the county jail, the torture, and the farcical nature of the forty-five-minute trials—and then plead with the Court to set a new precedent, one that would break with the past:

> If said judgement is permitted to stand uncorrected, unreversed, the discrimination against the Negro race through all the Circuit Courts of Arkansas . . . will go on, [and] their rights under the Fourteenth Amendment to the United States Constitution and under the Acts of Congress pursuant thereto [will] continue to be denied as they have been for more than 30 years past.

The entire proceedings, Jones and Murphy wrote, were nothing more than the "execution of a previously devised program" to sentence the six sharecroppers to death. The state had merely "pretended" to hold a trial. And so they asked: could this mockery of justice possibly be considered due process under the Fourteenth Amendment?

THE SUPREME COURT WOULDN'T rule on their petition until the fall, and on May 27, Jones and Edgar McHaney, who was Murphy's junior partner, met with NAACP officers in New York, laying out for them the difficult challenge ahead. "We are not very hopeful of any favorable result on this petition," McHaney confessed. They were also now so strapped for cash that they couldn't perfect the appeals in the Ware retrial cases. The stenographer they'd hired to produce the trial transcripts wouldn't release them until he was paid the $1,181 he was owed, and at the moment, the Citizens Defense Fund had already expended most of the $8,500 it had collected. "We do not believe that the colored people in this State can raise a fund sufficient to pay us and to pay Jones and the costs necessary to be incurred at each step in the procedure to be taken," McHaney said, adding that his firm was taking a financial beating because it had taken on this case. "We believe that the honest, God fearing,

Liberty loving white people of the United States ought to come to their assistance."

As a result of that meeting, the NAACP agreed to pay Jones and Murphy's firm up to $5,000 more for their work on the cases, leaving it up to them to decide how the money should be split. The NAACP had finally accepted the fact that Jones, this Southern black man they didn't fully trust, was acting at the very least as co-counsel. Nearly a year later, the NAACP's checkbook would show that Jones had received $3,500 under this contract and Murphy's firm $250, providing historical proof of who was doing the lion's share of the legal work.

On June 18, Jones and Murphy successfully defended V. E. Powell in federal court against the charge that he and Robert Hill had conspired to impersonate federal officers. The prosecution's case was so lacking that Judge Jacob Trieber ordered the jury to return a "not guilty" verdict. "In my judgment," Jones informed the NAACP, this "automatically acquits Robert Hill of said charge," and indeed, several months later, federal charges against Hill, who had been locked up in a Kansas jail, were dismissed as well.

There was that summer of 1920 another terrible stream of lynchings, and a smattering of news more directly related to the case. On June 15, three blacks were lynched in Duluth, Minnesota; a week later, a mob of thousands castrated and burned alive a black man in Georgia; on July 5, three thousand people cheered as a mob in Paris, Texas, lashed two sharecroppers to a flagpole at the county fairgrounds and set them on fire. The leaders paraded through town with the "barbecued niggers" tied to the back of a car, and then a group of twenty men took the victims' three sisters to the basement of the county jail and gang-raped them, "after which," one witness reported, the girls "were given a bucket of molasses, a small sack of flour and some bacon and told to hit the road." The violence went on and on, and as it did, the nation's legislators remained unable to agree that lynching should be made a federal crime.

In Helena, Mayor J. G. Knight resigned and moved to Atlanta. Sheriff Kitchens died and was carried to his grave by, among others, the sharecroppers' defense attorney, John Moore. Finally, on Octo-

ber 10, a fire erupted in Helena's black section, destroying fifty
homes and leaving two hundred homeless. "Men, women and children filled the streets and alleys, some sitting disconsolately about
piles of bedding, tables, chairs and other household furniture hastily
removed," the *Helena World* wrote.

It had been another dismal summer and early fall in America,
and on October 11 the U.S. Supreme Court did as Jones expected,
declining to review the Moore cases. "No opinion was announced by
the court in denying petition for certiorari," Court clerk James
Maher informed Jones. There was, apparently, nothing in this case
that raised any red flags for the nation's highest court, and when
Colonel Murphy, the ex-Confederate who had so courageously
taken up the sharecroppers' cause, died of cardiac complications that
same day, it seemed that surely he had died of a broken heart, disap-
pointed both in the Court and in his country. "I think," Jones told
Ovington, "that he died at the very hour" the Court turned down
their application.

The Moore six, the *Arkansas Democrat* reported, would now
"face death in the electric chair unless Governor Brough should commute their sentences," and in Helena, the town fathers quickly
mounted a campaign to make sure that Brough did no such thing.
The Richard Kitchens American Legion post, the Helena Lions Club,
the Helena Rotary, and the Helena Civitan Club all passed resolutions demanding that the six condemned men be electrocuted at
once. Sheriff Dalzell, John Miller, and the Committee of Seven wrote
to Brough as well, and the message from all these groups was the
same: on the night of October 2, the leading citizens of Helena had
stayed the lynch mob by making a "solemn promise that the law
would be carried out," and only if Frank Moore and the other five
men were now put to death—and "as soon as possible"—would
that "solemn promise be kept." If their sentences were commuted,
the town's leaders told Brough, it "would be difficult, if not impossible" to prevent lynchings in the future. "We think the law itself is on
trial," the Committee of Seven said.

On November 15, Brough told the press that he had heard the

Helena leaders loud and clear. "Every business, civic and other organization in [Helena], which refrained from mob violence, has taken a strong stand for carrying out the decree of the court to the letter," he said. As soon as he received official notice of the U.S. Supreme Court's October 11 decision (the written order had not yet been sent by the court clerk to Arkansas), he would set an execution date. Since Brough had decided not to run for reelection, he would be leaving office on January 12, and he assured the public that the men would be electrocuted before that date.

Announced the *Arkansas Gazette:* "Last Hope Gone for Six Negroes."

THERE WOULD SOON COME a moment when all hope truly was gone, but at this point, Governor Brough and the newspapers were, in fact, a little premature in their conclusions. Jones knew that he could go back to federal court one more time by petitioning for a writ of habeas corpus, and while that legal tactic had never been successfully used to overturn a verdict rendered in a state criminal court in a case that was clearly within its jurisdiction (as murder was), he could still use it to delay the executions. Yet the real hope for saving Frank Moore and the others, Jones reasoned, lay in publicly linking their fate to Ed Ware and the others. How could the state electrocute six of the men while it was still possible that the other six might go free? Weren't they all theoretically guilty of the same crime of conspiring to kill whites?

On November 16, Jones fired off a letter to the Little Rock newspapers, and this time he dropped his usual measured tone: "All agree that the death penalty was promised, solemnly and religiously, if the mob would stay its hand. This is not news to us. We had understood from the very beginning that somebody had to be executed because the mob had been promised blood, and like Shylock of old, it is still insisting on blood. [But] the statements contained in the morning paper purporting to give the facts with reference to the cases mentioned are not borne out by the records, but are simply conclusions arrived at by the writer of the article. And when it becomes known, and it will become known, how the evidence was obtained which formed the basis of the convictions in all these cases, we predict a change of sentiment, even in Phillips County."

Although neither Little Rock paper published Jones's letter, it had its effect, for the *Arkansas Democrat,* in an editorial the next day, suddenly wondered why the state had to be in such a "rush" to execute the men. "Is it known that the six cases now pending in the Arkansas Supreme Court are to be affirmed, and further appeal denied? . . . Let us not speed these cases unduly. There is no cause for haste. Let the courts function, and when they have completed their work, if there is then to be no executive clemency, let the sentences fall."

Old Sparky was not to be fired up just yet. Jones's logic had put a brake on the state's thirst for vengeance, and on December 6, the Arkansas Supreme Court applied the brake a little more. The court reversed the Ware convictions, this time because Judge Jackson had refused to hear evidence regarding the exclusion of blacks from the juries. These six men would have to be tried yet again.

"While [the decision] vitally and directly affects our present Elaine cases, we are very proud of the fact that in its larger aspects it is a victory for the Race," Jones wrote to Walter White. "I am pretty sure that execution in the other six cases will be stayed pending the outcome of the trials in the six cases just reversed." And then, in this letter, he added a personal note, something that he rarely did: "I am selfish enough to be very proud of the reversal in the Elaine cases, for the reason that, on account of the sudden illness of Colonel Murphy, I had to try all of the cases, except Martin's, in the lower court myself."

Frank Moore and the others still had reason to believe that their lives might be spared. The news of the reversal, the *Arkansas Democrat* reported, was "received with considerable rejoicing" by all twelve men in the death house.

JONES'S STRATEGY FOR SAVING the condemned men was clear: if he could get the Ware six acquitted at their retrials, he would then petition Arkansas's new governor, Thomas McRae, to pardon Frank

Moore and the others. Although McRae, a sixty-nine-year-old lawyer, had promised in his campaign speeches that he would "uphold our courts and juries" by refusing to issue pardons, stating that "few criminals are unjustly punished," Jones nevertheless considered him a reasonable man, someone who could be swayed by the opinions of others. "A committee of prominent white citizens" from the Second Presbyterian Church in Little Rock, Jones told the NAACP, had asked the new governor to not set any execution date until the other trials could be held, and McRae, in his first few months on the job, showed no inclination to do so.

With the retrials scheduled for May, the NAACP, which was no longer trying to hide its involvement, renewed its fund-raising effort. It was necessary to raise $5,000 "within a short time if the lives of the men in Arkansas are to be saved," Du Bois told *Crisis* subscribers, and they sent back envelopes filled with the small contributions they could afford. "We decided to make a plea to every colored man of our little town for one dollar each to assist in seeing justice in these cases of the doomed men of Phillips County," wrote a reader in Tonopah, Nevada, "and every colored man in our town, which are very few, gave one dollar each without being coaxed."

Jones, meanwhile, pulled out all the stops. First, he prodded his friends in the Arkansas House of Representatives to introduce a law that would require a circuit court judge to grant a change of venue whenever it was requested in a murder case. The bill, he informed the NAACP on February 16, had been approved by the House and was pending in the Senate, the legislature as a whole—and this subterfuge clearly pleased Jones—unaware that it "was introduced for the benefit of the Elaine victims." Next, he hired a white detective, at a cost of $125 a week, to determine what could be learned from Helena whites who had been part of the posses. Finally, he sought to hire a white attorney who could serve as his co-counsel at the Ware trials. With Murphy dead, this duty seemingly fell to McHaney, but neither Jones nor Bratton, who was keeping up on the case from his new home in Detroit, thought McHaney was right for the job. "McHaney has absolutely no interest [in the case] other than to get the money," Bratton told the NAACP. "McHaney was grumbling all along as to the cases and fee. He was scared to death for fear of the local feeling, and besides, said the bunch at Helena were his special friends." Jones convinced a former U.S. congressman from Arkansas, Colonel Stephen Brundidge Jr., to help him with the retrials, and got the NAACP to agree to pay half of Brundidge's requested $2,500 fee.

On March 25, a determined Jones wrote to White:

> I know not how to convince you of my deep appreciation to raise half of Colonel Brundidge's fee, provided we raise the other half. I don't know where I can get the money. Our Defense Fund Commission is not raising any funds at present, but your money will be matched, even if I have to pay every dollar of it myself. This is a life and death struggle with us and I am unwilling for you to do more for us than we do for ourselves. These men should not and must not go to the electric chair if it can be prevented, and it can! I know that we are engaged in a just cause, a righteous fight and we must win. These men have lived under the shadow of the electric chair long enough. With marshalled forces, united and untiring efforts, we must meet our enemies, and I hope—for the last time—I hope that you and those who are associated with you will feel assured that we are not going to surrender.

They would be telling the sharecroppers' story once more, and if Judge Jackson granted their motion for a change of venue, Jones was optimistic that all twelve men could be saved: "I think if we succeed in acquitting the six men who are entitled to new trials, the Governor will be forced by public sentiment and a sense of fairness to pardon the rest of the convicted men," he told the NAACP.

FRANK MOORE AND THE other eleven men at The Walls passed those first months of 1921 in a relatively tranquil manner. Joe Knox "held daily services for his companions," the *Arkansas Gazette* reported, and at times Ed Ware also led them in prayer, for he had become a preacher in prison. They spent hours singing—"They sing one or two songs that would move any audience to tears," Jones told the NAACP—and the new warden, E. H. Dempsey, even let them out of their cells each day so they could exercise on the prison lawn. Dempsey "also gave them light work," the *Gazette* noted, "which he thought would help their mental and physical condition."

On April 29, however, all twelve men rose at a much earlier hour than usual, long before daybreak. Knox had spent the last few nights providing comfort to twenty-one-year-old Revertia Reynolds, another death house inmate, and after a round of prayers that morning, he and Ware accompanied him to the death chamber. Reynolds had asked both men to be with him at this final hour, and thus, a little before 6:00 A.M., Knox and Ware stoically watched as Reynolds was strapped into the electric chair. Their eyes met his one last time and then Reynolds's executioners dropped a hood over his head.

This was the first time that any of the twelve men had seen the electric chair in use. "When they first put the charge to you," said *Arkansas Gazette* police reporter Joe Wirges, who'd witnessed many executions, "it runs a little better than 2,000 volts but only two or maybe three amperes. The executioner [then] increases the amperes and decreases the voltage. The amperes are what kills you and the voltage is what burns you up." Flames, on occasion, flew from the headpiece, and even witnesses could smell the burning flesh. "Of course there is a sickening odor. The brain is dehydrated, just cooked and fried. The whole system, it just burns up."

Knox and Ware returned to their cells badly shaken. Nobody wanted to talk about that death scene, and then, at day's end, Governor McRae issued a proclamation: Knox, Frank Moore, Paul Hall, Ed Coleman, Frank Hicks, and Ed Hicks were to be electrocuted on June 10.

Jones was stunned. "I had inferred from my last interview [with McRae] that he would await the results of the future trials of the other six men," he told the NAACP. So too was the *Arkansas Democrat* surprised—"Either all twelve of these negroes are guilty and ought to die, or all twelve are innocent and ought to go free," it wrote—and a few days later Jones got his first glimpse of how Helena authorities, now that a date had been set, were planning to make certain that the men were put to death.

On May 9, Jones filed a motion in Phillips County Circuit Court for a change of venue in the Ware trials. Given that the Arkansas Supreme Court had already twice reversed verdicts in these cases, Jones expected that Judge Jackson would have to grant his motion, sending it to neighboring Lee County. That county "will be hostile to us; still any place is preferable to Helena," Jones informed the NAACP. However, rather than rule on the motion, Jackson said that he would take it "under advisement." This was clearly puzzling— "We do not quite understand the judge's position in not rendering the decision," Jones wrote—and then days and weeks passed, and gradually it became evident that Jackson did not intend to make any decision prior to June 10. Apparently, Jackson and the Helena planters feared the retrials for the same reason that Jones wanted them: if they were held before the execution date, the sharecroppers would get another chance to tell their story. In one of his earlier court filings, Jones had even offered to call *fifty* men to the stand to testify that they'd been tortured to give false testimony. This was the very information that Jones, in his November letter to the Arkansas newspapers, had promised would sway public opinion and derail the executions. "It looks to me," White told Jones, "as though they now realize that they will never be able to have the convictions stand in the six cases now pending in the Phillips County Court, and they are determined to execute the other six men to appease the mob spirit."

And so the final countdown to June 10—and a nation's moment of truth—began.

OVER THE COURSE OF the past five months, the nation had been forced to confront, time and again, the shame of peonage and the horrors of mob violence. The year had gotten off to a ghastly start with a barbaric lynching in Nodena, Arkansas, that produced perhaps the most bizarre paragraph ever to be published in an American newspaper. On January 26, a mob chained Henry Lowry, a sharecropper alleged to have killed his landlord in a settlement dispute, to a log and placed leaves soaked with gasoline around his feet. After dragging his wife and little girl to the scene, they lit the brush. "Every few minutes fresh leaves were tossed on the funeral pyre," wrote *Memphis Press* reporter Ralph Roddy, and in this manner "inch by inch the negro was fairly cooked to death." As the flames burned away Lowry's flesh, Roddy added, the mob conducted what it considered to be a trial:

> One witnessing the scene might have easily pictured themselves in a courtroom. The negro was burned in a natural amphitheater between two bluffs, with the Mississippi on one side and a huge lake, caused by backwater, on the other. As the negro slowly burned to death two men stood near his head and questioned him . . . A big six-footer put the question to the condemned man, while another wrote the questions and answers down in a notebook. It reminded me of a lawyer and court reporter. Other members of the mob crowded around, but not once did they attempt to interrogate the negro, leaving this to the pair who appeared to have been assigned this duty.

Although Lowry tried to "pick up the ashes and thrust them into his mouth in order to hasten death," Roddy nevertheless concluded that, during those moments of absolute agony, Lowry properly "confessed" to the crime. "The general impression was that he was telling the truth," Roddy said. The *Memphis Press*'s editors, picking up on this theme, compared the lynching to courtroom proceedings that, while equally certain to send an "atrocious criminal" to his death, were slower. Both achieved the desired end, with the paper—apparently in all sincerity—asking its readers: "Which Is the Better Way?"

The NAACP collected Roddy's article and other newspaper reports of the burning into a pamphlet—"500 Watch Slayer Roast for 30 Minutes," the *Memphis News Scimitar* shouted—and mailed a copy to newspapers throughout Latin America, encouraging them to "comment on the phases of American civilization which this publication reveals." Unfortunately, even as newspaper editors in South America gasped in disbelief, there was more shameful news about the United States on the way. In April, a planter in Georgia facing federal peonage charges killed eleven blacks in order to "remove" the evidence, and soon after that Georgia governor Hugh Dorsey published a report on how "the negro" in his state was being enslaved, lynched, and in some counties "driven out as though he were a wild beast." Newspapers and magazines announced that blacks were being held in conditions "worse than outright slavery" in other states as well, and suddenly the nation was forced to wonder whether the Thirteenth Amendment had, in essence, been repealed in much of the South.

Arkansas had its own lynching spree that spring. On March 15, a black man in Hope, Arkansas, was taken from a county jail and hanged; the following week a mob in Monticello, Arkansas, did the same to a prisoner there. Next, on May 13, fourteen-year-old Leroy Smith, who had been out frog hunting, tried to hitch a ride on a country road near McGehee, apparently thinking that the car coming his way belonged to the foreman at the company where he worked. It turned out that it was being driven by a white couple, and that faux pas ended with his being hanged from a tree. Nationwide, the Ku Klux Klan that spring of 1921 was in the midst of a recruiting drive that resulted in another one hundred thousand American men donning the white robes, and then, on May 30, a nineteen-year-old black shoeshine boy in Tulsa stumbled while entering an elevator operated by a seventeen-year-old white girl, and that proved to be the match that ignited what was perhaps the nation's worst racial violence ever. The boy either bumped the girl or grabbed her arm as he stumbled—in one way or another he *touched* her—and she screamed and he ran, and soon the *Tulsa Tribune* was reporting that she'd been sexually assaulted. The following evening whites gathered outside the courthouse in order to lynch the shoeshine boy, and then seventy-five armed blacks showed up to prevent them from doing so, and shooting broke out. There was scattered fighting throughout the night, and then at 5:00 A.M., ten thousand whites—armed with machine guns, rifles, pistols, dynamite, and oil—launched a full-scale assault on Tulsa's black neighborhood, a thirty-five-square-block area known as the Greenwood District. They methodically looted homes and set them ablaze, and as part of their attack, they sent eight planes into the air, either for reconnaissance purposes or in order—as numerous black witnesses asserted—to drop firebombs. By the time the assault was over, the white mobs had destroyed more than a thousand black homes, killed between forty and three hundred blacks, and wounded several hundred more.

All across the country, blacks—and some whites—now saw the planned execution of the Elaine sharecroppers as more of the same. Lowry, the murder of eleven sharecroppers in Georgia, the enslavement of blacks, and Tulsa—they were all chapters in a never-ending tale of white violence. The story of the "Arkansas peons," as the *Crisis* referred to this case, had begun with the massacre of black farmers and a mass arrest of blacks, and now it was coming to a conclusion that, if anything, made for the most morally objectionable moment of all. The electrocution of the six men would be nothing more than a *court-ordered* burning. A U.S. Supreme Court–approved burning. How was this so different from the Lowry killing? Governor McRae, the *Arkansas Gazette* wrote, was "besieged with requests and petitions for a postponement," with the loudest protest of all coming from a white English professor at Virginia Military Institute, Robert Kerlin. In his May 25 letter, which the *Arkansas Democrat* published, Kerlin asked the governor to search his "Christian conscience":

> Not in the history of our Republic has a more tremendous responsibility before God and the civilized world devolved upon the shoulders of the chief executive of any state than has devolved upon yours *in re* the Negroes of Phillips County. . . . In the case of six of those condemned men the sentence of death has been sanctioned by you and you have appointed the day of their execution. It is a deed to be contemplated with extreme horror. In the execution of those men a race is suffering

crucifixion. I entreat you to take the matter into your private chamber and give it an hour's earnest consideration, as before the Eternal Judge. Have those men been dealt with according to justice, according to the principles of civilized and humane governments?

All of Arkansas—and many people around the nation—were awaiting McRae's answer.

ALMOST TO THE END, Jones believed that McRae would be swayed by the logic of his argument. "I entertain some hope that the governor will postpone indefinitely the electrocution of the six men until after the trials of the other six men," he told White on May 30. He and McHaney had their habeas corpus papers ready, but they were deliberately waiting until the last moment before taking their petition to federal judge Jacob Trieber, for they thought that McRae, with the lives of the six men in his hands, would be forced to do the right thing and put off the executions until the fate of the other six was resolved. Even the *Arkansas Democrat* agreed: "All 12 of these cases rest upon the same bottom. Let us be calm, unrushed, unswayed by blind unreasoning passion." Their strategy made sense, but it backfired horribly, for on June 2 Jones and McHaney learned that Judge Trieber, who'd been away in St. Paul, Minnesota, helping with federal trials there, would not return until after June 10.

"The matter is now up to Governor McRae," McHaney told the Little Rock newspapers. "Unless the governor grants the postponement, we have no tribunal due to recess of the federal court to which we may make any further appeal."

That day, June 2, McRae did waver a bit. He asked the prosecutor, John Miller, to provide him with a summation of the cases, one that would presumably refute Kerlin, who'd made much of the fact that the blacks who'd testified against Frank Moore and the others had been tortured to give false testimony. This apparent hesitancy on the governor's part stirred much of Helena into a frenzy, with both Miller and Judge Jackson hurriedly writing to put McRae at ease.

"Mr. Kerlin," Miller wrote, in a letter that reached McRae on Monday, June 6, "is not advised of the facts." The entire trouble, he said, arose because Robert Hill and the men condemned to die had organized "for the purpose of acting in concert to gain their fancied rights." The "citizens of Phillips County," he added, had no knowledge of the sharecroppers' union and their plan to commit "premeditated" murder. Pratt and Adkins were innocently passing by the Hoop Spur church when they were "fired upon" by the Negroes. "Not a single shot was fired into the lodge by the officers," and over the course of the next two days, not "a single Negro was killed unnecessarily," Miller said. Nor had any prisoners ever been whipped: the Committee of Seven and the deputy sheriffs "were not vindictive and used no cruel methods in their investigation, but worked to arrive at the facts." Finally, Miller advised, the governor needed to think about the feelings of the whites in Phillips County, for to commute the death sentences of Frank Moore and the others "would be the gravest insult that can be given to a body of law-abiding people."

Judge Jackson's letter, which also reached the governor on Monday, echoed these themes. Everything Kerlin had said was "a wicked lie," he wrote. Perhaps never before in American history, the judge said, had a racial clash "been handled with the same degree of absence of mob violence, leniency and respect for law as that which was shown in the Elaine insurrection." As for the affidavits by the defendants and witnesses stating that they'd been tortured, "careful investigation was made during the trials of alleged whipping of the negroes to obtain testimony, and all that human testimony can show this was not done." And Judge Jackson, like Miller, warned the governor that if he commuted the sentences, from here on he could expect lynching in the Arkansas Delta to flourish: "If the promises made to our people, promises by our Christian leaders, are not carried out, then no more promises will be made."

On Tuesday, June 7, whites in Helena held a public meeting to demand that the electrocutions proceed on schedule. The Richard Kitchens American Legion post passed a new resolution to that effect, and the next day John Moore and Sebastian Straub led a delega-

On their way to the woods, Governor Brough and the Camp Pike troops discovered a woman lying outside her cabin with a gunshot wound to the throat. Although the newspapers didn't identify her, the murdered woman was 55-year-old Frances Hall. *Courtesy of the Arkansas History Commission.*

Federal troops from Camp Pike hunting blacks in the canebrakes. Once the troops from Camp Pike were fired upon, Colonel Jenks ordered his men, some of whom were armed with machine guns, to "shoot to kill." *Courtesy of the Arkansas History Commission.*

Hundreds of blacks gathered along Route 44 on Thursday morning, hoping to be rescued by the federal troops from Camp Pike. The soldiers marched them to Elaine and locked them up in the town's schoolhouse. *Courtesy of the Arkansas History Commission.*

Altogether, federal troops rounded up more than 800 black farmers and "detained" them in Elaine. *Courtesy of the Arkansas History Commission.*

Left: D. A. E. Johnston. *Courtesy of the Butler Center for Arkansas Studies.*
Center: Dr. Louis Johnston. *Right:* Corporal Leroy Johnston. Photos of Louis and Leroy Johnston are from Ida B. Wells-Barnett's *The Arkansas Race Riot* (1920).

Helena dentist D. A. E. Johnston and his three brothers, on their way back from a hunting trip, were arrested in Elaine and killed. (The fourth brother, Gibson Johnston, isn't shown.)

U.S. BRATTON, JR. IS CHARGED WITH INCITING BLACKS

Son of Former Little Rock Postmaster Held for Murder

CLOSELY GUARDED

Accused of Having Preached Social Equality to the Negroes.

LONG UNDER SUSPICION

Arkansas Gazette,
Oct. 2

NEGROES HAD PLOT TO RISE AGAINST WHITES, CHARGED

Shooting of Officers From Ambush Started Wholesale Killings—All Negroes Said to Have Been Armed.

FIRST POSSE FROM HELENA IS ATTACKED

Attempt to Arrest Bootlegger Leads to Trouble—Propaganda Led Negroes to Secretly Organize.

Arkansas Democrat,
Oct. 2

GENERAL UPRISING HAD BEEN PLANNED, SAYS CORRESPONDENT

Arkansas Democrat Staff Representative Says Phillips County Trouble Had Long Been Planned by Negroes.

SLAIN NEGRO DENTIST WAS "BRAINS" OF PLAN

Guards Around Secret Meeting, Tuesday Night, Touched Off Plan Prematurely by Firing on Officers.

BY PAUL R. GRABIEL.
Staff Correspondent of the Arkansas Democrat.)

Arkansas Democrat,
Oct. 3

VICIOUS BLACKS WERE PLANNING GREAT UPRISING

All Evidence Points to Carefully Prepared Rebellion

BEGUN PREMATURELY

Blacks Suspected Officers Who Stopped Near Church by Accident.

Arkansas Gazette,
Oct. 4

PLANNED MASSACRE OF WHITES TODAY

Negroes Seized in Arkansas Riots Confess to Widespread Plot Among Them

HAD PASSWORD FOR RISING

And a " Paul Revere " Courier System—School House an Ammunition Depot.

New York Times,
Oct. 6

Headlines: Over the course of five days, newspapers in Arkansas and across the country reported that the Hoop Spur sharecroppers had been plotting to commit mass murder.

On October 7, the Citizens Committee in Helena put up this poster around town and published it in the *Helena World* newspaper. Two of the men on the committee, John Moore and Edwin Bevens, subsequently acted as the sharecroppers' defense attorneys. *Courtesy of Mary Louise Fiser.*

TO THE NEGROES
OF PHILLIPS COUNTY
Helena, Ark., Oct. 7, 1919

The trouble at Hoop Spur and Elaine has been settled.

Soldiers now here to preserve order will return to Little Rock within a short time.

No innocent negro has been arrested, and those of you who are at home and at work have no occasion to worry.

All you have to do is to remain at work just as if nothing had happened.

Phillips County has always been a peaceful, lawabiding community, and normal conditions must be restored right away.

STOP TALKING!

Stay at home---Go to work---Don't worry!

F. F. KITCHENS, Sheriff   COMMITTEE
Edward Bevens J. C. Meyers S. Straub E. M. Allen
T. W. Keesee D. A. Keeshan Amos Jarman
H. D. Moore J. G. Knight Jno. L. Moore E. C. Hornor

Nicholls Print, Helena, Ark.

Walter White. *Visual materials from the NAACP records; Library of Congress.*

When Walter White arrived at the Helena train station, he feared that he was being watched and might be lynched. *Courtesy of the Department of Arkansas Heritage, Delta Cultural Center Archives.*

Profiteered for Years on the Negro Share Croppers.

FARM TENANTS WERE ROBBED

Effort to Stop Fraudulent Practices Incensed White Owners, Who Started Trouble.

(Special Correspondence to THE NEW YORK AGE.)

WINCHESTER, ARK.—It is clearly and definitely established, by an exhaustive investigation made personally by a reliable correspondent, that the sole cause of the race troubles at Elaine, Phillips County, in this State, lay in the fact that the white men, owners of the land, objected to giving the Negro men, tenants on the land, a fair deal and honest treatment in the adjustment of rent contracts.

For years the white owner has profiteered on the labor of the Negro farm tenant in the yearly settlement for the crops raised, and when the tenants devised a plan by which the dishonest practices could be stopped, the whites determined to use radical and illegal methods to perpetuate their scheme for pauperizing and impoverishing the tenant and for maintaining control of their services as farm laborers. A statement from the investigator shows conclusively that the report of an organization among the Negroes for an uprising against the whites is simply a part of the plan to cover up the true facts.

On October 25, 1919, the *New York Age*, in an article headlined "Arkansas Landowners Defraud Tenants," ran Walter White's report on the "race troubles at Elaine."

John E. Miller, who would later be elected to the U.S. Congress, prosecuted the sharecroppers. *John Elvis Miller Papers, Special Collections, University of Arkansas Libraries, Fayetteville.*

Phillips County Courthouse. The county jail was attached to the rear of the building. *Courtesy of the Butler Center for Arkansas Studies.*

The twelve men condemned to die. *Courtesy of the Arkansas History Commission.*

This photo of Scipio Jones was published in a 1924 book on the history of the Mosaic Templars. *Courtesy of the Butler Center for Arkansas Studies.*

Above: In 1919, the *National Cyclopedia of the Colored Race* ran this picture of "Judge Scipio A. Jones." *Courtesy of the Butler Center for Arkansas Studies.*

The NAACP hired Colonel George Murphy, a Democrat and Confederate war hero, to appeal the death verdicts. *Courtesy of the Butler Center for Arkansas Studies.*

Top left: Arkansas governor Thomas McRae was besieged with requests to pardon the condemned men. *Courtesy of the Arkansas History Commission.*

Top center: Chancery court judge John Martineau issued the writ of habeas corpus that saved the Moore six from certain execution. *Library of Congress.*

Top right: NAACP president Moorfield Storey argued the case before the U.S. Supreme Court. *Visual materials from the NAACP records; Library of Congress.*

Below: The Taft Court. *Back row (left to right):* Pierce Butler, Louis Brandeis, George Sutherland, Edward Sanford. *Front row:* Willis Van Devanter, Joseph McKenna, William Howard Taft, Oliver Wendell Holmes, James McReynolds. Sanford was not on the court in January 1923 when *Moore v. Dempsey* was heard. *Collection of the Supreme Court of the United States; Courtesy of the Oyez Project.*

Oliver Wendell Holmes wrote the
Moore v. Dempsey decision.
Library of Congress.

Scipio Jones with the Ware six.
Back row: Alf Banks, John Martin, Ed
Ware. *Front row:* Joe Fox, Albert Giles,
William Wordlow. *Courtesy of the
Butler Center for Arkansas Studies.*

Scipio Jones with the Moore six.
Back row: Ed Hicks, Frank Hicks,
Frank Moore. *Front row:* J. C. Knox,
Ed Coleman, Paul Hall. *Courtesy of the
Butler Center for Arkansas Studies.*

tion of Helena's leaders that called upon McRae in Little Rock. "There are people in Phillips county," they warned, "who will not stand for law and order if these men are not executed."

The letters from Miller and Jackson, along with Moore's wholehearted endorsement of electrocuting his former clients, provided McRae with the public cover he needed.* They had sworn that witnesses had not been tortured and their letters were published in Arkansas's newspapers, and that enabled McRae to at least publicly maintain that the trials had been "fair," even though he surely knew that Miller and Jackson were lying. Indeed, if he'd wanted proof that they were, he could have read the transcript of the Ware retrials, which included this exchange between Miller and Will Wordlow:

> *MILLER:* When did they give you the first whipping—how long after you had been in jail?
> *WORDLOW:* About four or five days, I think.
> *MILLER:* When did they whip you next?
> *WORDLOW:* About three or four days after that.

That exchange had come in a hearing outside of the jury's presence, which Jones had forced Judge Jackson to hold because the prosecution wanted to read Wordlow's testimony from the first round of trials into the record (testimony that Wordlow had disavowed at the retrials). Miller, with these questions, was trying to make the argument that since Wordlow had been whipped shortly after he and the others were jailed, nearly a month before the trials, then his testimony could not be said to have been coerced. The issue at hand wasn't whether the sharecroppers had been whipped but when the whippings had stopped. Furthermore, Miller—as Jones surely pointed out to McRae—had never made any effort at the retrials to deny that the men had been whipped. The sharecroppers had named the deputy sheriffs who'd tortured them, but Miller

---

* Undoubtedly, Greenfield Quarles would have joined Moore in pleading that the men he defended be put to death, but he had died in January.

hadn't brought any of those deputies to the witness stand to counter this testimony. "Why did he not call one or more of the deputy sheriffs if it was not true?" Jones had written in his brief appealing those verdicts. "The trouble about it was that it was all true, and there was more yet that might be brought to light if the perpetrators were subjected to cross examination."

Those were the "facts" that Miller and Judge Jackson should have told the governor if they had wanted to be honest; at the retrials, the whipping of the defendants had been conceded by the prosecution. But that was not the sort of information that would help McRae proceed with the executions, and so they had simply lied in their letters.

During this final week, Jones and other black leaders also lobbied the governor hard. Jones and McHaney met with him twice to plead for clemency, Jones providing him with affidavits from the Elaine sharecroppers attesting to how they'd been tortured to falsely testify. On Tuesday, June 7, there was a steady stream of black delegations that called upon the governor—a group of ministers from Little Rock, another from Pine Bluff, and then Frank Moore's father, mother, wife, and children. Similar pleas for mercy came from around the country: "Telegrams continue to pour into the office of the governor, insisting that he manifest executive clemency," the *Arkansas Democrat* reported.

The clock was winding down for the six condemned men, and on Tuesday, eight students and two professors from Arkansas Baptist College, all of whom were members of the school's "jubilee chorus," came to The Walls to comfort them. The time had come for Frank Moore and the others to prepare to meet their maker, and for several hours, the visitors and the Elaine farmers "conducted an old-fashioned prayer and song service." All during their imprisonment, Frank Moore and the others had found solace in song, and on this Tuesday, their voices filled the penitentiary:

> My Lord, he calls me
> He calls me by the thunder

The trumpet sounds within my soul
I ain't got long to stay here.

On the following morning, the *Arkansas Gazette* announced that the governor remained firm in his decision "not to intervene." The first electrocution would go off at 6:00 A.M. on Friday, and then the remaining five men would be put to death one by one in short order, this the first time, the papers reported, that six men will "have died in the electric chair on the same day." Warden E. H. Dempsey and other prison officials began their final preparations that Wednesday, "the death chamber cleaned and the apparatus tested." All was ready; even the "coffins had been ordered."

In Helena, Clinton Lee's parents and others prepared to travel by train to Little Rock so they could witness the electrocutions—the town had been waiting for this moment for a long time. A promise to the mob had been made twenty months ago, on that Thursday evening, October 2, 1919, and it was finally going to be kept. The *Arkansas Gazette* sent a reporter to the penitentiary to record the sharecroppers' last words, the paper perhaps hoping for a dramatic last-minute confession. The black farmers could finally acknowledge their guilt, admit that they had indeed plotted to massacre whites, but the reporter returned with a disappointing story. The six condemned men were "not despondent" at all, but rather were convinced "they will be saved in the last minutes."

"Mr. Jones," the sharecroppers explained, "won't let us die."

Great Writ of Liberty

W ITH IT APPARENTLY SET in stone that the men would be executed at 6:00 A.M. on June 10, a Chicago newspaper, eager to be the first to report the news, carried an account in its Friday edition—as the *Helena World* later reported—"of the electrocution of the six Negroes. This story gave the order in which the men were led to the chair and even the last words of several of them." The *Helena World* didn't name the paper that had published this report, but it had apparently set its type on Wednesday afternoon, unaware that while it was doing so, Jones and McHaney were on their way to the Pulaski County Courthouse with a last-ditch—and outrageous—plan for delaying the executions.

In early May, the two attorneys had prepared habeas corpus petitions to submit to federal judge Jacob Trieber, hoping that they could convince him that the trials had been so unfair that the state could be said to have "lost its jurisdiction" over the men. That was the only legal argument that remained for them to make. However, once they learned that Trieber was away and couldn't be reached, they had reworked the petitions into a similar plea—and this was the outrageous part—to the Pulaski Chancery Court. Chancery courts handled property disputes and other civil matters—they had no authority over criminal matters. Moreover, the chancellor who presided over the Pulaski court, John Martineau, knew this better than any chancery judge in Arkansas. Seven years earlier, he'd issued a writ of habeas corpus to stay the execution of an insane man, and

the Arkansas Supreme Court had subsequently given him a good ver-
bal spanking. Chancellor Martineau, the court wrote with evident
exasperation, "was wholly without jurisdiction" to have done such
a thing.

And now Jones and McHaney, standing before Chancellor Martineau at 3:00 P.M., were asking him to do it again.

Forty-seven years old, Martineau was a Catholic whose father
was French Canadian, a heritage that did provide him with an outsider's perspective and a streak of stubborn independence. He was
known, one Arkansas historian wrote, for being "liberal in his views
and as a humanitarian in his rulings." Moreover, he "was always
ready to cut through anything that seemed to stand in the way of justice." He also liked and admired Jones, and would, a few years later,
ask him to preside over a divorce case in his chancery court, a temporary appointment that would make headlines in legal circles
nationwide. There was one other part of his personality—rare in
lower-court judges—that was critical to his decision-making process
in this case: he didn't mind being reversed.

Martineau issued two orders. First, he prohibited Warden E. H.
Dempsey from executing the six men on Friday morning. Second, he
issued a writ of habeas corpus to Dempsey, demanding that he bring
the six condemned men to his court on Friday at 2:00 P.M. and "then
and there state in writing the terms and cause of their imprisonment,
and produce your authority for so doing."

Although Jones immediately telegraphed the NAACP with the
good news—"Petition for Habeas Corpus filed Chancery Court
which stays execution" he wrote at 4:20 P.M.—it remained touch
and go all day Thursday on whether this maneuver would, in fact,
block the Friday morning electrocutions. Early Thursday, Arkansas's
attorney general, J. S. Utley, told reporters that since Chancellor
Martineau had no jurisdiction in criminal matters and everyone
knew that was so, the state might simply "carry out the sentences
without regard to the injunction." This was what the Committee of
Seven urged the state to do—"What has a chancery judge in Pulaski
County to do with Phillips County's affairs after State and United

States courts have passed on the legality of an execution?" they asked in disbelief—and yet, as the day wore on, Utley and Governor McRae came to see that as something of a bad idea. It would expose Dempsey to a contempt-of-court charge, as it was up to a higher court to point out to Martineau the error of his ways, and it would also open up the state to criticism that it had ignored the law. Executing the men, the *Arkansas Democrat* reasoned, would be "an official act of anarchy."

Late Thursday afternoon, Utley appealed to the Arkansas Supreme Court to annul Martineau's orders so that the electrocutions could proceed as planned. While Chief Justice Edgar McCullough wanted to do just that, the four associate judges decided that it would be best to hear arguments the following Monday. And it was then, at that moment, that Jones and McHaney and the six condemned men could finally breathe a sigh of relief. Although the Arkansas Supreme Court was certain to scold Martineau and remind him that he was never, ever to intrude into criminal matters again, it didn't matter. The executions had been delayed, a new round of state proceedings was under way, and that would give Jones and McHaney the opportunity to seek habeas relief for the six condemned men in federal court.

"No imminent danger of electrocution," Jones happily told White.

THE WRIT OF HABEAS corpus—Latin for "you shall have the body"—stands at the very heart of English law, its roots dating back to the early 1200s, when English courts were in their early stages of evolution. At first, it was simply used by a judge to command a sheriff to bring a prisoner (or someone in the community) into court so that judicial proceedings could be had. But in the early 1300s, prisoners turned it into a writ of a different sort. A jailed person would petition a judge to order a sheriff to bring him into court so that the court could inquire into the legality of his imprisonment. Under what process of law was he being held? If the jailer could not answer that question adequately, the court would free the prisoner. The writ now served as a protection against arbitrary arrest.

Prisoners also began using habeas petitions to challenge a court's jurisdiction. There was a helter-skelter mix of courts in England during this period, and if one court ordered a person to be held, the prisoner would appeal to a second or even a third court for relief, arguing that the first court lacked the jurisdictional authority to imprison him. This broadened the reach of habeas corpus, as a prisoner could now use it to challenge both police and judicial authority. The prisoners' court shopping also helped English courts sort themselves into a hierarchy, as clearly one court could deem another court's jurisdiction insufficient only if, in some manner or another, it was superior to it. The prisoners' habeas petitions forced England to create a more unified judicial system.

In the 1600s, the writ evolved into a check even on the king's power. In 1627, Charles I ordered wealthy landowners to make loans to the Crown, and when five knights refused, he ordered them jailed. The knights petitioned the Court of King's Bench for habeas relief, arguing that the king, under the Magna Charta, could not imprison a free man "except by lawful judgment of his peers or by the law of the land." The Crown responded by maintaining that the king's order was the law of the land, a dispute that ultimately led England's Parliament, in 1641, to pass an act decreeing that the king's word was not, in fact, a sufficient reply to a habeas petition. A free man could be held in prison only under the process of law. This was the moment that habeas corpus came to be enshrined as the Great Writ of Liberty.

The Founding Fathers of the United States, intent on protecting the rights of the people, declared in the Constitution that "[t]he Privilege of the Writ of Habeas Corpus shall not be suspended, unless when in Cases of Rebellion or Invasion the public Safety may require it." The Judiciary Act of 1789 then explicitly authorized all federal courts "to grant writs of habeas corpus for the purpose of an inquiry into the cause of commitment." However, neither the Constitution nor the Judiciary Act directly addressed the question of whether federal judges were authorized to release prisoners in state courts, and in 1807, U.S. Supreme Court Justice John Marshall, in *Ex parte Bollman,* ruled that they did not have such power. State prisoners could seek habeas relief only from state courts.

After the Civil War, Republicans in Congress, worried that the Rebel states would seek to imprison blacks unfairly as a way to control their labor, made habeas reform a cornerstone of Reconstruction law. The Fourteenth Amendment guaranteed all Americans due process under the law, and the Habeas Corpus Act of 1867 provided state prisoners with the access to federal courts necessary to secure that guarantee. It authorized federal judges to conduct habeas reviews "in all cases where any person may be restrained of his or her liberty in violation of the Constitution, or of any treaty or law of the United States." The act also allowed state prisoners in habeas proceedings to present "material facts" not included in the state trial records. As such, a habeas petition was more than just an appellate review of state actions; it was a de novo (new) proceeding. "It is a bill of the largest liberty," said Ohio congressman William Lawrence.

Together, the Fourteenth Amendment and the Habeas Act of 1867 set the stage for the nationalization of criminal justice standards. In fact, defendants in state criminal trials now had, at least in theory, two ways to challenge their imprisonment in federal court. A convicted prisoner could file a writ of error (or writ of certiorari) appeal to argue that some element of the trial proceedings—jury selection, his right to confront witnesses, and so on—violated his due process rights under the Fourteenth Amendment. The prisoner would first make this argument to a state appellate court, and if he lost there, he could then appeal to the U.S. Supreme Court. In addition, with the passage of the Habeas Act, a state prisoner could challenge his incarceration with a habeas appeal to a federal court either before or after the trial was held. The prisoner would argue that his imprisonment, in some manner or another, violated his constitutional rights.

Like so much of Reconstruction law, this was a radical change, and it was immediately evident that the U.S. Supreme Court would have to interpret the boundaries of this newly granted federal power to hear habeas petitions from state prisoners. However, because of political complications, it wasn't until 1886 that the Court attended to that task, and by that time the die was cast.* The Court had ruled that it was the states and not the federal government that were the principal protectors of civil rights, and it had decreed in *Hurtado* that the Bill of Rights didn't limit the states. That last decision made it nearly impossible for state criminal defendants to get any federal relief via writ of error appeals, and the Supreme Court quickly shut the habeas corpus door as well. In *Ex parte Royall* (1886), the court declared that federal judges should not step on the toes of state courts:

> The forbearance which courts of coordinate jurisdiction, administered under a single system, exercise towards each other, whereby conflicts are avoided, by avoiding interference with the process of each other, is a principle of comity, with perhaps no higher sanction than the utility which comes from concord; but between state courts and those of the United States it is something more. It is a principle of right and of law, and, therefore of necessity.

Guided by this principle of "comity," the court ruled time and again in ways that narrowed the availability and scope of federal habeas review. It decided that a state prisoner could not petition a federal court until all state remedies were exhausted, and that habeas corpus could not serve as a means for correcting procedural errors. A

---

* In 1868, a white newspaper editor in the South imprisoned by a military commission filed a habeas petition in federal court, and Congress, worried that if the U.S. Supreme Court granted him relief it would undercut the militarization of the South necessary for Reconstruction to proceed, suspended the Court's authority to review the habeas decisions of lower federal courts. In 1885, Congress finally lifted this suspension, the House Judiciary Committee declaring that it was time for the U.S. Supreme Court to define the "true limits of the Federal courts."

convicted prisoner would have to raise such complaints through writ of error (or certiorari) appeals. Moreover, those appeals would have to be concluded before a habeas petition could be heard. Indeed, the only time a federal court could provide habeas relief to a state prisoner, the U.S. Supreme Court repeatedly concluded in the 1890s and early 1900s, was if the prisoner was being held under a state law "repugnant" to the Constitution, or if the state had lacked jurisdiction in the case. "Upon habeas corpus, the court examines only the power and authority of the [state] court to act, not the correctness of its conclusions," the U.S. Supreme Court determined. And given that murder, theft, assault, and nearly all other crimes clearly fell under state jurisdiction, this meant that the U.S. Supreme Court had, in essence, rendered its own habeas powers moot in regard to state prisoners. Those convicted of crimes in state courts simply couldn't hope for habeas relief from a federal court.

And that's where matters stood until 1915. That year, in *Frank v. Mangum*, the Supreme Court opened the habeas door just a crack— a small opening that was truly the Elaine sharecroppers' last hope.

ALTHOUGH THE ISSUE THAT technically was before the Arkansas Supreme Court when it met on June 13, 1921, was that of Martineau's authority to intervene in the case, the general public knew that it was, in a broader sense, about whether the six condemned men had any chance to escape the electric chair. Black and white spectators, the *Arkansas Democrat* reported, filled "every available seat." The crowd that Monday morning also included a "large number" of attorneys from around the state who had come to hear Jones and McHaney articulate why, under the precedent set by *Frank,* the six condemned men deserved to go free, or to at least get a new trial. This hearing would preview the arguments that would be made later in federal court.

In 1913, twenty-nine-year-old Leo Frank was accused of murdering a thirteen-year-old girl at the Atlanta pencil factory where they both worked. He was Jewish, and at the end of four weeks of testimony, with the jury ready to begin its deliberations, a large throng gathered outside the courtroom and chanted, "Hang the Jew." The clamor was such that the judge feared that if the jury acquitted Frank, the mob would immediately lynch the defendant and his attorneys. After Georgia's Supreme Court upheld the death penalty verdict, Frank petitioned the U.S. Supreme Court for habeas relief, his attorney Louis Marshall arguing that because of the mob's "dominance" of the proceedings, the state had "lost its jurisdiction." While writing the majority opinion, Justice Mahlon Pitney took a comprehensive—and fresh—look at federal habeas powers.

The Habeas Corpus Act of 1867, Pitney wrote, authorized federal courts to conduct "a more searching investigation" of a state criminal case than the usual "bare legal review" allowable when it considered writ of error appeals. The federal courts could "look beyond [procedural] forms and inquire into the very substance of the matter, to the extent of deciding whether the prisoner has been deprived of his liberty without due process of law," and then, after "determining the facts by hearing testimony and arguments, dispose of the party as law and justice require." Pitney concluded:

> If a trial is in fact dominated by a mob, so that the jury is so intimidated and the trial judge yields, and so that there is an actual interference with the course of justice, there is, in that court, a departure from due process of law in the proper sense of that term. And if the state, supplying no corrective process, carries into execution a judgment of death or imprisonment based upon a verdict thus produced by mob domination, the state deprives the accused of his life or liberty without due process of law.

That paragraph was the habeas door cracking open. Jurisdiction could be *lost*. However, Pitney was not finished. If a state appellate court had conducted its own inquiry into this question of mob dominance, which Georgia's Supreme Court had done, then that review provided a "corrective process" that allowed the state to retain its jurisdiction. "If a violation be threatened by one agency of the state but prevented by another agency of higher authority, there is no violation by the State," Pitney said. The Supreme Court denied Frank habeas relief, and since appellate review was a regular feature of every state's judicial system, this provision suggested that a state would never, in fact, lose its jurisdiction in criminal proceedings. And that was the habeas door seemingly slamming shut once again.

Perhaps not surprisingly, both sides in the June 13 hearing pointed to the *Frank* case to bolster their positions. Jones and McHaney argued that *Frank* set a precedent for a judge to find that a trial court, for one reason or another, had lost jurisdiction in a criminal case. That, they said, was what had happened here. The state was represented by assistant attorney general Elbert Godwin, who denounced the prisoners' habeas petitions as "one of the bitterest attacks ever made on a court of any community," and then argued that under *Frank,* the six condemned sharecroppers simply had no argument to make. There had been appellate review and that closed the matter.

In a written decision rendered on June 20, the Arkansas Supreme Court ventured to look ahead. After chastising Martineau for having stepped out of line and ruling that he had no authority to hold a habeas hearing, Chief Justice McCullough moved on to a discussion of the *Frank* precedent and its possible application to this case. Not only had there been appellate review of the sharecroppers' convictions, the *Frank* decision made it clear that the right of federal courts to intervene in state criminal trials was a very limited one:

> The court [in *Frank*] said that "this familiar phrase 'due process of law' does not mean that the operations of the state government shall be conducted without error or fault in any particular case, nor that the federal courts may substitute their judgment for that of the State courts, or exercise any general review over their proceedings, but only that the fundamental rights of the prisoner shall not be taken from him arbitrarily or without the right to be heard according to the usual course of law."

That was the bottom line: a federal court would have no valid reason to intervene in this case. "Further discussion," McCullough concluded, "would seem to be useless."

WITH THE ARKANSAS SUPREME Court having given Governor McRae the green light to reschedule the executions, Judge Jackson in Helena quickly allowed the Ware retrials to go forward, ruling on June 20 that the trials would be moved to Marianna, in neighboring Lee County. However, when Phillips County sheriff J. D. Mays and four deputies arrived at the state penitentiary to pick up the Ware six for transport to Marianna, Warden Dempsey—mindful that a few weeks earlier Helena's leaders had not so subtly warned that if Frank Moore and the others were not executed, then lynch mobs might go to work—refused to hand them over. As the Little Rock papers admitted, state officials were afraid of "mob violence."

After a day of tense negotiations, the state agreed to release the men into the joint custody of Mays and a squad of armed agents from Missouri Pacific, who promised that they would keep the Ware defendants safe. But even as the party departed for the depot in North Little Rock, intent on catching a 3:10 P.M. train, the state caught wind "of a plot to lynch the Negroes somewhere on the way to Marianna." It seemed that a mob might already be gathering to attack the train, and as Mays and the other law enforcement officers drove past the state capitol, seemingly on their way to the bridge that crossed the Arkansas River into North Little Rock, they suddenly veered off course and raced to the Missouri Pacific depot, just west of downtown. They hustled Ware and the others up a rear stairway to the third floor, where they hid them for the next eleven hours. At 2:40 A.M., they secreted their prisoners onto a "special coach attached to the Memphis Sunshine Special."

The next morning, Mays successfully dropped off Ed Ware and the others at the Marianna jail. There, deputy sheriff John Jones and his men prepared for an assault. But the hours clicked by without incident, and when an *Arkansas Gazette* reporter called late that night, needing a final update for Sunday's edition, Deputy Jones was able to tell him that "up to midnight, no efforts had been made to take the six Elaine negroes from the jail." The prisoners, he added, "appeared to be satisfied with their new home," having spent their first day in Lee County, in the midst of all this turmoil, calmly "singing and praying."

ON AUGUST 12, GOVERNOR McRae set September 23 as the new electrocution date, and the countdown began once again. There was, over the course of the next few weeks, a bit of case-related news. Ulysses Bratton briefly returned to Little Rock on business, and Helena authorities indicted him for barratry, a charge that prosecutor John Miller had previously filed against his son Ocier, only to let it drop. This new prosecutorial effort, Bratton railed in a letter to Governor McRae, was simply a ruse by the Helena planters to get him into Phillips County so that he could be "assassinated." This second barratry charge went no further than the first. In Virginia, Robert Kerlin was also under fire, and in mid-August, Virginia Military Institute told him that his continued presence there "would prove harmful and detrimental, and embarrassing" to the institution, and so he too was chased from the South. "It all shows how tense the feeling is regarding these Arkansas cases," Ovington said.

Bratton and Kerlin were simply paying the price of having broken tribal ranks. There was always a high cost to pay for doing that, and this case stirred up the most primal tribal passions imaginable. For anyone in Helena to break ranks would be unthinkable, which is why everyone at the NAACP's office in New York was so stunned when, on August 30, this message arrived from McHaney: "We now have two white witnesses who were in the trouble at Helena and Elaine from beginning to end, and who are going to testify for us."

Henry Smiddy had come knocking on McHaney's door. And he had brought with him his old boss, T. K. Jones.

There is not a clear historical record of how this came about. One possibility is that the detective Scipio Jones had hired in the spring convinced the two men to contact Scipio. "Mr. Scipio Jones,"

NAACP secretary Johnson told the board, "got in touch with them and after some time succeeded in getting them to tell the truth about the case." Other correspondence, however, suggests that Smiddy made the decision to step forward on his own. Either way, it's evident that ultimately Smiddy was moved by the demands of his conscience. "I did what I did for the Colored People," he explained in a letter to Walter White. "I knew the streight of the thing and I wanted to see them come out of it, and I did this for them. . . . I could not get another white man down their to make a affidavit to help save them only a man by the name of T. K. Jones and he did not want to give the streight facks about it until I got right in behind him."

At the moment they stepped forward in this way, both Smiddy and T. K. Jones were employed and thus doing fairly well financially. Jones had recently left his job at the Missouri Pacific Railroad to take a similar supervisory position with the Illinois Central Railroad, and Smiddy was working there too. Both men understood that their lives were now going to be ruined, and that was particularly true for Smiddy. After the trials in 1919, he had gone to work for the Helena City Police, and in early 1920, Kitchens had hired him as a deputy sheriff. He had remained in that post until Mays was elected. Smiddy had been at the very center of this dispute, and he was now crossing a line that no Southern lawman ever dared to cross. At the very least, Smiddy—who was the father of three girls and a boy, with his youngest only a few months old—was going to be chased from his job with the Illinois Central Railroad. McHaney promised that he would try to help him out financially "until I could get on my feet again," Smiddy said.

McHaney made a similar promise to T. K. Jones, and he and Smiddy dutifully laid out the entire story in their affidavits. Together, they told of how the planters had "objected to the Negroes having this union," and how Adkins and Pratt—and apparently some other whites—had gone to Hoop Spur that night "for the purpose of breaking up the meeting." Smiddy described how he'd found "where the church had been shot into from the north side," and both told of how the church was subsequently burned "to destroy the evidence that it had been fired into." They related how Helena posses descended upon Hoop Spur the next morning and began shooting blacks, with Smiddy providing a step-by-step account of how he and fifty or sixty others marched down both sides of the Govan Slough and shot the black farmers hiding there, with James Tappan apparently killed by their own crossfire. As for Clinton Lee's death, both swore that while they'd seen a party of Negroes, about one-half mile to the south, scurry across the road moments before Lee was shot, they hadn't seen anyone kneel down and squeeze off a shot. The Negroes "seemed to be scared and seemed to be trying to get out of the way of the white folks," Smiddy said. He told too of how the white posses had killed hundreds of black men, women, and children. They described how Camp Pike troops conducted a mass roundup of blacks, and of how, on Thursday night, the Committee of Seven and other Helena leaders promised a lynch mob that the black prisoners would be duly "punished." Next they described the torture—the whippings, the use of the electric chair, the simulated suffocation— they and others inflicted on the black prisoners to get them to testify to whatever the Committee of Seven wanted. They both swore that Frank Moore and the others had not been given the opportunity to appear before the grand jury, as the law required, and as for the trials, they related how the sharecroppers' attorneys had made no effort to defend them. Posse members, Smiddy said, served as jurors in the trials. When it was his turn to step onto the witness stand, Smiddy added, "I was instructed by those in authority that I should give no testimony of any character favorable to the defendants."

They had confirmed every last detail of the black narrative of events. Theirs was an extraordinary defection, and T. K. Jones, in the last line of his affidavit, wrote: "I make this affidavit freely and voluntarily to the end that justice may be done."

As expected, the backlash came fast and furious. Smiddy was immediately fired and thrown into jail. "The Arkansas officers," Smiddy said, "bent on executing the Negroes, began to make various charges against me for the sole purpose of compelling me to withdraw the affidavit." With his star witness in jeopardy, Scipio Jones rushed to Helena and got Smiddy released on $1,000 bail, the mob nipping at Smiddy's heels even as he fled to Memphis. "My life was threatened," Smiddy told Jones, and after Arkansas authorities cooked up a new criminal charge against him, hoping to extradite him from Memphis to Little Rock, Jones gave him some "traveling money" and Smiddy hurried from Tennessee. He was now a man on the run, and three months later, he turned up at the NAACP's branch office in Topeka, Kansas—broke, hungry, and lonely for his wife and kids.

"I want to get them up hear with me for my Wife is worring her self to death about me and the Four little children we have," Smiddy wrote, in a letter to Walter White. "Neither one of the children are big enough to take care of themselves, so you see I am in a bad shape write now. . . . Now they have a Federal charge against me in Little Rock, which is trumped up on me for making this affidavit for the Boys, so they want to get me back down their to kill me. . . . Please help me out of this if there is any chance to, I am not a bad fellow at all or no cruckor."

Jones did what he could to help. He traveled to Memphis to provide Smiddy's wife with some money, and after T. K. Jones was fired, he helped out his family too. Over the course of several months, he shelled out $1,400 to the two families. But that financial assistance could not begin to repair their lives. Smiddy and T. K. Jones were now pariahs, and they and their families were suffering the consequences. They had known this was to be their fate when they had signed those affidavits, which is why, by doing so, they surely had performed acts of bravery and heroism, and acts of personal redemption too.

A WEEK BEFORE THE scheduled electrocutions, Scipio Jones was hit by a new bombshell. In late August, McHaney had asked the NAACP for another $5,000, but the NAACP had refused, and on September 16, McHaney resigned. His "withdrawal from the cases at this stage of the proceeding will, doubtless, weaken our cause, but his requirements are so unreasonable, I am sure no one will attempt to comply with them," Jones told the NAACP. "I expect to live up to my contract with the Association."

The NAACP too was stunned: "It is difficult for us to conceive that Messrs. Murphy, McHaney and Dunaway would desert these cases at this juncture," NAACP secretary James Weldon Johnson told Jones. "And not for a moment do we think that you will do anything else but stand by these men until the very last resource is exhausted. These Arkansas cases are no longer mere legal cases. These constitute a fight for common justice and humanity and those who are aiding in the fight are doing a great public service. Indeed, the monetary consideration ought to be secondary."

Jones hustled to finish the habeas petitions. With the affidavits of Smiddy and T. K. Jones in hand, it was easy for him to tell a story of gross injustice—he now had both torturers and the tortured attesting to that fact. Jones also had secured affidavits from the three sharecroppers—Walter Ward, George Green, and John Jefferson—who, in one manner or another, had provided the testimony that was used to convict the Moore six. All three recanted that earlier testimony, attesting to how it had been secured through torture or threats of it. Yet Jones knew that a narrative of torture being used to send innocent men to the electric chair was not going to save his clients. As the U.S. Supreme Court had explicitly noted in *Frank,* "the essential question" before a federal court in a habeas hearing was "not the guilt or innocence of the prisoner." What Jones needed to do, if he was going to exploit the sliver of hope offered by *Frank,* was tell a story of a state judicial system that had *lost jurisdiction* over Frank Moore and the others.

As a first step, Jones focused on the Committee of Seven's actions. This group, Jones argued, had usurped the Court's jurisdiction, with this usurpation process having begun on the night of October 2, when the Committee—and other Helena leaders—promised the mob that the "law" could be used to "execute" the sharecroppers:

> Petitioners say . . . that their real trial and condemnation had already taken place before said Committee of Seven; that said

Committee, in advance of the sitting of the court, had sat in judgment upon them and had assumed and exercised the jurisdiction of the court by determining the guilt or innocence of those in jail. [The Committee] decided which of the defendants should be electrocuted and which sent to prison and the terms to be given them, and which to discharge; when court convened, the program laid out by said Committee was carried through and the verdicts against petitioners were pronounced and returned, not as the independent verdict of an unbiased jury, but as a part of the prearranged scheme and judgment of said Committee.

This was a carefully crafted legal argument. The Committee of Seven had taken over the judicial proceedings, the actual trials had been "but an empty ceremony," and by consenting to this, Jones wrote, "the court did not exercise the jurisdiction given it by law."

However, this argument had an obvious weakness: this was a story of a *mob-conducted* trial, not a mob-dominated trial, and while the former was clearly more insidious, the fact that the town fathers of a small Southern town had orchestrated a trial involving black defendants was hardly an extraordinary thing. Everyone knew that wealthy planters ran their towns like they were their private fiefdoms, and everyone knew that white juries in the South were not fair to black defendants, and that when a case involved both white and black parties, they would reach a race-based decision. In such trials, the fix was always in, and the U.S. Supreme Court, by allowing for the exclusion of blacks from juries, had given its blessing to such a system. So how was this "empty ceremony" any different from the thousands of such trials that had taken place ever since Democrats had "redeemed" the South?

Jones needed to piggyback on the *Frank* decision in a more precise manner, and he and McHaney, when they had worked with Smiddy and T. K. Jones on their affidavits, had prepared for this. In his 1919 motion for new trials, Jones had not claimed that a "mob" had dominated the court, and that was because no such thing had happened. None of the newspapers covering the trials had described such a scene, but rather had reported that the courtroom was filled with both black and white spectators, with the white crowd occasionally *laughing* at the proceedings. With John Moore and Greenfield Quarles as the sharecroppers' defense attorneys, and with posse members such as Charlie Afflick and Louis Anselman in the jury box, there had been no need for a mob to gather outside the courthouse in order to intimidate the jury. However, it was true that whites had crowded into the courtroom, and that they all wanted the defendants to be given the death penalty, and that if any other verdict had come down, they almost certainly would have rioted. With details like that to work with, it hadn't been too much of a stretch for the two attorneys to have Smiddy and T. K. Jones, in their affidavits, declare that "large crowds thronged the court house and grounds, all of whom were unfriendly to the defendants, and desired their condemnation and death."

Thronged—that word, Jones well knew, would help transform a crowd into a mob in the reader's mind.

Jones presented the habeas petitions for the six men—Frank Moore, Ed Hicks, Frank Hicks, Joe Knox, Ed Coleman, and Paul Hall—to Judge Jacob Trieber on September 21, and Trieber granted the writ, ordering the state to respond by Monday, September 26. The state could have contested the allegations, but—and this was a huge break for the condemned men—it responded with a "demurrer," arguing that even if everything the condemned men said was true, it didn't matter. "The question of mob domination at the time of the trial of the Elaine rioters had been ruled upon by the state courts," Arkansas attorney general J. S. Utley explained to reporters, and thus, under the *Frank* decision, "was not admissible as a cause for a review by the federal court."

Because Trieber had lived for a time in Helena, he recused himself from presiding over the September 26 hearing. Jones and Utley argued instead before Judge John Cotteral from Oklahoma, and since the state had demurred to the habeas petitions, Cotteral was to treat the prisoners' allegations as fact.* This was a case in which white planters shot up a church where black sharecroppers were meeting, and then, over the course of the next few days, white posses and federal troops killed more than two hundred black men, women, and children. Next, white authorities rounded up hundreds of blacks, promised a lynch mob that leaders of the farmers union would be executed, and tortured witnesses to falsely testify at trials where white posse members served as jurors and angry throngs gathered outside the courtroom. While Cotteral acknowledged this was indeed a disturbing set of facts, he noted that by law he was "forced to rely on the decisions of the state Supreme Court as to the regularity of the proceedings in the trial court," and the Arkansas Supreme Court "had held that the trial had been regular and that the negroes had been given a fair and impartial trial."

Frank Moore and the other five condemned men had lost again. But Cotteral did authorize an appeal of his decision to the U.S. Supreme Court, and this, in fact, was precisely the ruling that Jones wanted. "The sustaining of the demurrer of the State was really a victory for the petitioners," he explained to the NAACP. "You know that we have been trying to get these cases in the Supreme Court of the United States for almost two years, without success, but we are now sure that the cases will reach the Supreme Court with the facts stated in our petition undenied. Had Judge Cotteral overruled the state's demurrer to our petition, we would have been put to the test of proving the allegations in our petition."

Jones had thirty days to perfect the appeal. However, he needed to turn his attention first to the Ware retrials, which were now slated to begin October 10. Here too he had a surprise up his sleeve. "With the assistance of a few of my friends, I have succeeded in raising $6,000 . . . for payment of fees to two law firms at Marianna for their services in the trial of the six cases," he told Ovington, and

---

* McHaney appeared with Jones at this hearing; his resignation apparently was to take effect immediately afterward.

then, in a follow-up letter, he explained just who these mystery attorneys were. One was a former Marianna *judge*, J. C. Smith, and the second was a partner from the prominent Marianna firm of Mann and *McCullough*. Mr. McCullough, Jones noted with evident pleasure, "is a son of Chief Justice McCullough of the Supreme Court of this state."

Jones pulled this off—including raising the $6,000—during the last week of September. Like Helena, Marianna was a town run by planters, and yet Jones had succeeded in recruiting attorneys who were leaders in that community to serve as his co-counsel. He'd fractured the town's white leadership, which meant that the retrials would no longer fit neatly into a white-versus-black box. "Mann and McCullough," Jones told the NAACP, "are well connected in Lee County and in position to control public sentiment in their county." Prosecutor John Miller apparently saw it that way too, for he told the court on October 10 that the state needed "further time to perfect its evidence," and Judge Jackson granted his request, putting off the trials until the following spring.

Jones perfected the appeals to the U.S. Supreme Court on October 21, and it was possible, at that moment, to see how skillfully—and triumphantly—he had handled these cases. Two years earlier, the story that had been told in the Helena courtroom was that savage blacks had conspired to kill whites and take over their land. Now the state feared to return to the courtroom to retry the six Ware defendants, and the U.S. Supreme Court, as it considered the habeas petitions of the Moore group, would be confronted by a narrative, one agreed to by both parties, that told of a white massacre of blacks and of judicial proceedings of the most grotesque sort. Jones had turned the narrative completely around, and not just in the court of public opinion, but also in the legal record. He had fought and fought, and by doing so, he had served not only the Elaine farmers well, but also the entire nation. The U.S. Supreme Court would now have to think deeply about the country's makeup, and how it was, more than fifty years after the Fourteenth Amendment remade the Constitution with its promise of equality under the law to all, that the country had reached such a moment as this. There would be the past to consider, and then the court would have to decide whether the country should continue down the path it was on, or head in a new direction.

Roared W. E. B. Du Bois: "The greatest case against peonage and mob law ever fought in the land, and involving 12 human lives, comes before the highest court!"

Taft and His Court

T HE BACKLOG OF CASES at the U.S. Supreme Court was such that Jones didn't expect his appeal to be heard for at least a year, and yet, even so, he immediately asked the NAACP to help him "secure the services of the ablest Constitutional lawyer obtainable." He and Walter White and Mary Ovington were all imbued with a sense of great hope—"We have never had so exciting a time in the history of our work here," Ovington wrote in one of her letters—and they agreed that NAACP president Moorfield Storey was the perfect person for the job. "I hope that he will accept employment in these cases," Jones wrote to White on October 28.

There was perhaps no white man in the country who had so steadfastly argued for equal rights for blacks as Moorfield Storey. Born in Boston in 1845, he'd served as secretary to Massachusetts senator Charles Sumner from 1867 to 1869, and during that time he'd soaked up Sumner's abolitionist values. Sumner was the architect of the 1875 Civil Rights Bill, and Storey never wavered in his belief that federal law should protect the basic rights of all Americans. At the moment of the NAACP's founding, he'd been elected president by acclamation.

Storey had argued before the Supreme Court in 1915 and again in 1917, and while the NAACP counted both decisions as great victories, neither one—and Storey knew this as well as anybody—had resulted from a newfound interest in black rights by the court. In

*Guinn v. United States,** the U.S. Supreme Court agreed that Okla-homa's use of a grandfather clause in its voting laws—the provision enfranchised only those who had ancestors eligible to vote prior to 1866—was unconstitutional. Since the grandfather clause was clearly a proxy for race, it violated Supreme Court law that prohibited states from enacting race-based voter eligibility laws. The Supreme Court required states to use more subtle provisions to disenfranchise blacks, and this decision was consistent with that wink-wink stan-dard. In the 1917 case *Buchanan v. Warley,* the Supreme Court agreed with Storey that a residential segregation law enacted by Louisville, Kentucky, violated the Constitution. However, the court's primary objection to the law was that it harmed the property owner's right to sell to whomever he wished. White property owners soon began writing whites-only covenants into their deeds, and the court subse-quently gave its approval to that owner-initiated segregation.

There was, in short, nothing in the two decisions to make one think that the court had changed its stripes, and that was why, when Ovington and White asked Storey to argue the Arkansas cases, he begged off. "I am an old and very busy man," he replied, and, more-over, he didn't really see how this appeal could be won. "I do not wish to refuse absolutely to appear for the Arkansas Negroes in the Supreme Court of the United States, but I must be satisfied before I do appear that they have a good case. I do not mean by that that they have a case that is good on the facts, but that there is some authority which will sustain their present application to the court." At last, Storey agreed not to make any decision until Jones had prepared the record on appeal for his review. "If I find that I can speak with some conviction, I will try to do so," he said, "but I do not want to appear in court with a case that I cannot maintain."

The NAACP now began a final round of fund-raising, and while Storey's hesitation may have dimmed the organization's optimism

---

* This case was originated by the U.S. Department of Justice, with Storey and the NAACP filing a friend-of-the-court brief.

about winning the appeal, Ovington and others knew at once how to raise more money. The NAACP reprinted Jones's habeas petition as a pamphlet titled "The Arkansas Peons: Not a Description of Conditions in Mexico or the Belgian Congo, but in the United States!" and mailed it to Julius Rosenwald and other previous donors to the Arkansas Defense Fund. This petition, Walter White told friends, is "one of the most human and thorough legal documents ever printed in America." The *Crisis* also published it, Du Bois urging subscribers to "read carefully this amazing document which portrays so clearly the vicious methods which have been used in the attempt to murder these innocent men."

This praise unwittingly revealed a certain truth. Storey, or some other attorney known for his constitutional expertise, might lend his prestige to the case, but there was nothing that any attorney could do now that would improve on what Jones had already done. Jones, born into slavery and raised in an illiterate household, had penned the most eloquent and convincing argument that could possibly be made, and it consisted, ultimately, of a powerful narrative that left no question about what the nation's highest court, if it was concerned about justice, should do.

OVER THE NEXT TWELVE months, there were a handful of twists and turns in the case that made news. Whites in Helena had threatened that they would begin lynching Negroes accused of crimes if the "Elaine rioters" were not executed, and on November 18, 1921, they made good on that promise. After eighteen-year-old Will Turner was arrested that morning for assaulting a seventeen-year-old white girl, a mob grabbed him from deputy sheriffs, pumped him full of bullets, and ceremoniously burned his corpse in the park across from the county courthouse. While the *Helena World* editorialized that the lynching was to be regretted, as Phillips County would no longer be able to boast that it had never hosted such an affair, it reasoned that surely everyone, given that the Elaine twelve had yet to be electrocuted, would understand why it had occurred: "Who can say truthfully that [the county's] provocation was not great, or that her forbearance had not been taxed beyond that of any community in the American Union? There must be an end to everything except Eternity, and so there was an end to the patience of those who have hitherto borne much."

From Little Rock, there came the strange news that a white bandit had held up the penitentiary and offered the six condemned men "their freedom," but, Walter White informed a friend, they "refused to leave their cells." Ed Ware and the five men in the Marianna jail similarly made headlines, a brouhaha erupting after newspapers reported that deputy sheriff John Jones, having apparently concluded that they were a harmless bunch, began letting them out of their cells to cook, with Jones, on at least one occasion, using Ware as his personal chauffeur as he ran errands. Judge Jackson, who presided over both counties, immediately ordered the six prisoners transferred to Phillips County jail, as deputies there were certain to keep them locked up twenty-four hours a day.

The spring term of criminal court in Lee County came and went without the retrials being held, Utley declaring that the state would delay those prosecutions until the U.S. Supreme Court ruled on the Moore appeals. Smiddy grew ever more desperate in Topeka, Kansas, and briefly lashed out at Scipio Jones, telling the NAACP that while he'd come to think of Jones as his "friend," Jones was not doing enough to help him. Jones responded to Smiddy with disbelief—"He ba[w]led me out good and plenty," Smiddy confessed—and with good reason: he was now carrying much of the financial burden of these cases himself. There was the $6,000 he had raised to pay the Marianna attorneys, the $1,000 bail he'd posted for Smiddy, the $1,400 he had given to Smiddy and Jones and their families, and the $795 he'd sent to the U.S. Supreme Court to cover court costs. Not so long before, Jones had run around Little Rock in a chauffeured Cadillac, but now, he told White, he was a "financial wreck."

Nationwide, there was the usual spate of lynchings, with thirty-three recorded in the first six months of 1922. May was a particularly bad month, with six blacks hung, shot, or beaten to death, and another six set on fire. "The South has triumphed!" the *Messenger* declared. "The spirit of Dixie holds the nation in its grip." Harvard University showed its Dixie spirit that summer by banning its black students from dining rooms and dormitories, President Abbott Lowell reasoning that "we owe to our Negro students the best possible education, but we do not owe to them inclusion in a social system with white people."

The country continued to careen down the same awful road it had been on for so long. The notion that blacks were not really fit human beings continued to hold sway, and Jones and the NAACP, as they looked ahead to the coming oral arguments, could only have been disquieted by the court's rapidly changing makeup. In the summer of 1921, President Warren Harding had named former President William Taft to be chief justice, and with three more seats on the court in the process of becoming vacant, Harding was certain to fill them with men who shared Taft's ideology. That meant that the Moore appeals would be heard by a court that was even more conservative than the one that had ruled in *Frank,* and it would be dominated by judges who shared a judicial philosophy—one that had first taken hold in the 1880s—that blacks found utterly infuriating.

AFTER THE CIVIL WAR ended, the country began to go through a period of rapid industrialization, and while the captains of industry—the owners of railroad, steel, and oil companies—reaped great fortunes, farmers and laborers were, in many ways, crushed by this surge of unfettered capitalism. These latter groups, beginning in the 1880s, elected "populists" to fight for their economic interests, and their representatives did so by passing laws to regulate business, which in turn produced disputes that made their way to the Supreme Court.

In this particular battle, Republicans were the party of big business, and Democrats—at least in the North—were the party of the workingman. Because the Republicans had controlled the presidency since the end of the Civil War, the Court was filled with Republicans, and naturally most of the justices came from the upper class. Many had worked as corporate attorneys, and thus it was not surprising that they, like their wealthy peers, were deeply influenced by social

Darwinism, a school of thought that rich capitalists were eagerly embracing. In the struggle for survival, social Darwinists argued, those who emerged on top in society—that is to say, the rich—were the "fittest." The poor failed to prosper because they were "weak" and "unfit." This was the natural state of things, and the United States could best grow and prosper in a laissez-faire economy where the fit were unencumbered by government regulations.

The U.S. Supreme Court began turning this social Darwinist philosophy into law in 1886, when it ruled in *Santa Clara Co. v. Southern Pacific Railroad* that corporations were to be considered "persons" under the Fourteenth Amendment. As such, no state could deprive them of their "property without due process." In 1890, the Court, in *Chicago, Milwaukee & St. Paul Railway v. Minnesota,* provided a corporate "person" with its first Fourteenth Amendment victory, voiding a Minnesota law that barred railroads from challenging in court the tariffs set by the state's railroad commission. This rate-fixing process, absent any judicial appeal, deprived the railroad "of the lawful use of its property, and thus, in substance and effect, of the property itself, without due process of law," the Court ruled. Other similar decisions soon followed, the Court even holding in *Smyth v. Ames* (1897) that railroad commissions had to set rates that provided railroads with a "fair return" on invested property— apparently the Fourteenth Amendment guaranteed their owners a profit deemed "just" and "reasonable" by the Court. The Court also issued Fourteenth Amendment decisions that protected big business from labor unions—strikes and picketing could be stopped by court order if they deprived a business of the "rightful" use of its property. Big corporations flocked to the Supreme Court for Fourteenth Amendment relief so frequently that in 1912, when a scholar reviewed the history of the Court's Fourteenth Amendment cases, he determined that only 28 of the 604 cases dealt with black rights. "It is not the Negro, but accumulated and organized capital which now looks to the Fourteenth Amendment for protection from State activity," he concluded.

This was a transformation of an amazing sort: an amendment

that had been enacted in 1868 to protect the basic rights of the freed-men had been turned into a shelter for the rich, and what particu-larly infuriated blacks was that it required, on the part of the Court, the most blatant hypocrisy. Whenever the Court ruled on Fourteenth Amendment cases involving the civil rights of blacks, it invoked the "states' rights" principle. That was why the federal government couldn't stop mobs from lynching blacks, or from burning them at the stake, or from driving them from jobs. The federal government—and federal courts—had "limited powers." The Court may have wanted to do the right thing, but it couldn't—its hands were tied by the Constitution. Yet when it came to protecting the property rights of the wealthy, the Court trampled all over states' rights, voiding law after law that state legislatures had enacted. Blacks could conclude only one thing: "states' rights" was a fig leaf that the Court hid be-hind whenever it ruled against the Negro's interests, which it did nearly all the time.

"The United States Supreme Court has easily found grounds for jurisdiction where economic rights are concerned, but just as easily disclaims jurisdiction where human rights are involved in cases in which Negroes happen to be the complainants," wrote Carter Wood-son, editor of the *Journal of Negro History,* in 1921. "Such sophistry deserves the condemnation of all fairminded people, when one must conclude that any person even without formal education, if he has heard the English language spoken and is of sound mind, would know better than to interpret a law [the Fourteenth Amendment] so unreasonably."

Taft had long been one of the country's most avid proponents of this laissez-faire judicial philosophy. As a U.S. Circuit Court judge in 1894, he'd argued that "princely profits" were a just reward to "men of judgment, courage, and executive ability," and that it was only right and fair that federal courts keep that property safe from the greedy hands of the populists: "The poor are the majority. The ap-peal of the rich to the Constitution and courts for protection is still an appeal by the weak against the unjust aggressions of the strong." However, he didn't see any need to provide defendants in criminal trials with the protections set forth in the Bill of Rights. The Fifth Amendment right not to incriminate oneself, he told Yale law students in 1905, was of "doubtful utility." Nor did he necessarily think that defendants should have the right to confront witnesses. "We must cease to regard [these rights] as fetishes to be worshipped without reason and simply because they are." Concern for the property rights of the wealthy and a lack of concern for the basic rights of criminal defendants were, for Taft and so many laissez-faire judges, the two sides of the same judicial coin.

As president, Taft also had done much to alienate blacks. At his presidential inauguration in 1909, he declared that he would not appoint any Negroes to federal posts in the South, and by the time he left office, only six held such positions. Federal peonage prosecutions, an effort that Theodore Roosevelt had begun, declined and faded away under his leadership. Taft's unpopularity with blacks was such that more than 100,000 of them voted for Woodrow Wilson in 1912, as they abandoned the Republican party that had been their home for so long.

Given Taft's record as federal judge and as president, black leaders expected little from him as chief justice. Taft, reasoned the *Chicago Defender,* hadn't challenged white-supremacist policies in the South while president, so why would he as head of the Supreme Court? "Mr. Taft," Du Bois wrote in the *Crisis,* "is not an enemy of the Negro race, he is worse than that; he is a luke-warm friend whom enemies of the race have used and will use to its hurt." The *Messenger* sounded an equally hopeless note: "The court formerly represented capital and the corporations; so does Taft. The court has consistently stood on a caste status for the Negro; Taft concurs with it. The 13th, 14th, and 15th Amendments have not been enforced by the Court previously (except insofar as their enforcement benefited the corporations). Negroes need not expect their enforcement now."

This man now presided over the Court, and a justice-by-justice review of the other members could not provide Jones and the NAACP with much reason for optimism, either.

Joseph McKenna, 79, was a former railroad lawyer who had

ruled with the majority in the *Frank* case, and to make matters worse, he was now sliding into senility. "He is not able to grasp the point" of a legal argument, Taft confessed, "or give a wise and deliberate consideration of it." Willis Van Devanter, who likewise had voted with the majority in *Frank,* had ruled so consistently in favor of big business that Taft, upon ascending to the bench, called him "my chancellor." Next in the line of laissez-faire judges was James McReynolds, a Tennessee Democrat who'd been appointed by Wilson in 1914. He too had voted with the majority in *Frank,* and he also happened to be the most virulent racist ever to sit on the bench, with even Taft remarking—despite their shared economic beliefs— that he was "fuller of prejudice than any man I've ever known." George Sutherland and Pierce Butler, the two men new to the Court in the fall of 1922, had been practically handpicked by Taft. Sutherland, a former senator from Utah, treated big business so kindly that Woodrow Wilson once quipped: "In my few dealings with Justice Sutherland, I have seen no reason to suspect him of either principles or brains." Butler was a millionaire railroad attorney from Minnesota who, as one Court historian said, "displayed no sympathy for the poor." *

That made six justices in the Taft mold. However, the remaining two justices—the ninth seat was about to be vacated—could be expected to look favorably upon the sharecroppers' case. Oliver Wendell Holmes had dissented in *Frank,* arguing that if a habeas petition presented evidence that trial proceedings had been grossly unfair, a federal court had both the authority and a duty to "examine the facts" and determine for itself if the allegations were true, regardless of what the state's appellate court had concluded. "Otherwise," Holmes concluded, the right of habeas corpus "will be a barren one." As for Louis Brandeis, whom President Wilson had appointed

---

* Harding picked Butler over Tennessee senator John Shields, who may have sabotaged his chances when he publicly explained why he was opposed to giving the ballot to "nigger women": "You see, we couldn't treat the wenches as we do the men; we just club the niggers if they come to the polls."

to the bench in 1916, he was Taft's ideological opposite. The first Jewish justice in the Court's history, he had gained fame for his fights against the railroads and on behalf of labor, struggles that had earned him the moniker the "people's lawyer." Blacks had cheered his appointment, Du Bois writing that "with the nomination of Mr. Brandeis we have a man who, as a Jew, knows what it is to be 'despised and rejected of men,' and, as a friend and advocate of laboring men, he knows what the curse of poverty means and what its abolition involves."

Such was the Court that would decide the fate of Frank Moore and the other five condemned men. There were six laissez-faire justices who were hostile to unions and thought that the Fourteenth Amendment was best employed to protect the property rights of the rich, and this group was led by a chief justice who didn't think that criminal defendants deserved the protections in the Bill of Rights. On the other side were Holmes and Brandeis. The voting numbers for the Elaine sharecroppers didn't look promising, and Storey, after finally agreeing in September of 1922 to appear in the cases, concluded the obvious: "I am very much afraid," he told Mary White Ovington, that "we shall not be able to win the case, but I am going to try."

THAT OCTOBER, JONES ONCE again prepared for the Ware retrials, and once again the state requested that they be delayed. Ed Ware and the others would have to remain locked up in the Helena jail and wait yet again for the next term of court. However, Jones did have a bit of good news to report that fall: he had succeeded in getting all of the men serving five- or six-year terms at Cummins State Farm released on parole, such that there remained only fifteen men—Milligan Giles and the fourteen sharecroppers sentenced to twenty-one-year-terms—still at the farm.

Storey waited until mid-November to begin his work on the brief. Jones prepared the record on appeal, and as Storey reviewed it his pessimism began to lift. The record was so compelling. There were the affidavits from the sharecroppers recanting their testimony, and the affidavits from Smiddy and T. K. Jones, and there were the pleas from the Helena American Legion and other Helena businesses that the men be executed—those letters provided evidence of the mob spirit at work. And Jones had woven all of this factual information into a powerful narrative in his habeas petition, one that seemingly would move even the hardest heart. "It is rather my habit when I enlist in a case to grow more and more confident that my cause is just, and that process is going on in the Arkansas case," he told White. "The Supreme Court in the *Frank* case made it clear that a case can be presented on which habeas corpus will issue, and I cannot help thinking that if that is so, it would be impossible to find a stronger case than the one which we have."

Storey made Jones's narrative the centerpiece of his brief. His was more an appeal to the Court to do what was "just" and "right," rather than an argument of law. However, he did try to distinguish this case from *Frank* in terms of the state appellate review that had occurred. The Georgia Supreme Court had conducted its own investigation into whether the jury had been dominated by a mob and concluded that it hadn't been. But in this case, the Arkansas Supreme Court had "assumed" that all of the sharecroppers' allegations were true and had then concluded that it didn't matter. As such, Storey reasoned, the Arkansas Supreme Court had given its blessing to torture and to farcical trials that did not provide any semblance of due process, and thus had not provided a "correction" to the unfair trial proceedings. "Nowhere in the history of the case from beginning to end is there any indication that prior to the conviction there was any serious attempt made to ascertain whether the defendants were really guilty," he wrote. "The evidence on which they were convicted was manufactured, the witnesses were beaten and terrorized, and the record of the whole case shows what, if consummated, is only judicial murder."

The entire state process had been nothing more than a judicial lynching—this was Storey's legal argument. The Arkansas Supreme Court had lost its jurisdiction for the same reason that the trial court had, and that was because it had given its consent to this lynching. And then Storey raised the constitutional issue at stake:

> If this Court on reading this petition, these affidavits and this record is not satisfied that if there ever was a case in which habeas corpus should be granted this is the case, no argument of counsel will convince them, and we submit with confidence that either habeas corpus should be granted in this case or habeas corpus is not a practical remedy for such outrages as the evidence in this case discloses.

The state, for its part, did not try to argue that the trials had been fair. Instead, in his brief, Utley pointed to the existing standards of habeas corpus law. A state law prohibiting murder, he noted, was clearly not "repugnant" to the Constitution. All that a state was required to do, he wrote, citing *Frank,* was to provide defendants with trials "conducted according to the well established course of judicial proceedings as established by the laws of said State," and Arkansas had met that requirement. The Moore appellants had been tried before a jury, and the state's Supreme Court had signed off on the conduct of those trials. All told, Utley cited more than a dozen habeas corpus decisions as applicable precedent. The past was all on the state's side, and to stray from that precedent—and pay any heed to affidavits filed at the last moment, such as the ones from Smiddy and T. K. Jones—would "open an avenue for every criminal charged with violating our State laws" to appeal to federal courts for relief.

With this case, the evolution of habeas corpus law—and thus of all American criminal law—had clearly reached the proverbial fork in the road. In *Frank,* the court had raised the *possibility* of federal courts providing habeas relief to state prisoners who had been convicted at trials that were grossly unfair. If the court now ruled in favor of the Elaine farmers, then that possibility would become a reality, and that would mean that federal habeas review could become a means by which federal courts established basic fairness standards that all states would be required to meet. But if the court ruled against the Elaine farmers and sent the six men to their death, then this possibility of reform would disappear. The habeas door would be fully shut once again, for as Storey had said in his brief, if this case didn't merit habeas relief, then it was impossible to imagine one that ever would.

THE CHANCE TO APPEAR before the U.S. Supreme Court is any good lawyer's dream, and for a black man who'd been born a slave, it must have represented the achievement of the impossible dream. Yet in the fall of 1922 this dream began to slip from Jones's grasp, and it was the NAACP that was the unwitting culprit, this unsettling turn beginning when Walter White, without checking with Jones first, asked Ulysses Bratton if he would appear along with Storey and Jones. "I assure you that it will indeed be a pleasure to me to render any possible service in the way of assisting in getting the real facts and conditions before the Supreme Court," Bratton replied. The NAACP had first discussed this possibility a year earlier, and at that time Jones had quietly explained his objections to Arthur Spingarn, head of the organization's legal committee. As Spingarn informed the board: "He stated that the defense would be allowed only two arguments [by the Taft court], and that he had planned to make one of the arguments himself."

Now, with Bratton having accepted White's invitation, Jones was in a bind. This was *his* case. He had fought and fought to keep the six men alive, and he wanted to tell their story to the nation's highest court. Storey could argue the law, while he would inform the court of the facts. But in order to protect his opportunity to speak, he now had to object, once again, to Bratton's participation, and what made that so difficult was that he and Bratton had long been friends. Fifteen years ago, they had fought the lily-whites in Little Rock together. In his letters, Bratton still addressed him as "Friend Sip." However, Jones did have a practical reason, one that didn't involve his own ambitions, for not wanting Bratton to appear. If he showed up in Washington representing the sharecroppers, this would infuriate whites in Little Rock. "I am of the opinion that Mr. Bratton's connection with these cases will be used against us should we be forced to apply again for executive clemency," Jones informed White on November 25. "Personally, I would like to have him in the case."

The letter provided an easy way out for White. All he had to do was read between the lines, sense that Jones was understandably protecting his turf, and then he could explain to Bratton why, for political reasons, it was best that he not appear. But White, apparently unaware of the only-two-attorneys-may-speak rule of the Taft court, instead asked Jones to reconsider: "We want to do nothing that would endanger the lives of the men now in jail in Arkansas, nor to jeopardize the success of the [Ware] trials. On the other hand, it will have a splendid psychological effect if Mr. Bratton, a white man from Arkansas who knows conditions behind these cases thoroughly, should open the argument."

After that, White and Jones exchanged a couple more telegrams, as did Storey and White, and none of that cleared up the miscommunication. To White and Storey, it seemed that Jones was being a bit difficult, and finally Jones relented, asking White to simply leave Bratton's name off the brief, as at least that way Little Rock whites wouldn't think that Bratton had been hired by the six condemned men. "If he should just appear and participate in the argument, I can say that he volunteered and was not selected by the defendants," Jones wrote on December 21.

Once the new year arrived, Bratton and Jones prepared for their trips to Washington, D.C. "Judge Storey advised me that the cases would likely be reached sometime the latter part of this month," Bratton wrote to White, "but suggested that I hold myself in readiness to come sometime around the second week in January." Jones was told the same thing, that the case was set for the "third week of January," and on Saturday, January 6, hoping to finalize his travel plans, he wired the clerk of the Supreme Court. Could he confirm that the Moore case would be heard during the week of January 15–19?

The clerk's reply—that the case had been moved up a week on the calendar—must have broken Jones's heart. "Am advised by clerk cases will probably be reached Tuesday," Jones telegraphed White. "Don't fail to have Judge Storey there."

Even at this late hour, it would have been possible for Jones to make it to Washington in time. From Little Rock to the nation's capital took forty-four hours by train, and if he hustled down to the station right away, he could catch an overnight train to St. Louis, and that would get him to Washington by 4:00 P.M. on Monday. But the trip would be exhausting—as a black man, he would not be able to obtain a sleeping berth in a Pullman car on the ride to St. Louis—and he would also have to suffer the disappointment of not having the opportunity to speak. Jones, that gray Saturday afternoon, returned to his home at 1911 Pulaski Street. It seems that he spent that night mulling over the possibility of catching a train early Sunday, and he may even have gone to the station that morning with packed suitcase in hand, but by then, the timetable no longer worked at all. Fate had thrown him a most unkind curveball, and so he slowly walked over to the Western Union office instead.

"Don't expect to be able to be in Washington," he telegraphed White. "Depending on Mister Bratton and Judge Storey to appear."

THE COURT, AT THAT time, was housed in the Capitol, as the magnificent Supreme Court building that graces Washington, D.C., today had not yet been built. Ever since 1860, the Court had heard oral arguments in an old Senate chamber that, one court historian noted, was "small, badly ventilated and poorly lighted," and on that Tuesday afternoon, January 9, Taft, who weighed nearly 300 pounds, entered first. The other seven justices followed in order of seniority, and their places on the bench reflected that pecking order as well. As the most senior member of the court, McKenna sat on Taft's right, and Holmes, second to McKenna in seniority, sat on Taft's left. Then it went back and forth in that way, with the two newcomers, Sutherland and Butler, at the far ends of the bench.

The justices had familiarized themselves with the case, and as such, their minds that afternoon must have flitted back to the newspaper headlines from the past few days, given that they so hauntingly echoed the matter now before them. The previous Thursday, a "race war" had broken out in the tiny community of Rosewood, Florida. Whites from as far as 75 miles away had flooded into Rosewood to join in the "fighting," and at latest count, six blacks had been killed, all of the Negro homes in town had been burned, and white posses were in the process of hunting blacks who had "taken refuge in nearby woods out of fear." The United States had yet another shameful chapter to add to its history, and Bratton, striding to the lectern, went right to the heart of the matter. "The conditions that have grown up in the Arkansas Delta are worse now than before the Civil War," he said. "I speak from my knowledge gained during my 12 years of experience as a legal representative of the Department of Justice."

Bratton spoke with his usual fire. He told the court about peonage, and about how the Elaine sharecroppers had come to him for help in receiving a fair settlement. "Whites," he said, "killed some 200 innocent Negroes." Next, he described how his son had almost been lynched. "I endeavored to get a mental picture in the minds of the Court as to the exact conditions in Arkansas," he later wrote, and while none of this was directly relevant to the legal question at issue, of whether the trials had been so unfair that the state could be said to have lost jurisdiction, it did serve to remind the court of the larger context of the case. Not so long ago, the United States had enslaved blacks, and since the end of Reconstruction the country had treated them in a most unfair manner, with sharecroppers still laboring in near bondage. The Red Summer of 1919 had ended with the massacre at Elaine, and then had come Tulsa and Rosewood—Arkansas was all part of a larger history. And if the Supreme Court wanted to know whether the Helena court was biased, it should consider this fact: "Wholesale murders on the part of the whites were committed, and yet not a single indictment was returned," Bratton said. "If the influence of those in control of the [Phillips County] court was such as to prevent an indictment, the same influence was sufficient to indict and condemn the Negroes they had marked for execution." It was, he concluded, "preposterous to imagine a fair trial was had."

Storey spoke in a much more deliberate manner. Slightly stooped with age, he was bald except for tufts of white hair above his ears, and yet, dressed in a waistcoat as always, he radiated dignity. He picked up the narrative where Bratton had left off. The citizens of Helena, he told the eight justices, "were determined that the men should be convicted" and they "manufactured the evidence for that purpose." The Arkansas courts, the newspapers, the Helena Rotary Club, the American Legion, and other business organizations—all of them, Morey said, had joined together to "railroad the Negroes to death."

"Your contention," asked Holmes, leaning forward, "is that the whole procedure was one dominated by a mob and that the conditions surrounding the trial was such as to render the whole trial a nullity, and that under the decision of this Court in such cases, we have the jurisdiction and it is our duty to give relief?"

"Yes, your honor. If the record in this case does not warrant the relief demanded, then that part of the Constitution [on habeas corpus] should be eliminated as it would mean nothing."

Utley had listened to all this with growing frustration and anger, his face turning red, and upon stepping to the lectern, he immediately protested that the narrative told by the appellants, in their briefs and again here today, wasn't true. There had been no massacre of blacks, there had been no coercion of witnesses . . . Taft held up his hand for Utley to stop. "Yes, but you demurred to the petition, thereby admitting the allegations."

All that Utley could do now was argue the law. Once again, he went over the points he'd made in his brief. The Arkansas Supreme Court had signed off on the trial verdicts, and thus the state had met the "corrective process" standard the court had set in *Frank*. He concluded by reminding Taft and the seven other justices that this was a habeas corpus appeal. "Mere errors in point of law, however serious, committed by a criminal court in the exercise of its jurisdiction over a case properly subject to its cognizance, cannot be reviewed by habeas corpus."

Holmes sat up straight. "You do not contend that if the whole affair was a mere sham, that however irregular the proceedings may have been, that this court would be deprived of the right of going into the case and granting the relief?"

"No," Utley stammered, that was not what he was contending.

After that, the justices peppered the attorneys for both sides with questions about "issues of jurisdiction." Did the U.S. Supreme Court have the authority to provide relief? The entire proceedings didn't last much more than an hour, but both Storey and Bratton, as they exited the Capitol into the streets of Washington, felt that the oral arguments had gone well. Utley, with his "nasal twang," had been sharply rebuked once and mildly rebuked a second time, and even McReynolds, Bratton noted, had muttered that it appeared that the appellants had gotten a "rotten deal." "I feel very hopeful for a reversal," Bratton said.

And yet Utley, walking off in a different direction, was just as confident. "It is well recognized," he told reporters, "that questions of fact are for the jury and not for the court to decide, and these matters have already been settled in the circuit court of Phillips County. Every appellate court to which the cases have been carried, so far, has sustained the action of the trial court." The NAACP and its attorneys, he added, were just trying "to stir up trouble . . . It would be a sad state of affairs in this country if propaganda should be substituted for law in the trial of criminal cases."

Each of the two sides had a different perspective, and both had good reason to believe they would emerge victorious. The Moore appellants had justice on their side, while the state of Arkansas had nothing less than 136 years of historical precedent on its side. Ever since the people of the United States had come together to form "a more perfect union," the states had always maintained jurisdiction over ordinary crimes like murder, and federal courts had never before granted habeas relief to a state prisoner because he hadn't received a "fair trial." This was a case where justice and precedent law clashed, and who could know how the court would decide?

"The cases," White wrote in a January 12 letter to Jones, now "lie on the laps of the Gods."

Hardly Less than Revolutionary

ON SATURDAY, JANUARY 13, Taft and the other seven justices convened for their weekly discussion of cases. Their conference room was located in the dusty confines of the Capitol's basement, and there was nothing about the dingy space that attested to its importance, that it was here that a handful of men regularly made the decisions that so profoundly affected the course of American history. "The room," remembered one justice, would become "overheated and the air foul. . . . [It was] not conducive to good humor. I suppose that no high court in the country had fewer conveniences." Taft and the others stood around for a few moments, each man shaking hands with every other, a tradition that dated to the Fuller Court in the 1880s, and then they took their seats around the oval conference table. Their clerks made certain they had everything they needed— briefs, law books, and so on—for the cases to be decided that day, and then they exited so that the eight men could deliberate in complete privacy.

There was, at the table, a surprising collegiality given the Court's ideological split. This was Taft's doing; he was, one justice said, a "good sport," and during his eighteen months as chief justice, he had made a point of fostering a sense of camaraderie among the Court's members. The one justice who had resisted Taft's leadership in this regard was McReynolds. In his usual loutish manner, McReynolds made it abundantly clear that with Brandeis on the Court, he found it disagreeable to even have to shake the hand of a "Hebrew." But—and this was the truly surprising part—Taft, Holmes, and Brandeis were now getting along well.

Taft, upon being named chief justice in 1921, had expected to tangle with both Holmes and Brandeis. He had long loathed Brandeis's progressive politics, and in 1916, when Woodrow Wilson nominated Brandeis for the Court—a post that Taft had always longed for—he'd exploded in a jealous fury. He denounced Brandeis as a "socialist" and a "hypocrite" who had much "power for evil," and joined five other past presidents of the American Bar Association in publicly declaring that he was "not a fit person" for the Court. He considered Holmes to be a "noisy dissenter," and vowed to friends that he would not let this "dangerous twosome"—these "Bolsheviki"—get control of the Court. Yet during the 1921–22 term, Taft had come to think of them in a new light. They were by far the most able members of the Court when it came to writing opinions, and, from a practical point of view, that was the very heart of the Court's business. McKenna was no longer capable of such work—"he does not know what he means," Taft concluded—while Van Devanter was "opinion shy," which was Taft's polite way of saying that Van Devanter struggled mightily to produce an opinion and preferred that others handle the writing. McReynolds, of course, was an impossible person to work with—"a continual grouch," Taft said—and lazy to boot. In contrast, Brandeis was a workhorse, his opinions "admirable, compact, forcible, and clear," Taft noted. The same was true of Holmes, who, in spite of the fact that he was now past eighty years of age, churned out eloquent, crystal-clear opinions in a week's time. By January 1923, Taft's feelings toward Brandeis and Holmes had so softened that he gave them a ride home following every Saturday conference, and this feeling of warmth was now mutual. "We are very happy with the present Chief," Holmes remarked. "Never before have we gotten along with so little jangling and dissension." Marveled Brandeis: "It's very difficult for me to understand why a man who is so good a Chief Justice could have been so bad as President."

This softening of feeling naturally worked its way into the Court's decision-making process. Taft wanted the Court, whenever possible, to speak with a unanimous voice. He discouraged dissents, and Brandeis had come to understand that this provided the "Bolsheviks"—Holmes and himself—an opportunity. In cases where he and Holmes were destined to lose and there was no important principle at stake, "I sometimes endorse an opinion with which I do not agree," Brandeis explained to friends. "I acquiesce." By showing himself to be a good team player, Brandeis figured that Taft, in response, would become more willing to listen to the views that he and Holmes shared on cases dear to their hearts. And if they could woo Taft to their side, then others would likely follow. "They will take it from Taft but wouldn't take it from me," Brandeis privately confessed. "If it is good enough for Taft, it is good enough for us, they say—and a natural sentiment."

Such was the group dynamic at work in this case. As Taft went, so would the majority go.

THE COURT'S DELIBERATIONS ARE kept confidential, and so there is no record of the discussion that occurred that fateful Saturday afternoon. There would have been talk about the *Frank* precedent, and most likely there was some discussion about the real-life end to that case. After the court in 1915 upheld the death penalty verdict for Leo Frank, Georgia governor John Slaton—convinced that Frank was innocent—commuted his sentence to life imprisonment. This so angered Georgia whites that a pack of twenty-five men, which included two former superior court justices, abducted Frank from the state prison and lynched him. This was the very demonstration of mob spirit that the Supreme Court had, in essence, excused in its 1915 decision, and thus the lynching—as Brandeis later wrote—"subjected the reputation of the court to severe strain."

Holmes, it is fair to surmise, asked everyone to consider again the principle of justice that had animated his dissent in *Frank:* "Whatever disagreement there may be as to the scope of the phrase 'process of law,' " he'd written, "there can be no doubt that it embraces the fundamental conception of a fair trial." Yet, as all of the justices knew, the Supreme Court had never before set aside a state criminal verdict because the proceedings had been unfair. That was the weight of precedent law that bore down on this decision-making process: did they dare cross a federal-state boundary line that had been so firmly drawn over the previous 136 years? Perhaps the debate lasted thirty minutes, perhaps an hour, and it seems that McReynolds, judging by what he later wrote, gradually grew ever more sour. This habeas petition was based on affidavits from eight "ignorant convicts" and "two white men" who were "low villains according to their own admissions," he believed. The Moore appellants had been convicted of an "atrocious crime." To grant them habeas relief would violate "principles which are essential to the orderly operation of our federal system." The court should be guided by *Frank,* the doctrine in that case "right and wholesome."

At last Taft called for a vote. Brandeis and Holmes were lined up on one side, and McReynolds on the other, and the three men had spent the discussion period fighting for the votes in the middle. Taft cast his vote first, then all of the others did in order of seniority, and the final tally ended up, numerically speaking, just as one would have predicted: six in the majority with two dissenters. Only then Taft, having voted with the majority, assigned Oliver Wendell Holmes to write the decision that would change America.

HOLMES IS REMEMBERED TODAY as one of the greatest jurists ever to sit on the court. However, he was not a man who had any particular empathy for the plight of blacks in American society. Born in Boston in 1841, he was the son of the prominent physician and writer Oliver Wendell Holmes Sr., and as a member of New England's Brahmin caste, he'd enjoyed a life of privilege. He was an elitist in attitude and bearing, and, in fact, a social Darwinist in his beliefs. Even so, he didn't think that the Fourteenth Amendment had been drawn up to protect wealthy corporations. Rather, he believed that its purpose was to protect the basic rights of all American citizens. That had been the legislative intent, and he thought that it was the Supreme Court's duty to honor it. He also believed that constitutional law should "evolve," pushed along by the "felt necessities of the time."

The 6–2 vote at conference was not yet etched in stone. Holmes now needed to frame the opinion in such a manner that all of the other majority judges—Taft, McKenna, Van Devanter, Butler, and Brandeis—would stay on board. A justice could always change his vote during the opinion-writing process, and in this case, Holmes clearly had to proceed cautiously. According to the principal of *stare decisis,* Latin for "let the decision stand," the Supreme Court was not supposed to overturn earlier rulings of the Court. Both McKenna and Van Devanter had voted with the majority in *Frank,* and thus if he wrote an opinion that made it evident that *Frank* had been overturned, he faced losing their votes. On the other hand, Holmes naturally wanted the principle that he had outlined in his *Frank* dissent—that a federal court had a duty to provide habeas relief to state prisoners who'd been convicted in proceedings that were grossly unfair, regardless of whether a state appellate court had signed off on the trial verdict—to become the precedent that would guide federal courts in the future. The dissent in *Frank* needed to become the new precedent without the majority realizing it. As Holmes confided to a friend, "I have a case on burning themes, at which the boys have had their whack at the conference and which I must tinker [with] to get by those who are shy and inclined to kick. I think I can keep nearly all [the justices], if not perhaps get all, but it will need a little diplomatic adjustment."

This was an instance where the opinion needed to be clear in spots and murky in others, and Holmes, ever deft with the pen, rose to the occasion. First, he asserted that federal courts could overturn state criminal verdicts even if a state supreme court had approved the trial proceedings:

If the case is that the whole procedure is a mask—that counsel, jury and judge were swept to the fatal end by an irresistible wave of public passion, and that the State Courts failed to

correct the wrong, neither perfection in the machinery for correction nor the possibility that the trial court and counsel saw
no other way of avoiding an immediate outbreak of the mob
can prevent this Court from securing to the petitioners their
constitutional rights.

Next, he cautioned that the Court, in this case, wasn't explicitly
addressing the appellate review standard articulated in *Frank*.

We shall not say more concerning the corrective process af-
forded to the petitioners other than to say it does not seem to
us sufficient to allow a Judge of the United States to escape the
duty of examining the facts for himself when if true as alleged
they make the trial absolutely void.

In short, Holmes articulated the very position he'd argued for in
his *Frank* dissent, and then he told his colleagues not to worry. *We
shall not say more concerning the corrective process* . . . they weren't
necessarily straying from the majority opinion in *Frank*. There was
nothing for McKenna and Van Devanter to worry about, and on
Monday, January 22, he sent his opinion to the other justices for
their review. "My cases are all written up to date," he told a friend.
"One" was on "burning themes," and he wondered whether any of
the judges, upon reading it, would, as a "child" might say, "swallow
up." But his decision sailed through; none of the other majority
judges—as Holmes had joked—"vomited" when they read it. Taft
quickly affixed his initials to the draft, as did McKenna, Butler, and
Louis Brandeis. "I like this opinion much," Taft scribbled in the mar-
gin, and Van Devanter also gave it his blessing: "As you say," he told
Taft, "the opinion has been framed on a line which makes it impossible to write in anything that is worth while; and the more I think
about it the more I am disposed to believe the opinion will not constitute an unhappy precedent."

The court released its *Moore v. Dempsey* decision on February
19, with McReynolds, who was joined by Sutherland, writing a

stinging dissent. He thought that Holmes had pulled a fast one, and argued that the Court, with this decision, was overturning *Frank:* "This matter is one of gravity. . . . I can not agree now to put [the Frank doctrine] aside and substitute the views expressed by the minority of the Court in that case."* McReynolds understood the importance of the decision, and certainly the other justices did too, which is why Holmes referred to it as a "burning theme," and yet the *New York Times* and other leading newspapers made little note of it, probably because at first glance the decision didn't seem all that dramatic. Although the Court had reversed the ruling of the federal district court, it hadn't set the Elaine sharecroppers free. Instead, it had ordered the district court to hold a trial to determine whether the allegations that the sharecroppers had made in their habeas petitions—the allegations that the state had demurred to— were in fact true. If so, then the federal court was to order Arkansas to release the prisoners. The endless criminal proceedings were now going through yet another step. However, many others—legal scholars, the NAACP, and a handful of magazines and smaller newspapers—understood at once that this was a watershed moment for the country.

"I regard it as a great achievement in constitutional law," said Louis Marshall, the prominent constitutional attorney who had argued the *Frank* case. *Moore v. Dempsey,* he told the NAACP, would serve as the "cornerstone" for building a new "temple" of justice. The *Crisis* pronounced it "a milestone in the Negro's fight for justice, an achievement that is as important as any event since the signing of the Emancipation Proclamation." This decision, reasoned the *Toledo*

---

* Louis Marshall also thought that the court, in *Moore v. Dempsey,* "overturned its former decision." Walter White thought so too, telling the *Outlook* editor that "the decision in the Arkansas cases is diametrically opposite" to the *Frank* ruling. However, none of the majority justices, in their private correspondence, described it as a reversal of *Frank,* and scholars in habeas corpus law have advanced varying opinions on whether *Moore* overruled *Frank* or expanded on it. This lasting uncertainty surely would have delighted Holmes, for it is a testament to how he employed just the right dose of murkiness to keep the majority together when he wrote the opinion.

Times, would "spur state courts to conduct trials fairly." Blacks in the South would now "feel a greater sense of security in knowing that the strong arm of Uncle Sam stands between them and prejudiced courts." At last, the *New Republic* rejoiced, "the Fourteenth Amendment guarantees to every man" the "substance" of a real trial. The ACLU hailed the decision, as did the *Nation, Outlook* magazine, and numerous black newspapers. The *Louisville Courier Journal* perhaps summed up its importance best: "The principle that the Federal Government may constitute itself a reviewer of the decisions of the criminal courts of States, overruling the authority of state courts of last resort, will, if established, constitute a change hardly less than revolutionary."

That was the history-altering aspect of this decision: It set a clear precedent for federal review of state criminal proceedings *in their entirety,* and that meant that the U.S. Supreme Court was finally delivering on the promise that Congress made to the nation's black citizens when it passed the Fourteenth Amendment. The federal government would become the protector of their basic rights to life, liberty, and due process under the law. If the Moore precedent was allowed to stand, the *Arkansas Gazette* editorialized with evident alarm, "the powers of the state courts will in large measure be nullified." While that was an exaggeration—the powers of the state courts would not be nullified by this decision, but rather constrained by a reinvigorated Fourteenth Amendment—it spoke to a larger truth: this decision threatened the very foundation of white supremacy in the South. All of Jim Crow society relied on previous Supreme Court decisions that, under the states' rights principle, limited federal intervention in state matters, and *Moore v. Dempsey* was a sharp break with that past. "U.S. High Court Orders 'Fair Trial,' " the *Little Rock Daily News* shouted, and readers in that city could only be astonished by such startling news.

There now remained one last challenge for Scipio Africanus Jones: securing the freedom of the Elaine sharecroppers. In one manner or another, he had to turn this monumental legal victory into a real-world triumph.

Thunderbolt from a Clear Sky

THE LEGAL TRIUMPH WAS so monumental that there briefly appeared, in the correspondence of Walter White and others, a sense that the battle had been won, and that all there remained to do now was a final tidying up. "The NAACP can take credit for saving the lives of these poor and unfortunate victims, and I trust that this victory will enable you to add many new members," Bratton told White on February 26. But Jones knew that it was too early to celebrate. Although he appreciated the fact that a great victory in constitutional law had been achieved, his focus remained, first and foremost, on the sharecroppers, and there were still twenty-seven men locked up. There were the Moore six at the state penitentiary, the Ware six in the Helena jail, and fifteen men at Cummins. And what complicated matters for Jones was that the legal statuses of the three groups were quite different. The Ware six were awaiting trial on murder charges. The Moore six were headed toward a hearing in federal court to determine whether their trials had, in fact, been mob-dominated charades. The men at Cummins were serving out ten-to-twenty-one-year sentences and thus seemingly had no hope of gaining their freedom. Jones had to figure out how to leverage the U.S. Supreme Court victory so that, in the end, *all* of the men went free.

A few weeks earlier, Ed Ware had written Jones a letter that spoke of their desperation. Ware, Alf Banks, Joe Fox, Albert Giles,

John Martin, and Will Wordlow had been penned up in county jails in Marianna and Helena ever since June 1921, and with their lives ticking away, they were reaching their breaking point:

> *Dear Sir this comes in Secret to Let you no How We are. all is not so Well Really non of us isn't Well But Some is Better than others. i My Self seems Like i Have compleetly Lost My Healyth. i Hope this Letter will find you and your family well. also your friends. Listen Mr. Jones if there is any Way that you can give me Some Relief now is the time i Wish you Would if you please Sir Because we is Suffering so much so much Here on this Hard concreet floor. and We is kep so confine and is fed so Bad untill we are Just about Woe out. Please Sir Help us if you can. Because it is not near as good as it is at the Walls Where a man can Walk on the ground and catch some fresh air. i dont Look for No ans. from this But i Will Look for Some Relief all the Boys Joins me in Sending Love to i am*
>
> *You Client*
E. D. Ware

As Jones read this heart-wrenching letter, he took solace in knowing that at least this group of men would likely soon be free. They were scheduled to go on trial in April in Lee County, but Jones, attentive as always to the finer points of the law, had a surprise prepared for the state. The previous year, the prosecution, while waiting for the U.S. Supreme Court to rule on the Moore appeal, had twice asked for a continuance of their trials. Each time, Jones had played possum: he'd not made any vigorous objection to the prosecution's motion, and yet, at the same time, he'd informed the court that the defendants were "ready for trial." By doing so, he had created a record of the defendants not having consented to the state's request for a continuance, and under Arkansas law, if the state failed to prosecute criminal defendants for two consecutive terms of court without their consent, they were—at the next term of court—to be set free.

Jones had played the state perfectly, and on April 16, he filed a "motion for discharge" in Lee County Circuit Court. Although Judge E. D. Robertson denied his motion, Jones appealed, and on June 25, the Arkansas Supreme Court ordered "the sheriff of Lee County to discharge the appellants from custody." *

"Abundant congratulations to you upon the Supreme Court decision," White excitedly telegraphed Jones. "This marks the beginning of the end of the greatest fight of its kind in the history of America. To you all honor and glory and I extend my sincere and hearty congratulations in which all in the office join with me."

All that Jones had to do now was arrange for the release of the men, which seemed simple enough, and yet this process quickly hit a snag. The state had fifteen days to file for a rehearing of the Court's decision, and in Marianna, Judge Robertson wasn't sure whether the six men were to be freed immediately or whether he was to hold them for another two weeks. Fearful that news of the Court's decision might stir a lynch mob to attack the Marianna jail—the *Helena World* was already typesetting a headline that read: "Murder of Two Helena Legionnaires Unavenged"—Robertson ordered Lee County sheriff A. F. Calloway to transport Ware and the others to The Walls in Little Rock. Authorities there, he figured, could decide whether to let them go or hold them until the fifteen days were up.

JONES WAS WAITING FOR Ware and the others when they arrived at The Walls at 11 P.M. that night. He was hoping that they would immediately be set free, and so he had hired cars and armed guards to whisk them away. The cars were parked a ways off, at the bottom of a long hill, and Jones had also asked the sharecroppers' wives and friends to wait there too. Ware and the others weren't shackled—they were free, and yet not quite free—and Calloway left

---

* McHaney reemerged as co-counsel for the Elaine sharecroppers during these proceedings. While he had quit the case before the appeal to the U.S. Supreme Court, his firm had signed a contract stating it would represent the sharecroppers in all other proceedings, and apparently Jones asked McHaney to help him while he pursued the discharge of the Ware group through this failure-to-prosecute statute.

them with Jones while he and his two deputies disappeared inside the prison to talk to warden Hamp Martin. *Arkansas Gazette* reporter Joe Wirges whipped out his notepad and asked the six sharecroppers how they felt.

"Mighty fine," Ware said. "When I first got in this trouble, I consulted my God and He told me He would take care of me."

All of the other five men nodded in agreement. "I now know that the good Lord listened to our prayers," Ware added. "I worried a great deal when I first came here, and these other boys did too. After consulting God, we made up our minds that if we would have to die in that chair, we would be ready to meet Jesus. We all know that Jesus took care of us."

Ware continued to answer Wirges's questions, even relating a few "funny incidents" that had occurred during their incarceration. Several of the men, when asked whether they would return to farming, joked that they'd been locked up for so long that they'd grown "lazy." Ware said he could never return to Phillips County, for he would never be able to relax. "I'd plow up all the cotton, watching and looking around."

A little after midnight, Calloway and his deputies exited from the prison's front gate. They shook hands with the night watchman, and then—without saying a word to Jones or the six men—hopped into a waiting taxi, leaving Jones and everyone else quite bewildered. They didn't dare "move from the prison," Wirges said, "because they were not convinced that the prison guards would not shoot them with their high-powered rifles." Finally, the night watchman stepped from the prison and yelled that they were free to go, and they all began backing down the hill, one cautious step after another, their eyes on the guard towers, until finally it seemed they were out of gunshot range, and then they all turned and scrambled down the hill as fast as they could, each man dropping his suitcase when he reached the bottom and jumping into the arms of a loved one. Ware lifted his wife in his arms, Martin was pounded on the back by his children as he hugged his wife, Edna, and Sallie Giles took her son Albert's head into her hands—this was the moment that they had feared would never come.

"You never heard such shouting and singing and praising the Lord in your life," Wirges said. "It woke up the whole town out there."

Only Jones remained calm. He stood off to one side, smiling and yet not joining in the raucous celebration. Six down, twenty-one to go.

THERE WAS, THE NEXT day, a small item in the Little Rock newspapers that surely caught Scipio Jones's eye, for it told of an event in Elaine that, in terms of its timing, seemed to have been scripted by a short-story writer. Twelve hours after Ed Ware and the others were released, Kid Collins had stormed into a lumber camp and tried to kill his wife, who was employed there as a cook. The camp was owned by Lynn Smith, who'd been one of the posse leaders during the Elaine "riots," and as he tried to arrest Collins, there was a struggle and Smith shot Collins dead. The irony was impossible to miss: Collins, the *Arkansas Gazette* admitted, was the jail trustee who, during the trials of the Elaine rioters, had emerged as a "hero" to the Helena planters.

JONES NOW TURNED HIS attention to the Moore six. The legal process that was looming was straightforward: if he could prove at a trial before a federal judge that the facts he'd set forth in their habeas petitions were indeed true, then the men would be set free. But, he feared, this was going to be very difficult. The first problem—and Moorfield Storey agreed with Jones on this point—was that it was unlikely they could get T. K. Jones and Smiddy to testify. "I have always thought that it is going to be very difficult to prove the allegations in our petition," Storey confessed, "for the white witnesses who testified would hesitate very much to come and testify in person before the District Court, since they might well be lynched themselves and probably would be unwilling to risk their lives." Without their testimony, the trial would devolve into a black-versus-white contest, and that was a contest that blacks always lost. The second problem was one that only Scipio appreciated. The habeas petitions had told of large throngs gathered outside the Phillips County Court-house during the trials. Jones had put in that detail to provide a visceral sense of a mob mentality at work, a scenario that provoked a helpful comparison to the *Frank* case. The problem was that this particular detail didn't happen to be true. No newspaper had reported the presence of such a throng, and the state could easily point out that blacks in Helena had attended the trial. Would they have dared to do that, Utley might ask the federal judge, if angry white mobs had surrounded the courthouse? These trials had been mob-conducted, not mob-dominated, which was a much subtler kind of injustice that would be much harder to prove. And if Jones lost the federal trial, Frank Moore and the others would be executed.

There was one other thing that Jones had to consider: the fifteen men at Cummins. If he negotiated a settlement of the Moore cases, he could insist that those men be pardoned too. That was the only means he had for securing their freedom. The decision wasn't an easy one—who wouldn't want complete vindication of the share-croppers?—but Jones, as he'd explained to the NAACP several months earlier, wanted to explore this possibility. "Do you think it would be advisable to dispose of these cases by accepting short sentences for our Elaine clients?" he'd asked White on April 2. The NAACP had been lukewarm to the idea—"It is most important to work this matter out so as to save the lives and restore the liberty of these unjustly accused Negroes, while at the same time keeping intact the very great moral victory which has been won," the NAACP had told him—and Jones quickly discovered that the state, in the wake of the freeing of the Ware six, wasn't particularly amenable to negotiations either.

The rather bizarre end to the Ware cases had stirred anew, in many white Arkansans, a spirit of revenge toward the Elaine share-croppers. "Never before," the *Arkansas Gazette* railed, "has any one incident so discredited our courts and never before has the public had more just grounds for complaint." Other papers wrote bitterly that these "convicts" had gone "scot free." The *Fort Smith Sentinel-Record* explicitly threatened the freed men: "They should get out of

Arkansas at once. They were leaders in a movement to kill white people because of racial prejudices, and the evil is still lurking in their hearts." The animosity was such that Jones thought it wise for Ed Ware and the others to leave the state, and he helped them all move north, the NAACP soon reporting that they were "living and working in Chicago and St. Louis." In August, Jones met with Utley, hoping that he might be reasonable, but Arkansas's attorney general warned that even if the state lost the federal habeas trial, he would urge Phillips County to indict the Moore six once more and start the whole process all over again. "I found [Utley] more determined now than ever before to prosecute vigorously these cases," Jones told the NAACP in early September.

Although Jones began preparing for the trial, he decided to make one last effort to secure the freedom of the men without going to court. On September 14, he presented Governor McRae with a petition signed by several hundred people that urged him to "grant a full and complete pardon" to Frank Moore and the others. The state had failed to prosecute the Ware group, a tacit admission that it "lacked evidence" that the Elaine sharecroppers had committed a crime, and thus, the petitioners said, "it would be fair and right, and in keeping with justice," if the rest of the men went free. At the same time, Jones asked several of his white friends to push settlement talks along. Did the state—and the Helena planters—really want a trial to be held in federal court that would focus on whether the initial trials had been grossly *unfair*? Did they want a reairing of testimony that the sharecroppers had been whipped and tortured to testify falsely? Jones was now calling the state's bluff in the same way that Utley had tried to call his, and in late September, Helena authorities—the mayor, the Committee of Seven, John Moore, and other business leaders—responded with a petition of their own. They asked McRae to commute the sentences of the Moore six "to second-degree murder" and reduce their sentences to "twelve years each in the penitentiary." Under Arkansas law, prisoners were eligible for parole once they'd served one-third of their sentence, and thus the men would be immediately eligible for release.

The two sides were getting closer, and on Friday, November 2, Jones hammered out a final compromise with state officials. The Moore six would not plead guilty to any charge, but if McRae commuted their sentences to twelve years and promised that *all* of the Elaine prisoners would be released within twelve months, the Moore group would not pursue their freedom through a federal trial. For the Helena planters and the state, the face-saving part of this deal was that McRae wouldn't pardon the men, only commute their sentences, and since a twelve-year sentence was the usual punishment for second-degree murder, that would at least give the impression that the sharecroppers were guilty of that crime.

It wasn't perfect, but it would provide for the freedom of all the men. Jones quickly wired the NAACP to explain the terms of the deal:

> Before agreeing to accept the compromise I consulted Judge Trieber and two or three other white friends, and I have been satisfactorily assured that a full and complete pardon will be granted to my clients in less than a year, and that reduction of sentences or full pardons will be granted to the 21-year men, and I am of the opinion that we would be justified in accepting this proposition, in view of the fact that it is very doubtful about our being able to make the proof that would be required by the [federal] court before granting us the relief prayed for in our petition, and even if we would succeed in making the necessary proof to sustain the allegations in our petition, still, the grand jury of Phillips County would be at liberty to indict my clients and force their return to the county jail to await trial, and I do not think it is safe for them in Phillips County. At any rate, I hesitate to assume the responsibility of turning down an offer that will at least save the lives of six men and in a short time will release them from further imprisonment.

Although the NAACP had misgivings about the deal, as it worried that the acceptance of the twelve-year sentences would be misunderstood by the public—"Personally, I have been opposed to the acceptance of any compromise, but perhaps this is the wisest way out," White reasoned—the *Arkansas Democrat* saw it as something of a complete victory for Jones and his clients. The six men would be immediately "eligible for parole," the paper reported, and "it is further understood that as soon as certain phases of the cases are cleared up, the penitentiary board and the governor will be approached for such paroles and in all probability for a complete pardon and restoration of citizenship."

It didn't seem that anything could go wrong now. In six to twelve months, Jones had good reason to believe, all of the Elaine sharecroppers would be free.

ANY MISGIVINGS THAT THE NAACP may have had about the deal quickly dissipated. "There is no question now but that the State of Arkansas admits that it was wrong," White wrote in a letter to donors to the Arkansas Defense Fund. "Not only have the lives of innocent men been saved but the falsehood that Negroes had organized to kill white people has been exploded for all time."

Now it truly did appear that there was nothing left to do in this case but tidy up a few loose ends. The epic fight had been won, and Jones suggested to Walter White that perhaps it would be good to have Robert Kerlin write a book about it. When White didn't reply to his first letter, Jones brought up the issue a second time: "You never did favor me with your opinion as to advisability of writing a history of the Elaine cases. I shall be glad to have you advise me what you think of the proposition."

There clearly was so much to be revealed by such a project. Up to that moment, the "history" had been told entirely from the NAACP's perspective. A book would allow for a fuller picture to emerge: Jones and his Little Rock colleagues could tell of how they had begun planning an appeal even as the initial set of trials got under way, and Jones could describe all that he had gone through to investigate the matter and what he'd done to keep safe during the Ware retrials. Kerlin or some other writer could interview the freed sharecroppers and further document the massacre of black men, women, and children. A book would help flesh out the entire history, but White, who had his own turf to defend here, splashed cold water on the idea.

"This has practically been done already in the accounts which have been given, beginning with the articles which I wrote for the *Nation, Survey,* and *Chicago Daily News* in 1919," he told Jones. "It would be largely the editing of these running accounts and whipping them into shape. What is your idea of the salability of such a book? Unless we had a specific audience largely arranged in advance of publication I am quite sure that no publisher would be willing to run the financial risk of bringing out a book."

Jones never brought up the subject again. White's response must have stung, but he was ever the graceful man, and when White prepared a summary of the cases for the NAACP's 1923 annual report, Jones assured him that it was "very ably done." Jones also spent some time that year traveling through Arkansas telling blacks that it was their duty to join the NAACP, and he and a handful of his Mosaic Templars friends subscribed to $500 lifetime memberships. "Arkansas," Jones told blacks in his state, "owes the Association an obligation it can never pay."

Six months came and went. Although McRae said nothing publicly about the imprisoned Elaine sharecroppers, seven of the fifteen men at Cummins were released, and so there was no reason for Jones to panic. The promise was that they would all be free within a year. All of the men except for Paul Hall were at Cummins, with even Ed Coleman, who was now eighty-three years old, back out in the prison's cotton fields, dragging a burlap bag behind him that fall of 1924 as he plucked the cotton bolls clean. September passed, and still no word came from the governor's office, and then on October 7, 1924, McRae informed penal authorities that "until the crop of cotton is substantially gathered, I am not issuing any furloughs to able-bodied prisoners." This meant that the release of the men would be put off until at least November, and it was then that Jones began to fret. Next the anniversary of the settlement came and went, and still there was no word from McRae. A promise had been made, but it wasn't being carried out, and then, on December 19, McRae officially reneged.

McRae that day released the eight men still serving twenty-one-year terms—Will Barnes, Sykes Fox, John Ratliff, Gilmore Jenkins, Sam Wilson, Charles Jones, Ed Mitchell, and Will Perkins—on "indefinite furloughs." But, McRae told reporters, that would be it for the Elaine sharecroppers. He would be leaving office on January 14, and the Moore six would "not receive clemency."

Jones did not say one word to the newspapers critical of McRae. There was, he knew, nothing to be gained by calling him on his betrayal. That would only serve to set his decision in stone, and Jones was certain that if McRae didn't change his mind before he left office, then Frank Moore and the others would stay locked up for at least two more years. The incoming governor, Thomas Terral, had been elected with the backing of the Ku Klux Klan.

Within hours of McRae's announcement, Jones began circulating a new petition, one urging the governor to issue a "full and complete pardon" to the men. Then, on December 21, he hurried by train to Helena. There was one group of signatures, Jones believed, that could force McRae to set the men free. Upon his arrival at the train station on Cherry Street, he marched directly to the Solomon Building, with his petition in hand, where he called upon John Moore and the other town fathers. The Helena planters must have been startled by the sight of Jones, but Jones apparently reminded them that they had signed off on the deal a year ago and that it was now up to them to do the honorable thing, for he left that building with a number of their signatures. He then stopped off in the county courthouse to call on the elected officials there, and just to make the point crystal clear to the governor, he made certain that, prior to returning to Little Rock, he also obtained the signatures, as the *Arkansas Democrat* reported, of "many prominent Elaine citizens." On Christmas Eve, Jones presented the governor with a petition signed by "700 to 800" people. The planters of Phillips County were now asking the governor to release the men, former prosecutor John Miller was as well, and so too were many prominent whites and blacks from around the state.

And still McRae said nothing.

This flurry of activity—and his despair—wore Jones out. "Your secretary," White wrote to Jones on January 5, told "me that you were quite ill." He remained in his bed, battling fevers and a hacking cough, and all the while watching with disbelief as the clock ticked down. Day after day passed without a word from McRae. This seemed to be a rerun of June 1921, when the execution date grew ever nearer and McRae remained mute. Jones had promised Frank Moore and the others that they would be released. That had been the deal that everyone had agreed upon. Jones had *trusted* McRae. January 10 clicked by, then January 11 and 12. Finally, on the morning of January 13, Jones roused himself from his bed. He still was not well, but he put on a suit, his gold watch as always hanging from a pocket chain, and knocked on the governor's door one last time. He took his seat and placed his straw hat in his lap, and then he spoke softly to the governor. He didn't stay long, perhaps fifteen minutes or so, then the two men rose and shook hands.

"Just concluded presentation of our matter," he wired the NAACP moments later. "Anticipate favorable results by tomorrow."

This had been such a long, long battle. More than five years had passed since Jones and his fellow blacks in Little Rock—J. M. Conner, John Hibbler, Thomas Price, and Joseph Booker—had formed a defense committee for the sharecroppers. Again and again, Jones had needed to call on his considerable political and legal skills and, most of all, his relentless will. He had chipped away and chipped away, fighting battle after battle, and now at last the end had come. Late in the day on January 13, in his last act as governor, McRae—stating that he was acting in response to the petition "signed by officers and well-known residents of Phillips county"—granted Frank Moore and the other five men "indefinite furloughs."

That next morning, Jones traveled to Cummins to pick up Moore, the Hicks brothers, Preacher Joe Knox, and Ed Coleman. Each man was carrying his few possessions in a worn suitcase, just as

Ed Ware and the others had done that night outside The Walls, and then they all hurried back to the state penitentiary, where Paul Hall was waiting. He was the last of the eighty-seven Elaine sharecroppers to be freed, and as Jones and his six clients sped away, they left behind a *Gazette* reporter, who could only reflect on how utterly improbable this all was. "Coffins were constructed for [the sharecroppers'] burial," he wrote. "The execution of the sentences seemed assured." But the coffins on this day were out in the prison yard, weathered and unused, their presence, the reporter concluded, a fitting "symbol" of the entire affair.

NEWS OF THE RELEASE of the Moore six triggered a burst of jubilation among blacks around the country. All eighty-seven men *free*. Ever since the end of Reconstruction, that brief period when their hopes had burned so bright, blacks in America had grown accustomed to losing, to having their hopes and dreams crushed at every turn. Their right to vote in the South—gone. Their right to sit on juries in the South—gone. The U.S. Supreme Court had given its blessing to Jim Crow laws that left them riding in dirty railroad cars and confined to balconies in movie theaters. Their elementary schools were poorly funded and their high schools closed. Month after month, year after year, white mobs hanged blacks from trees and nothing was ever done about it. The country's scientists and artists opined on how blacks were inferior to whites. There simply was no justice or equality under the law in the United States of America if you had black skin. The Elaine massacre and the subsequent imprisoning of eighty-seven sharecroppers started out as just one more chapter in that miserable history, the climax to the awful Red Summer of 1919, and then—and this was the miracle of it all—the NAACP and a lone black attorney from Little Rock had turned it all around. The eighty-seven men were free, and the story of what had happened in Phillips County—the writing of that history—had been turned on its head. It was the black narrative of events that now carried the aura of truth.

The freeing of the last six Elaine prisoners, rejoiced Reverend J. R. Maxwell, in a letter to the NAACP, "was like a thunderbolt from a clear sky. Had it not been for the masterly work done by the Association, long before this those innocent men would have answered the roll call in judgment. . . . Ask for what you wish from this day on." The *Crisis* celebrated, as did the *Messenger* and the *Chicago Defender;* donors to the Arkansas Defense Fund sent congratulations to the NAACP; and the *Dallas Express,* like many black newspapers, spoke of how it hinted of a better America ahead. The "victory is one of greater significance to the race than can now be imagined. . . . Not only the race but America as well has profited by the freeing of these men."

And all now praised Scipio Jones. "You have rendered a service not only to the men whose lives were saved and who were freed from prison, but you have benefitted all America," the NAACP told him. They asked that he come speak at their annual conference that summer in Denver so that all NAACP members could "see the man who has made such a brave and brilliant fight in Arkansas." The Associated Negro Press crowed that the job done by Scipio Jones was "the greatest achievement of any Negro lawyer in the history of the country," and, in an editorial titled "Scipio Africanus Maximus," it threw all restraint to the winds:

This Scipio is the REAL "Africanus," not by the artificial vote of the Roman Senate, but by actual ties of blood. He was the legal heart and brains of the Arkansas Cases, and is not to be honored for destroying Africans but for saving them. The Romans had their artificial Scipio Africanus Minor and their Scipio Africanus Major. To these we add Scipio Africanus Maximus, of Arkansas, the present, the living, the real . . . Publius Cornelius Scipio Africanus Major defeated Hasdrubal and Hannibal and conquered Carthage in the third century B.C. Publius Cornelius Scipio Africanus Minor destroyed Carthage in the second century B.C. But our Scipio Africanus Maximus, of the fame of Elaine in Phillips County, Arkansas, in the 20th century A.D., has not destroyed but saved, and is not so much a conqueror as a defender of his kind.

And in Little Rock, the *Arkansas Survey*—a black publication—triumphantly pronounced that "We Are Proud of Him."

> Mr. Jones went down to Helena and took charge of that case when it was a tangled mess after the defendants had been beaten into making damaging statements. He went down there and gathered the data for his case when Helena was a seething cauldron of Hate; when the least indiscretion meant death. . . . For four years he travelled and investigated and pled until the 13th of January when Governor McRae opened the prison gates to the last of the alleged rioters. And during the four years he has maintained his poise. At all times he has conducted his case so as to retain the friendship and the help of the good people of the state. All hail Judge Jones! Praise him for his knowledge of law, his nerve, his patience and his sagacity.

Such was the outpouring of praise and gratitude. And all this for a man who, sixty-two years earlier, had been born a slave.

Birth of a New Nation

TODAY IT IS EASY to see, through a sweeping review of American history, how *Moore v. Dempsey* remade the nation. At the moment of the country's founding, Thomas Jefferson and the other signers of the Declaration of Independence proclaimed that "all men are created equal" and that "they are endowed by their Creator with certain inalienable rights." That declaration, however, didn't include men with black skin, and when the Founding Fathers drew up the Constitution in 1787, they made the federal government the protector of the slave owner's property rights. As such, the Constitution was ultimately a pro-slavery document, rather than a pro-freedom one. Moreover, the Bill of Rights, as interpreted by the U.S. Supreme Court, did not prevent the states from abridging the freedoms of their "citizens."

The passage of the Fourteenth Amendment, with its promise of equality under the law for all, marked the birth of a new nation, so different from the old one. The United States now had a Constitution consistent with the principles articulated in the Declaration of Independence. Furthermore, the role of the federal government, in its relation to the states, was diametrically opposite to what it had been before. The federal government was no longer the protector of slavery but rather the guarantor of the basic rights of all Americans. The Bill of Rights—or so Bingham and the other architects of the Fourteenth Amendment believed—would now limit the states.

That was a radical leap for a nation to make, and the revolution was quickly short-circuited by the U.S. Supreme Court. With its *Slaughterhouse* and *Cruikshank* decisions, the Court carved the heart out of the Fourteenth Amendment, and with such decisions as *Plessy v. Ferguson* and *Williams v. Mississippi,* it gave its blessing to an apartheid-like legal system in the South. As a result, the United States began a long slide, a moral descent that brought the country to the brink of a racial civil war in the Red Summer of 1919. The United States had become a nation that reeked with hypocrisy: it espoused democratic values, and yet it was a country where the fundamental rights of blacks were abridged in every manner possible. Many blacks still labored in a peonage system that was only a step removed from slavery, and white racial violence went so unchecked that lynchings were a regular feature of American life. The Elaine massacre, in which federal troops turned their machine guns on farmers hiding in the woods, was in so many ways the climactic event of that long slide.

There was, in short, a vast gulf between the promise of the Fourteenth Amendment and the reality of 1919 America, and it was in *Moore v. Dempsey* that the country began to reclaim the promise. As one legal scholar wrote: "For the first time, and for the benefit of all Americans, it was decided that citizens' rights under the United States Constitution could not be trampled on at state court trials, that life and liberty (not merely property, as had been the case until then) were shielded by the pledge of due process of law, and that the duty and the right to redeem that pledge lay with the federal judicial system acting under the Fourteenth Amendment." This was the case in which the U.S. Supreme Court began to free itself from the precedent law of the past and turned instead toward building a body of common law consonant with the Declaration of Independence, that all men are created equal and enjoy certain inalienable rights.

As a result of the *Moore* case, the U.S. Supreme Court now had a precedent for overturning state trials that were unfair, and this principle guided the revolution in due process law that unfolded, step by step, over the next forty-five years. In *Powell v. Alabama* (1932), the

U.S. Supreme Court ruled that defendants in a capital case had a right to counsel. In *Norris v. Alabama* (1935), the Court decreed that black defendants were denied due process if blacks were deliberately excluded from juries; the lengthy absence of blacks from jury service in a community would now be seen as proof of racial discrimination that violated the Fourteenth Amendment. That same year, in *Mooney v. Holohan,* the Court ruled that the prosecution could not present testimony that it knew was false. In *Brown v. Mississippi* (1936), the Court declared that confessions obtained through torture were void. As it made these decisions during the 1930s and 1940s, the Court officially adopted a "fairness" standard: state criminal trials were to be voided, the Court explained in *Palko v. Connecticut* (1937), if the proceedings violated the "fundamental principles of liberty and justice which lie at the base of all our civil and political institutions."

The Court still had not embraced the notion that the Fourteenth Amendment incorporated the Bill of Rights. The *Hurtado* precedent, which decreed that the amendment did no such thing, continued to haunt the Court during the 1930s and 1940s. However, even many states began to complain that the Court's "fairness" standard ultimately seemed quite subjective, and asked that it set down more precise rules for the conduct of criminal trials. The Bill of Rights provided such precise rules, and finally, in 1947, U.S. Supreme Court justice Hugo Black, after researching the legislative debate that John Bingham and others had engaged in when drafting the Fourteenth Amendment, concluded that the Reconstruction Congress had intended to nationalize the Bill of Rights. Thus, in *Adamson v. California,* Black argued for "total incorporation" of the Bill of Rights, and while he failed to prevail in that case, the issue was now front and center before the Court. Finally, in 1961, the Court declared in *Mapp v. Ohio* that the Fourth Amendment's protection against unreasonable searches and seizures applied to the states through the Fourteenth Amendment, and the process of "selective incorporation" was on. In *Robinson v. California* (1962), the Court decided that the Fourteenth Amendment prohibited cruel and unusual punishment, thus incorporating the Eighth Amendment; in *Malloy v. Hogan*

(1964), the Court incorporated the Fifth Amendment right against self-incrimination. The old *Hurtado* rule had been abandoned, and during the next five years, under the leadership of Chief Justice Earl Warren, the Court finished the job. It ruled that the Fourteenth Amendment guaranteed the right to confront witnesses *(Pointer v. Texas)*, the right to a trial by an impartial jury *(Parker v. Gladden)*, and the right to a speedy trial *(Klopfer v. North Carolina)*, such that by 1969 the incorporation of the Bill of Rights, having been accomplished through a piecemeal process, was basically complete.

This revolution in due process was a key part of the larger civil rights movement, and again, it is possible to see how *Moore v. Dempsey* was the seed for that broader remaking of American society. Jim Crow society had blossomed under the states' rights umbrella. That apartheid society could not be torn down as long as the U.S. Supreme Court allowed states' rights to, in essence, trump the Fourteenth Amendment. In *Moore v. Dempsey,* the Court finally set a precedent for federal interference in state matters if such interference was required to protect the basic rights of all Americans. That limit on the right of states to self-governance was what allowed the remaking of American society to proceed. This case also marked the moment that the Supreme Court began to emerge as the institution that would prompt the United States to become a more fair society.

And thus the remaking of a nation: out of the ashes of the Elaine massacre came a legal victory that set the country on a new course, until finally, in the 1960s, with the incorporation of the Bill of Rights into the Fourteenth Amendment and the passage of civil rights legislation, the United States became a society that honored, in its constitutional law, the noble and democratic sentiment that "all men are created equal." This was the gift that Scipio Jones and the NAACP gave the nation. "You have benefitted all America," the NAACP told Jones, and indeed, the *Moore v. Dempsey* victory was one that surely would have made James Madison and John Bingham proud.

THIS WAS A HISTORY with many characters, and not surprisingly, it is hardest to track down what became of the sharecroppers. After

Frank Moore and the others were freed, they went their separate ways, and all of them quickly slipped back into obscurity. Even the 1930 census provides a faint trail for only a few of the men. Frank Moore was one of those who fled to the North, and in 1930, it appears he was working as a night watchman for a real estate company in Chicago. Several of the men returned to sharecropping, although not in Phillips County. John Martin worked on a cotton plantation south of Little Rock; Ed Hicks settled in Crittenden County, north of Helena; and Paul Hall moved to Chicot County, in the very southern part of the Arkansas Delta, which is where he had been born. And one of the men—most likely Ed Ware—looked up Ida B. Wells-Barnett in Chicago, recalling for her family how, during her visit to The Walls, she told the men to pray to God "to open our prison doors like he did for Paul and Silas," and how "after that we never talked about dying any more."

Although the Progressive Farmers and Household Union may have been crushed in 1919, sharecroppers in the Arkansas Delta did not completely give up their dream of organizing a union, and on a hot July night in 1934, eleven white and seven black tenant farmers met in Tyronza, about 90 miles north of Hoop Spur, to do just that. It was an unusual coalition: several of the white farmers had formerly belonged to the Ku Klux Klan. Two of the seven black farmers were veterans of the Hoop Spur union, and one of them, Isaac Shaw, articulated why it was so important that the usual racial divide among poor farmers be bridged: "As long as we stand together, black and white together in this union, nothing can tear it down." That meeting led to the founding of the Southern Tenant Farmers' Union, which grew into an organization with thirty-one thousand members in seven states. The planters once again responded with violence. Union leaders were beaten and jailed; sharecroppers who joined were threatened and driven from their farms; a Presbyterian minister and a white Memphis woman who supported the union were kidnapped and whipped; black churches where union meetings were held were burned. The union, which had vowed at its founding to "turn the other cheek" to such violence, as otherwise it feared there would be a repeat of the Elaine massacre, managed to pull off several strikes, and although it never succeeded in improving the plight of sharecroppers to any real extent, the union did survive, eventually metamorphosing into the United Farm Workers.

The lives of the other main characters in this history played out, for the most part, in expected ways. In Detroit, Ulysses Bratton labored as a union attorney and ran a law firm with his sons. His "fame" as an advocate for blacks, his son Ulysses later recalled, drew many "colored" clients to their door. Moorfield Storey passed away in 1929, black newspapers declaring that "no American of his day had a more useful career." In 1931, Walter White became executive secretary of the NAACP, and when he published his autobiography, *A Man Called White,* he devoted a chapter to his trip to Little Rock and Helena in October 1919. When he died in 1955, "Mr. NAACP," as he'd come to be known, must have felt great satisfaction with his life's work, having lived long enough to see the NAACP's great victory in *Brown v. Board of Education.* That 1954 U.S. Supreme Court decision ordered the integration of public schools, a case that at last discarded the separate-but-equal standard established by the Court in *Plessy v. Ferguson.*

After Brough left office in 1921, he worked for the Arkansas Advancement Association, which was the state's chamber of commerce. He traveled around the country promoting Arkansas, always presenting it as a progressive state, one that was fair to the Negro, just as he had done during the dark days of 1919. McRae died in 1929, not too long after leaving office; in 1926, John Martineau was elected governor and then, fourteen months later, he vacated that office to accept an appointment to the federal bench. He served as a federal judge for nine years, remembered at his death for his devotion to justice. John Miller, the prosecutor in the Elaine cases, was elected to Congress in 1931 and served ten years, resigning from the Senate in 1941 to become a judge in the U.S. District Court in Arkansas, a post he held for twenty-six years. As a federal judge, he resisted implementing the *Brown v. Board of Education* decision ordering the desegregation of Little Rock's schools, but he did, in a

1976 interview with an Arkansas historian, confess to all he knew about the Elaine massacre—the mass killing of blacks and the whipping of defendants, and how the entire affair arose because of the planters' systematic defrauding of the sharecroppers. In that interview, he seemed to unburden his mind of a wrong that had been nagging his conscience for fifty-six years.

Perhaps somewhat surprisingly, Helena turned into a mecca for Mississippi Delta blacks in the 1930s and 1940s. After Prohibition ended in 1930, the downtown filled with saloons, pool halls, and juke joints. Whites shopped and played on Cherry Street, while blacks flocked to Walnut Street, which was only one block away. "There was gambling houses all over downtown," recalled blues musician Robert Junior Lockwood, who grew up in the Helena area. "Helena was wide open, like Las Vegas." Muddy Waters and Howlin' Wolf regularly performed at dance halls on Walnut Street, and in 1941, Lockwood and Sonny Boy Williamson created a live blues radio program on Helena station KFFA that featured such legends as Robert Nighthawk, David "Honeyboy" Edwards, and Houston Stackhouse. All of this enabled Helena, years later, to lay claim to being the birthplace of modern blues, as the great Helena performers, in the 1940s, took their music to Memphis and Chicago.

The introduction of mechanical cotton pickers in the 1940s led to the demise of sharecropping, and Phillips County's population began a long slide. The Helena public high school was integrated in 1969, but nearly all of the white students immediately fled to De Soto School, a private academy that was established, and that pattern of segregation—Helena whites attending De Soto and blacks in the public schools—still held true in 2005, when Helena and West Helena were consolidated into one municipality. Helena's downtown remained vibrant into the 1970s, but then its shops went bust after a Wal-Mart opened in West Helena, and today its downtown is nearly vacant. That emptiness is even more pronounced in Elaine, as its lone commercial street has the look and feel of a ghost town.

As with many racial histories of this kind, the "Elaine Riot" was largely forgotten for many years, one of those shameful events best not talked about. Today, if you talk to people in Elaine and Helena, you can hear many different accounts. Many older whites relate a story that closely hews to the account given by the Committee of Seven, and they dispute the notion that black deaths numbered more than twenty-five. "It's like when you catch a fish, and every time you tell the story, the fish gets bigger," says Mary Louise Fiser, whose grandfather came to Elaine in 1913, opening a general store that her family ran for decades. "That's what has happened. It's been blown out of proportion." Blacks who've heard of this history—and many haven't—recall a massacre: "They shot women and children," says Raymond Willie, whose grandfather worked for the Tappans. "It was open season on black people." His father-in-law, J. W. Banks, worked as a sharecropper in the 1940s, and that is the story he remembers too: "You could smell nothing but death. You couldn't pick up the bodies. They were in the woods hiding when they were killed." The official version, which you can read in the Delta Cultural Center housed in the old train station at the south end of Cherry Street, states that "although accounts vary, five whites and 23 blacks are reported killed."

There are still Hornors and Tappans in Helena, and in 2005, Robert Miller—a nephew of D. A. E. Johnston, the dentist who was killed in the riot—was mayor, the first black ever elected to that position. Those names provide a springboard to the past, and if you go to the Maple Hill Cemetery, you can find the headstones for James Tappan, Clinton Lee, Greenfield Quarles, E. C. Hornor, Frank Kitchens, and many others. A number of the great Victorian mansions still remain, with Jerome Pillow's house now open for tours, and if you walk from the old train station north on Cherry Street, you'll pass the Solomon Building, where E. M. Allen, John Moore, and Greenfield Quarles had their offices, and it's fairly easy to figure out where—a little farther along and across the street—Ulysses Bratton had his. The ghosts of 1919 still haunt the streets, and if you walk up the stairs of the county courthouse and turn right, you can enter the courtroom where, during the first week of May 1920, Scipio Jones called Vina Mason to the stand and asked her to describe how she cradled her baby in the Hoop Spur church on that fateful September night.

SCIPIO JONES, AS COULD only be expected, spent the remainder of his days fighting in various ways to "better his race." The spirits of Booker T. Washington and W. E. B. Du Bois animated his actions in the manner they always had. He sought to help blacks prosper economically, he fought political and legal battles to secure their basic rights, and he tried to nurture good relations between the races.

He was involved in two major business ventures during the 1920s. He invested in the People's Ice and Fuel Company, which constructed a $120,000 ice plant and provided jobs for scores of blacks, and he served as its chairman of the board. In 1929, he and other blacks drew up plans for a very ambitious "negro colonization program," which they called "Hollywood." They announced that they would build, on 6,000 acres south of Conway, Arkansas, a canning factory, an industrial school, and a plant for producing motion pictures. However, that was the year that Wall Street went bust, kicking off the Great Depression, and their colonization program never took full flight. The Mosaic Templars also failed during the Depression, with Jones's personal finances taking a nosedive during this time.

Many blacks during the 1930s switched their allegiance, at the national level, to the Democratic party, but Jones remained a loyal Republican. He had come of age when the Republicans were the party that provided a home to blacks in the South, and he never gave up trying to prod the party to reject lily-whitism and return to its roots. In 1928 and again in 1940, he was elected as a delegate to the national Republican Convention, and in 1927, he raised a ruckus when it appeared that President Calvin Coolidge was going to appoint Wallace Townsend, a prominent lily-white Republican in Little Rock, as a federal judge. Townsend, Jones raged, is the "archenemy of our people . . . he is the most obnoxious lily-white Republican in this State." Jones and his fellow protesters won this battle, for Coolidge appointed Martineau to the bench instead. Even though Martineau was a Democrat, he and Jones went way back, and their friendship was such that in 1924 Martineau recused himself from a case in Pulaski Chancery Court so that Jones could serve as chancellor for a day. This was his second stint as a judge, and since a chancery court was much more prestigious than a municipal court, at least a few papers outside of Arkansas made note of it. "This was the first time in the history of the South, and possibly in the United States, that such an honor has been paid a Negro lawyer," the NAACP wrote in its press release.

Although there was a certain coolness that developed between Jones and Walter White after the Elaine cases came to a conclusion, the two men always addressing each other in formal terms, Jones handled several high-profile criminal cases during the 1920s and 1930s that drew the support of the NAACP, with Jones assisted at times by the NAACP's in-house counsel, Charles Houston and Thurgood Marshall, both of whom addressed him fondly as "Judge Jones." The most dramatic of those criminal cases was reminiscent, in many ways, of the Elaine battle. In January 1935, a sheriff in Blytheville, Arkansas, who had been harassing the Southern Tenant Farmers' Union was shot and slightly wounded while he was parked on the side of a rural road. Authorities picked up two black sharecroppers, Bubbles Clayton and Jim Caruthers, and tortured them to confess to the shooting. When they refused, the authorities threatened that they would bring a white woman into the jail to accuse them of rape. Still Clayton and Caruthers maintained their innocence, and so a charge of rape was drawn up. The two men, who vigorously protested that they were being framed, were given only a few days to prepare a defense; their court-appointed attorneys were local whites friendly with the prosecution; the courtroom was dominated by a mob; and no blacks were allowed on the jury. The two men were sentenced to die in the electric chair, and that's when Jones and Hibbler entered the case. With the Depression raging, Jones and Hibbler struggled to finance an appeal, with Hibbler at one point selling his law books to keep the case moving through the courts. It all came down to the wire in June 1939, with Jones and Hibbler preparing a writ of habeas corpus petition to the U.S. Supreme Court. However, they were so financially strapped that they had to ask Arkansas governor Carl Bailey to stay the executions so they could raise money to perfect the appeal, and Bailey not only refused, he rushed the electrocutions, the two men put to death on June 30. This undoubtedly was one of the bitterest defeats that Jones ever experienced.

In addition to such criminal defense work, Jones waged several notable struggles against Jim Crow laws. In 1930, he, Hibbler, and Joseph Booker sued the Arkansas Democratic party, arguing—albeit unsuccessfully, in a case they appealed all the way to the U.S. Supreme Court—that it was unconstitutional for the party to ban Negroes from voting in its primaries. In 1941, Jones pressured the University of Arkansas to provide tuition assistance to a black college graduate so that he could attend law school at Howard University. With the University of Arkansas closed to blacks, there was no way for blacks to study law in Arkansas, and after this initial case was brokered by Jones, the state began setting aside a pool of money to provide out-of-state tuition assistance to blacks whenever they wanted to pursue studies that weren't offered at Arkansas AM&N, the publicly funded black college in the state. A year later, at age seventy-nine, Jones initiated what would be his last legal struggle for the rights of "his people." He, Hibbler, and Booker boldly sued the Little Rock school district for paying black schoolteachers and administrators less than their white counterparts. This was a legal dart aimed at the heart of Jim Crow society, and while Jones died before the case came to a conclusion, it eventually came to a successful end, with Thurgood Marshall arguing the case before the Eighth Circuit Court of Appeals. *Morris v. Williams* marked yet another step forward for blacks in America, and it served as a fitting and symbolic capstone to Jones's life: he had been one of the country's first great black attorneys, and in this instance he handed off the baton to the man who would argue *Brown v. Board of Education* and subsequently become the first black to sit on the U.S. Supreme Court.

Jones passed away at his home in Little Rock on March 28, 1943. He was survived by his wife, Lillie, and three grandchildren, his daughter, Hazel, having died in 1927. The cause of his death was inflammation of the kidneys, although his friends noticed that in his last years he had "a nervous twitch that caused his head to bobble," which might have been a symptom of Parkinson's disease. He died a man of very modest means: he owned his home at 1872 Cross Street and a small building lot, and beyond that his only assets were the tools of his trade—an oak desk, a typewriter, two filing cabinets, a library table, six office chairs, one gold watch, and a law library, the last worth $1,000.

Both the *Arkansas Gazette* and the *Arkansas Democrat* remembered him for his support for Negro fraternal groups and his devotion to Bethel A.M.E. Church, and hailed him as one "of the foremost Negro lawyers in the country." But neither mentioned the Elaine case, apparently deciding that it was better left forgotten. However, the *Arkansas State Press,* a black publication, published a much longer obituary, recalling his Elaine triumph and detailing how he'd been a "liaison man in the time of misunderstanding between the races." Even prior to his death, an all-white Little Rock school board had honored him for a similar reason, renaming the black high school in North Little Rock the Scipio A. Jones High School.

Such was the character of Scipio Africanus Jones. He'd spent his entire life fighting against the wrongs of a Jim Crow America, and yet he'd always waged those fights in such a genial manner that most whites could not help but think well of him. At the time, that surely was the only effective way to wage a struggle for equal rights in the South, and yet it also was a reflection of who Jones was: born a slave, he believed in the promise of a United States that was democratic in both law and in spirit, and that meant, for him, nurturing good relations between the races. The possibility of such a future was even in evidence at his funeral, which was held at his beloved Bethel A.M.E. Church. This was located in the very heart of black Little Rock, which was a segregated city, and yet on that day, March 31, 1943, one section of the church had to be cordoned off, "reserved," the *Arkansas Democrat* noted, for his many "white friends."

Epilogue

THE STORY OF THE Elaine massacre, which for various reasons is unknown—even in its broadest details—to most Americans, serves as a reminder that the struggle to make our society, as
Theodore Roosevelt put it, "juster and fairer," was a long and hard
one. We often think of the civil rights movement springing to life on
December 1, 1955, when Rosa Parks refused to give up her seat at
the front of a bus in Montgomery, Alabama. But we can see in this
history that the modern civil rights movement was simply the culmi-
nating chapter to a hundred-year struggle, one that began in the
summer of 1865, when the freedmen met in their state conventions
and expressed their hopes for equal rights under the law. Scipio
Jones devoted his life to that struggle, and we can see too that the
Hoop Spur sharecroppers, by daring to hire an attorney to represent
their rights at settlement, were showing the same courage as those
who traveled to Mississippi during the Freedom Summer of 1964 to
help blacks register to vote. Blood was spilled on the fields of Hoop
Spur in 1919, and it was spilled again during that year of "Mississippi Burning."

Although the *Moore v. Dempsey* legal case is similarly unknown
to most Americans, legal scholars regularly cite it as a "turning
point" in American law. This case, explained law professor Curtis
Reitz in a 1961 article in the *Harvard Law Review,* was the "point of
departure" for the "great expansion of the due process clause as a
regulator of state procedures." David Fellman, in his 1976 book *The
Defendant's Rights Today,* noted that it was in *Moore* that the
Supreme Court, at long last, abandoned its "position of extreme
comity with regard to state courts." In his 2003 book on habeas corpus, Larry Yackle, a professor of law at Boston University, wrote

that "after Moore," the Supreme Court regularly began to use "habeas corpus to investigate deprivations of liberty by virtue of unlawful criminal convictions." All of these observations speak to the same point: we often think that the Constitution, as written in 1787, guaranteed United States citizens a fair trial, but in fact it took nearly two centuries before such a fundamental guarantee was fully incorporated into our national law.

This history also provides a foil for thinking about our country's commitment to such principles of fairness today.

In 1969, the Warren Court called the writ of habeas corpus "the fundamental instrument for safeguarding individual freedom against arbitrary and lawless state actions," and for the next twenty-five years it proved to be just that for many Americans. From 1973 to 1995, federal courts provided relief to 40 percent of the 599 death-row prisoners who filed habeas petitions, with the boxer Rubin "Hurricane" Carter one of those given relief. All of the prisoners given a new lease on life had been convicted at trials that, under the Constitution, could not be considered "fair."

Congress's erosion of the Great Writ of Liberty began in 1996 when it passed the Antiterrorism and Effective Death Penalty Act. The legislation decreed that federal courts can provide habeas relief to state prisoners only if a state court has issued a ruling that is "unreasonably wrong" as opposed to just plain wrong. Since federal judges aren't likely to consider state courts "unreasonable" in their rulings, this is an almost impossible standard to meet. Congress, in essence, undid much of the *Moore* precedent with this law. "Federal habeas jurisdiction," the *New York Times* explained, "is now only a shadow of what it was."

Then came 9/11 and our country's "war on terror." In December 2001, President George W. Bush asserted that he had the authority to detain indefinitely noncitizens suspected of a connection to terrorists. He declared that the prisoners, whom he deemed "unlawful enemy combatants," would have no access to U.S. courts to challenge their imprisonment. More than 650 men and boys from forty different countries were subsequently rounded up and imprisoned at Guantánamo Bay. There is now considerable evidence that many of the detainees were tortured, with the *New York Times* reporting that it appears that a "large portion, if not a majority" of those detained at the U.S. naval base in Cuba are, in fact, "innocent men."

Beginning in 2002, the Guantánamo prisoners sought to challenge their detention by filing petitions for writs of habeas corpus in federal courts, this legal work done by the Center for Constitutional Rights and other U.S. attorneys concerned with protecting civil liberties. Although President Bush and his administration argued that the Guantánamo prisoners had no right to petition a federal court because they were not being held on U.S. soil, the Supreme Court ruled in *Rasul v. Bush* (2004) that they did. The Supreme Court also subsequently ruled in *Hamdan v. Rumsfeld* (2006) that the military commissions set up by the Bush administration to try the detainees violated both the Uniform Code of Military Justice and the Geneva Conventions, as the commissions' procedural rules did not meet those two legal codes for trying prisoners of war.

Congress responded by passing the Military Commissions Act in late 2006. The act decreed that federal courts shall have no jurisdiction to hear a petition for a writ of habeas corpus filed by an "alien detained by the United States who has been determined by the United States to have been properly detained as an enemy combatant or is awaiting such determination." In essence, under this act, the United States has declared that it has the right to kidnap and imprison anyone who is not a U.S. citizen and hold that person indefinitely, with the detainee having no right to challenge his or her imprisonment in court. If the detainee is eventually tried by a military commission, the military, under this new U.S. law, may rely on hearsay, secret evidence, and coerced testimony.

Just as *Moore v. Dempsey* proved to be a turning point in our country's history, so too may the Military Commissions Act of 2006 prove to be one. Habeas corpus, the great writ that saved Frank Moore and his co-appellants from the electric chair, is losing its place at the heart of our law. The United States is headed down a new path, and suddenly—and this is what is truly astonishing about this new turn in American law—the machinations of justice in the Helena courthouse, at the end of that awful Red Summer of 1919, no longer seem quite so foreign.

Appendix: The Killing Fields

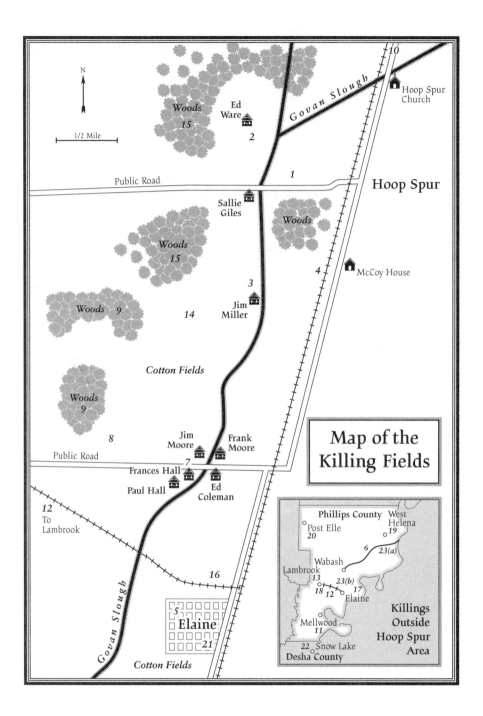

N

1/2 Mile

Woods
15

Ed
Ware

2

Govan Slough

10

Hoop Spur
Church

Public Road

1

Hoop Spur

Sallie
Giles

Woods
15

Woods

Woods
9

14

Jim
Miller

3

4

McCoy House

Cotton Fields

Woods
9

8

Jim
Moore

Frank
Moore

7

Public Road

Frances Hall

Paul Hall

Ed
Coleman

12
To
Lambrook

16

5
Elaine

21

Govan Slough

Cotton Fields

Map of the
Killing Fields

Phillips County   West
Helena

Post Elle
20

19

6

23(a)

Wabash

Lambrook

13

23(b)

18   12

17

Elaine

Mellwood
11

22   Snow Lake

Desha County

Killings
Outside
Hoop Spur
Area

The Killing Fields

Place	Approximate Time	Who Did the Killing	Reports of Blacks Killed
	OCTOBER 1:		
1. Road west of Hoop Spur	10:30 A.M.	Helena posse	Lemon
2. Ed Ware's house	11:00 A.M.	Helena posse	Charlie Robinson
3. Govan Slough near Jim Miller's house	11:30 A.M. to noon	Helena and Elaine posses	Jim Miller, Arthur Washington, and at least six or seven others; posse member Henry Smiddy says many more killed
4. Corn patch near McCoy's	Noon to 3:00 P.M.	Helena and Elaine posses	Several, as reported by Henry Bernard
5. Elaine	1:00 P.M.	Elaine residents?	Newspapers report fifteen slain in Elaine; researcher Bessie Ferguson reports in 1927 that blacks were killed and mutilated in Elaine
6. Route 44 between Helena and Wabash, and possibly in Hoop Spur area as well	1:00 to 5:00 P.M.	Outside posses	*Memphis Press* reports posses killing blacks working in cotton fields near road; witnesses say that these posses began indiscriminate killing of black men and women
	OCTOBER 2		
7. Frances Hall's house, on road that ran west from Route 44, about one mile north of Elaine	6:30 A.M.	Outside posses	Frances Hall
8. Road running west from Frances Hall's house and into woods	7:00 A.M. to 8:30 A.M.	Outside posses	Posses reported they killed at least four blacks that morning
9. Two wooded areas northwest of Frances Hall's house	10:00 A.M. to noon	Camp Pike troops	There were 150 black men reported to be "hiding" in these two patches of woods; troops were acting under "shoot to kill orders" and opened fire with machine guns; only one reported survivor

Place	Approximate Time	Who Did the Killing	Reports of Blacks Killed
10. Route 44 just north of Hoop Spur church	10:00 A.M.	Amos Jarman and others	D. A. E. Johnston and his three brothers
11. Mellwood	9:00 A.M. to noon	Mellwood residents	Three blacks
12. Railroad line between Elaine and Lambrook	9:00 A.M. to noon	Local posse members hiding in gondola car	Report that the men "picked off" several negroes that morning
13. Lambrook	2:00 P.M. to evening	Camp Pike troops	One sharecropper burned to death; not known whether others were killed
14. Hoop Spur cotton fields; big area north from where Frances Hall lived to Ed Ware's place	1:00 to 4:00 P.M.	Camp Pike troops	Unknown number; Arkansas newspaperman L. Sharpe Dunaway reported in 1925 that troops marched through fields "committing one murder after another"
15. Woods west of Hoop Spur (west of where Ed Ware and Albert Giles lived)	3:00 to 5:00 P.M.	Camp Pike troops	Newspapers that afternoon reported that at least one hundred men were trapped in the woods and that it would be a "fight to the finish"; no further reports of numbers killed or whether any blacks survived
	OCTOBER 3		
16. Outskirts of Elaine	3:00 A.M.	Camp Pike troops	Dan Dixon and one other black killed by machine gun fire
17. Canebrakes three miles east of Elaine	7:00 A.M. to early afternoon	Camp Pike troops	There were fifty blacks reported to be in the woods at the start of the fight; fifteen were captured, no reports on whether the remaining thirty-five escaped or were killed
18. Lambrook	Sometime Friday	Camp Pike troops	Four or five blacks reported killed
	OCTOBER 4–7		
19. West Helena		Locals	One
20. Post Elle		Locals	One
21. Elaine schoolhouse		Camp Pike troops	Isaiah Murphy

Place	Approximate Time	Who Did the Killing	Reports of Blacks Killed
22. Snow Lake		Locals	One
OTHER ANECDOTAL ACCOUNTS			
23. a) Bridge four miles south of Helena	a) Uncertain	a) Camp Pike troops	a) Sixteen blacks hung from bridge
b) Railroad line from Elaine to Lambrook, or from Elaine to Helena	b) Uncertain	b) Camp Pike troops	b) Prosecutor John Miller later said that one hundred blacks who approached the train were killed

Notes

To view court documents and other source materials, go to onthelapsofgods.com.

ABBREVIATIONS

Publications
AD   *Arkansas Democrat*
AG   *Arkansas Gazette*
AHQ   *Arkansas Historical Quarterly*
HW   *Helena World*
MCA   *Memphis Commercial Appeal*
PCHR   *Phillips County Historical Review*
PCHQ   *Phillips County Historical Quarterly*

Source Documents
BJ   Interviews by J. W. Butts and Dorothy James, December 7, 1960, Phillips
        County Library, Helena, Arkansas
BP   Papers of Charles Brough, University of Arkansas at Fayetteville, Special
        Collections
DC   Tom W. Dillard Black Arkansiana Collection, Butler Center for Arkansas
        Studies, Central Arkansas Library System, Little Rock
DYT   David Yancey Thomas Collection, University of Arkansas at Fayetteville,
        Special Collections
FSAA   *Federal Surveillance of Afro-Americans, 1917–25*
NAACP   *Papers of the National Association for the Advancement of Colored People*
PF   *Peonage Files of the U.S. Department of Justice, 1901–1945*
PFHU   Progressive Farmers and Household Union documents
WF   NAACP files of Elaine riot copied by Arthur L. Waskow, Wisconsin State
        Historical Society Library, University of Wisconsin, Madison

Libraries
AHC   Arkansas History Commission, Little Rock
BC   Butler Center for Arkansas Studies, Central Arkansas Library System, Lit-
        tle Rock
SC   Schomburg Center for Research in Black Culture, New York Public Li-
        brary, New York City
UAL   University of Arkansas Libraries, Fayetteville, Special Collections

UALR   University of Arkansas at Little Rock/Pulaski County Law Library, Special Collections

NOTES

Full citations for books and journal articles that are referenced in the notes can be found in the bibliography.

Chapter 1: *A Union in Hoop Spur*

Personal information about the Hoop Spur sharecroppers can be found in U.S. census records, World War I military records, Arkansas State Penitentiary records, *Arkansas Race Riot* by Ida B. Wells-Barnett, and the various trial proceedings that were part of the *Moore v. Dempsey* case.

1 "house was packed" *Ware v. Arkansas,* 1920, brief and abstract of record, 61. UALR.

2 "I had those [union] books" Wells-Barnett, *Arkansas Race Riot,* 32.

2 "We've just begun" Committee of Seven report, Oct. 7, 1919. *Moore v. Dempsey* brief and record. UALR.

2 "two hundred head of men" Wells-Barnett, *Arkansas Race Riot,* 14.

3 "White people don't want" *Ware v. Arkansas,* brief and abstract of record, 60, 61.

3 "The whites are going" Wells-Barnett, ibid., 34.

4 "nothing of their own" Ferguson, 14.

4 "could study astronomy" Auerbach, 114.

6 "Pulling the cotton" Wolff, 34.

6 "I'm down" Delta Cultural Center, Helena, Arkansas.

7 "They didn't give" Lankford, 320.

8 "Nought's a nought" William Pickens, "These Colored United States," *The Messenger,* Jan. 1923.

8 "The negro is then bound" J. Shillady to *Albany Journal,* Oct. 30, 1919. WF.

9 "acute unrest" Basil Manly. "Memoranda on Tenancy in the Southwestern States," 1916, WF.

9 "by the droves" U. S. Bratton to D. Y. Thomas, March 1, 1920, and Sept. 15, 1921, DYT, box 1, file 2.

10 "their chance had come" Wells-Barnett, *Arkansas Race Riot,* 7.

10 "The object of this organization" PFHU bylaws, FSAA, reel 21.

11 "the Grand Circuit badge" PFHU incorporation papers, FSAA, reel 21.

11 "We did all" R. Hill to U. S. Bratton, Dec. 4, 1919, WF.

11 "I lend my best services" ibid.

11 "O you laborers" PFHU circular, BP, series 8, box 22, folder 13.

12 "Will you defend" PFHU examination certificate, BP, series 8, box 22, folder 13.

13 "Ye farmers" Ferguson, 39.

13 "It was a fact" Hill to Bratton, Dec. 4, 1919.

13 "detective on the case" R. Hill to NAACP, Nov. 26, 1919, WF.

14 "They inquired of us" Bratton to Thomas, March 1, 1920.

14 **"Let us see"** Wells-Barnett, *Arkansas Race Riot,* 8.

15 **"Negroes should be made"** Holmes, 117.

15 **"to keep their racks"** McElveen to Justice Department, Oct. 10, 1919, FSAA, reel 12.

16 **"going to resign"** Wells-Barnett, *Arkansas Race Riot,* 31; *Ware v. Arkansas,* brief and abstract of record, 74.

16 **Ware's conversation with McCullough** Wells-Barnett, *Arkansas Race Riot,* 32; *Ware v. Arkansas,* brief and abstract of record, 74.

17 **Ware's threatened lynching** Wells-Barnett, *Arkansas Race Riot,* 13, 16, 17, 19, 33.

18 **"bravest man"** Ibid., 19, 33.

18 **"was threatening"** Ibid., 17.

18 **"A car has driven"** *Ware v. Arkansas,* brief and abstract of record, 71.

Chapter 2: *The Path to Hoop Spur*

19 **"What shall we do"** Richardson, 39.

20 **"the slaves of society"** Meyer, 48.

20 **"We simply ask"** Litwack, 521.

20 **"the restoration"** Lincoln, 102.

21 **"If the color is not right"** Kennedy, 37.

21 **"Let us rather"** Hahn, 158.

22 **"a covenant with death"** Newman, 2.

22 **"I admit"** Irons, 192.

23 **"We must see"** Curtis, 51.

23 **"arm the Congress"** Ibid., 70.

24 **"Why should this not pass?"** Ibid., 55.

24 **"The black man is free"** Richardson, 80.

25 **"They are *crazy*"** Litwack, 474.

25 **"The time has arrived"** DeBlack, 178.

26 **"We have broken"** Newman, 14.

27 **"The American people"** Meyer, 77.

28 **"When the decision"** Irons, 105.

29 **"A Republican Supreme Court"** Foner, *Voice of Black America,* 505.

29 **"so-called emancipation"** Foner, *Frederick Douglass,* 711.

29 **"the Court has been serving"** Irons, 215.

30 **"eliminate the nigger"** Wormser, 70.

30 **"The greatest mistake"** Klarman, 44.

30 **"When there is a row"** Albert Bushnell Hart, "The Outcome of the Southern Race Question," *North American Review,* July 1908.

30 **"This is the barbecue"** James Allen, 174.

30 **"sweethearting"** Wells-Barnett, *On Lynchings,* 37.

31 **"If the people"** Ginzburg, 36.

31 **"fundamental principles"** Heaney, 445.

31 **"We have three"** Friedman, 375.

32 **"From the standpoint"** Kellogg, 24.

32 **"inferior to whites"** Jefferson, 270.

32 **"facial angle"** Stoskopf, 45.

33 "anatomically constructed" Kolchin, 192.
33 "that negroes are not *men*" Fredrickson, 86.
33 "separate species" Stoskopf, 49.
33 "raise his race" Dray, 100.
34 "cannot comprehend" *American Medicine*, April 1907, 197.
34 "half child, half animal" Frederickson, 280.
34 "lecherous ape" *Crisis*, April 1915, 276.
34 "there's just as much difference" *Crisis*, May 1917, 25.
35 "civilized white men" Kellogg, 172.
35 "The federal government has set" *Crisis*, Oct. 1913, 298.
36 "It's like history" Dray, 198.
36 "into a Southern partisan" Wormser, 121.
36 "Burn him slow" *Crisis,* July 1917, suppl. 1.
37 "It was the biggest" *Crisis*, Feb. 1918, 178.
37 "the application of red-hot irons" As cited by the *Crisis,* May 1918, 25.
37 "The common people" *Crisis,* May 1918, 24.
37 "not simply insolent" NAACP, "Newspaper Comment During 1918 Regard-ing Lynching," part 7, series a, reel 1.
37 "writhe in agony" Walter White, "The Work of a Mob," *Crisis,* Sept. 1918.
37 "You ought to have heard" Walter White, "I Investigate Lynchings," NAACP, part 7, series a, reel 3.
38 "We are asking" Negro Womanhood of Georgia to W. Wilson, May 29, 1918, FSAA, reel 14.
38 "The law, as laid down" C. Porter to P. G. Cooper, March 13, 1919, FSAA, reel 14.

Chapter 3: *The Red Summer of 1919*
39 "not more than 50" Harris, 184.
39 "The most wonderful" Ibid., 188.
40 "Will [the Negro] accept" Arnesen, 90.
40 "If thousands" Finley, 250.
40 "his protest" Harris, 83.
40 "We are not stopping" Finley, 258.
41 "If the war lasts" *Crisis,* Dec. 1917, 80.
41 "juster and fairer" Richard Dalfiume, Introduction to "Discrimination in the U.S. Armed Forces, 1918–1955," NAACP, Part 9.
41 "Out of this conflict" David Levering Lewis, "The Race of War," *Nation,* Feb. 20, 2006.
41 "The *Crisis* says" *Crisis,* Sept. 1918, 217.
41 "Our great American" Harris, 178.
42 "As a result" Harris, 202.
43 "One could not find" *Crisis,* Feb. 1919, 167.
43 "I am awful proud" Finley, 264.
43 "A large faith" *Crisis,* March 1919, 288.
43 "We return" *Crisis,* May 1919, 14.
43 "niggers," "coons" NAACP, part 9, introduction.

44 **"Secret Information"** Du Bois, "Documents of the War," *Crisis,* May 1919.
44 **"Niggers keep out"** *Crisis,* March 1919, 222.
44 **"niggers are rapists"** Charles Williams, War Department report, May 17, 1919, FSAA, reel 20.
44 **"The things that happened"** Cyril Briggs, "Fighting Savage Hun and Treacherous Cracker," *Crusader,* April 1919.
45 **"strutting about"** F. Sullens, "Memorandum for Maj. Brown, War Department," Nov. 30, 1918, FSAA, reel 21.
45 **"If the black man"** James Weldon Johnson, "Terrorism—How It Could Be Met," *New York Age,* Nov. 1, 1919.
45 **"for any Negro"** Kerlin, 136.
45 **"If you wish"** Seligmann, 257.
46 **"colored soldiers who find"** *Crisis,* April 1919, 289.
46 **"not heretofore open"** *Crisis,* Feb. 1919, 186.
46 **"head south"** *Crisis,* May 1919, 31.
46 **"their duty"** Kerlin, 37.
46 **"accused of writing"** *Crisis,* July 1919, 155.
46 **"niggers get off"** Kerlin, 103.
46 **"cut to pieces"** "Why Congress Should Investigate Race Riots and Lynchings," NAACP, part 7, series a, reel 2.
47 **"anything known in ancient"** William Reedy, "The Black Man's Burden," *St. Louis Mirror,* June 19, 1919; NAACP, part 7, series a, reel 6.
47 **"This is how we treat"** Kerlin, 101.
47 **"Three Thousand Will Burn"** U.S. House of Representatives, "Segregation and Antilynching Hearings," 66th Congress, 2nd session (1920).
48 **"We are demanding"** *Crisis,* May 1919.
48 **"The Negro race is united"** Kerlin, 43.
48 **"to know itself"** Monroe Work, "The Negro Press in the United States," *Messenger,* May 1923.
48 **"exist in a Hell"** Editorial in *Crusader,* cited in U.S. Senate, "Radicalism and Sedition Among the Negroes as Reflected in their Publications," 66th Congress, 1st session (1919), doc. no. 153.
48 **"The South is more Hellish"** "American Huns," *Challenge,* cited in U.S. Senate, "Radicalism and Sedition."
48 **"stands before the world"** *Crusader,* editorial, April 1919.
48 **"Men, Women and Children"** *Veteran,* June 18, 1919, FSAA, reel 13.
48 **"the most damnable"** *Negro Age,* cited in U.S. Senate, "Radicalism and Sedition."
49 **"have purchased arms"** Herbert Seligmann, "Protecting Southern Womanhood," *Nation,* June 14, 1919.
49 **"Negroes are not planning"** *Crisis,* Oct. 1919, 298.
49 **"Civilization trembles"** Kerlin, 114.
49 **"Oh! Say can you see"** *Messenger,* July 1919.
49 **"A new Negro is rising"** "The Hun in America," *Messenger,* July 1919.
49 **"If we must protect"** *Chicago Defender,* June 28, 1919, FSAA, reel 13.
49 **"too brutally inhuman"** *Veteran,* "The Remedy for Mob Violence," June 28, 1919, cited in U.S. Senate, "Radicalism and Sedition."

49 "The only recourse" William Bird, "Herald Correspondent Urges Negroes to Defend Their Lives at All Cost," *Baltimore Daily Herald*, NAACP, part 7, series a, reel 6.

50 "loyalty of the Negroes" Murray, 178.

50 "Reds Try to Stir" Ibid., 178.

50 "financed from Russia" Newspaper article, "Reds Accused of Stirring Up Negro Rioters," FSAA, reel 8.

50 "no use in shutting" Murray, 178.

50 "organized alignment" U.S. Office of the Postmaster, "Radicalism and Sedition Among the Negroes as Reflected in Their Publications." July 2, 1919, FSAA, reel 12.

50 "employing reliable negroes" Henry Sebastian, "Activities of Department of Justice on Negro Question," FSAA, reel 21.

51 "As long as the Negro" Kerlin, 151.

51 "Get all the niggers" Chicago Commission on Race Relations, 596.

53 "the Negroes stood" Charles Edward Russell, *Reconstruction*, Oct. 1919, NAACP, part 7, series a, reel 6.

53 "now assumed" B. Thomson to L. Winslow, July 29, 1919, FSAA, reel 17.

53 "The time for cringing" Kerlin, 70.

53 "an eye for an eye" U.S. Senate, "Radicalism and Sedition."

53 "If it is to be a Land" *Crisis*, Sept. 1919.

54 "No one who was in the United States" Murray, 17.

Chapter 4: *Helena*

55 Hornor, . . . cleared 12,000 acres Mills, 27.

55 Keesee, . . . had cotton . . . on 2,000 acres Herndon, *Annals of Arkansas*, 812; *HW*, Feb. 20, 1919.

56 Rising cotton prices in 1919 "Hold Your Cotton," *HW*, Feb. 8, 1919; "Cotton Prices May Be High," *HW*, May 28, 1919; "Dollar Day Bargains," *HW*, June 22, 1919.

56 "$300 worth of cotton" "Eastern Arkansas and the Garden of Eden," *AD*, Oct. 27, 1919.

57 "reported that the niggers" Brooke Tappan, "Reminiscence of Charles Madison Young," 1977, Folklore Class Reports, 1958–1999, UAL.

57 "Bratton was an old carpetbag" Ferguson, 68.

58 "sink of crime" Worley, 4.

60 "Everywhere they are devouring" Moneyhon, *The Impact of the Civil War and Reconstruction on Arkansas*, 30.

60 "The people through here" Crisler, 17.

60 "The ridges and ravines" Whayne, *Arkansas Delta*, 85.

60 "My God!" DeBlack, 140.

60 "With proper energy" Moneyhon, *The Impact of the Civil War and Reconstruction on Arkansas*, 187, 189.

60 "The nigger is going" Litwack, 415.

60 "They take all the cotton" Baskett, *Persistence of the Spirit*, 22.

60 "the colored people are being swindled" DeBlack, 156.

60 "when the settlement" Freedmen's Bureau for Arkansas, Nov. 24, 1866, Bureau of Refugees, Freedmen and Abandoned Lands, 1865–1869, National Archives microfilm M979, roll 52.

62 Planters regain control of county politics Todd Lewis, "Racial Politics in Jefferson and Phillips Counties," 1997, UAL; Todd Lewis, "Racial Politics in Arkansas, 1865–1894," UAL; Dillard, "To the Back of the Elephant"; Underwood; Justice.

63 "Except for that dark" Susan Huntsman, "Race Relations in Phillips County, 1895–1920," Stockley papers, BC.

64 "in a manner" Whayne, The Arkansas Delta, 226, 235.

64 "soil more fertile" E. M. Allen, 22.

65 History of Elaine Ibid.; Mary Jones; John Moore; Mills; Kyte.

65 Lambert's story Lambert.

67 "land of opportunity" Helena Business Men's League, Push and Pull: Hustling Helena Has Both, 1910.

68 "fabulous parties" Frances Hornor Curtis, "Folklore of Phillips County," 1958, Folklore Class Reports, 1958–1999, UAL.

68 "snatching fruits" Street, 35.

68 throw chickens Frances Hornor Curtis, "Folklore."

69 "good for a turnout" Parmelee.

69 "all the latest coon" HW, June 24, 1919.

69 Mrs. Pat Parham reported "West Helena Negro Accused of Grave Crime," HW, May 11, 1917; "Angry Citizens Gather Around the County Jail," HW, May 13, 1917; "Will Dial Gets 21 Years in Prison," HW, May 16, 1917.

70 "In the present crisis" "Negroes Feared Threats of Men," HW, Aug. 30, 1917.

70 "Helena Negroes" "Army Post Will Use No More Negro Labor," HW, Aug. 10, 1917.

71 "stripped and beaten" Crisis, Oct. 1914, 273.

71 "spiritual wickedness" "Many Names on Petition Are Negroes," HW, July 21, 1916.

71 "This is bad literature" E. J. Kerwin to A. Bielaski, May 7, 1917, FSAA, reel 9.

72 "is an asset" "More Agitation," HW, May 14, 1919.

72 "has again demonstrated" Letter to the editor, MCA, Jan. 26, 1919.

72 "Here we had a tinderbox" Lambert, 74.

73 "Even a blind man" "Printer Charges Neglect by Federal Official," AG, Oct. 12, 1919.

73 "to find out" Charles Straub interview, Oct. 15, 1960, BJ.

73 Bio for Bratton Hempstead, 719; Ulysses S. Bratton Jr. interview, 1978, Stockley papers, BC.

74 "it is the practice" U.S. Attorney General to Whipple, Jan. 20, 1905, PF, reel 2.

75 "in the penitentiary" U. S. Bratton to Terrell, July 5, 1905, PF reel 2.

75 "nothing more than slavery" U. S. Bratton to D. Y. Thomas, Sept. 15, 1921, DYT, box 1, file 2.

75 "did not know" "Plead Guilty to Peonage Charges," AG, April 9, 1905; Whipple to U.S. Attorney General, April 18, 1905, PF, reel 2.

75 **Quackenbos's investigation** Quackenbos to U.S. Attorney General, 1907, PF, reel 4.

76 **"These people are held"** Black to Trieber, March 18, 1912, PF, reel 13.

76 **"The sympathy was with the planters"** Whipple to U.S. Attorney General, May 23, 1912, PF, reel 13.

77 **"I am glad"** Bratton to Thomas, Sept. 15, 1921.

77 **"degenerate white man"** Brooke Tappan, "Reminiscence of Charles Madison Young."

77 **"Kill the Coons!"** *HW*, July 30, 1919.

78 **"guards [were] sitting on the steps"** Kyte, 49.

78 **"famine"** "To the Public," *HW*, Aug. 8, 1919.

78 **$5,000 worth of shotguns** "Eleven Negroes to Pay with Their Lives for Greed of One," *New York World*, Nov. 16, 1919.

78 **"It is expected"** "To Mothers, Wives, Sweethearts of Phillips County Soldiers," *HW*, Aug. 11, 1919.

78 **"could provide troops"** Senn; "Major General Sturgis Guest of Helena," *HW*, Aug. 13, 1919.

78 **"rumors upon rumors"** Kyte, 49.

78 **Black men were reported to be** Letter to the editor, *HW*, Sept. 23, 1919.

78 **"to get ready for trouble"** Statement by J. W. Butts, Oct. 17, 1960, BJ.

79 **"Hill had the ability"** E. M. Allen to Governor Allen, May 9, 1920, as cited by Cortner, *A Mob Intent on Death,* 82.

79 **"few darkies"** Lynn Smith interview, Oct. 28, 1960, BJ.

79 **"Southern white capitalists"** "Strikes," *Messenger,* Sept. 1919.

79 **"designated citizens"** Straub interview.

79 **"They realized"** Lambert, 74.

80 **"We crawled"** Henry Bernard interview, Dec. 7, 1960, BJ. Bernard recalled crawling under the Elaine church on the same night that Adkins was shot; however, that meeting was held the previous Thursday night, and thus he was evidently recalling that earlier meeting.

80 **"I was too sleepy"** Affidavit by H. F. Smiddy, Sept. 19, 1921, *Moore v. Dempsey* brief and record, UALR.

81 **"get some whiskey"** Ibid.

Chapter 5: *The Killing Fields*

83 **Sharecroppers' description of church shooting** *Ware v. Arkansas* brief and record, 34, 69, 72, 105, 31, 58, 32, UALR.

85 **Officers' examination of church** Affidavit by T. K. Jones, Sept. 19, 1921, *Moore v. Dempsey* brief and record, UALR: affidavit by Smiddy; *Arkansas v. Martin and Banks,* transcript, 14. UALR.

87 **"substantial and prosperous"** Hempstead, 819.

88 **"We have ways"** John Elvis Miller, interview, March 18, 1976, UAL.

88 **"Nothing could have suited"** H. Anderson to Brough, Oct. 7, 1919, BP, series 1, box 4, folder 54, item 87.

88 **"ambushed"** "Negroes Had Plot to Rise Against Whites, Charged," *AD*, Oct. 2, 1919.

89 "unable to direct" "U.S. Bratton Jr. Is Charged with Inciting Blacks," *AG*, Oct. 2, 1919.

89 "He told us some white people" *Ware v. Arkansas* brief and record, 91.

90 Shooting at Ware's house Ibid., 90, 93.

91 "We heard the shooting" *Arkansas v. Giles and Fox*, transcript, 19, UALR.

91 "told us if they didn't bother" and "Lay close" Ibid., 26, 37.

91 "The white people" shooting "at the women" *Ware v. Arkansas*, brief and record, 83.

91 Smiddy's description of Govan Slough shootings Affidavit by Smiddy.

92 "I saw some six" Henry Bernard interview.

92 "Look out, we are shooting" Affidavit by Smiddy.

93 "the fact that even ONE WHITE MAN" Dunaway, 101.

93 "shot in the head" *Ware v. Arkansas*, brief and record, 85

93 "to kill all the Negroes" Wells-Barnett, *Arkansas Race Riot*, 32.

93 "Don't you all hear" *Hicks v. Arkansas*, transcript, 17. UALR.

94 "tried to cut us off" Wells-Barnett, *Arkansas Race Riot*, 17.

94 "It was only two shots" Ibid., 18.

94 "I slipped back" Ibid., 17.

94 "I am hit" *Hicks v. Arkansas*, transcript, 6.

94 "After the shooting of Lee" Affidavit by Smiddy.

95 "Circuit and county judges" "500 Camp Pike Soldiers Sent to Quell Riot," *AG*, Oct. 2, 1919.

95 Negroes "were assembling" "10 Dead, Dozen Hurt," *AG*, Oct. 2, 1919.

95 "I got in this corn" H. Bernard interview, Dec. 7, 1960, BJ.

95 Bratton's near lynching O. S. Bratton to U. S. Bratton, Nov. 19, 1919, WF.

96 "Mr. E. C. Hornor advised" Statement by J. W. Butts, Oct. 17, 1960, BJ.

96 "fighting was in progress" "10 Dead . . . ," *AG*, Oct. 2, 1919.

96 "negroes had been driven" Ibid.

97 "at least 15 negroes" "U.S. Bratton, Jr. Is Charged with Inciting Blacks," *AG*, Oct. 2, 1919.

97 "Barbarism such as cutting" Ferguson, 83.

97 "It is alleged that Bratton" "U.S. Bratton, Jr. Is Charged."

98 "My negroes don't belong" Affidavit by T. K. Jones.

98 "Dead bodies were lying" "Press Reporter Spends Two Days at Helena and Elaine," *Memphis Press*, Oct. 4, 1919, WF.

99 "Plenty of them" "500 Soldiers Arrive at Elaine with Brough," *Memphis News Scimitar*, Oct. 2, 1919.

99 "struck by 26 bullets "Believe Memphian Slain," *MCA*, Oct. 2, 1919.

99 "During that afternoon" Affidavit by Smiddy.

99 "numerous clashes" "4 Negroes, One White Man, Killed," *AD*, Oct. 2, 1919.

99 "armed bands of whites" Ferguson, 61, 83.

99 "when that damn Mississippi" John Miller, interview, March 18, 1976, UAL.

99 "We formed a cordon" Statement by Butts.

100 "The quiet, however" "10 Dead."

100 "I had eight women" Wells-Barnett, *Arkansas Race Riot*, 14.

100 Moore's military service Discharge record for Frank Moore, serial number 3848337, Arkansas World War I Discharge Records, AHC.

Chapter 6: *They Shot Them Down Like Rabbits*

102 **"Four whites said to be killed"** Brough to Newton Baker, Oct. 1, 1919, FSAA, reel 16.

103 **"only person in human history"** Cook, 11.

103 **Brough's treatise** Brough, "Clinton Riot."

104 **"As an American"** Brough, "Work of the Commission," 55.

105 **"I am not in favor"** Cook, 79.

105 **"Congratulations from Phillips County"** S. Stoaks to Brough, April 2, 1916, BP, box 2, file 27, item 274.

105 **"only Confederate General"** "Inaugural Message of Charles H. Brough," Jan. 10, 1917, BC.

105 **"use of federal troops"** U.S. War Department to McRae, March 26, 1921, FSAA, reel 16.

106 **"sufficient supply of ammunition"** "500 Camp Pike Soldiers," *AG*, Oct. 2, 1919.

106 **"Every one of the 500"** "Agitators Blamed for Negro Revolt," *AG*, Oct. 6, 1919.

106 **"The machine guns are expected"** "500 Camp Pike Soldiers."

106 **"paraded the streets"** "Negroes Had Plot to Rise Against Whites," *AD*, Oct. 2, 1919.

106 **"above fever heat"** "Race Riot Excites Phillips County," *MCA*, Oct. 2, 1919.

107 **"a small army"** "Quiet at Elaine During Night," *AD*, Oct. 2, 1919.

107 **"They are known"** "4 Negroes, One White Man, Killed," *AD*, Oct. 2, 1919.

107 **Beating of Lula Black** Wells-Barnett, *Arkansas Race Riot*, 21.

107 **"tying her clothes"** Ibid., 21; *Ware v. Arkansas* brief and record, 91, UALR.

108 **"heavy firing"** Isaac Jenks to Commanding General of Camp Pike, Oct. 14, 1919, WF.

108 **"small groups of white people"** and **"We were met"** Edward Passailaigue, Oct. 7, 1919, FSAA, reel 16.

108 **"sent notice"** "Three Whites, 11 Negroes Killed in Race Fights," *AG*, Oct. 3, 1919.

108 **"discharged soldiers"** "4 Negroes."

108 **"The engagement in progress"** Jenks to Commanding General.

109 **"shotguns, rifles"** "Three Whites."

109 **"The troops are all"** "4 Negroes."

109 **"I took the children"** Wells-Barnett, *Arkansas Race Riot*, 17.

110 **"I stayed in the bushes"** Ibid., 15; *Ware v. Arkansas* brief and record, 84.

110 **"I stayed [in the woods] until the soldiers"** Wells-Barnett, *Arkansas Race Riot*, 16.

110 **"hardly any had guns"** "Press Reporter Spends Two Days at Helena and Elaine," *Memphis Press*, Oct. 4, 1919, WF.

110 **"I saw several hundred"** Brooke Tappan, "Reminiscence of Charles Madison Young," 1977, Folklore Class Reports, 1958–1999, UAL.

110 **"Gangs of them"** "Agitators Blamed."

110 **"Negro women"** "Three Whites."

110 **"With the arrival"** "Unknown Assailant Attempts to Shoot Governor Brough," *Little Rock Daily News*, Oct. 2, 1919.

110 **"On route"** Jenks to Commanding General.
111 **posses had killed at least four other blacks** "4 Negroes."; "Three Whites."
111 **"Major Callen deployed"** Passailaigue, Oct. 7, 1919.
111 **150 Negroes in the woods** "4 Negroes."
111 **"The soldiers immediately"** Statement by J. W. Butts, Oct. 17, 1960, BJ.
111 **"I saw many persons"** "Press Reporter Spends."
112 **"This terrain was uncleared"** Jenks to Commanding General.
112 **"gave them orders to shoot"** Tappan, "Reminscence of Charles Madison Young."
112 **"were shooting them down like rabbits"** U. S. Bratton Jr., oral interview, 1978, Stockley papers, BC.
112 **"tearing away part"** "Corporal Earles' Body at Camp Pike," *AG*, Oct. 4, 1919.
112 **"We captured several prisoners"** Jenks to Commanding General.
112 **"many negroes killed"** "Blacks Fight to Finish," *Memphis Press*, Oct. 2, 1919, WF.
112 **"killed many negroes"** Statement by Butts.
112 **"Situation quiet"** S. Sturgis to Adjutant General, Oct. 2, 1919, FSAA, reel 16.
112 **"This group of helpless people"** Passailaigue, Oct. 7, 1919.
113 **Biographical information on Johnstons** Walter White, "The Real Causes of Two Race Riots," *Crisis*, Dec. 1919; "Lived at Pine Bluff. Bodies of Four Johnston Brothers Taken There for Burial," *AG*, Oct. 4, 1919; Wells-Barnett, *Arkansas Race Riot*; Calvin Smith.
114 **"very prominent niggers"** Tappan, "Reminiscence of Charles Madison Young."
114 **"instrumental in getting"** "Phillips County Uprising Halted," *MCA*, Oct. 3, 1919.
114 **"distributing ammunition"** Ferguson, 54.
115 **"We met a car"** "How O. R. Lilly Was Murdered," *HW*, Oct. 3, 1919.
116 **"We had to go off"** Tappan, "Reminiscence of Charles Madison Young."
116 **"lunches and coffee"** "Three Whites."
116 **"been made to lynch"** Jenks to Commanding General.
116 **"records and all other obtainable evidence"** Ibid.
116 **"steel gondola"** Lambert, 76.
117 **Burning of "colored ringleaders"** Ibid., 77.
117 **"about 400 guns"** C. M. Walser and C. R. Maxey, "Negro Insurrection at Hoop Spur and Elaine in Phillips County, Arkansas," Oct. 9, 1919, FSAA, reel 12.
118 **"best known newspaperman"** "Veteran Newsman L. S. Dunaway Dies," *AG*, Sept. 4, 1959.
118 **Dunaway's account of killing by troops** Dunaway, 101, 102, 117.
118 **"When I got there"** Wells-Barnett, *Arkansas Race Riot*, 18.
119 **"They put a board"** *Arkansas v. Giles and Fox*, transcript, 33. UALR.
119 **perhaps as many as four hundred trapped** "Eleven Negroes to Pay with Their Lives for Greed of One," *New York World*, Nov. 16, 1919.
119 **"The riots are raging"** "Unknown Assailant."
119 **"The negroes are surrounded"** "Blacks Fight to Finish," *Memphis Press*, Oct. 2, 1919, WF.

119 "There can be no correct" "4 Negroes."

120 "It was a good many" Letter from ex-soldier to E. Scott, Nov. 12, 1919, WF.

120 "I do not know how many negroes" Affidavit by Smiddy.

121 "radius of several miles" Walser and Maxey, "Negro Insurrection."

121 Planters at interrogation *Hicks v. Arkansas,* transcript, 24, UALR; "Negroes Duped and Inflamed Against Whites," *AG,* Oct. 7, 1919.

121 "Here, in a large bare" Lambert, 75.

121 "Those found to be interested" "Phillips County on Peace Basis Again," *MCA,* Oct. 5, 1919.

121 "before they would be allowed" "Agitators Blamed."

121 "that they were law abiding" Jenks to Commanding General.

122 Arrest of Duker, Powell "Negroes' Office at Winchester Raided Saturday," *AD,* Oct. 5, 1919.

122 "One negro's body" "Soldiers Trail Desperate and Armed Negroes," *AG,* Oct. 4, 1919.

122 Troops "cornered" fifty Negroes "Brough Believes Phillips County Situation in Hand," *AD,* Oct. 3, 1919.

122 "badly warped head" "Sergt. Maj. Lorbert Effected Capture of Negro Suspect," *AD,* Oct. 4, 1919.

122 "shoot on sight" "Three Whites."

122 "machine gun squad" "More Outbreaks Reported Daily in Race Riots," *Hot Springs New Era,* Oct. 4, 1919.

123 Negroes shot in West Helena and Snow Lake "Soldiers Hunt for Revolt Leaders," *AG,* Oct. 7, 1919.

123 "Two men calmly" Lambert, 78; "Sentry Slays Negro, Party to Revolt," *Pine Bluff Daily Graphic,* Oct. 12, 1919.

123 "Order restored" S. Sturgis to Adjutant General, Oct. 7, 1919, FSAA, reel 16.

124 "in celebration" John Miller, interview, March 18, 1976, UAL, 13, 15.

124 "coming to aid them" "Eleven Negroes."

124 "people who had their hands" "Filling the Gaps," *Arkansas Review: A Journal of Delta Studies,* 32 (2001): 159.

125 "knew personally" George Washington Davis, Nov. 30, 1920, WF.

125 "The militia would kill" Steve Fronabarger, "Violence," 1961, Folklore Class Reports, 1958–1999, UAL.

125 "thrown into a pit" Dunaway, 104.

125 "The stench of dead bodies" White, "The Real Causes of Two Race Riots."

125 "dead niggers were stretched" Stockley, 52.

126 Dan Dixon's death "Elaine Insurrection Is Over, Committee of 7 in Charge," *HW,* Oct. 3, 1919.

126 three more black men burned *NAACP's Tenth Annual Report* (1919), 19.

Chapter 7: *Whitewash*

127 "outbreak" "Outbreak Reported at Elaine," *AD,* Oct. 2, 1919.

127 "when his party" "Bootleggers Ambush 3 Peace Officers," *HW,* Oct. 1, 1919.

128 "repair a punctured tire" "Negroes Had Plot to Rise Against Whites," *AD,* Oct. 2, 1919.

128 **"nothing of the negro meeting"** "General Uprising Had Been Planned." *AD,* Oct. 3, 1919.

128 **"fired upon from the church"; "organized band"; "force of armed negroes"** "Ten Dead, Dozen Hurt, Race War at Elaine, Ark.," *AG,* Oct. 2, 1919.

128 **"high-powered rifles"** "Federal Troops Have Situation Under Control," *AG,* Oct. 3, 1919.

128 **"promiscuous firing"** "Two Whites, Seven Negroes Are Slain," *Pine Bluff Daily Graphic,* Oct. 3, 1919.

128 **"greatly outnumbered"** "Two Whites."

128 **"crossing a field"** "Quiet at Elaine."

128 **"brave men"** "General Uprising."

128 **"wholesale killings"** "Negroes Had Plot."

128 **"It has been established"** "Quiet Reigns After Day of Wide Unrest," *HW,* Oct. 2, 1919.

129 **Bratton's preachings to union** "U.S. Bratton Jr. Is Charged with Inciting Blacks," *AG,* Oct. 2, 1919; "Federal Troops"; "Negroes Inflamed by a White Man," *AG,* Oct. 3, 1919; "Negroes Have Been Aroused by Propaganda," *AG,* Oct. 3, 1919.

129 **"socialistic literature"** "Casey and Bratton Law Offices at Helena Are Raided," *AD,* Oct. 3, 1919.

129 **"they believed that their plan"** "Vicious Blacks Were Planning Great Uprising," *AG,* Oct. 4, 1919.

129 **"Vicious Blacks"** *AG,* Oct. 4, 1919.

129 **"Trouble Traced to Socialist Agitators"** *New York Times,* Oct. 3, 1919.

129 **"assassinate" Governor Brough** "Unknown Assailant Attempts to Shoot Governor Brough," *Little Rock Daily News,* Oct. 2, 1919.

129 **"narrowly escaped death"** "22 Dead in Helena Riot," *Fayetteville Democrat,* Oct. 3, 1919.

129 **"Fallen cane"** "Phillips County Blacks Planned Uprising Today," *AG,* Oct. 6, 1919.

130 **"none of the refugees"** "Quiet Reigns."

130 **"dissuaded" from acting** O. S. Bratton to U. S. Bratton, Nov. 5, 1919, WF.

130 **"threatened lynching"** "Lynching Discussed?" *AG,* Oct. 3, 1919.

131 **"very anxious to reassure"** "Great Drive for Insurgents Now Underway," *HW,* Oct. 6, 1919.

131 **"machine guns and would shoot"** Bratton to Bratton.

131 **"A solemn promise"** Resolution by Richard L. Kitchens Post, Oct. 19, 1920, WF.

131 **"ten and fifteen"** Bratton to Bratton.

131 **Brough's press conference** "No Lynching in Phillips County," *AG,* Oct. 4, 1919.

132 **"determined little fellow"** "Sergeant Major Louis Lorber Effected Capture of Negro Suspect," *AD,* Oct. 4, 1919.

132 **"The Negro uprising"** "Confidence Everywhere Restored," *HW,* Oct. 5, 1919.

132 **"terribly exaggerated"** "Elaine Insurrection Is Over, Committee of 7 in Charge," *HW,* Oct. 3, 1919.

132 **"14 dead"** "Inner Workings Negroes' Society Being Uncovered," *AD*, Oct. 4, 1919; "Confidence Everywhere Restored," *HW*, Oct. 5, 1919; "Phillips County on Peace Basis Again," *MCA*, Oct. 5, 1919.

132 **"nipped in the bud"** "General Uprising."

133 **"large landowners"** G. Quarles to D. Y. Thomas, Jan. 5, 1920, DYT.

133 **Committee of Seven's findings** "Insurrection Planned to Be Begun Today," *HW*, Oct. 6, 1919; "Negroes Had Planned General Slaughter," *MCA*, Oct. 6, 1919; "Inward Facts about Negro Insurrection," *HW*, Oct. 7, 1919.

135 **"expressed amazement"** "Negroes Duped."

135 **"go to work!"** "Proclamation Is Addressed to Negroes."

136 **"Massacre of Whites"** *Dallas Morning News*, Oct. 6, 1919.

136 **"Negroes Seized in Arkansas Riots"** *New York Times*, Oct. 6, 1919.

136 **"The mind is chilled"** "A Hideous Conspiracy," *Seattle Times*, Oct. 6, 1919, WF.

136 **"This is the first"** *Shreveport Weekly Caucasian*, Oct. 9, 1919, WF.

136 **"Arkansas negroes are"** "Arkansas Race Riot," *Nashville Banner*, Oct. 4, 1919, WF.

136 hopeless **"ignorance"** "Ignorance Is to Blame," *Portland Oregonian*, Oct. 8, 1919, WF.

136 **"The unusual thing"** "Some Branch Normal," *Hot Springs Sentinel Record*, Oct. 7, 1919.

136 **"line of duty"** "Important Correction," *HW*, Oct. 2, 1919; Gladin, 3.

137 **Congratulatory messages to Brough** R. Rice to Brough, Oct. 8, 1919, BP, box 4, file 54, item 90; W. Fitzsimmons to Brough, Oct. 6, 1919, BP, box 4, file 54, item 82; W. McElroy to Brough, Oct. 3, 1919, BP, box 4, file 54, item 75; "Rejoice over Brough's Escape," *MCA*, undated article in Brough's scrapbook, AHC.

137 **"The behavior of the troops"** Isaac Jenks to Commanding General, Oct. 14, 1919, WF.

137 **"tireless in their apprehension"** Brough to Newton Baker, Oct. 10, 1919, FSAA, reel 16.

137 **"they are not partisans"** "Troops Will Act to Stop Disorder," *New York World*, Oct. 16, 1919. WF.

137 **"citizens of Helena"** "Grateful for Prompt Relief," *HW*, Oct. 12, 1919.

137 **"hospitality, friendliness"** "Grateful for Cooperation," *HW*, Oct. 9, 1919.

137 **"courage and bravery"** Gladin, 4.

138 **"The Law and No Mob"** *AG* editorial, Oct. 7, 1919.

138 **"absence of race hatred"** "Gives High Praise to Phillips County," *AG*, Oct. 12, 1919.

138 **"white people of the South"** "Tells Negroes Who Their Friends Are," undated newspaper article, Brough scrapbook, AHC; "The Negroes' Best Friends," *HW*, Oct. 9, 1919.

138 **"does not hate the negro"** "If Elaine Were in Cook County, Illinois," *AD*, Oct. 13, 1919.

138 **"We have set"** "Back to Normal," *HW*, Oct. 6, 1919.

139 **"stopped their car"** McElveen to Department of Justice. Oct. 7, 1919, FSAA, reel 12; C. M. Walser and C. R. Maxey, "Negro Insurrection at Hoop Spur and Elaine in Phillips County, Arkansas," Oct. 9, 1919, FSAA, reel 12.

140 **"where according to the hotel"** Walser and Maxey, "Negro Insurrection."
140 **"in an upcoming settlement"** Ibid.
140 **"The contract Bratton"** McElveen to Department of Justice.
140 **"It does not appear"** Walser and Maxey, "Negro Insurrection."
140 **"about 20 negroes"** Edward Passailaigue, Oct. 7, 1919, FSAA, reel 16.
140 **"Anywhere from fifty to eighty"** McElveen to Department of Justice.
141 **"Some information has been secured"** and **"Pipkin advised"** McElveen to Department of Justice, Oct. 5, 1919, FSAA, reel 12.
141 **"Rioters had small amount"** McElveen to Department of Justice, Oct. 9, 1919, FSAA, reel 12.
141 **"Only evidence of intended murder"** McElveen to Department of Justice, Oct. 7, 1919 and Oct. 9, 1919.
142 **"Every piece of literature"** "Kerwin Fnds Negroes Acted in U.S. Name," *Pine Bluff Daily Graphic,* Oct. 7, 1919.
143 **"The United States will not countenance"** "Exploiting Simplicity," *HW,* Oct. 12, 1919.
143 **"annihilation of the Negroes"** "Work for Negro Leaders," *AG,* Oct. 8, 1919.
143 **"they would be protected"** "The Negroes' Best Friends," *HW,* Oct. 9, 1919.
143 **"unanimously reaffirm"** "Negroes Make Emphatic Denial That Uprising in St. Francis County Planned," *Times Weekly Herald,* Forrest City, Ark., Oct. 24, 1919.
143 **"there are no Bolshevists"** "Negroes of Jackson Declare Themselves," *Clarion,* Jackson, Mississippi, Nov. 19, 1919.
143 **"We urge that the race"** "Colored Baptists Strong for Peace," *Dallas Morning News,* Oct. 31, 1919.
143 **"civilized country"** "Negro Preacher Says Prayer Is Best Method," *Hot Springs Sentinel Record,* Oct. 7, 1919.
144 **"There have been seditious"** "Race Riots Denounced," *AG,* Nov. 4, 1919.
144 **"negroes are returning"** "Phillips County Returns to Normal," *HW,* Oct. 8, 1919.
144 **"Few negroes can be secured"** Taylor, 282.
144 **Sharecroppers' wives return home** Wells-Barnett, *Arkansas Race Riot,* 12, 15, 18–20.

Chapter 8: *The Longest Train Ride Ever*

146 **"The propaganda"** Church to White, Oct. 6, 1919, WF.
147 **"Shillady" had been "received"** Kellogg, 240.
147 **"Your organization"** NAACP Annual Report, 1919.
147 **"His great gaiety"** White, 46.
147 **"In view of the critical situation"** White to Shillady, Oct. 7, 1919, WF.
148 **Bio on White** White, 3–44.
149 **McIlherron's burning** Walter White, "The Burning of Jim McIlherron," *Crisis,* May 1918, 16–20.
151 **"certain facts"** White to Robert Scott, Oct. 9, 1919, WF.
151 **"I want these facts"** White to James Johnson, Oct. 10, 1919, WF.
151 **"want a complete article"** White to C. H. Dennis, Oct. 9, 1919, WF.

151 **"read the leading Arkansas"** Walter White, "Hell Breaks Out in Arkansas," WF.

152 **"rushed into Elaine"** Walter White, "Arkansas Race Riots Laid to Bad System," *Chicago Daily News*, Oct. 18, 1919.

152 **"fired into the church"** Statement by Walter White, Oct. 17 (and Oct. 20 press release), WF.

152 **"I purposely led him"** White, 49.

152 **"unpunished murder"** Shillady to Brough, Sept. 4, 1919, NAACP, part 7, series a, reel 8.

152 **"The entire trouble"** "Arkansas Race Riots Laid."

152 **"Northern agitators"** White, 50.

152 **autographed picture** Ovington, *The Walls Came Tumbling Down,* 156.

152 **White walked into Bratton's office** White to U. S. Bratton, Feb. 23, 1923, WF.

153 **"knew nothing of the affair"** U. S. Bratton to Sheriff Kitchens, Oct. 15, 1919, WF.

153 **"The Negroes at Elaine"** U. S. Bratton to Frank Burke, Nov. 6, 1919, WF.

154 **"Everything favorable"** "Francis" (Walter White) to J. W. Johnson, Oct. 13, 1919.

154 **$1,000 bounty** Affidavit of Hugh Fisher, May 18, 1920, WF.

154 **"I was advised"** U. S. Bratton to D. Y. Thomas, Sept. 15, 1921, DYT, box 1, file 2.

154 **"crowd of men"** Walter White, "I Investigate Lynchings," *American Mercury,* Jan. 1929, 62–72.

155 **"We did not know whom to trust"** Walter White, "Hell Breaks Out in Arkansas," WF.

155 **"Negroes here live in fear"** Walter White, "The Real Causes of Two Race Riots," *Crisis,* Dec. 1919.

155 **"overheard the conversations"** White, "Hell Breaks Out in Arkansas."

155 **"Several white men"** Walter White, "The Race Conflict in Arkansas," *Survey,* Dec. 13, 1919.

155 **"Negroes who did not know"** Walter White, "Massacring Whites in Arkansas," *Nation,* Dec. 6, 1919.

155 **"brazenly admitted"** "Arkansas Race Riots."

155 **"the most dangerous situation"** White to Charles Bentley, Oct. 24, 1919, WF.

156 **"No matter what the distance"** White, 51.

157 **"Riots Caused by Profiteering"** *Afro American,* Oct. 24, 1919.

157 **"Arkansas Land Owners Defraud Tenants"** *New York Age,* Oct. 25, 1919.

157 **"Expose Arkansas Peonage System"** *Chicago Defender,* Nov. 1, 1919.

157 **"Congressional investigation"** "The Elaine Horror," *Baltimore Daily Herald,* Oct. 9, 1919, WF.

157 **"bloodthirsty mobs"** "Elaine, Arkansas Riots," *Boston Chronicle,* editorial, Nov. 1, 1919, WF.

158 **"Considerable indignation"** "Statement by Committee of Seven," HW, Oct. 12, 1919.

158 **"slings and arrows"** "Setting a Community Right Before the Country," *AG,* Oct. 19, 1919. WF.

158 **"far from the truth"** W. L. Jarman to First Assistant Postmaster General, Oct. 10, 1919, FSAA, reel 13.

158 **"I personally"** Brough to H. L. Donnelly, Nov. 4, 1919, FSAA, reel 13.

158 **"It is highly imperative"** Brough to A. S. Burleson, Oct. 17, 1919, FSAA, reel 9.

Chapter 9: *A Lesson Made Plain*

159 **"18 tool-proof apartments"** Frances Hornor Curtis, "Folklore of Phillips County," 1958, Folklore Class Reports, 1958–1999, UAL.

160 **"There were a great many negroes"** Affidavit by William Wordlow, Dec. 18, 1919, *Moore v. Dempsey* brief and record, UALR.

160 **Committee of Seven expanded** "Proclamation Is Addressed to Negroes," *HW*, Oct. 7, 1919.

160 **Torture of prisoners** Affidavits by H. F. Smiddy, Sept. 19, 1921; T. K. Jones, Sept. 19, 1921; Walter Ward, May 18, 1921; Alf Banks Jr., Dec. 18, 1919; George Green, May 18, 1921; John Jefferson, May 18, 1921; William Wordlow, Dec. 18, 1919. All in *Moore v. Dempsey* brief and record, UALR. Also see Wells-Barnett, *Arkansas Race Riot*, 18–19; "Judge Orders Destruction of Electric Chair Used by Arkansas Sheriff for Confessions," *New York Times*, Nov. 23, 1929.

165 **Miller's investigation** John Elvis Miller, interview, March 18, 1976, 11, 16, 19, 21, UAL.

165–166 **"said that he knew the conditions"** Guy Bratton to U. S. Bratton, Nov. 9, 1919, WF.

166 **men of "good character"** *Eastling v. State*, 69 Ark. 189 (1901).

166 **planters as jury commissioners** *Moore v. Dempsey* brief and record, UALR.

167 **"His friends in Helena"** Herndon, *Centennial History*, 405.

167 **"Judge Jackson has always given"** Ibid.

167 **"evidence . . . is very strong"** "100 Negroes Will Be Tried for Uprising," Marianna *Courier Index*, Oct. 24, 1919.

167 **Indictments** "73 Are Held as Murderers," *HW*, Oct. 28, 1919; "Murder Cases Start Monday," *HW*, Oct. 30, 1919; "Entire Number Are Indicted," *HW*, Oct. 31, 1919.

168 **"The indictments were based"** "Uprising Report Varies from Facts," *AG*, Nov. 23, 1919.

169 **Bio for John Moore** Obituaries in Phillips County Library; Gladin; Ledbetter; Hempstead, 1074; Whayne, *The Arkansas Delta*, 21; "Helena in 1900," *PCHQ* 5 (1967): 28; "Some Helena Business Houses," *PCHQ* 2 (1964): 20–25.

170 **Bio for Quarles** Hempstead, 1117; "Helena Loses a Beloved Citizen in Death of Judge Greenfield Quarles," *HW*, Jan. 14, 1921; "Cotton Planters Favor Reduction of Acreage," *HW*, Oct. 20, 1919.

170 **Bevens was a planter** "Cotton Planters"; "4 Negroes."

170 **"giving his heart"** Hempstead, 826.

171 **"in the posses"** Affidavit of Smiddy.

171 **Afflick and Anselman on jury** "Insurrection Trials Begin," *HW*, Nov. 3, 1919; affidavit of Smiddy; Gladin.

171 **"dressed in ragged"** "Eleven Elaine Rioters Must Die in Electric Chair," Marianna *Courier Index*, Nov. 7, 1919.

171 "ignorant plantation negro" Ibid.

171 "clinching the seams" "Insurrection Trials Begin," *HW,* Nov. 3, 1919.

172 There was nothing in Hicks's life Arkansas State Penitentiary admission form, Frank Hicks, Stockley papers, BC.

172 Service of indictment to Hicks *Moore v. Dempsey* brief and record, UALR; White to Bruno Lasker, Dec. 15, 1919, WF.

172 "to kill planters" "Alleged Slayer of Helena Man During Rioting on Trial," *AD,* Nov. 3, 1919.

172 "I ask for a fair, impartial trial" "Insurrection Trials Begin," *HW,* Nov. 3, 1919.

172 Testimony at Hicks's trial *Hicks v. Arkansas,* transcript, UALR.

174 more than one hundred blacks sitting up in the gallery "Five Others Found Guilty," *HW,* Nov. 4, 1919.

175 "Record time was made" "Six Negroes Found Guilty," *HW,* Nov. 4, 1919.

176 Tully Hornor and Miles on jury "Five Others"; Bealer.

177 "going to kill the white people" *Moore v. Dempsey,* brief and record.

177 "not to let nobody" *Arkansas v. Wordlow,* transcript, UALR.

177 "They told me" Banks affidavit.

178 "take a leak" *Arkansas v. Martin and Banks,* transcript, UALR.

178 "something went wrong with their car" "Two More Are Found Guilty," *HW,* Nov. 4, 1919.

179 Fox and Giles's trial *Arkansas v. Giles and Fox,* transcript, UALR.

179 "a bullet hole in each side" "A Verdict in Six Minutes," *HW,* Nov. 4, 1919.

180 seventy-three who had been convicted Arkansas Department of Corrections, admissions records for 1871–1974.

181 "absence of witnesses" "Ten Negroes Get Light Sentences," *HW,* Nov. 7, 1919.

181 "nervous and ill at ease" "11 Sentenced to Electric Chair," *AG,* Nov. 12, 1919.

181 "Frank Moore, you have been convicted" Ibid.

181 "dead, dead, dead" *Moore v. Dempsey* brief and record.

181 70 cents a pound "Cotton Brings Record Price," *HW,* Nov. 2, 1919.

182 burned a fifty-year-old "Negro Who Shew Sheriff Is Burned at Stake by Mob," *AD,* Nov. 11, 1919.

182 "antagonistic to the white race" "Radicalism and Sedition Among the Negroes as Reflected in Their Publications," 66th Congress, 1st session (1919), document no. 153.

182 "indicted for first-degree" "Eleven Negroes to Pay with Their Lives for Greed of One," *New York Sun,* Nov. 16, 1919.

182 "admitted the organization" *Congressional Record,* 66th Cong., 1st session, Nov. 19, 1919, 8818–21.

182 Whipping of inmates at Cummins Abington, 49.

183 "Their black faces were ashen" "Hundreds Visit the Walls to Get Glimpses of Rioters," *AD,* Nov. 24, 1919.

183 "stood in hushed silence" "12 Negroes Under Death Sentences Arrive at Prison," *AD,* Nov. 22, 1919.

183 "shaggy, slovenly creatures" "Condemned Negroes Are Victims of Ignorance," *AG,* Nov. 23, 1919.

184 "Considerable hope up" "Hundreds Visit."

Chapter 10: *Scipio Africanus Jones*

185 **"His whole professional career"** Bush, 237.

185–186 **"He is the best"** "Scipio Jones Endorsement," *AD,* May 9, 1909.

186 **Scipio Jones's bio** Dillard collection on Scipio Jones, ms 0010, series 1, box 9, DC; Dillard, "Scipio A. Jones"; Coke, 312–14; Woods, 59; *The National Encyclopedia of the Colored Race,* 459; Ovington, *Portraits in Color,* 92–103; "Scipio Jones State Negro Leader, Dies," *AG,* March 29, 1943; "Noted Attorney Passes," *Arkansas State Press,* April 2, 1943; "High Honor for Scipio A. Jones," *Twin City Star,* March 1, 1916 (Hampton University clippings, microfiche 381); United States Census 1870, 1880, 1900, 1910, 1920, 1930.

187 **"I used to say master"** Lankford, 91.

187 **"I went to school"** Ibid., 109.

188 **"intercourse between the two races"** Love, 2.

188 **"The meager prejudice"** Gordon, 1.

189 **"We slept on pool tables"** Lankford, 315.

189 **"pick up crumbs"** Ovington, *Portraits in Color,* 92.

189 **"He was exceptionally friendly"** Louis Tarlowski interview by Tom Dillard, June 22, 1971, DC, ms 00-10, series 1, box 9.

190 **"great nation of ours"** "Appeals to the Negroes," *AG,* May 17, 1917.

190 **"devoid of any mercenary"** Bush, 238.

190 **"ever-present eating"** Niswonger, 118.

190 **"when we have no doubt"** Vinikas, 549.

191 **"manly self-respect"** David Levering Lewis, 288.

192 **"assist in establishing"** Woods, 59.

193 **"Win a glorious victory"** Fred Williams, 177–80.

193 **"to eliminate the Negro"** *Crisis,* Aug. 1912, 175.

193 **"crushing defeat"** Fred Williams, 177–80.

193–194 **"humble in appearing"** Tarlowski interview.

194 conducted **"himself in such a way"** Coke, 312.

194 **"his vigilant eye"** D. B. Gaines, *Racial Possibilities as Indicated by the Negroes of Arkansas,* 1898, DC.

194 **"finest cross-examiner"** Coke, 312.

194 **"Scipio could get them released"** Joseph Crenchaw interview by Tom Dillard, April 24, 1971, DC, ms 00-10, series 1, box 9.

194 **"It is hard to find language"** Gaines, *Racial Possibilities.*

194 **"successful and unpretentious"** Woods, 59.

194–195 **"He was an inspiration"** William Pickens, "Scipio Africanus Maximus," Associated Negro Press, Pickens papers, 1906–1957, reel 4, a, SC.

195 **"Nigger lawyer"** Fred Williams, 167.

195 **"had nothing else"** *Arkansas Democrat,* Oct. 18, 1906.

195 **"Scipio Jones Buys a Mule"** *Arkansas Gazette,* Feb. 6, 1909.

195 **"This had some influence"** Will Sheppard interview by Tom Dillard, April 15, 1971, DC, ms 00-10, series 1, box 9.

195 **"I suppose all the white lawyers"** Dillard, "Scipio A. Jones," 206.

196 **"there are white men"** "High Honor for Scipio A. Jones," *Twin City Star,* March 1, 1916.

196 **"had only a chair"** Coke, 312.

196 **"You put down the riot"** "Local Negroes Commend Brough for His Action," *AG,* Oct. 19, 1919.
197 **"betrayed"** Gwendolyn Floyd interview by Tom Dillard, July 17, 1972, DC, ms 00-10, series 1, box 9.
197 **"Scipio, you take charge"** J. M. Conner to White, Aug. 28, 1920, WF.
198 **Murphy bio** *Quapaw Quarter* newsletter, Stockley files, BC; J. L. Carmichael, "Colonel George W. Murphy," 1921 Year Book of the Arkansas Law School, UALR.
198 **"suffer bodily harm"** John Hibbler to R. Church, Nov. 22, 1919, WF.
198 **"Mr. Scipio A. Jones and myself"** Thomas Price to White, Nov. 26, 1919, WF.

Chapter 11: *The Constitutional Rights of a Race*
200 **"If there is one infamy"** *Baltimore Daily Herald* editorial, Nov. 8, 1919, WF.
200 **"judicial lynching"** "Judicial Lynch Law," *New York Age,* Nov. 15, 1919.
200 **"enemies of humanity"** David Elliott to the Inspector, re the *Favorite* magazine, Jan. 14, 1920, FSAA, reel 13.
200 **"the contemplated murder"** "The Arkansas Challenge," *Crusader,* Jan. 1920.
200 **"would immediately take steps"** "Condemned Arkansas Rioters Look to Chicago for Help," *Chicago Defender,* Dec. 13, 1919.
201 **"their only crime"** "Boston Negroes Ask Rioters Be Spared," Parke-Harper News Service, Dec. 1, 1919, Brough scrapbook, AHC.
201 **"nationwide protests"** "Legalized Lynching," *Messenger,* Feb. 1920.
201 **"assassinated"** "Governor Scorns Outside Advice on Race Problems," *AD,* Nov. 24, 1919.
201 **"I was on the ground"** "Governor Scores Action of Equal Rights League," *AD,* Nov. 16, 1919.
201 **interracial conference** "Racial Meeting at Little Rock Monday," *HW,* Nov. 24, 1919.
201 **"be no doubt"** "Condemned Negroes to Be Granted Reprieves until High Court Acts," Brough scrapbook, AHC.
202 **"I have your letter"** White to Thomas Price, Dec. 1, 1919, WF.
202 **"thoroughly astonished"** U. S. Bratton to Shillady, Nov. 22, 1919, WF.
202 **"investigation showed no grounds"** Meeting of NAACP Board of Directors, Nov. 10, 1919, NAACP, part 1, reel 1.
202 **"secure counsel"** Ovington to Edith Wharton Dallas, Nov. 11, 1919, WF.
203 **"is a man of attractive personality"** Ibid.
203 **"We have never yet"** Ibid.
203 **"not yet been completed"** R. P. Stewart to Carl Hayden, Nov. 8, 1919, WF.
203 **"He is one"** U. S. Bratton to Shillady, Aug. 15, 1920, WF.
203 **"There would have been no probing"** Ovington to Julius Rosenwald, Dec. 12, 1919, NAACP, part one, reel 17.
203 **"It would queer"** Ovington to Edith Wharton Dallas, Dec. 9, 1919, WF.
204 **"very grave danger"** White to William Aery, Nov. 28, 1919, WF.
204 **"noble work"** G. W. Mitchell to NAACP, Jan. 10, 1921, NAACP, part 7, reel 20.
204 **"bootlickers"** Ovington to U. S. Bratton, Dec. 10, 1919, WF.
204 **"would do more"** John Milholland to Ovington, Dec. 4, 1919, WF.

204 **"A white one"** White to William King, Nov. 29, 1919, WF.

204 **"We do not want"** James Johnson to R. Church, Dec. 2, 1919, WF.

205 **"I am not yet"** "Will ask appeal of Elaine cases," Brough scrapbook, AHC.

205 **"I first told my lawyer"** *Ware v. Arkansas,* brief and record, 39, UALR.

206 **"never been at a trial"** Motion for a new trial, *Moore v. Dempsey,* brief and record, UALR.

206 **"I would have written"** Monroe Work, "A Report on the Elaine Riots," April 8, 1920, WF.

206 **"most important case"** White to Julius Rosenwald, Nov. 16, 1923, NAACP, part 1, reel 24.

Chapter 12: *I Wring My Hands and Cry*

207 **"I Stand and Wring"** Wells-Barnett, *Arkansas Race Riot,* 5.

207 **Description of men** 1920 U.S. Census and Arkansas State Penitentiary admission forms. There are admission forms for seven of the twelve condemned men in the Stockley files (BC), and all show that the men had no prior convictions. Jones also noted in legal documents that none of the men had been in trouble before.

208 **"was heart rending"** U. S. Bratton to NAACP, no date, WF.

208 **"The principle at stake"** "Condemned Arkansas Rioters Look to Chicago for Help," *Chicago Defender,* Dec. 13, 1919.

208 **"This is one of the 12"** Wells-Barnett, *Arkansas Race Riot,* 4.

208 **Wells-Barnett's penitentiary visit** Ibid.; Wells-Barnett, *Crusade for Justice,* 401–2.

211 **"He was extremely kind"** "Mrs. Barnett in Arkansas," *Chicago Defender,* Feb. 28, 1920.

211 **"unsafe to visit"** Monroe Work, "A Report on the Elaine Riots," April 8, 1920, WF.

211 **"would be protected"** U. S. Bratton to NAACP.

211 **"We are hard at work"** Work, "A Report."

212 **"The report from Arkansas"** Ovington to Archibald Grimké, Dec. 4, 1919, WF.

214 **"in use almost everywhere"** Skolnick, 45.

214 **"inherited" the chair** "Judge Orders Destruction of Electric Chair Used by Arkansas Sheriff for Confessions," *New York Times,* Nov. 23, 1929.

214 **"Where would be the virtue"** Forman, 927.

215 **"remarkably similar sentences"** Ibid., 930.

216 **"I have defended Negroes"** "The Art of Being Just," *Crisis,* March 1916, 230.

216 **"A Negro accused"** Moorfield Storey, "The Negro Question," NAACP pamphlet, 1918.

216 **Jones had lost four murder cases** See *Eastling v. State,* 69 Ark. 189 (1901); *Kinslow v. State,* 85 Ark. 515 (1908); *Hunter v. State,* 93 Ark. 275 (1910); *Robinson v. State,* 99 Ark. 208 (1911).

217 **"Colonel Murphy assisted"** Jones to White, March 15, 1924, NAACP files, part 7, series a, reel 8.

217 **NAACP testimony to House Judiciary** U.S. House of Representatives, "Segregation and Antilynching," 66th Congress, 2nd session (1920).

218 "The killing of Negroes" "Antilynching Bill," 66th Congress, 2nd session (1920), report 1027.

218 "The colored people that were killed" James Guy to Shillady, Jan. 28, 1920, NAACP, part 12, series d, reel 6.

218 "The troops used machine guns" "Insurrection to Second Trial Defendants Go," *HW,* May 3, 1920.

219 "It has been made evident" U. S. Bratton to Senator Dillingham, Feb. 21, 1920, WF.

219 "just where Mr. Scipio A. Jones" Shillady to Work, April 10, 1920, WF.

219 "Mr. Jones is an able lawyer" Work to Shillady, April 19, 1920, WF.

220 "they should be shunned" "Hill Betrayed by Own Race," *Chicago Defender,* Feb. 14, 1920.

220 "Judas" U. S. Bratton to Shillady, Feb. 25, 1920, WF.

220 "You and I know" William Pickens to Bishop Conner, Feb. 6, 1920, WF.

220 "Last Saturday" J. M. Cox to Pickens, Feb. 13, 1920. WF.

221 "uprising of the niggers" James Guy affidavit, May 18, 1920, WF.

221 "You Kansas nigger lover" Cortner, *The Supreme Court and the Second Bill of Rights,* 74.

222 "that the temper of that community" *Crisis,* June 1920, 90.

222 "impersonated a federal officer" "Hill Is Immediately Arrested by Officer," *HW,* March 23, 1920.

222 "Everybody knew" "Supreme Court Reverses Six Arkansas Riot Cases," *Chicago Defender,* April 3, 1920.

222 "fatally defective" *Banks v. State,* 143 Ark. 154 (1920).

222 "fair and impartial" *Hicks v. State,* 143 Ark. 158 (1920).

223 Jones's fight with lily-whites Tom Dillard, "Fighting the Lily Whites," DC, ms 00-10, series 6, box 2, file 11, BC. Also see "Negroes in G.O.P, 100 Strong, Plan to Storm Meeting," *AD,* April 13, 1920.

224 "poisoned" Coke, 313.

224 "had to shift" Ibid.

224 "When the day" Ovington, *Portraits in Color,* 98.

224 "detail a deputy sheriff" John Miller interview, March 18, 1976, UAL.

225 "I made a good record" Report of the Secretary, June 1920, NAACP, part one, reel 4.

225 Trial testimony *Ware v. Arkansas,* brief and record, UALR.

227 "to rely on the former statements" "Second Trial of John Martin Still Continues," *HW,* May 4, 1920.

229 "masterly" Ovington, *Portraits in Color,* 98.

229 "Is it not striking" *Ware v. Arkansas,* brief and record, 141.

229 "Scipio Jones, his skin was black" John Miller interview.

229 "We feel that they never" "Negroes Hope to Escape the Chair," *AG,* May 17, 1920.

Chapter 13: *All Hope Gone*

231 "If said judgement" Petition for a writ of certiorari, *Moore v. Dempsey* brief and record, UALR.

231 **"We are not very hopeful"** E. L. McHaney to Arthur Spingarn, June 18, 1920, NAACP papers, part 7, reel 20.

232 **"In my judgment"** Jones to Arthur Spingarn, June 26, 1920, WF.

232 **"barbecued niggers"** Ginzburg, 138–40.

232 **Kitchens died** "Frank Kitchens Succumbs After Long Hard Fight," *HW,* Oct. 4, 1920.

233 **"Men, women and children"** "Helena Loses $300,000 from Sunday's Fire," *Helena World,* Oct. 11, 1920.

233 **"No opinion was announced"** James Maher to Jones, Nov. 9, 1920; petition for a writ of certiorari, *Moore v. Arkansas* papers, UALR.

233 **"I think that he died"** Ovington, *Portraits in Color,* 99.

233 **"face death"** "U.S. Court Refuses to Review Trials of Elaine Rioters," *AD,* Oct. 11, 1920.

233 **Helena resolutions** *Moore v. Dempsey* brief and record, UALR. Also see D. R. Dalzell to Brough, Nov. 10, 1920, WF; John Miller to Brough, Nov. 14, 1920, WF; and Helena Civitan Club Resolution, Nov. 11, 1920, WF.

234 **"Every business"** "No Clemency for 12 Elaine Rioters," *AG,* Nov. 16, 1920.

234 **"Last Hope Gone"** *AG,* Nov. 30, 1920.

234 **"All agree"** Scipio Jones, "Statement Made to the Evening Paper Today," Nov. 16, 1920, WF.

235 **"Is it known"** "Why Rush These Cases?" *AD,* Nov. 17, 1920.

235 **"While [the decision] vitally"** Jones to White, Dec. 15, 1920, NAACP, part 7, series a, reel 8.

235 **"received with considerable rejoicing"** "Elaine Negroes' Sentences Are Again Reversed," *AD,* Dec. 6, 1920.

236 **"uphold our courts"** "Speech of Hon. Thomas C. McRae, Candidate for Governor," *AG,* June 6, 1920.

236 **"A committee of prominent"** Jones to James Johnson, Feb. 16, 1921, NAACP, part 7, series a, reel 8.

236 **"within a short time"** "Funds Needed to Fight Arkansas Cases," *Crisis,* Dec. 1920: 65.

236 **"We decided to make a plea"** C. L. Stewart to *Crisis,* Dec. 28, 1920, NAACP, part 7, reel 20.

236 **"was introduced for the benefit"** Jones to Johnson, Feb. 16, 1921.

236 **"McHaney has absolutely"** U. S. Bratton to Shillady, Aug. 15, 1920, WF.

237 **"I know not how"** Jones to White, March 25, 1921, NAACP, part 7, series a, reel 8.

237 **"I think if we succeed"** Jones to Johnson, Feb. 16, 1921.

237 **"held daily services"** "Young Woman Sees Negro Go to Death," *AG,* April 30, 1921.

238 **"They sing one"** James Johnson (quoting Jones) to White, Aug. 3, 1923. WF.

238 **"also gave them light work"** "Six Elaine Insurrectionists Still Hope for Favorable Act," *HW,* June 7, 1921.

238 **"When they first put the charge"** "Only One Condemned Man Sat in Chair and Walked Away Under Own Power," *AG,* Jan. 21, 1973.

238 **"I had inferred"** Jones to Arthur Spingarn, April 30, 1921, NAACP, part 7, series a, reel 8.

238 **"Either all twelve"** "Habeas Corpus vs. Haste," *AD*, April 30, 1921.

239 **"will be hostile"** Jones to Spingarn, April 30, 1921.

239 **"We do not quite understand"** Jones to White, May 13, 1921, NAACP, part 7, series a, reel 8.

239 **"It looks to me"** White to Jones, June 22, 1921, NAACP, part 7, series a, reel 8.

239 **Henry Lowry lynching** *An American Lynching* (New York: NAACP, 1921).

241 **"driven out as though"** "Georgia Declares War on Peonage," *Literary Digest,* May 14, 1921:17.

241 **"worse than outright slavery"** NAACP's 12th Annual Report, 58.

242 **"besieged with requests"** "Six Elaine Insurrectionists."

242 **"Not in the history"** Robert Kerlin to McRae, May 25, 1921, NAACP, part 7, series a, reel 8.

243 **"I entertain some hope"** Jones to White, May 30, 1921, NAACP, part 7, series a, reel 8.

243 **"All 12 of these cases"** "Sanity Wins in the Elaine Cases," *AD,* June 11, 1921.

243 **"The matter is now up to Governor"** "Will Plead for Elaine Negroes," *AG,* June 2, 1921.

244 **"Mr. Kerlin is not advised"** John Miller to McRae, June 6, 1921, WF; "Elaine Cases Are Explained to Governor McRae," *HW,* June 8, 1921.

244 **"a wicked lie"** J. M. Jackson to McRae, undated, WF.

245 **"There are people"** "Protests Court Action," *AD,* June 9, 1921.

245 **Wordlow testimony** *Ware v. Arkansas* brief and record, 50, UALR.

246 **"Why did he not call"** Ibid., 141.

246 **"Telegrams continue to pour"** "State Seeks Legal Course to Carry Out Executions of Negroes Friday Morning," *AD,* June 9, 1921.

246 **"conducted an old-fashioned"** "Negro Ministers Ask Mercy for Rioters," *AD,* June 7, 1921.

246 **"My Lord, he calls me"** Leroy Williams, "Tell 'Em We're Rising, 1900–1954," essay in *The Persistence of the Spirit* (Helena: Delta Cultural Center, 1991).

247 **"not to intervene"** "Governor Silent on Elaine Cases," *AG,* June 8, 1921.

247 **"have died in the electric chair"** "Six Elaine Insurrectionists."

247 **"death chamber cleaned"** "Decide to Go into Courts if McRae Finally Refuses Stay for Rioters Sentenced to Die," *AD,* June 8, 1921.

247 **"not despondent"** "Six Elaine Insurrectionists."

247 **"Mr. Jones won't let us die"** Ovington, *The Walls Came Tumbling Down,* 160. Ovington quotes the men as saying that "Scipio Jones won't let us die," but the men regularly called him "Mr. Jones," or "Attorney Jones," rather than Scipio. The *AG* also quoted the men as expressing confidence that they would be saved at the last minute.

Chapter 14: *Great Writ of Liberty*

248 **"of the electrocution"** "Late Advices by Wire from State Points," *HW,* June 14, 1921.

249 **"was wholly without jurisdiction"** *Ferguson v. Martineau,* 115 Ark. 317.

249 **"liberal in his views"** Fay Williams, 219, 209.

249 **"then and there state"** "Late Advices," *HW*, June 14, 1921.

249 **"Petition for Habeas"** Jones to NAACP, June 8, 1921, NAACP, part 7, series a, reel 8.

249 **"carry out the sentences"** "State Seeks Legal Course to Carry Out Executions of Negroes Friday Morning," *AD*, June 9, 1921.

249 **"What has a chancery"** "Protests Court Action," *AD*, June 9, 1921.

250 **"an official act of anarchy"** "Sanity Wins in the Elaine cases," editorial, *AD*, June 11, 1921.

250 **"No imminent danger"** Jones to White, June 21, 1921, NAACP, part 7, series a, reel 8.

252 **"It is a bill"** Steiker.

254 **"Upon habeas corpus"** *Harlan v. McGourin*, 218 U.S. 442 (1910).

254 **"every available seat"** "Contention Is Lost by Attorneys for Six Elaine Negroes Sentenced to Die," *AD*, June 13, 1921.

255 **"Hang the Jew"** Dinnerstein, 60.

256 **"one of the bitterest"** "Elaine Negroes Get New Delay," *AG*, June 14, 1921.

256 **"The court [in *Frank*] said"** *State v. Martineau*, 149 Ark. 237.

257 **Transfer of prisoners from Little Rock to Lee County** "Prison Warden Refuses to Surrender Elaine Negroes," *AD*, June 23, 1921; "Negroes to Lee County," *AD*, June 24, 1921; "Elaine Negroes on Way to Marianna," *AG*, June 25, 1921; "Elaine Rioters, Now in Jail at Marianna, Were Secreted in Little Rock for 12 Hours," *AD*, June 25, 1921; "Phillips County to Pay Bill for Rioters," *AG*, June 26, 1921.

258 **"assassinated"** "U.S. Bratton Is Arrested Here on Second Barratry Indictment from Helena," *AD*, July 8, 1921.

258 **"would prove harmful"** "How the V.M.I. Disposed of the Kerlin Incident," *HW*, Aug. 24, 1921.

258 **"It all shows"** Ovington to McHaney, Aug. 26, 1921, NAACP, part 7, series a, reel 8.

258 **"We now have"** McHaney to Ovington, Aug. 30, 1921, NAACP, part 7, series a, reel 8.

258 **"Mr. Scipio Jones"** Secretary's report to the Board, June 1922, NAACP, part 1, reel 4.

259 **"I did what I did"** Smiddy to White, Feb. 15, 1922, NAACP, part 8, reel 3.

259 **"until I could get"** Ibid.

259 **Affidavits** H. F. Smiddy, Sept. 19, 1921; T. K. Jones, Sept. 19, 1921; *Moore v. Dempsey* brief and record, UALR.

260 **"The Arkansas officers"** Smiddy to NAACP, Feb. 3, 1922, NAACP, part 8, reel 3.

261 **"I want to get them"** Smiddy to White.

261 **"withdrawal from the cases"** Jones to James Johnson, Sept. 23, 1921, NAACP, part 7, series a, reel 8.

262 **"It is difficult"** James Johnson to Jones, Sept. 20, 1921, NAACP, part 7, series a, reel 8.

262 **"Petitioners say"** *Moore v. Dempsey* brief and record, UALR.

264 **"The question of mob domination"** "Decision Today on Elaine Cases," *AG,* Sept. 27, 1921.

265 **"forced to rely"** "State Sustained in Elaine Negroes' Cases," *AD,* Sept. 27, 1921.

265 **"The sustaining of the demurrer"** Jones to Ovington, Sept. 30, 1921, NAACP, part 7, series a, reel 8.

265 **"With the assistance"** Ibid.

265 **"is a son"** Jones to Arthur Spingarn, Oct. 8, 1921, NAACP papers, part 7, series a, reel 8.

265 **"Mann and McCullough"** Ibid.

265 **"further time to perfect"** "Trials of Elaine Negroes Deferred," *AD,* Oct. 8, 1921.

267 **"The greatest case"** *Crisis,* Jan. 1922, 117.

Chapter 15: *Taft and His Court*

268 **"secure the services"** White to James Johnson, Oct. 27, 1921, NAACP, part 7, reel 8.

268 **"We have never"** Ovington to Storey, Oct. 24, 1921, NAACP, part 1, reel 20.

268 **"I hope that he will"** Jones to White, Oct. 28, 1921, NAACP, part 7, series a, reel 8.

269 **"I am an old"** Storey to White, Oct. 25, 1921, NAACP, part 1, reel 24.

269 **"I do not wish"** Storey to James Johnson, Nov. 3, 1921, NAACP, part 1, reel 24.

270 **"one of the most human"** White to Edward Lasker, Oct. 14, 1922, NAACP, part 7, series a, reel 20.

270 **"read carefully"** *Crisis,* Dec. 1921, 27.

270 **Will Turner's lynching** "17-Year-Old Girl Attacked by Negro Brute," *HW,* Nov. 18, 1921; "Helena Breaks Her Record for Law and Order," *HW,* Nov. 20, 1921.

270 **"Who can say"** "Helena's Tragedy," *HW,* Nov. 20, 1921.

271 **"their freedom"** White to William Fuerst, Dec. 12, 1921, NAACP, part 11, reel 17.

271 **"He ba[w]led me out"** Smiddy to White, Feb. 15, 1922, NAACP, part 8, reel 3.

271 **"financial wreck"** Jones to White, Feb. 9, 1922, NAACP, part 8, reel 3.

271 **"The South has triumphed!"** "The South's Triumph," *Messenger,* April 1922, 386.

272 **"we owe"** *The Messenger,* Aug. 1922, 459.

273 **"It is not the Negro"** Berger, 80.

274 **"The United States Supreme Court"** Woodson, 15, 53.

274 **"princely profits"** Mason, 45–49.

275 **"Mr. Taft is not"** *Crisis,* July 1921, 101.

275 **"The court formerly"** *Messenger,* Aug. 1921, 236.

276 **"He is not able"** Mason, 214.

276 **"my chancellor"** Severn, 168.

276 **"fuller of prejudice"** Mason, 215.

276 **"In my few dealings"** Schwartz, 214.

276 **"displayed no sympathy"** Irons, 286.

277 **"with the nomination"** *Crisis,* March 1916, 243.

277 **"I am very much afraid"** Storey to Ovington, Nov. 13, 1922, WF.
278 **"It is rather my habit"** Storey to White, Nov. 16, 1922, WF.
278 **"Nowhere in the history"** "Brief for the Appellants," Moorfield Storey, UALR.
279 **"repugnant" to the Constitution** "Brief for the Appellee," J. S. Utley, UALR.
280 **"I assure you"** U. S. Bratton to White, Nov. 28, 1922, WF.
280 **"He stated that the defense"** NAACP board meeting, Nov. 14, 1921, NAACP, part 1, reel 1.
280 **"Friend Sip"** U. S. Bratton to Jones, March 20, 1922, NAACP, part 12, series a, reel 4.
281 **"I am of the opinion"** Jones to White, Nov. 25, 1922, WF.
281 **"We want to do"** White to Jones, Dec. 4, 1922, WF.
281 **"If he should just appear"** Jones to White, Dec. 21, 1922, WF.
281 **"Judge Storey advised"** U. S. Bratton to White, Jan. 1, 1923, WF.
281 **"third week of January"** Storey to White, Dec. 18, 1922, NAACP, part 1, reel 24.
281 **"Am advised by clerk"** Jones's telegram is copied in White to Storey, Jan. 6, 1923, WF.
282 **"Don't expect to be able"** Jones's telegram is copied in White to Storey, Jan. 8, 1923, WF.
282 **"small, badly ventilated"** Schwartz, 206.
283 **Rosewood riot** "Whites and Blacks Clash in Florida Following Attack on Woman by Three Brutes," *HW*, Jan. 5, 1923; "Florida Race Riot Is Believed Ended," *AD*, Jan. 8, 1923.
283 **"The conditions that have grown"** U. S. Bratton to White, Jan. 11, 1923, WF.
284 **"were determined"** "Elaine Riot Cases in Supreme Court," *AG*, Jan. 10, 1923.
284 **"Your contention"** Bratton to White.
284 **"Yes, but you demurred"** Ibid.
284 **"Mere errors"** "Negroes Beg Lives of Supreme Court," *New York Times*, Jan. 10, 1923.
285 **"You do not contend"** Bratton to White.
285 **"nasal twang"** White to Jones, Jan. 12, 1923, WF.
285 **"rotten deal"** Bratton to White.
285 **"It is well recognized"** "Utley Replies to Propaganda in Rioters' Appeal," *AD*, Jan. 10, 1923.
285 **"The cases lie"** White to Jones.

Chapter 16: *Hardly Less than Revolutionary*

286 **"The room"** Schwartz, 207.
286 **"good sport"** Mason, 236.
287 **"socialist" and a "hypocrite"** Purcell, 117.
287 **"not a fit person"** Mason, 74.
287 **"noisy dissenter"** Ibid., 161.
287 **"Bolsheviki"** Irons, 286.
287 **"he does not know"** Mason, 214.
287 **"opinion shy"** Ibid., 209.

287 "a continual grouch" Ibid., 215.

287 "admirable, compact" Ibid., 215.

287 "We are very happy" Schwartz, 214.

287 "It's very difficult" Ibid., 213.

288 "I sometimes endorse" Mason, 201.

288 "They will take it from Taft" Ibid., 203.

288 "subjected the reputation" Freedman, 65.

289 "ignorant convicts" Dissent in *Moore v. Dempsey,* 261 U.S. 86 (1923).

290 "felt necessities" Frankfurter, 13.

290 "I have a case" Freedman, 197.

291 "My cases" DeWolfe, 110.

291 "I like this opinion" Freedman, 197.

291 "As you say" Ibid., 83.

292 "I regard it" Louis Marshall to White, March 12, 1923, NAACP, part 7, series a, reel 20. In this letter, Marshall slightly mangled the cornerstone analogy; White later recast it in *A Man Called White,* 53.

292 "a milestone in the Negro's fight" Walter White, "The Defeat of Arkansas Mob Law," *Crisis,* April 1923, 261.

293 "spur state courts" *Toledo Times* editorial, Feb. 22, 1923, WF.

293 "the Fourteenth Amendment guarantees" *New Republic,* "Legal Lynching and the Constitution," March 21, 1923, 84–85.

293 "The principle that" *Crisis,* April 1923, 279.

293 "the powers of the state courts" "The Decision in the Elaine Case," *AG* editorial, Feb. 21, 1923.

293 "U.S. High Court Orders 'Fair Trial' " *Little Rock Daily News,* Feb. 19, 1923.

Chapter 17: *Thunderbolt from a Clear Sky*

294 "The NAACP can take credit" U. S. Bratton to White, Feb. 26, 1923, WF.

295 "Dear Sir" Ware to Jones, Feb. 12, 1923, WF.

296 "sheriff of Lee County" *Ware v. State,* 159 Ark. 540 (1923).

296 "Abundant congratulations" White to Jones, June 25, 1923, WF.

296 "Murder of Two Helena Legionnaires Unavenged" *HW,* June 26, 1923.

297 Wirges's interview with Ware "Negroes Get Rapid Action on Decision Freeing Them," *AG,* June 26, 1923.

297 "move from the prison" "Only One Condemned Sat in Chair and Walked Away Under Own Power," *AG,* Jan. 21, 1973.

298 "hero" to the Helena planters "Elaine Negro Is Shot and Killed," *AG,* June 27, 1923.

298 "I have always thought" Storey to Ovington, April 14, 1923, WF.

299 "Do you think" Jones to White, April 2, 1923, WF.

299 "It is most important" Herbert Stockton to Robert Bagnall, April 18, 1923, WF.

299 "Never before" "The Breakdown of the Law in the Elaine Cases," *AG* editorial, June 26, 1923.

299–300 "They should get out of Arkansas" "Was Not Justice," *Fort-Smith Sentinel Record,* WF.

300 "living and working" "The Arkansas Cases," Sept. 1, 1923, NAACP, part 7, series a, reel 21.

300 **"I found [Utley]"** Jones to White, Sept. 14, 1923, WF.

300 **"grant a full"** Petition for pardon of Frank Moore (and others) to T. C. McRae, Sept. 14, 1923, WF.

300 **"to second-degree murder"** Committee of Seven Petition to Hon. T. C. McRae, undated, WF.

301 **"Before agreeing"** Jones to White, Nov. 3, 1923, WF.

302 **"Personally, I have been opposed"** White to Storey, Nov. 7, 1923, WF.

302 **"eligible for parole"** "Elaine Negroes Escape Death," *AD,* Nov. 4, 1923.

302 **"There is no question"** White to Julius Rosenwald, Nov. 16, 1923, NAACP, part one, reel 24.

302 **"You never did favor"** Jones to White, Sept. 14, 1923, WF.

303 **"This has practically"** White to Jones, Sept. 19, 1923, WF.

303 **"very ably done"** Jones to White, May 14, 1924, NAACP, part 7, series a, reel 8.

303 **"Arkansas owes the Association"** *Crisis,* May 1925, 49.

303 **"until the crop of cotton"** McRae to Sheriff A. J. Collins, Oct. 7, 1924, McRae papers, book 1, box 2, folder 62, AHC.

304 **"not receive clemency"** "Eight of Elaine Negroes Released," *AG,* Dec. 20, 1924.

304 **"full and complete pardon"** "Governor Will Be Petitioned to Free Six Elaine Negroes," *AD,* Dec. 21, 1924.

304 **"many prominent Elaine"** "Clemency Hearings Completed by McRae," *AD,* Dec. 24, 1924.

305 **"Your secretary"** White to Jones, Jan. 5, 1925, NAACP, part 7, series a, reel 21.

305 **"Just concluded presentation"** Jones to White, Jan. 13, 1925, NAACP, part 7, series a, reel 21.

305 **"signed by officers"** "Furloughs Issued Last of Rioters," *AG,* Jan. 14, 1925.

306 **"Coffins were constructed"** Ibid.

306 **"was like a thunderbolt"** J. R. Maxwell to NAACP, Jan. 22, 1925, NAACP, part 7, series a, reel 21.

307 **"victory is one"** "Colored Editors Comment on Arkansas Victory," Jan. 30, 1925, NAACP, part 7, series a, reel 21.

307 **"You have rendered"** White to Jones, May 7, 1925, NAACP, Part 7, series a, reel 21.

307 **"the greatest achievement"** William Pickens, "The Last of the Arkansans," Associated Negro Press, Pickens papers, 1906–1957, reel 4, SC.

307 **"This Scipio"** William Pickens, "Scipio Africanus Maximus," Associated Negro Press, Pickens papers, 1906–1957, reel 4, SC.

308 **"We Are Proud of Him"** *Arkansas Survey,* NAACP, part 7, series a, reel 21.

Chapter 18: *Birth of a New Nation*

310 **"For the first time"** Meyer, 171.

313 **"to open our prison"** Wells, *Crusade for Justice,* 404.

313 **"As long as we stand"** Biegert.

314 **"fame" as an advocate** Ulysses S. Bratton Jr. interview, 1978, Stockley papers, BC.

314 **"no American"** "Moorfield Storey," *Amsterdam News,* Oct. 30, 1929.

315 **"There was gambling"** Delta Cultural Center exhibit, Sept. 2005, Helena, Ark.

316 **"It's like when you catch"** Interview with Mary Louise Fiser, Sept. 13, 2005.

316 **"They shot women"** Interview with Raymond Willie, Sept. 12, 2005.

316 **"You could smell"** Interview with J. W. Banks, Sept. 12, 2005.

317 **"archenemy of our people"** Jones to James Johnson, Oct. 29, 1927, and Jan. 9, 1928, both in NAACP, part 12, series a, reel 4.

318 **"This was the first time"** NAACP press release, "Scipio A. Jones Elected Chancellor in Arkansas Court," Sept. 5, 1924, NAACP, part 7, series a, reel 8.

318 **Caruthers case** NAACP, part 8, reel 4.

320 **"a nervous twitch"** Mrs. George Smith interview with Tom Dillard, July 25, 1971, ms 0010, series one, box 9, file 9, DC.

320 **Scipio's obituaries and funeral** "Scipio Jones, State Negro Leader Dies," *AG*, March 29, 1943; "Scipio A. Jones," *AD*, March 29, 1943; "Noted Attorney Passes," *Arkansas State Press*, April 2, 1943.

Epilogue

321 **"turning point"** Cortner, *A Mob Intent on Death*, 189.

321 **"point of departure"** Reitz, 1329.

321 **"position of extreme comity"** Fellman, 17.

322 **"after Moore"** Yackle, 38.

322 **"the fundamental instrument"** *Harris v. Nelson*, 1969.

322 **"Federal habeas jurisdiction"** "The Rehnquist Reins," *New York Times*, Oct. 6, 1996.

323 **"large portion"** "After the Lawyers," *New York Times*, April 27, 2007.

Abington, E. H. *Back Roads and Bicarbonate*. New York: Vantage Press, 1954.

Aikman, Daryl. "The Confederate Memorial in Helena." *PCHQ* 17 (1979): 28–32.

Allen, Desmond Walls. *Index to Arkansas' World War I African American Soldiers*. Conway, AR: Arkansas Research, Inc., 2002.

Allen, E. M. "The Story of Elaine, Arkansas." *PCHQ* 4 (1966): 22–24.

Allen, James. *Without Sanctuary: Lynching Photography in America*. Santa Fe, NM: Twin Palms Publishers, 2005.

Amar, Akhil Reed. *The Bill of Rights*. New Haven: Yale University Press, 1998.

Arnesen, Eric. *Black Protest and the Great Migration*. Boston: Bedford/St. Martin's, 2003.

Auerbach, Jerold. "Southern Tenant Farmers." *AHQ* 27 (1968): 113–131.

Barton, Glen. *Recent Changes in Farm Labor Organization in Three Arkansas Plantation Counties*. Fayetteville: University of Arkansas College of Agriculture, 1939.

Baskett, Tom, Jr. *The Arkansas Delta*. Helena, AR: Delta Cultural Center, 1990.

———, ed. *Persistence of the Spirit*. Helena, AR: Delta Cultural Center, 1991.

Bealer, Harry. "The Last Man's Club." *PCHQ* 17 (1978): 29–33.

Bennett, Harrison. "The Phillips County Riot Cases." *Chickenbones*. Accessed on November 1, 2006, at www.nathanielturner.com.

Berger, Morroe. *Equality by Statute*. Garden City, NY: Doubleday, 1954.

Biegert, M. Langley. "Legacy of Resistance." *Journal of Social History* 32 (1998): 73–99.

Blake, Tom. "Phillips County, Arkansas, Largest Slaveholders from 1860 Slave Census Schedules," 2003. Accessed on October 30, 2006, at www.freepages. genealogy.rootsweb.com/~ajac/arphillips.htm

Bodenhamer, David. *Fair Trial*. New York: Oxford University Press, 1992.

Bradford, Gene. "Barton." *PCHR* 34 (1996): 3–12.

Brough, Charles. "The Clinton Riot." *Mississippi Historical Society* 6 (1902): 53–63.

———. "Work of the Commission of Southern Universities on the Race Question." *Annals of the American Academy of Political and Social Science* 49 (1913): 47–57.

Bruce, John Edward. *The Blood Red Record*. Albany, NY: Argus Co., 1901.

Buckelew, Richard A. "Racial Violence in Arkansas, Lynchings, and Mob Rule, 1860–1930," Ph.D. dissertation, University of Arkansas, 1999.

Bush, A. E. *History of the Mosaic Templars of America*. Little Rock: Central Printing, 1924.

Chicago Commission on Race Relations. *The Negro in Chicago*. Chicago: University of Chicago Press, 1922.

Cochran, Robert. "George W. Featherstonhaugh's Contribution to the Bad Name of Arkansas." *AHQ* 18 (1989): 1–16.

Coke, Octavius. *The Scrapbook of Arkansas Literature*. Little Rock: American Society Caxton Press, 1939.

Cook, Charles. "Arkansas's Charles Hillman Brough, 1876–1935." Ph.D. dissertation, University of Houston, 1980.

Cortner, Richard. *A Mob Intent on Death*. Middletown, CT: Wesleyan University Press, 1988.

———. *The Supreme Court and the Second Bill of Rights*. Madison: University of Wisconsin Press, 1981.

Crisler, E. T. "The Battle of Helena." Helena, AR: Helena Centennial Association, 1963.

Curtis, Michael. *No State Shall Abridge*. Durham, NC: Duke University Press, 1986.

DeBlack, Thomas. *With Fire and Sword*. Fayetteville: University of Arkansas Press, 2003.

De Man, George. *Helena: The Ridge, The River, The Romance*. Little Rock: Phillips County Historical Society, 1978.

Dillard, Tom. "Golden Prospects and Fraternal Amenities: Mifflin W. Gibbs's Arkansas Years." *AHQ* 35 (1976): 307–33.

———. "To the Back of the Elephant." *AHQ* 33 (1974): 3–15.

———. "Scipio A. Jones." AHQ 31 (1972): 201–19.

Dinnerstein, Leonard. *The Leo Frank Case*. Athens: University of Georgia Press, 1966.

Douglass, Frederick. *Frederick Douglass: Selected Speeches and Writings*. Ed. Philip Foner. Chicago: Lawrence Hill, 1999.

Dray, Philip. *At the Hands of Persons Unknown*. New York: Modern Library, 2003.

Duker, William. *A Constitutional History of Habeas Corpus*. Westport, CT: Greenwood Press, 1980.

Dunaway, L. S. *What a Preacher Saw Through a Keyhole in Arkansas*. Little Rock: Parke-Harper, 1925.

Fellman, David. *The Defendant's Rights Today*. Madison: University of Wisconsin Press, 1976.

Ferguson, Bessie. "The Elaine Race Riot." Master's thesis, George Peabody College for Teachers, Nashville, 1927.

Fink, Jacob. "What I Know About Helena's Public Schools." *PCHQ* 6 (1967): 15–19.

Finley, Randy. "Black Arkansans and World War One." *AHQ* 49 (1990): 249–77.

Foner, Philip, ed. *The Voice of Black America*. New York: Simon & Schuster, 1972.

Forman, James, Jr. "Juries and Race in the Nineteenth Century." *Yale Law Journal* 113 (2004): 895–938.

Frankfurter, Felix. *Mr. Justice Holmes and the Supreme Court*. Cambridge, MA: Belknap Press, 1961.

Fredrickson, George. *The Black Image in the White Mind*. New York: Harper and Row, 1971.

Freedman, Eric. *Habeas Corpus.* New York: New York University Press, 2001.

Friedman, Lawrence. *Crime and Punishment in American History.* New York: Basic Books, 1993.

Froelich, Jacqueline. "Total Eclipse." *AHQ* 58 (1999): 131–58.

Ginzburg, Ralph. *100 Years of Lynchings.* Baltimore: Black Classic Press, 1962.

Gladin, Ivey. "Early Days of the Richard L. Kitchens Post of the American Legion." *PCHR* 27 (1989): 1–4.

Gordon, Louise. *Caste and Class.* Athens: University of Georgia Press, 1995.

Graves, John William. "Negro Disfranchisement in Arkansas." *AHQ* 26 (1967): 199–25.

———. "The Arkansas Separate Coach Law of 1891." *AHQ* 32 (1973): 148–65.

———. "Jim Crow in Arkansas." *Journal of Southern History* 55 (1989): 420–48.

Green, E. G. "A Brief History of West Helena." *PCHQ* 3 (1965): 20–24.

Hahn, Steven. *A Nation Under Our Feet.* Cambridge, MA: Harvard University Press, 2003.

Harris, Stephen. *Harlem's Hell Fighters.* Washington, D.C.: Potomac Books, 2003.

Haynes, George. *Negro Migration in 1916–1917.* New York: Negro Universities Press, 1969.

Heaney, Gerald. "Jacob Trieber." *University of Arkansas at Little Rock Law Journal* 8 (1985–86): 421–78.

Hempstead, Fay. *Historical Review of Arkansas.* St. Louis: Lewis Publishing, 1912.

Herndon, Dallas, ed. *Centennial History of Arkansas.* Chicago: S. J. Clarke Publishing, 1922.

———. *Annals of Arkansas.* Little Rock: Historical Record Association, 1947.

Hixson, William B. *Moorfield Storey and the Abolitionist Tradition.* New York: Oxford University Press, 1972.

Holmes, Oliver Wendell. *Holmes-Pollock Letters.* Ed. Mark Howe. Littleton, CO: Rothman and Company, 1994.

Holmes, William. "The Arkansas Cotton Pickers Strike of 1891 and the Demise of the Colored Farmers's Alliance." *AHQ* 32 (1973): 107–19.

Hornor, Albert A. "The Northeast Corner of Porter and Columbia." *PCHR* 32 (1994): 4–12.

Hornor, Joseph. "Some Recollections of Reminiscences by My Father." *PCHQ* 10 (1971): 9–23.

Hornor, Robert Moore. "Historic Moore-Hornor House Donated to the Delta Cultural Center." *PCHR* 33 (1996): 11–13.

Howe, M. S. DeWolfe. *Portrait of an Independent, Moorfield Storey.* Boston: Houghton Mifflin, 1932.

Howell, Jere. "Childhood Memories of Growing Up in Wabash." *PCHR* 33 (1995): 25–41.

Irons, Peter. *A People's History of the Supreme Court.* New York: Penguin Books, 1999.

James, Dorothy. "Courthouses of Phillips County." *PCHQ* 3 (1965): 1–3.

Janken, Kenneth Robert. *White: The Biography of Walter White, Mr. NAACP.* New York: New Press, 2003.

Jefferson, Thomas. *Notes on the State of Virginia.* E-text, University of Virginia Library, etext.virginia.edu/toc/mudeng/public/JefVirg.html

Jones, Mary L. Demoret. "Elaine, Arkansas." *PCHR* 34 (1996): 33–37.

Justice, Ernest. "James Camp Tappan," *PCHQ* 3 (1965): 5–17.

Kellogg, Charles. *NAACP: A History of the National Association for the Advancement of Colored People.* Baltimore: Johns Hopkins University Press, 1967.

Kennedy, Randall. *Race, Crime, and the Law.* New York: Pantheon Books, 1997.

Kerlin, Robert. *The Voice of the Negro, 1919.* New York: Arno Press, 1968.

Kirkman, Dale. "Early Days at Helena." *PCHQ* 3 (1964): 1–13.

———. "Early Helena Newspapers." *PCHQ* 4 (1966): 13–15.

———. "The Leased Plantations Below Helena." *PCHQ* 4 (1966): 8–15.

———. "The Road North from Helena." *PCHQ* 13 (1975): 14–20.

———. "Whatever Happened to the Seven Generals." *PCHQ* 22 (1983): 69–75.

———. "Early History of Helena." *PCHR* 32 (1994): 18–21.

Klarman, Michael. *From Jim Crow to Civil Rights.* New York: Oxford University Press, 2004.

Knowlton, Jean. "Anniversary of Phillips County Community College." *PCHQ* 28 (1990): 1–10.

Kolchin, Peter. *American Slavery, 1619–1877.* New York: Hill and Wang, 1993.

Kousser, J. Morgan. "A Black Protest in the 'Era of Accomodation': Documents." *AHQ* 34 (1975): 149–78.

Kyte, Willie Mae Countiss. "Elaine, Arkansas." *PCHR* 34 (1996): 38–51.

Lambert, Gerard. *All Out of Step.* Garden City, NY: Doubleday, 1956.

Lankford, George, ed. *Bearing Witness.* Fayetteville: University of Arkansas Press, 2003.

Ledbetter, Calvin. "The Constitutional Convention of 1917–1918." *AHQ* 34 (1975): 3–40.

Lewis, David Levering, *W. E. B. Du Bois: Biography of a Race.* New York: Henry Holt and Company, 1993.

Lewis, Todd. "Booker T. Washington and His Visits to Little Rock." *Pulaski County Historical Review* 42 (1994).

Lincoln, Abraham. *Collected Works of Abraham Lincoln,* vol. 7. New Brunswick, NJ: Rutgers University Press, 1953.

Lisenby, Foy. "Charles Hillman Brough as Historian." *AHQ* 35 (1976): 115–26.

———. *Charles Hillman Brough.* Fayetteville: University of Arkansas Press, 1996.

Litwack, Leon. *Been in the Storm So Long.* New York: Vintage Books, 1979.

Love, Berna. *End of the Line.* Little Rock: Center for Arkansas Studies, 2003.

Lynch, Teresa. "Interview with J. J. White." *PCHQ* 27 (1985): 8–17.

McCarty, Joey. "The Red Scare in Arkansas." *AHQ* 37 (1978): 264–77.

Mason, Alpheus. *William Howard Taft, Chief Justice.* New York: Simon & Schuster, 1964.

Meyer, Howard. *The Amendment That Refused to Die.* Lanham, MD: Madison Books, 2000.

Meyers, Christopher. "Killing Them by the Wholesale." *Georgia Historical Quarterly* 90 (2006): 214–35.

Mills, Margie. "Modoc." *PCHQ* 14 (1976): 22–32.

Mitchell, H. L. "The Founding and Early History of the Southern Tenant Farmers Union." *AHQ* 32 (1973): 343–69.

Moneyhon, Carl. *The Impact of the Civil War and Reconstruction on Arkansas.* Fayetteville: University of Arkansas Press, 2002.

———. *Arkansas and the New South.* Fayetteville: University of Arkansas Press, 1997.

———. "Black Politics in Arkansas During the Gilded Age, 1876–1900." *AHQ* 44 (1985): 222–45.

———. "Economic Democracy in Antebellum Arkansas, Phillips County, 1850–1860." *AHQ* 40 (1981): 154–72.

Moore, C. L. "C. L. Moore and Brothers." *PCHQ* 8 (1970): 31–33.

Moore, John Thomas. "Collections as Told to Me and How I Saw It." *PCHR* 35 (1997): 4–25.

Mosby, Winston. "The Lumber Industry in Helena and Phillips County." *PCHQ* 19 (1981): 1–12.

Murray, Robert. *Red Scare.* New York: McGraw-Hill, 1964.

Nash, Horace. "Blacks in Arkansas During Reconstruction." *AHQ* 48 (1989): 243–59.

National Encyclopedia of the Colored Race. Montgomery, AL: National Publishing Co., 1919.

Newman, Nathan. "A New Birth of Freedom." Brennan Center for Justice at NYU School of Law, 2004.

Niswonger, Richard. "A Study in Southern Demagoguery." *AHQ* 39 (1980): 114–124.

Ovington, Mary White. *The Walls Came Tumbling Down.* New York: Schocken Books, 1970.

———. *Portraits in Color.* New York: Viking Press, 1927.

Parmelee, L. R. "Helena and West Helena: A Civil Engineer's Reminscences." *PCHQ* 1 (1962): 1–8.

Perry, Michael. *We the People.* New York: Oxford University Press, 1999.

Pickens, William. "Lynching and Debt-Slavery." NAACP pamphlet, May 1921.

Pittman, Carolyn Holcomb. "A History of the Media in Helena–West Helena, Arkansas." *PCHQ* 26 (1986): 28–52.

Porter, Rusty. "Railroads of Phillips County." *PCHQ* 26 (1988): 1–24.

Purcell, Edward. *Brandeis and the Progressive Constitution.* New Haven: Yale University Press, 2000.

Quarles, Clarence. "War Experiences of Clarence Quarles." *PCHQ* 4 (1965): 1–5.

Reitz, Curtis. "Federal Habeas Corpus." *Harvard Law Review* 74 (1961): 1315–73.

Richardson, Heather Cox. *The Death of Reconstruction.* Cambridge: Harvard University Press, 2001.

Robinson, Charles F. "Most Shamefully Common." *AHQ* 60 (2001): 265–83.

Rohrscheib, Betty. "Gift of the Winds." *PCHQ* 5 (1967): 16–20.

Schwartz, Bernard. *A History of the Supreme Court.* New York: Oxford University Press, 1993.

Seligmann, Herbert. *The Negro Faces America.* New York: Clarence S. Nathan, 1920.

Semonche, John. *Keeping the Faith.* Lanham, MD: Rowman and Littlefield, 1998.

Senn, Gerald. "The Arkansas Council of Defense." *AHQ* 36 (1977): 280–304.

Severn, Bill. *William Howard Taft.* New York: Van Rees Press, 1970.

Sizemore, Jean. "Architectural Overview of the Helena Survey Area." *PCHR* 32 (1994): 24–63.

Skolnick, Jerome. *Above the Law.* New York: Free Press, 1993.

Smith, Calvin. "Serving the Poorest of the Poor." *AHQ* 57 (1998): 287–308.

Steiker, Jordan. "Incorporating the Suspension Clause." *Michigan Law Review* 92 (1994): 862–925.

Street, Bill. "Legendary Events Are Retold About Habib's Café in Helena." *PCHQ* 4 (1965): 34–43.

Stockley, Grif. *Blood in Their Eyes.* Fayetteville: University of Arkansas Press, 2001.

Stoskopf, Alan. *Race and Membership in American History.* Brookline, MA: Facing History and Ourselves Press, 2002.

Tappan, Thomas E. "President Taft at Helena." *PCHQ* 14 (1976): 24–29.

———. "Oldtown 1922." *PCHQ* 22 (1985): 27–38.

———. "Columbia Street, Helena Arkansas: 1909–1921." *PCHQ* 27 (1989): 45–73.

Taylor, Kieran. "We Have Just Begun." *AHQ* 58 (1999): 264–84.

Thomas, David Y., ed. *Arkansas and Its People, a History, 1541–1930.* New York: American Historical Society, 1930.

Underwood, Q. K. "Reminiscences of Helena." *PCHQ* 2 (1963): 27–30.

Vinikas, Vincent. "Specters in the Past." *Journal of Southern History* 65 (1999): 535–64.

Waskow, Arthur. *From Race Riot to Sit-In.* Garden City, NY: Doubleday, 1966.

Wells-Barnett, Ida. *Crusade for Justice.* Chicago: University of Chicago Press, 1970.

———. *The Arkansas Race Riot.* Chicago: Hume Job Print, 1920.

———. *On Lynchings.* Salem, NH: Ayer Company, 1991.

Whayne, Jeannie. "Low Villains and Wickedness in High Places." *AHQ* 58 (1999): 294–95.

Whayne, Jeannie, ed. *The Arkansas Delta.* Fayetteville: University of Arkansas Press, 1993.

———. *Arkansas: A Narrative History.* Fayetteville: University of Arkansas Press, 2000.

White, Walter. *A Man Called White.* New York: Viking Press, 1948.

Widener, Ralph. "Charles Hillman Brough." *AHQ* 34 (1975): 99–121.

Williams, Fay. *Arkansans of the Years,* vol. 2. Little Rock: C. C. Allard and Associates, 1952.

Williams, Fred, ed. *A Documentary History of Arkansas.* Fayetteville: University of Arkansas Press, 1984.

Wolff, Sally. "Cotton Pickin' at Cummins Prison." *AHQ* 52 (1993): 28–43.

Woods, E. M. *The Blue Book of Little Rock and Argenta.* Little Rock: Central Printing, 1907.

Woodson, Carter. "Fifty Years of Negro Citizenship as Qualified by the United States Supreme Court." *Journal of Negro History* 6 (1921): 1–53.

Work, Monroe. *Negro Year Book.* Tuskegee, AL: Negro Year Book Publishing, 1922.

Worley, Ted. "Helena on the Mississippi." *AHQ* 13 (1954): 1–15.

Wormser, Richard. *The Rise and Fall of Jim Crow.* New York: St. Martin's Press, 2003.

Yackle, Larry. *Federal Courts.* New York: Foundation Press, 2003.

Young, Porter. "Mr. and Mrs. Charles M. Young and the Helena World." *PCHQ* 20 (1982): 3–11.

Map Sources

Map of Phillips County in 1919. Drawn by Cary Cox. Dillard Collection, box 1, file 6, BC.

Map showing territory and vicinity of Hoop Spur and Elaine, drawn by Monroe and Parmelee, October 25, 1919, BC.

Acknowledgments

I owe a great debt to a number of people who provided me with encouragement and assistance while I researched and wrote this book.

At the very outset, Professor Eric Freedman at Hofstra University, one of the country's leading scholars on habeas corpus law, graciously allowed me to review and copy documents from his files on the *Moore* v. *Dempsey* case. Hofstra University librarian Cindie Leigh made certain that during my time at Hofstra I had full access to Professor Freedman's files.

While I was first working on the proposal for this book, Amanda Cook provided me with invaluable guidance. And I shall forever be indebted to Chris Jackson, who acquired the book for Crown.

While researching the book, I spent a great deal of time in libraries in Boston, New York City, Madison (Wisconsin), Little Rock, Fayetteville, and Helena. At every stop, librarians helped me find and copy documents, and helped me obtain photographs. In particular, I owe a thank-you to Cary Cox, Brian Robertson, Rhonda Stewart, Chris Stewart, and Linda McDowell at the Butler Center for Arkansas Studies in Little Rock; to Kathryn Fitzhugh at the William H. Bowen School of Law in Little Rock; to April Goff, Jane Wilkerson, and Lynn Ewbank at the Arkansas History Commission in Little Rock; and to Geoffrey Stark, Anne Prichard, and Andrea Cantrell at the Special Collections room in Mullins Library at the University of Arkansas in Fayetteville.

I owe a special thanks to Arkansas historians Tom Dillard and Todd Lewis. If it weren't for Mr. Dillard, Scipio Africanus Jones might be completely forgotten today. In 1972, he published an article on Scipio A. Jones in the *Arkansas Historical Quarterly,* and his research remains the primary source for information about Jones's life.

Todd Lewis's research on the "redemption" of Phillips County by whites in the late 1800s is a model of good scholarship, and I found it invaluable for telling that part of the story.

In Phillips County, the "Elaine Riots" can be a topic that many would rather not talk about, and yet I was graciously treated at every turn. I owe thanks to Helena librarians Pat Ward and Linda Bennett, and to librarian Clara Williamson in Elaine. A number of people in Helena provided me with insight into the town's history, including Annetta Beauchamp, Joe Madonia, and Paula Oliver. On my first stay in Helena, John Butkiewicz, owner of the Foxglove Bed and Breakfast, helped me find my way about town. At the Delta Cultural Center, Terry Buckalew and Gregg Cook provided me with assistance, and Mr. Buckalew graciously shared his research on the history of the blues in Helena.

There was one person in particular in Helena who took me under his wing—Raymond Willie. I met him at the Pillow Thompson house, and over the course of several days, he introduced me to a number of people, including Doris Miller Aubry, D. A. E. Johnston's niece. She shared her memories of what she had been told about the riot by her father, Robert D. Miller (whose sister was married to D. A. E. Johnston). Raymond Willie also introduced me to his father-in-law, J. W. Banks, who, during a long conversation on his porch step, recalled what it was like to grow up in a sharecropper's family in the 1930s and 1940s.

In Elaine, Mayor Poindexter Fiser and his wife, Mary Louise (Demoret) Fiser, spoke at length about the riot and the history of their town. Her family roots go back to the earliest days of Elaine, and together they gave me a tour of the now shuttered Demoret general store. The store, with its dusty shelves and wooden floor, provides a visceral sense of that past.

My agent, Theresa Park, provided me with encouragement, support, and guidance from start to finish. Every writer should have the good fortune to have an agent who works as diligently and as passionately as Theresa does on my behalf.

All writers fear that their manuscript may slip into a void when the acquiring editor leaves for another house, and I am grateful to Crown and editorial director Kristin Kiser for making sure that didn't happen after Chris Jackson left for a new Random House imprint, Spiegel & Grau. First, Rachel Klayman ably shepherded the project along, and then, once the manuscript was ready for editing, Sean Desmond made the book his own. He greatly improved the manuscript in ways both big and small, and in every manner possible championed the book. I am also grateful to Sue Warga for her skillful copyediting, to Lenny Henderson for his wonderful layout, to Julie Miesionczek for her diligent management of the project, and to the many others at Crown who have contributed their talents to this book.

While I was struggling to bring this book to completion, I received support of a most generous sort from the J. Anthony Lukas Prize Project. This prize, which is designed to help a writer finish his work, is the brainchild of Linda Healey, and is jointly administered by the Columbia University Graduate School of Journalism and the Nieman Foundation at Harvard University. The project is sponsored by the family of the late Mark Lynton. I am deeply grateful to all who contribute their time and energy to this wonderful project. I took the encouraging words of the three judges, Francis Clines, Joan Quigley, and Elinor Langer, to heart.

Finally, I am deeply thankful to my wife, Andrea, and to my three children, Rabi, Zoey, and Dylan, for their continued love and support. Andrea was the first to take a red pencil to the manuscript, and Rabi, Zoey, and Dylan all contributed, in one way or another, to the manuscript too.

Index

About the Author

Robert Whitaker is the author of two previous books, *The Mapmaker's Wife: A True Tale of Love, Murder, and Survival in the Amazon* and *Mad in America: Bad Science, Bad Medicine, and the Enduring Mistreatment of the Mentally Ill.* He's received numerous journalism awards, including (in May 2007) the J. Anthony Lukas Work-in-Progress Prize for *On the Laps of Gods.* He lives and writes in Cambridge, Massachusetts.